Hawthorne's Fuller Mystery

Thomas R. Mitchell

University of Massachusetts Press   AMHERST

Copyright © 1998 by Thomas R. Mitchell
All rights reserved
Printed in the United States of America
LC 98-19290
ISBN 1-55849-170-8
Designed by Sally Nichols
Printed and bound by BookCrafters, Inc.

Library of Congress Cataloging-in-Publication Data

Mitchell, Thomas R., 1950–
    Hawthorne's Fuller mystery / Thomas R. Mitchell.
      p.   cm.
    Includes bibliographical references and index.
    ISBN 1-55849-170-8 (alk. paper)
      1. Hawthorne, Nathaniel, 1804–1864—Political and social views.
    2. Feminism and literature—United States—History—19th century.
    3. Women and literature—United States—History—19th century.
    4. Hawthorne, Nathaniel, 1804–1864—Friends and associates.
    5. Fuller, Margaret, 1810–1850—Friends and associates.   6. Fuller,
    Margaret, 1810–1850—Influence.   7. Transcendentalism in literature.
    8. Transcendentalism (New England)   I. Title.
    PS1892.F45M57   1999
    813'.3—dc21   98-19290
                                                                   CIP

British Library Cataloguing in Publication data are available.
This book is published with the support and cooperation of the
University of Massachusetts, Boston.

Dedication

To the women in my life who have inspired me: my grandmothers,
Warrene East Mitchell and Lillie Rainbolt Coon;
my mother, Elsie Coon Mitchell; my wife, Linda Garcia Mitchell;
and my daughters, Lesley Warrene and Ashley Cynara.

Contents

Acknowledgments ix

CHAPTER ONE
The "Riddle" of Margaret Fuller 1

CHAPTER TWO
The "Scandal" of Margaret Fuller 12

CHAPTER THREE
"This Mutual Visionary Life"
The Hawthorne-Fuller Friendship 41

CHAPTER FOUR
"Rappaccini's Daughter" and the Voice of Beatrice 93

CHAPTER FIVE
"Speak Thou for Me!"
The "Strange Earnestness" of The Scarlet Letter 125

CHAPTER SIX
"Silken Bands" and "Iron Fetters"
Fuller at Fire Island, Hawthorne at Lenox 159

CHAPTER SEVEN
Dreaming the "Same Dream Twice"
The Ghost Story of The Blithedale Romance 180

CHAPTER EIGHT
*The Venus of the Tribune, the Pearl Diver,
and* THE MARBLE FAUN 220

Notes 257

Index 311

Acknowledgments

Hawthorne could not have asked for a more sympathetic reader than I have had over the years in Professor Larry J. Reynolds. Quite simply, this study would not have been attempted, much less completed, had it not been for his encouragement and remarkable generosity and kindness.

I also acknowledge the following scholars for offering their valuable suggestions and encouragement at various stages and on various parts of the manuscript: Sara Alpern, Charles Capper, Bell Gale Chevigny, Jeffrey Cox, Fritz Fleischmann, Gordon Hutner, John Idol, Buford Jones, Harrison T. Meserole, Robert Milder, Maria Ponce, Christina Zwarg, and the anonymous readers for the University of Massachusetts Press and for *American Literary History,* where a much-condensed version of chapter 2 first appeared. At the University of Massachusetts Press, I especially have Paul Wright to thank for his faith in my work and patient support. For permission to quote from Sophia Peabody Hawthorne's unpublished letters, I thank the Berg Collection of English and American Literature, New York Public Library, Astor, Lenox, and Tilden Foundations; and the Houghton Library, Harvard University.

Without family support, no study like this can be contemplated, much less accomplished, and I have been fortunate to have the generous support, patience, and encouragement of all my family, immediate and extended, but most especially: my wife, Linda Marie Garcia; my children, Lesley Warrene, Ashley Cynara, and Jackson Thomas; and my father and mother, Thomas and Elsie Mitchell, who made numerous trips from Louisiana to Texas to help out so that I had time to work.

Hawthorne's Fuller Mystery

The "Riddle" of Margaret Fuller

She remained inscrutable to me.
RALPH WALDO EMERSON

The solution to the riddle lies in this direction.
NATHANIEL HAWTHORNE

Margaret Fuller's determination to define and redefine the self challenged the nineteenth-century's constricting demarcations of the feminine. Living in the historical center of the nineteenth-century's "cult of domesticity," she claimed that since childhood she had known that she "was not born to the common womanly lot," and she spent her life exploring the territory beyond that "lot."[1] Her passionate aspirations would extend the boundaries of the feminine and keep her life forever unsettled, and unsettling.

An 18 August 1842 entry in her private journal speaks of the all-too-frequent effort she had to summon to retain her faith in the self that was and the self that was ever about to be, of the resistance she had to exert against the pressures of even her most intimate friends. Recounting a confrontation with Ellery Channing, her brother-in-law, in her room at Emerson's house, where both were houseguests, Fuller reports Ellery's attempts to sort out the ambiguities of his relationship with her. She records him as saying: "I shall not like you the better for your excellence. I dont know what is the matter, I feel strongly attracted towards you, but there is a drawback in my mind, I dont know exactly what. You will always be wanting to grow forward, now I like to grow backward too. You are too ideal. Ideal people (always) anticipate their lives, and they make themselves and every body around them restless, by always being beforehand with themselves, & so on in the very tone of William's [William Henry Channing's] damning letter."[2]

Fuller often heard such voices of "damning" criticism, for the intensity of her commitment to self-redefinition inspired both personal and ideological unease. "Most of her friends," Emerson would confess, felt around her "at one time or another, some uneasiness . . . as if she were ill-timed and mis-mated, and felt in herself a tide of life, which compared with the slow circulation of others as a torrent with a rill." Including himself among such friends, Emerson admitted: "She remained inscrutable to me; her strength was not my strength,—her powers were a surprise." As "she passed into new states of great advance," he conceded, "I understood these no better."[3]

Fuller claims in the 1842 journal entry that she listens to these voices for what she can "learn from them." But she reaffirms her intention to listen even more attentively to another voice, "the voice in the heart" that reminds her that such criticism had been made "of every prophetic, of every tragic character" and that a "path" has been "appointed" her that she must continue to follow with "great energy" and "self-reliance."[4] She could endure censure, but she would not become one "who after a whole life passed in trying to build up himself, resolves that it would have been far better, if he had kept still as the clod of the valley, or yielded easily as the leaf to every breeze." Fuller resisted the pressure of self-doubt exerted on her by her intense and ambivalent friendships with Emerson, William Henry Channing, and Ellery Channing. In the same journal entry, she vows, "Waldo must not shake me in my worldliness, nor William in the fine motion that . . . has given me what I have of life, nor this child of genius make me lay aside the armour without which I had lain bleeding on the field long since." "I am what I am," she writes, and "I will bear the pain of imperfection, but not of doubt."[5]

By listening to the "voice of her heart," she had become at this moment in her life a leading figure among the Transcendentalist circle, America's greatest contemporary scholar and champion of Goethe, the first editor of the *Dial,* an occasional poet, a literary and arts critic, and a pioneer feminist. She had briefly and successfully taken the conventional path of trying one of the few occupations open to women, school teaching, but she had rejected it, and had instead made it her vocation to help other women find their voices by organizing an intellectual discussion group that she led, the "Conversations." There she had made a feminist application of Transcendentalist faith, urging women to recognize their obligation to perfect the divinity within them, to commit themselves to a life of self-development and "become gods . . . able to give the life which we now feel ourselves able only to receive."[6]

After 1842 her commitment to women's rights deepened with the publication in the *Dial* of "The Great Lawsuit" (1843) and its expanded revision, *Woman in the Nineteenth Century* (1845). She simultaneously used her position at Horace Greeley's *New-York Daily Tribune* (1844–46) as one of America's first professional women journalists to become not only one of the country's most significant early literary critics but also the voice of oppressed groups, chastising a materialistic America for its failure to live up to its revolutionary ideals in its treatment of American Indians, slaves, Irish immigrants, the urban poor, and female convicts and prostitutes.[7]

In turbulent Europe (1846–50) she became increasingly radical in her searing indictments of economic and political oppression, writing firsthand reports from Rome for the *Tribune* of the republican revolution of 1848–49, working for the revolutionaries in a field hospital during the shelling of the city, and in the despair of the revolution's failure and the return of despotic rule, finding Europe's only hope in an even more radical revolution.[8]

Her path in Rome also led her to Giovanni Angelo Ossoli, a penniless marquis and soldier in the Republican Guard. She bore his baby, Angelino, in September 1848. Retreating during the latter stages of pregnancy from the American colony in Rome to the small mountain town of Rieti, she informed her family and friends in America of her child only months later and answered the transatlantic gossip with the still-doubted claim of a secret wedding ceremony.

Her revolutionary hopes defeated, Fuller resolutely ignored her friends' warnings about the reception she would face and instead set out for America to face down the gossip and earn a living for Ossoli and her baby. On 19 July 1850, just off the beach of Fire Island, their ship ran aground in a hurricane. Waiting futilely for rescue during the morning and early afternoon on the disintegrating decks of the ship, Fuller and Ossoli refused to join fellow passengers and the crew in a desperate swim to the beach. The baby drowned in the arms of a crew member trying at the last moment to swim him to shore, and first Ossoli and then Fuller were swept off the decks, their bodies never recovered.

Fuller's life and career thus transgressed both public and private boundaries set for mid-nineteenth-century American women. She knew the costs of such transgressions. As she once wrote in a moment of passionately romantic and prophetic self-fashioning, she had been willing to define herself according to her "own law" even if it meant that she must encounter "the tragic depths that may open suddenly" and become "like Oedipus . . . a criminal, blind and outcast." Failure to realize herself fully, however, seemed to her equally catastrophic. Writing of the intensity of her unfocused passions as "Italy glowing beneath" her intellect's "Saxon crust," Fuller feared burning "to ashes if all this smoulders here much longer . . . if I do not burst forth in genius or heroism."[9] Fuller's anticipation of herself in the forward dynamic of her own law found habitual representation in such romantic self-dramatizations of the heroic, the prophetic, the tragic.

Though Fuller sought to retain the right to follow her appointed path, her own law, she lost that control, of course, in death. First friends and then later-generations of biographers and literary historians followed the example of Ellery's attempt to account for the complex force that was Fuller and for the puzzling ambiguity of their attraction to her life, of their own restless unease. Always informed by Fuller's own self-dramatizations, accounts of Fuller's life have provoked divergent and contested representations. The meanings that biographers and literary historians have given to her life have defined them as much as her. One of her earliest biographers, James Freeman Clarke, opens the 1852 *Memoirs of Margaret Fuller Ossoli* with a candid acknowledgment of the problem: "The difficulty which we all feel in describing our past intercourse and friendship with Margaret Fuller, is, that the intercourse was so intimate, and the friendship so personal, that it is like making a confession to the public of our most interior selves. . . . [T]o reveal her is to expose ourselves."[10] While Clarke had been an intimate, lifelong friend of Fuller and certainly meant the admission only as the dilemma of a friend, his statement has proven remarkably prescient. Few figures in the history of American literature better illustrate the personal and ideological revelations of historical re-creation than Fuller. Bell Gale Chevigny's title for her 1976 feminist rewriting of the 1852 *Memoirs, The Woman and the Myth,* could serve appropriately as the title for all Fuller biographies.[11]

Contestation over the Margaret Fuller that would be defined by history began within four days of her death. Friend and employer Horace Greeley devoted almost a full page of the 23 July 1850 issue of his *New-York Daily Tribune* to an account of Fuller's death and to a personal tribute dedicated to her memory and the need to define that memory for history. Greeley, the social crusader, would have her remembered as a fearless agent of change. Claiming that "America has produced no woman who in mental endowments and acquirements has surpassed Margaret Fuller," Greeley adds: "It were a shame to us if one so radiantly lofty in intellect, so devoted to Human Liberty and Well-being, so ready to dare and to endure for the upraising of her sex and her race, should perish from among us and leave no memento less imperfect and casual than those we now have." But though he praises her for "conversing so profoundly" and laments that "her great thoughts were seldom irradiated by her written language," in fact were often "clouded and choked by it," he says that "it will be a public misfortune if her thoughts are not promptly and acceptably embodied" and calls for her relatives to select "a person to prepare a Memoir." Her relatives did just that.[12]

The 1852 *Memoirs* that her friends Emerson, Channing, and Clarke produced was "a work of love," as her brother Arthur B. Fuller described it, but it aimed to memorialize Fuller not so much as the daring and devoted intellectual working on behalf of "Human Liberty" and "her sex," as Greeley would have her remembered, but as the consummate "friend" and the devotee to what Clarke described as the "wholly religious, almost Christian" life purpose of "SELF-CULTURE."[13]

This version of Margaret Fuller was immediately challenged, as the following excerpt from an unsigned April 1852 review of the *Memoirs* attests: "Each of these gentlemen . . . turns Miss Fuller round and round until he gets her in certain lights familiar or propitious to himself, and then blows a succession of brilliant bubbles. . . . You are provoked by the feeling that it is owing to an act of will, or of discretion, on the part of the biographers that you are not getting the actual and substantial life of the woman." Finding the tone of the work presumptuous, the reviewer further complains that "it leaves too much the impression that they assume a right to treat with some familiarity an idol of their own making."[14]

Two months later in the *Democratic Review,* another unidentified reviewer (almost certainly Evert Duyckinck) complained even more strongly: "We heartily wish . . . that she were here to defend and save herself from her friends. Samuel Johnson used to say that he would take the life of any person who intended to write his; and indeed, we do not remember a case in which such an act could be perpetrated with more justification." Opening the review with the judgment that though Fuller "should have been by nature a woman among men, but by intellect she was a man among women," the reviewer laments that "whatever chance" Fuller had to be taken seriously as an intellectual "has been materially diminished" by her "friends": "These volumes detract much from our idea of Margaret Fuller; and we are certain there is no admirer of her high talents and brilliant capacities but will feel wearied and disgusted with the overweening vanity, inordinate ambition, and capricious characteristics which those books treasure up to her account. . . . [A]nd we more object to the exercise of the same faculties in the persons of, and as regards those editors themselves."[15]

The "idea of Margaret Fuller" contested in 1852 would continue being contested long after her first biographical representation in the *Memoirs.* Thirty-one years after the publication of the *Memoirs,* an aged James Free-man Clarke admitted to Thomas Wentworth Higginson, who was preparing to counter the *Memoirs* with his own biography of the "real" Margaret Fuller, that "Margaret had so many aspects of her soul that she might furnish mate-rial for a hundred biographers" and that "not all could be said even then." In 1915 Emerson biographer O. W. Firkins complained that Fuller was "one of the most inscrutable of personalities . . . in the wilderness of attributes one searches fruitlessly for the evasive character: one chases Margaret through Margaret." Inscrutable, evasive, and certainly provocative in her challenge to notions of the feminine, she has thus "belonged," as David Wat-son put it in 1988, "to many people, individuals as well as groups, each of whom with varying degrees of scrupulousness used her life work for their own purposes." Few figures who have puzzled over Fuller's complexities and their own "restless" ambivalence toward her used her life for their own pur-poses more than did Nathaniel Hawthorne.[16]

Almost fourteen years after parting forever from her as an intimate friend and eight years after her death, Hawthorne could be so moved to passion by petty gossip about Fuller's relationship with Ossoli that he could write in his journal what James R. Mellow has characterized as "the sharpest and most critical judgment he ever made on the human clay," creating, through "a kind of wrath, a secret animus," what Mellow praises as "the portrait of a difficult and vital woman—a woman more vivid and unkind, more instinct with life and passion, than he had ever quite created among his fictional heroines."[17]

Set within the often tedious descriptions of the *Italian Notebooks,* the pas-sage stuns the reader with the force of an eruption. After a visit from Ameri-can sculptor Joseph Mozier in Rome in April 1858, Hawthorne turned to his notebook to record his impressions of Mozier and their talk. He begins the Fuller passage by briefly repeating the gossip of the man he had condemned in the preceding paragraphs of the same journal entry as being made "not of the finest" clay:

> From Greenough, Mr. Mozier passed to Margaret Fuller, whom he knew well, she having been an inmate of his during a part of her residence in Italy. His developments about poor Margaret were very curious. He says that Ossoli's family, though technically noble, is really of no rank whatever; the elder brother, with the title of Marquis, being at this very time a working bricklayer, and the sisters walking the streets without bonnets—that is, being in the sta-tion of peasant-girls, or the female populace of Rome. Ossoli himself, to the best of his belief, was Margaret's servant, or had something to do with the

care of her apartments. He was the handsomest man whom Mr. Mozier ever saw, but entirely ignorant even of his own language, scarcely able to read at all, destitute of manners; in short, half an idiot, and without any pretensions to be a gentleman. At Margaret's request, Mr Mozier had taken him into his studio, with a view to ascertain whether he was capable of instruction in sculpture; but, after four months' labor, Ossoli produced a thing intended to be a copy of a human foot; but the "big toe" was on the wrong side.[18]

Hawthorne then seizes upon Mozier's revelations in an attempt to solve what to him has clearly been the long and deeply troubling puzzle of Fuller's character. In a voice remarkably similar to that of a betrayed admirer provoked by the unworthiness of a successful rival, Hawthorne gropes for some understanding of Fuller and Ossoli's relationship, finding it, despite the possible "revolt" of "conscience," in dismissing Ossoli contemptuously and quite literally as mere sexual object, "this hymen," and in contemplating bitterly the sexuality of Fuller that betrays the woman he suggests he thought he had known and that she attempted to be:

He could not possibly have had the least appreciation of Margaret; and the wonder is, what attraction she found in this boor, this hymen without the intellectual spark—she that had always shown such a cruel and bitter scorn of intellectual deficiency. As from her towards him, I do not understand what feeling there could have been, except it were purely sensual; as from him towards her, there could hardly have been even this, for she had not the charm of womanhood. But she was a woman anxious to try all things, and fill up her experience in all directions; she had a strong and coarse nature, too, which she had done her utmost to refine, with infinite pains, but which of course could only be superficially changed. The solution of the riddle lies in this direction; nor does one's conscience revolt at the idea of thus solving it; for— at least, this is my own experience—Margaret has not left, in the hearts and minds of those who knew her, any deep witness for her integrity and purity. She was a great humbug; of course with much talent, and much moral reality, or else she could not have been so great a humbug. But she had stuck herself full of borrowed qualities, which she chose to provide herself with, but which had no root in her. (14:155–56)

Though he attempts to deny Fuller the superficial sexual attraction suggested by the phrase "the charm of womanhood," the focus, tone, and diction of the passage betray his acknowledgment that the "riddle" of Fuller's character, and his interest in her, is centered in the sexual. Reminiscent of Melville's revealing use of sexually charged metaphor in "Hawthorne and His Mosses," Hawthorne's diction in this passage suggests his obsession with the sexuality of Fuller that informs his metaphorical representation of Fuller's character as one of deceptive and unstable "surfaces" and subversive but authentic "depths." Recalling the sexual terms of his ridicule of "handsome"

Ossoli as "hymen," Hawthorne represents Fuller's intense commitment to self-development as a desire to "*fill up* her experiences" in the "anxious" promiscuity of trying "all things" indiscriminately in "all directions." She cannot "refine" what, in deepest essence, is "coarse," and thus though she "*stuck* herself full of borrowed qualities," they take "no *root* in her," leaving no "*deep* witness for her integrity and purity." The passage, in other words, enacts Hawthorne's condemnation of Fuller's failure; he attempts to deny Fuller's sexual attractiveness while condemning her own irrepressible sexuality, her "strong and coarse nature." Yet he suggests his own attraction to her sexuality by the very act of making it the focus of his solution to her "riddle" and by unconsciously encoding that explanation in the sexually charged terms that betray the origins of his interest.

Fuller at this stage in the passage is the "false" woman, "great humbug," but Hawthorne cannot dismiss her, or his sense of betrayal and anger, so easily. He returns to a final revelation from Mozier's gossip:

> Mr. Mozier added, that Margaret had quite lost all power of literary production, before she left Rome, though occasionally the charm and power of her conversation would re-appear. To his certain knowledge, she had no important manuscripts with her when she sailed, (she having shown him all she had, with a view to his procuring their publication in America); and the History of the Roman Revolution, about which there was so much lamentation, in the belief that it had been lost with her, never had existence. (14:156)

Considering this final clue to the riddle, Hawthorne "refines" the "strong and coarse nature" of the Fuller character that he has just constructed. The simplicities of his portrait of Fuller as a "false" woman are now subsumed within the greater complexities of a tragic heroine whose Faustian aspirations are doomed to collapse of their own sheer folly. If all narratives originate in the desire to allegorize reality, as Hayden White has convincingly argued, the narrative that Hawthorne now creates for Fuller's life and character may be read as an attempt to resolve the "restless" ambivalence of the "riddle" that she has been to him by inserting it within the comforting ideological closures of a tragic allegory of feminine hubris.[19]

> Thus there appears to have been a total collapse in poor Margaret, morally and intellectually; and tragic as her catastrophe was, Providence was, after all, kind in putting her, and her clownish husband and their child, on board that fated ship. There never was such a tragedy as her whole story; the sadder and sterner, because so much of the ridiculous was mixed up with it, and because she could bear anything better than to be ridiculous. It was such an awful joke, that she should have resolved—in all sincerity, no doubt—to make her-

self the greatest, wisest, best woman of the age; and, to that end, she set to work on her strong, heavy, unpliable, and, in many respects, defective and evil nature, and adorned it with a mosaic of admirable qualities, such as she chose to possess; putting in here a splendid talent, and there a moral excellence, and polishing each separate piece, and the whole together, till it seemed to shine afar and dazzle all who saw it. She took credit to herself for having been her own Redeemer, if not her own Creator; and, indeed, she was far more a work of art than any of Mr. Mozier's statues. But she was not working on an inanimate substance, like marble or clay; there was something within her that she could not possibly come at, to re-create and refine it; and, by and by, this rude old potency bestirred itself, and undid all her labor in the twinkling of an eye. On the whole, I do not know but I like her the better for it;—the better, because she proved herself a very woman, after all, and fell as the weakest of her sisters might. (14:156–57)

The shocking potency of this passage is fueled by the very power that Fuller held over Hawthorne's imagination, but it is a power that cannot be contained by the tragic narrative that Hawthorne constructs for her life. The closure Hawthorne seeks in dismissing Fuller as, in the end, an ordinary woman felled by womanly "weakness" is belied not only by her extraordinary power to provoke Hawthorne after so many years but also by the "dazzling" "mosaic" of Hawthorne's own still-stubbornly ambivalent re-creation of her as tragic heroine. The instability of voices in the passage is the very sound of Hawthorne's ambivalences amplified. The cruelty of Hawthorne's endorsement of her and her family's untimely deaths as an act of Providence's kindness, the severity of his judgment of Fuller's nature as being "strong, heavy, unpliable, and, in many respects, defective and evil" are destabilized by the muted voice of an admiration that may have been betrayed but has not been silenced. The passionate logic of betrayal would make Providence "kind" if death saved a fallen Fuller from returning to the land of her early triumphs and many friends mated humiliatingly, for Hawthorne, to a "clownish husband" and unable to produce the masterpiece so long proclaimed and anticipated—a kindness that would save her, in other words, from facing the ridicule he says she could never bear but that, the passage subtly suggests, he could himself never bear to have her face. The "awful joke" of the "ridiculous" that Hawthorne would have as a mixture in Fuller's tragedy originates not in Hawthorne's sense of the comic folly of Fuller's unbounded aspirations but in his bitter contemplation of all that she seemed to promise and to him failed to be, all that once "dazzled" him. And still dazzles him. His attempt in the final sentence to find a new foundation for his admiration of her as an extraordinary example of a conventional woman who merely reaffirms patriarchal smugness about woman's "weakness" is undermined not only by the tentativeness of his "I do not know but" qualification but also by his very conception of her aspirations and fall in the mythic dimensions of a feminist Icarus, Pygmalion, Christ.

If Fuller was a riddle to Hawthorne, this passage suggests an even greater riddle. Namely, just why does Hawthorne care? And clearly, care so much. This study originated with that simple question. The answers, of course, are anything but simple, often less than certain, and it must be acknowledged from the beginning, frequently quite speculative. Given the limited historical record, the answers I propose to the riddle of Hawthorne's relationship with Fuller, like Hawthorne's own interpretation of the meaning of Fuller's life, must of necessity lie in the direction of biographical and intertextual interpretation. They point, however, toward the creative origins of much of Hawthorne's most highly regarded work—"Rappaccini's Daughter," *The Scarlet Letter, The Blithedale Romance,* and *The Marble Faun.* "There never was such a tragedy as her whole story," Hawthorne claims, but the narrative of Fuller's fall inscribed bitterly in his notebook is neither Hawthorne's first nor last revision of the tragedy he wrote her life to be. Quite simply, my reading of Hawthorne's relationship with Fuller suggests that Fuller had disturbed Hawthorne for a very long time, disturbed him so much that to one degree or another he wrote some of his most powerful fictions in an attempt to solve the "riddle" of her life. She was more than simply a partial model for the most complex and provocative women characters in his fiction, as critics have occasionally proposed. She was to an important extent the origin of their very conception, the problem at their heart. As a provocative, intimate friend and as the emblematic voice contesting the conventional ground on which the masculine and the feminine had been constructed, Fuller seems to have come to represent for Hawthorne, as Beatrice did for Giovanni, "the mystery which he deemed the riddle of his own existence" (10:110). Such a mystery, such a riddle, Hawthorne could best confront and attempt to resolve through the privacy and the control provided by the veiled allegories of narrative representation.

Obscured from the beginning by the very nature of these concealed and concealing fictions, Hawthorne's struggle with "the riddle" of Margaret Fuller has been further veiled by the contestations of literary history. If fiction allowed Hawthorne on a deeply personal level to engage in the contemporary effort to define Fuller and thereby confront the challenge she posed to conventional constructions of gender, publication of the notebook characterization twenty years after Hawthorne's death was itself employed to redefine both Fuller and Hawthorne and, of course, their personal and ideological relationship. The effect of that publication and the controversy surrounding it reduced Hawthorne's ambivalence to mere animosity and thus concealed the depth to which Hawthorne's art is shaped by his engagement with Fuller. Despite the immediate and furious defense of Fuller by her friends and relatives, the effect was also, for almost a century, to rescind her claim to a legitimate place in American literary history.

Before we can restore the Hawthorne-Fuller relationship to something like its full complexity and see its importance to his works, we must turn to the moment when Julian Hawthorne would attempt to domesticate his father's image at Fuller's expense. By discrediting Fuller, Julian sought to discredit the aspirations of Fuller's descendant, the New American Woman.

"The Scandal" of Margaret Fuller

Margaret Fuller has at last taken her place with the numberless other dismal frauds who fill the limbo of human pretension and failure.

JULIAN HAWTHORNE

The ideal of Margaret Fuller ... is one of high womanhood. We love it as a symbol. It is a golden image that we symbolically worship. If an iconoclast breaks it, proving it to be but gilded clay, what good? I have lost my idol, and have neither the absolute truth nor the image of gold in its place.

C. A. RALPH

When Emerson learned that Margaret Fuller had been swept off the decks of the *Elizabeth* just fifty yards from Fire Island, he dispatched Thoreau to recover her body and her book—the history of the Italian revolutions of 1848–49 that Fuller had said would be her masterpiece. He failed to find either. Emerson himself took over and transformed Thoreau's mission. Collaborating with two other Fuller friends, James Freeman Clarke and William Henry Channing, Emerson attempted to recover Fuller's life and work for literary history in the *Memoirs of Margaret Fuller Ossoli* (1852). "Because crowds of vulgar people taunt her with want of position," he confided in his journal, "a kind of justice requires of us a monument."[1] The monument that he raised was immediately challenged for its very lack of "justice" to the woman and her words. Nevertheless, anchored by Emerson's eminence, that monument would mark the site of Fuller's reputation for as long as he lived. Two years after his death, however, that monument would be disfigured and relocated.

When in late 1884 Julian Hawthorne published for the first time his father's now infamous 1858 notebook entry assaulting Fuller's marriage and her character, he intentionally provoked a literary scandal he hoped would realign and strengthen his father's position in literary history even as it destroyed Margaret Fuller's. Though Julian's two-volume *Nathaniel Hawthorne and His Wife* came to almost a thousand pages in length, the two and a half pages he devoted to the notebook entry on Fuller received almost the only detailed citation and comment from the reviewers. Her supporters were shocked to read of Hawthorne's assessment of Fuller's "defective and evil nature." Not only did they immediately assail Hawthorne's "solution to the riddle" of Margaret, but they also raised serious questions about the boundaries of propriety in publishing and the motives of Hawthorne and his son. Few literary feuds have been so public and so passionate.

Few have also been so damaging. Titillating as all scandals are, the feud that Julian constructed between the two dead friends and living literary legends is equally fascinating as an instructively dramatic exposure of the usually unarticulated, often unconscious politics behind the making and unmaking of literary reputations and national canons. In the rhetorical extremes with which the participants of the feud defended their chosen "idols," we see also just how fitting is literature's appropriation of the concept of "canonization" to describe the need to create and defend a faith in unblemished cultural saints. This chapter examines that moment in late 1884 and early 1885 when Julian succeeded in repositioning his father in American literary history by destroying Margaret Fuller's reputation, decanonizing damage that has only recently been repaired by revisionist histories of American literature that have raised a new monument to Fuller's reputation on the very grounds that Julian once destroyed it.

By 1884 Margaret Fuller occupied a prominent position in American cultural and literary history. When her *Memoirs* appeared in February 1852, the first thousand copies sold within twenty-four hours. Before the year ended, the two-volume edition had been reprinted four times; by 1884, eleven times.[2] Fuller's *Woman in the Nineteenth Century* (1845) had also enjoyed an active public presence during the three decades after her death, having been printed nine times by 1884. By that year her *Papers on Literature and Art* (1846) had been reissued six times and had originally been published along with Hawthorne's *Mosses,* Poe's *Tales,* and Melville's *Typee* as part of Evert Duyckinck's Library of American Books series for Wiley and Putnam.[3] Her brother Arthur's edited collections of her work, *At Home and Abroad* (1856) and *Life Within and Life Without* (1860), had been reissued, respectively, ten and four times. Of her *Summer on the Lakes, 1843,* Duyckinck in his private diary had written that it was the most genuinely American book he had ever read, and in 1855 he had included her in his groundbreaking *Cyclopaedia of American Literature.* In 1868 Horace Greeley had devoted an entire chapter in his autobiography, *Recollections of a Busy Life,* to Fuller, calling her "the best instructed woman in America" and "the loftiest, bravest soul that has yet irradiated the form of an American woman," judging her *Woman in the Nineteenth Century* "the loftiest and most commanding assertion yet made of the right of Woman to be regarded and treated as an independent, intelligent, rational being, entitled to an equal voice in framing and modifying the laws she is required to obey." The next year, Greeley had his publishing house issue a six-volume edition of Fuller's works.[4]

If Fuller's reputation seemed secure three decades after her death, the year 1884 initially promised improvement. Just the year before, Fuller's friend Julia Ward Howe had published *Margaret Fuller (Marchesa Ossoli)* for Roberts Brothers' Eminent Women series, the first biography of Fuller since the *Memoirs,* on which Howe depended heavily. In 1884 another friend, Thomas Wentworth Higginson, enshrined Fuller in the Houghton Mifflin American Men of Letters series with his still highly regarded biography *Margaret Fuller Ossoli.* Designed to compete with Macmillan's successful English Men of Letters series, of which Henry James's *Hawthorne* formed a part, the American Men of Letters series—along with the companion series American Statesmen and American Commonwealths—was initiated by Horace Scudder at Houghton Mifflin.[5] One of the first in the twenty-three volumes in the series of "the *men* who made" American literary history, Higginson's biography sought to elevate Fuller's reputation by redefining her as a serious thinker who was as committed to social action as to thought and thus explicitly challenging the Fuller who had been left "a little too much in the clouds" by the Emerson-Clarke-Channing *Memoirs.* Though Fuller had on Higginson "a more immediate intellectual influence" than "anyone except Emerson and Parker," she was not, as the *Memoirs* would suggest, an otherworldly, eccentric thinker, "a mystic, a dreamer, or a book-worm," but a woman determined to put thought into action, to engage what Higginson terms her "vigorous executive side."[6] If Higginson was challenging the *Memoirs* in 1884, Roberts Brothers was to make sure the public could judge for itself which of the two Fullers it preferred; that year alone Roberts Brothers followed up Howe's biography by reissuing the *Memoirs* four times and *Woman in the Nineteenth Century* once. In 1879 Henry James had written that Fuller had become such a "legend" that "the people who had known her well grew at last to be envied by later comers."[7] By the end of 1884, recovering and defining the memory of Margaret Fuller for "later comers" had become a cultural enterprise at its point of greatest energy. In that year there were to be not two but three Fullers to choose from—the Transcendentalist mystic Fuller of the *Memoirs* (and Howe's retelling), the social activist Fuller of Higginson, and the fallen-woman Fuller of the Hawthornes, Nathaniel and Julian.

Despite the fiery public defense of Fuller by her friends and family following Julian's publication of *Nathaniel Hawthorne and His Wife*, his vociferous insistence on his father's infallibility and his own vituperative attacks on Fuller clearly damaged her position within the American literary canon. After 1884 the *Memoirs*, for instance, would not be reprinted again until 1973, and even then only in a small run by a reprint house.[8] Fuller's *Woman in the Nineteenth Century*, in its twelfth printing in 1884, would be reprinted only once more (in 1893) before its resurrection in 1969. Other Fuller works and edited collections by her brother would suffer the same neglect.[9] Thus during the two crucial periods in which the American literary canon was institutionalized—the closing decades of the nineteenth century and its reformulation during the third and fourth decades of the twentieth century—Margaret Fuller was simply out of print and, of course, out of the canon, each to some extent both cause and effect of the other.[10]

Fuller's sudden devaluation in the very year that promised to raise her literary and historical currency was, in fact, part of Julian's strategy to strengthen his father's position as a celebrated American author. As Jane Tompkins and Richard Brodhead have so thoroughly demonstrated, by 1884 Hawthorne had long been served by the emerging literary institutions that had created and were busily marketing a canon of American literature as a "classic" American literature with a cultural difference.[11] Marketed as a classic first by Ticknor and Fields in their Blue and Gold edition and later by James R. Osgood and Company in their Little Classic edition, from 1880 on, as Brodhead has observed, Hawthorne was to be promoted vigorously by Osgood's successor Houghton Mifflin as a classic for all cultural levels—for the popular market in cheap paperbacks, for the collectors market in a deluxe edition, for the juvenile-educational market in the remarkably successful Riverside Literature series, and in 1883 for the burgeoning middle class and their home libraries in the Riverside edition of the Complete Works, the "format," says Brodhead, that "Houghton Mifflin perfected to identify the standard authors." Hawthorne's "extraordinary cultural status" in the second half of the nineteenth century, according to Brodhead, was such that not only did his greatness go completely unchallenged but he also began to define the fiction writer's "whole literary enterprise" as "no other figure in the history of American fiction . . . before or since." As French and Russian narrative models became influential, Hawthorne, instead of losing, gained in stature as he was reassessed in their light and each time found to prefigure them.[12] The 1883 twelve-volume deluxe edition of Hawthorne's works illustrates the bull market at work in Hawthorne's valuation as a national cultural treasure. The first of Houghton Mifflin's deluxe limited editions of American authors, the Hawthorne edition of 250 copies sold out immediately through subscription at six dollars a volume, many of the subscribers being "shrewd booksellers," according to Ellen B. Ballou; soon afterward volumes were reselling for fifteen dollars, prompting Houghton Mifflin to double the number of copies to 500 for the Emerson and Longfellow deluxe editions to follow.[13]

Using Hawthorne as her case study, Jane Tompkins has argued that classics "do not *withstand* change; they are always registering, or promoting, or retarding alterations in historical conditions as these affect their readers, and, especially, the members of the literary establishment." Julian's *Nathaniel Hawthorne and His Wife* illustrates this historically contingent process. Published in an identical format and binding as the prestigious Riverside edition of the Complete Works (in both trade and deluxe edition formats), and advertised as an optional supplement to the set, Julian's biography attempts to position Hawthorne as the thoroughly committed author and practitioner of the values of the market for which the edition was targeted—the middle-class American home.[14] Materially indistinguishable from his father's works in the edition, the biography makes a visual claim to Hawthorne's authority as an endorsement of Julian's reading of his life. Julian's "Hawthorne" registers the values of the conventionally domestic, and his cultural and literary prestige serves to champion the fight against those threatening to disrupt the harmony of the middle-class home. When Julian published the notebook entry and started a literary feud, more was at stake than simply domesticating Hawthorne for the marketplace.

Julian published *Nathaniel Hawthorne and His Wife* when the role of women in American society was undergoing rapid and profound redefinition, and his biography registers that change by resisting it with the weight of his father's prestige. Though the phrase the "New Woman" would begin to surface in the next decade to signify the end of the cultural hegemony of "the cult of True Womanhood," by the early 1880s the ideological underpinnings of "True Womanhood" were collapsing. Kate Gannett Wells's *Atlantic Monthly* article in December 1880, "The Transitional American Woman," assumes, in fact, that women had already rejected the most fundamental condition for the preservation of "True Womanhood": "Women do not care for their home as they did. . . . The simple fact is that women have found that they can have occupation, respectability, and even dignity disconnected from the home." Wells's article, indeed, is a complaint that "the imperative mood in which the times address modern women" to "do something, be of worth in yourself, form opinions" has led to "restlessness, wandering purpose, and self-consciousness." Assuming the triumph of the new vision of woman's life, Wells simply identifies, and laments, the aftereffects of the transition. The entire December issue of the *Atlantic,* in fact, works to redefine the concept of woman: Wells's article (817–23) is preceded by an installment of Henry James's *Portrait of a Lady* (740–66) and followed by George E. Woodberry's tribute to Mary Wollstonecraft (838–46).[15]

If Margaret Fuller in 1844 had become one of the first professional women journalists, by the 1880s James's "New Woman," Henrietta Stackpole, was no anomaly. Journalist Jan "Jennie June" Croly had started the first professional women's club, Sorosis, in 1868, after being denied admission to the all-male New York Press Club's dinner for Charles Dickens. By 1890, when the General Federation of Women's Clubs was founded, the women's club movement numbered more than a million members.[16] Though only 31 percent of American colleges accepted women in 1870, by 1890 that figure had more than doubled to 65 percent.[17] At the same time, first-rate colleges for women were being established: Vassar in 1865, Wellesley and Smith in 1875, Harvard Annex (Radcliffe) in 1882, and H. Sophie Newcomb in 1886. Expanded educational opportunities began to pay dramatic results: between 1890 and 1910, for instance, the number of women with college degrees soared from twenty-five hundred to almost eight thousand.[18]

As Wells observed in 1880, women were finding fulfillment outside the home, particularly women in urban areas, where the percentage of women ten years and older who worked grew from 16 percent in 1870 to 26 percent in 1890.[19] Whether or not they had jobs outside the home, many women entered the public arena to debate key social and political issues. The 1848 Seneca Falls Convention for women's rights, which Fuller's *Woman in the Nineteenth Century* is often credited with inspiring, had led, of course, to the women's suffrage movement; in 1878 the "Susan B. Anthony" constitutional amendment for women's suffrage was first introduced, as it would be virtually every year until its adoption in 1920. In 1874 the Women's Christian Temperance Union was founded; in 1889 Hull House was opened; and in 1895 the National Association of Colored Women was chartered.

The decisions Julian made in constructing his book respond to this social and historical context as much as they do to Fuller's individual impact. As contemporary reviewers were generally quick to praise, Julian gives his mother equal, but of course subordinate, billing. Her identity as a subject worthy of biography is equated with her duty. Julian claims that he has simply organized family documents and allowed his subjects to speak for themselves without his caring "to comment or to apologize" and not having been "concerned to announce or confirm any theory." But revealingly he dedicates the biography to his own wife as "Records of a Happy Marriage" and allows himself one interpretative "remark": "If true love and married happiness should ever be in need of vindication, ample material for that purpose may be found in these volumes."[20] And, implicitly acknowledging the "morbid" shadows haunting his father's image, he adds that the family closet has "no skeleton in it," that indeed "there was nothing to be hidden" in the first place. He assures his reader that he has indeed emptied that closet, excluding materials only because of considerations of "taste rather than of discretion," a claim that Fuller's friends would challenge.[21]

Julian's purposes embrace discrete but complementary goals. Allusions in reviews of the biography to the image of a morbid, reclusive Hawthorne whose sensibilities were perhaps slightly effeminate suggest why Julian recast his father's public image in the mold of a domesticated, manly Hawthorne. With one significant exception, every contemporary reviewer of *Nathaniel Hawthorne and His Wife* seemed to breathe a sigh of relief at the revelation of Hawthorne's "happy marriage" and the effect it had on dispelling any lingering doubts about Hawthorne the man.[22] The review in the *New York Times* illustrates the extent of Julian's success: "Here and there idle gossips have hinted at skeletons in the Hawthorne closets, and . . . his admirers will be glad to have this full record extant ready to stop busy mouths. Hawthorne's life was as pure and transparent as his own matchless English prose style, and, despite his shyness and retiring ways, he was at heart as manly as the best of us, and he had absolutely nothing to conceal." The reviewer for the *Nation* also praises the masculine sanity of Hawthorne by contrasting him with the "effeminate" intellectual environment surrounding him, Transcendentalism, "a species of intellectual measles which was then very contagious among the feminine minds of the neighborhood": "Certainly by comparison with the life out of which Hawthorne came, and perhaps even more clearly by comparison with the Transcendentalists, the Brook Farm reformers, the prophets and prophetesses among whom he was thrown, moral health and mental sanity and the vigor of an uncorruptible common sense seem to be peculiarly his possession—one is almost tempted to say, his alone." As if to prove further that "moral health and mental sanity" are inherently masculine, the reviewer associates masculine sexuality with healthy thought. The Transcendentalist Sophia, he notes, not only found a cure for her headaches when she married Hawthorne but "with the headache, apparently, disappeared also that peculiar Bostonian malady already mentioned. There is nothing more about 'paly golden-green letters,' or Mr. Emerson in his incarnation as 'Pure Tone.'" If the reviewer for the *New-York Daily Tribune* is not as explicit as reviewers of the *New York Times* or the *Nation* in declaring with relief that Hawthorne was "as manly as the best of us," he comes close. He praises "the Hawthorne whom his son presents" for being far from "the mystical, weird, and morbid romancer known to the sentimental imagination of would-be analysts" and asserts, now confidently, that "the Hawthorne of real life was a man of thoroughly sane mental habits, of healthy sensibilities and large sympathies." That Julian's portrait of his parents' marriage was a success in reshaping Hawthorne's image would be understating it, judging at least by one reviewer, *Chicago Tribune* columnist Hattie Tyng Griswold, who stated flatly that "no more beautiful record of a perfect marriage has ever been made than this life of the Hawthornes presents."[23]

As Julian proclaimed, however, his portrait of his parents' "perfect marriage" had broader purposes. Given the erosion of women's commitment to a life centered exclusively upon the home, the idyllic and conventional marriage that he portrays is meant to "vindicate" traditional "true love and married happiness" against the emergent forces threatening them. In a follow-up to her review of the biography, Hattie Tyng Griswold in "The Reasons for Hawthorne's Dislike of Margaret Fuller" made Julian's implicit polemic explicit. After identifying Hawthorne's dislike of Fuller as the result of his love for "simple, natural, unaffected people, and the part of a sibyl" therefore "very distasteful to him," Griswold praised Sophia as being "so different a person from the noble army of literary and artistic women who are so numerous today but who in his time had just begun to assert themselves— that, believing her to be the perfect flower of womanhood as he did, he could scarcely be expected to appreciate the Zenobias of that or of the present time." So powerful is the persistence of the ideal of the domestic "perfect flower of womanhood" that Griswold also contrasted Sophia with her sister Elizabeth Peabody, "one of the women of the new era" who "has spent her entire life in noble efforts to improve the world into which she was born," and can end the contrast only in the puzzled indecision born of the pull and counterpull of two conflicting gender ideologies: "Who shall say whether Mrs. Hawthorne or Miss Peabody was the highest type of woman?"[24]

Julian has no problem at all answering that question. For him, "Miss Fuller" (pointedly *not* Higginson's "Margaret Fuller Ossoli" or, much less, Howe's "Marchesa Ossoli"), then legendary as the almost mythic "creator" and symbol of the "New Woman," becomes useful as a foil to Sophia as wife and to Hawthorne as artist. Fuller's "tainted" marriage and "fall" provide Julian with a dark allegory about all "New Women," who, like Fuller, lose themselves as they stray from the home, an allegory against which Julian may highlight the "true love and married happiness" that Sophia found in the ideological confines of her conventional home—the very type of home, Julian suggests, requisite for nurturing great artists like his father.

Though ample evidence indicates that Sophia greatly admired Fuller before her marriage and that both Nathaniel and Sophia were intimate friends with her during their residence at the Old Manse, Julian selects and provides an interpretative frame for those materials that will portray Fuller as a potentially disruptive influence on his parents' marital "bliss," a misguiding influence on women in general, and a "fallen" woman whose radical feminism merely masked the desire for and subverted the attainment of the "bliss" that his parents found in their marriage.[25]

In portraying Fuller as a potentially disruptive influence on the Hawthorne marriage, Julian sets up his citation of Hawthorne's letter to Fuller declining the proposal to board her sister Ellen and Ellen's husband, Ellery Channing, by describing "Miss Fuller" as "a very clever woman" of whom "most people stood in some awe." He presents his father as being unintimidated, in fact as more than her match, for Julian adds as a postscript that the letter "finished the episode" and that if Miss Fuller "felt any dissatisfaction" she did not think it "advisable to express any." His mother is also not among those standing in "some awe" of Fuller. Julian cites Sophia's letter to her own mother reacting to Fuller's *Woman in the Nineteenth Century* ("What do you think of the speech which Queen Margaret Fuller has made from the throne? It seems to me that if she were married truly, she would no longer be puzzled about the rights of women.").[26] To be sure that his contemporary reader recognizes the wisdom of his mother's rejection of Fuller's misguided feminism, he prefaces the letter with his own patronizing dismissal of Fuller's and his own generation's concern for "the never-to-be-exhausted theme of Women's Rights":

> Miss Fuller was at this time in her apogee, and had to be doing something; and accordingly . . . she produced a book in which the never-to-be-exhausted

theme of Women's Rights was touched upon. The book made the rounds of the transcendental circle, and was sufficiently discussed; and doubtless there are disciples of this renowned woman now living who could quote pages of it. But married women, who had in their husbands their ideal of marital virtue, and whose domestic affairs sufficiently occupied them, were not likely to be cordial supporters of such doctrines as the book enunciated.[27]

Julian's desire to legitimize his own antifeminism through the authority of his parents may have led him, in fact, to rewrite and misdate his mother's letter in order to strengthen her condemnation of Fuller's "book." First of all, the now-lost letter that Julian cites condemns Fuller's 1845 "book" yet includes Sophia's praise of Emerson's review of Carlyle in the *Dial*, a review that appeared in July 1843, the same month as Fuller's "Great Lawsuit."[28] If Sophia was instead commenting on "The Great Lawsuit" and not *Woman in the Nineteenth Century,* as seems reasonable, then Sophia's and Hawthorne's relationship with Fuller certainly was not damaged in the least by her feminism, which Julian's "dating" of the letter has encouraged. As the next chapter demonstrates, the friendship between Fuller and both Hawthornes, in fact, was more intimate than ever in 1844.[29] In 1845 Sophia did indeed comment in a letter to her mother on Fuller's *Woman in the Nineteenth Century,* but her condemnation of the book is considerably milder than her comments in the letter reproduced by Julian. Sufficient parallels exist, however, to raise the possibility that Julian revised the letter to further his own purposes, just as he revised (as we shall see shortly) his father's notebook entry on Fuller. On 6 March 1845, Sophia wrote her mother that she "had no time to read any thing excepting my little daughter—with which belle literature I am quite content," but in the very next sentence of a new paragraph she indicated that she had made time to read *Woman in the Nineteenth Century:*

> I have read Margaret's book once but have not fully possessed myself of it yet. The impression it left was disagre[e]able. I did not like the tone of it—& did not agree with her at all about the change in woman's outward circumstances. But I do not think a single woman can possibly have any idea of the true position of woman. Neither do I believe in such a character of man as she gives. It is altogether too ignoble. I suspect a wife only can know how to speak with sufficient respect of man. I think Margaret speaks of many things that should not be spoken of.[30]

In the letter offered by Julian, Sophia shifts abruptly from a panegyric on Emerson's wisdom to an attack on "Queen Margaret Fuller's" impertinence:

> What do you think of the speech which Queen Margaret Fuller has made from the throne? It seems to me that if she were married truly, she would no longer be puzzled about the rights of woman. This is the revelation of wom-

an's true destiny and place, which never can be *imagined* by those who do not experience the relation. In perfect, high union there is no question of supremacy. Souls are equal in love and intelligent communion, and all things take their proper places as inevitably as the stars their orbits. Had there never been false and profane marriages, there would not only be no commotion about woman's rights, but it would be Heaven here at once. Even before I was married, however, I could never feel the slightest interest in this movement. It then seemed to me that each woman could make her own sphere quietly, and also it was always a shock to me to have women mount the rostrum. Home, I think, is the great arena for women, and there, I am sure, she can wield a power which no king or conqueror can cope with. I do not believe any man who ever knew one noble woman would ever speak as if she were an inferior in any sense: it is the fault of ignoble women that there is any such opinion in the world.[31]

The letter cited by Julian rings false in the very first sentence, for not only was sarcasm as alien to Sophia's temperament as it was integral to Julian's, but, as in Sophia's 6 March 1845 letter, Sophia habitually referred to Fuller in her letters as simply "Margaret," never "Margaret Fuller," much less "Queen Margaret Fuller."[32] If indeed Julian did revise his mother's letter, Sophia's supposed condemnation of "ignoble women," of "false and profane marriages," and of Fuller's views in general because she was not "married *truly*" conveniently complement the purposes for which Julian employs his father's 1858 notebook reaction to Fuller's marriage.[33]

Sophia chose to suppress Hawthorne's 1858 notebook entry on Fuller when she had control of her husband's texts, an act of discretion Fuller's friends were to praise in their condemnation of Julian's impropriety. Sophia, it may be supposed, wished not only to observe the propriety of not tainting Fuller's name and offending Fuller's friends and relatives but also to suppress what one reviewer of the passage labeled "the dark quality" of Hawthorne's "genius."[34] Julian had no fear that his father's immense reputation would be tainted, at least not among those who really count: "The majority of readers," he claims confidently during the heat of the ensuing feud with Fuller's supporters, "will . . . not be inconsolable" that Hawthorne has exposed Margaret so candidly even though Julian knew beforehand, as he says contemptuously, that the exposure "would create a fluttering in the dove cotes of Margaret's surviving friends, and of the later disciples."[35]

Julian, however, is not as candid as his father. He edits the notebook passage and frames it to put his father in the best possible light. He introduces the passage by dubbing Mozier's gossip about Fuller as "facts regarding her marriage" and by sarcastically terming his father's analysis of Fuller's character as "not too eulogistic."[36] He is also careful to exclude his father's own frame for the passage on Fuller, a frame that would detract from the credibility of Mozier's "facts" in that it is critical of Mozier's character and suggests that Hawthorne probably accepted Mozier's account with considerably more skepticism than Julian would have his readers feel.[37] Within the passage that he does quote, he makes several significant editorial changes that further his purposes. After the first sentence introducing Mozier's account of Fuller, Julian omits his father's statement that Mozier's "developments about poor Margaret were very curious"; the omission furthers Julian's effort to turn gossip into "fact" and to suppress any possibility of reading ambivalence in his father's reaction. More important, he makes editorial changes that preserve the image he seeks to create of his father as a righteous and courageous exposer of moral, feminist fraud and that protect him from charges of an ungentlemanly, indeed gratuitously profane and somewhat prurient, interest in Fuller's sexuality. To suppress his father's repeating of Mozier's implication that Fuller and Ossoli lived "in sin," he deletes Margaret's name in the identification of Ossoli as "Margaret's servant" ("———'s servant") or having "something to do with the care of her apartments" (". . . of ———'s apartments"). For his father's puzzlement over what "attraction" Margaret could have "found in this boor, this hymen without the intellectual spark," Julian censors "hymen" and substitutes "man." Where his father finally identified the only possible attraction Margaret could find in Ossoli as being "purely sensual," Julian deletes the entire phrase and leaves the reader with the impression that Hawthorne's chaste imagination had found its limits ("As from her towards him, I do not understand what feeling there could have been"). To cover his tracks, Julian must also recast "as from him towards her, there could hardly have been even this [the "attraction" of the "purely sensual"]" into "as from him towards her I can understand as little."[38]

Despite Julian's best efforts to preserve the severity of his father's judgment of Margaret without impugning the character of the judge, Sarah Clarke, one of Margaret's closest surviving friends, was quick to accuse Hawthorne of having clearly implied that Margaret "was not married to Ossoli," revealing how sensitive Fuller's family and friends were to the still-current suspicion that Fuller had not really been officially married or that, if she had, she had done so only after her baby was born. Julian takes hypocritical umbrage at Clarke's interpretation, and his reaction suggests the image of his father that he had hoped an edited version of the notebook entry would help preserve: Of Fuller not being married, he insists that his father "never entertained such an idea; he was not the man, under any circumstances, to make an insinuation; and the language he uses will not bear Miss Clarke's gratuitous interpretation."[39]

The fury of Fuller's friends and relatives over Julian's publication of his father's notebook entry on Fuller originated primarily, of course, in their desire to defend her memory from malicious and false attack, but the context in which they rallied to her defense suggests that their defense was informed by broader and more complex considerations than personal loyalty. Fuller had become more than just their friend; she had become a national symbol that guided their efforts to redefine woman's "proper sphere." One participant in the debate that followed, C. A. Ralph, a man who identifies himself as being "a later-day lover of Margaret Fuller ... one who has learned to look upon her as combining with distinct originality many of those characteristics of true womanhood which are so needful now as high ideals," complains bitterly against the increasing tendency toward iconoclasm. After stating that the defamation of an author's character does not negate the truths of his works, he explicitly identifies the larger import of Julian's attack:

> It is in this respect that the question of post-mortem criticism more nearly affects the case of Margaret Fuller, for it is rather by the ideal conception of her as an admirable woman than from her writings that she is worthy of remembrance. The existing symbol of her is every way worthy, and is the creation of those who best knew her. Its truth or falsity *cannot* be proven now. Let it stand. If it is true, as a most noble and loveable example; if it is false, then it is the same, but purely ideal. Its influence is only for good; why destroy it? The ideal of Margaret Fuller that remains is one of high womanhood. We love it as a symbol. It is a golden image that we symbolically worship. If an iconoclast breaks it, proving it to be but gilded clay, what good? I have lost my idol, and have neither the absolute truth nor the image of gold in its place.[40]

Ralph's reference to Fuller as a "symbol" created "by those who best knew her" alludes to the biographical projects that, three decades after the publication of the *Memoirs*, two of Fuller's friends had just completed—Julia Ward Howe in 1883, with *Margaret Fuller (Marchesa Ossoli)*, and Thomas Wentworth Higginson in 1884, with *Margaret Fuller Ossoli*. These biographies, together with the four reissues of the *Memoirs* and the one reissue of *Woman in the Nineteenth Century* in 1884, had consolidated Fuller's position as the "idol" of "high womanhood" in American cultural and literary history. Indeed, Higginson's overriding purpose was to strengthen that position even as he redefined it.

Higginson, who would match Julian insult for insult in the feud, was both personally and ideologically linked with Fuller. As a child, he had known her as a friend of his older sister, and as an adult he had married Ellery Channing's sister and had thus become the brother-in-law of Margaret's sister, Ellen Fuller Channing, acting frequently as her and her child's (Margaret Fuller Channing's) protector by making his home their refuge when Ellen and Ellery's marriage suffered one of its many storms. When he finally had a child of his own late in life, by his second wife, he named her Margaret Waldo Higginson after two of his idols. A committed intellectual who wrote prolifically throughout his life, Higginson was also a man of social conscience determined to act upon his beliefs. Among the most militant of abolitionists, he led a company of black soldiers in the Civil War and was a charter activist in the temperance, women's suffrage, and civil service reform movements. Early on he had taken up Fuller's challenge in *Woman in the Nineteenth Century*, joining the women's movement at its formal inception in the early 1850s, and he was among the leaders who formed the American Suffrage Association in 1869, acting for years as one of the contributing editors for its newspaper, *Woman's Journal*.[41]

By openly attempting in his biography to rescue Fuller from the image of the "mystic" eccentric created in large part by the *Memoirs*, Higginson emphasized "that vigorous executive side which was always prominent in her aspiration for her self and which was visible to all after she reached Italy."[42] The Transcendental "idea of Margaret Fuller," in other words, was to be supplanted by the feminist, social activist "idea," an idea that was not only more attractive to an intellectual social activist like Higginson but one in which Fuller could serve as an "ideal" of womanhood in an age, as Ralph proclaimed above, that was so "needful" of that ideal.

Higginson's biography goes a long way toward rescuing Fuller from the "clouds," but to recenter her life in the arena of social activism and to establish her credentials as a noble example to contemporary women, Higginson nevertheless clearly feels obligated thirty-four years after her death to put to rest any lingering hint of scandal regarding her marriage to Ossoli. Though he tries to portray her "vigorous executive" side, ironically he ends up committing almost a fifth of the book to her marriage—quoting at length both Mr. Cass's and Mrs. Story's full account (the *Memoirs* having abbreviated it) of Margaret's assurances to them of the propriety of her marriage and devoting an entire chapter to quotations from the love letters "between husband and wife." Higginson concludes the biography by vigorously attacking suggestions that Margaret's life had been a tragic failure. For Higginson, her life was "a triumphant rather than a sad one," for "she shared in great deeds, she was the counselor of great men, she had a husband who was a lover, and she had a child. They loved each other in their lives, and in their death they were not divided. Was not that enough?"[43]

Higginson's efforts to redefine Margaret's image for his age were inspired by lifelong personal and ideological commitments, but they were also quite timely, as was Julian's attempt to discredit her, for though the role of women was rapidly changing during this period, the suffrage movement had been rocked in the past fifteen years by dissension and scandal.[44]

Upset over Elizabeth Stanton's radicalism and particularly her racist remarks opposing the Fifteenth Amendment to give suffrage to *male* blacks while still denying it to all females, in 1869 the New England contingent of the movement split from the National Woman Suffrage Movement, led by Stanton and Susan B. Anthony, and formed the American Suffrage Association, led by former Fuller friends and supporters: Thomas Wentworth Higginson, Julia Ward Howe, Lucy Stone, Henry Blackwell, Rev. Henry Ward Beecher, and Theodore Tilton. The New England group formed its own periodical, *Woman's Journal,* in 1870, to provide an alternative to Stanton and Anthony's *Revolution.* From the beginning, efforts were made by the New England group, particularly by Higginson, to heal the split, but the movement was not to be united again until 1890. The New England group to which Higginson belonged was decidedly more conservative than Stanton's group. Higginson's Fuller—loving mother and wife *and* social and feminist activist—may be interpreted as his and his group's alternative ideal to the militant feminist they saw in Stanton.

Julian's blunt perception of Fuller as a "fraud" in need of exposure may have been inspired by, and almost certainly inspired memories of, the moral scandal that had earlier shaken the American Suffrage Association and all the country. In 1872 Rev. Henry Ward Beecher, the first president of the American Suffrage Association and nationally famous as a religious leader and moral spokesman, was accused of having seduced and maintained a long-term affair with the wife of one of his chief supporters and best friends, Theodore Tilton, a founding member of the American Suffrage Association and the president of the Union Association, an organization formed to reconcile the two suffrage groups. The public charge of adultery was made by the irrepressible spokeswoman for "free love" and avowed enemy of hypocrisy, Victoria Claflin Woodhull, in her Commodore Vanderbilt–subsidized *Woodhull & Claflin Weekly.* Briefly jailed for "obscenity" through the efforts of Anthony Comstock and eventually acquitted, Woodhull pressed the attack on Beecher in follow-up articles and persuaded Tilton, by then her own lover, to file suit against Beecher. The suit led to a nationally publicized trial that ended with a hung jury.

If the thirty-four years that had passed since the death of Fuller had not been sufficient time for Higginson to feel that rumors about her marriage had been silenced, then certainly the twelve years since the Beecher affair had not lessened the sensitivity of Higginson and Fuller's friends to the consequences of another scandal. Nor could they ignore the furor in the 1884 presidential election over Grover Cleveland's illegitimate son. Higginson, a Cleveland supporter, had in fact split with the American Woman Suffrage Association and left his position at the *Woman's Journal* (carrying his column on women to *Harper's Bazaar*) when Lucy Stone, supporting the graft-tainted Republican Blaine, used the *Woman's Journal* to denounce the Democratic reformer Cleveland as immoral, claiming that his election would "defile the purity of the American woman and endanger the sanctity of the American home."[45] Given the lingering memories of the embarrassment of the Beecher scandal and the bitter divisiveness of the election just concluded, Fuller's supporters could not but have been enraged with Julian's attempt not only to promote his father's characterization of Fuller as "fallen" but also to follow it up in the press with his own indictment of Fuller as a "dismal fraud."

In general, the sales and the reviews of *Nathaniel Hawthorne and His Wife* were very positive. Released in late October with a trade printing in the Riverside format of 3,000 copies, the biography had to be reprinted by December, this time in a 1,000-copy press run. A limited edition of 350 numbered copies was also released in the deluxe, collector's Riverside edition format, a hundred more copies of the edition than had been printed the year before of his father's works.[46]

Reviewers praised the inspiring example of the Hawthornes' "happy marriage," and throughout November the reviewers also either accepted Hawthorne's assessment of Margaret Fuller or raised no serious objections. The reviewer for Fuller's former paper, the *New-York Daily Tribune*, praised Julian's decision to publish Hawthorne's love letters and announced that "the world should be grateful for the records of so wise and noble a sentiment, so unselfish, and wholesome a passion." Of the Fuller passage, the reviewer said that it revealed Hawthorne's "positive aversion" to the "high priestess" of Transcendentalism and that, though it was "a rather harsh analysis of her character and career" and may be "partially mistaken and prejudiced," it nevertheless "has in it many elements of truth, and is, perhaps, quite as trustworthy as the unduly worshipping estimates of her followers." The reviewer for the *New York Times* praised the "pure and transparent" life Julian portrayed of his father, observed that Hawthorne's "opinions of others was [*sic*] severe and searching" and that consequently they were "likely to create discussion," and then singled out the Fuller passage as an example, quoting it in full. The reviewer followed the quotation with praise: "Hawthorne, we may be sure, never wrote those lines for publication. But how worthy of his powers of insight they are! She was a person 'anxious to try all things.' Who that knows anything about Margaret Fuller but will feel the truth of that sentence?" The reviewer for the *Boston Herald* said the propriety of publishing the passage on Fuller "may be questioned" but that it "discloses more truth about her than her friends and biographers have seemed willing to have told."[47]

In the first review of the book in the *Boston Evening Transcript*, on 15 November, the reviewer also hailed Hawthorne's "insight" into Fuller's perplexing character, saying that Hawthorne's "severe" judgment of her "reconciles all the others" and that though "it is not a pleasant solution of the riddle . . . it is better to know precisely what sort of Isis is behind the veil." In the second review in the *Boston Evening Transcript*, on 28 November, the writer reported that the biography had "already created a profound stir in literary circles" in reaction to Julian's decision to open up "private and confidential correspondence which in other hands and under other circumstances would have never seen the light." The reviewer indicts Julian for demonstrating "little delicacy or regard for the eternal fitness of things" but then pardons him because "there are few living to be wounded by any of these betrayed confidences" and "there does not seem to be a single expression in them inspired by a feeling of spite, bitterness or prejudice." Of the Fuller passage, the reviewer accepts Julian's version of the Fuller-Hawthorne relationship and concludes, as generations of scholars would afterward, that "Margaret Fuller was . . . an acquaintance—it can hardly be said a friend—of Hawthorne's" and that "he always disliked and distrusted her." The reviewer then proceeds to quote the entire Fuller passage without further comment. The irony of condemning Julian for the impropriety of publishing private and confidential papers and then proceeding to quote the most sensational and severe passage among them seems to have escaped this reviewer. Indeed, most reviews and even some of the letters written in Fuller's defense quote all or extensive parts of the passage even as they condemn not only its portrayal of Fuller but Julian's lack of propriety in making it public.[48]

The "profound stir in literary circles" became a very public feud by December. If the early reviews largely accepted Julian's presentation of Hawthorne's attitudes toward Fuller and barely questioned Hawthorne's judgment of her and Julian's discretion in publishing the passage, later reviews became much more critical, particularly after Fuller's supporters began to challenge the "idea of Fuller" that seemed to be gaining ascendancy over the rehabilitated image that Higginson had created earlier in the year.

On 6 December, Henry B. Blackwell, husband of Lucy Stone, reviewed the biography for the *Woman's Journal.* Reflecting the double ideological commitment of the *Woman's Journal* and its sponsor, the American Suffrage Association, to preserve the sacredness of the domestic even as it fought to secure a place for women outside the home, Blackwell uses half of the review to praise the "pure and happy home life" of the Hawthornes and half to condemn a series of passages in the biography that he identifies as being "on the wrong side of public questions." Among them, of course, is the Fuller passage, which Blackwell condemns as being "so cruelly unfair and so bitterly unjust." He rebukes the "settled prejudice" of both Hawthorne and Julian, particularly the "sneer" with which Julian dismisses the women's movement and Fuller's *Woman in the Nineteenth Century,* a work that "seems to-day a series of truisms so generally accepted as to have lost their novelty."[49]

On 12 December, Fuller's longtime friend Sarah Clarke began the full-fledged counterattack on both Hawthorne and Julian with a letter in the *Boston Evening Transcript,* and three days later another Fuller intimate, Caroline Healey Dall, entered the fray with her book review, "The Hawthorne Book Censured," in the *Springfield Republican.* The notebook entry, Clarke writes, is "discreditable" to Hawthorne's "judgment of character" and is "full of untruths," but Hawthorne "was too wise to publish anything so crude." Claiming that Hawthorne implies that Fuller "was not married to Ossoli," the most damaging and seemingly unsuppressible insinuation haunting Margaret's image, she counters by citing the *Memoirs* account of an Ossoli wedding. She also defends Ossoli's intelligence, his family's social rank, and Margaret's integrity. Praising Sophia's "delicate discrimination" in previous publications to omit "things not characteristic" of Hawthorne's "genius or his normal temper," Clarke can only lament that Julian did not show the same discrimination "that distinguished his mother." Dall also laments Julian's shortcomings as a son for not following his mother's example. Acknowledging that Julian's book is "the great literary sensation of the season," she charges that the notebook passage is a "revolting extract, which lowers greatly one's former estimate of Hawthorne" and "seems to be printed with a sort of elation, which makes one suspect that Margaret had in some way offended the self-love of both Hawthorne and his son." Testifying personally to the high national regard with which Fuller was held, Dall recalls a trip across the continent three years earlier during which she met many who "poured into my listening ear many a noble story of Margaret Fuller," and she found herself "welcome in many obscure places because I had known and honored her." Dall casts doubt on Julian's accuracy as well as judgment, challenging the details of his family genealogy in the book's "Ancestral Matters" section, specifically regarding William Hathorne and Francis Peabody. Mischievously, Dall implies that Julian's family biography blackens its own name in blackening Fuller's, for the "blood" of both William Hathorne and Francis Peabody, she claims, also "ran in Margaret Fuller's veins." Most of the other major counterattacks by Fuller supporters would follow Sarah Clarke's format—challenging the truth of Hawthorne's accusations with counter evidence, lamenting his misjudgment, and condemning Julian's impropriety.[50]

Thomas Wentworth Higginson, however, attempted to undermine the very foundation of Julian's monument to his parents. Anticipating T. Walter Herbert's provocative deconstruction of the idyllic image of the Hawthornes' "marital bliss," Higginson, in a 20 December article for *Woman's Journal* entitled "Wedded Isolation," warns his readers against the temptation to see the Hawthorne marriage as "ideal." Calling Nathaniel and Sophia "two very peculiar temperaments" who had led lives of "seclusion," Higginson states that by marrying "they simply admitted each other to that seclusion, leaving the world almost as far off as before." "A perfect conjugal devotion may create a beautiful atmosphere at home," Higginson warns, "and yet may bring with it danger, when it leads a husband and wife to entrench themselves, as it were, against the world outside, and live only for each other." Higginson condemns the hermetic quality of the marriage for producing an "antagonism" that is especially directed toward "those who took hold of life more actively," citing as examples Hawthorne's opinion of Margaret Fuller and Sophia's of Theodore Parker.[51]

Julian fought back. In the first of three letters he would write in his defense, Julian on 2 January 1885 responded to Clarke and Higginson. Rubbing salt deeply into the wound, he begins by citing virtually the entire Fuller notebook entry. To Clarke's lament that he lacked his mother's "delicate discrimination," Julian claims, basically, that his mother almost did not have it either. He says that his mother decided only at the last minute not to publish the Fuller passage, fearing that it would be interpreted as "revenge," since Margaret had treated Sophia with a "deficiency of good taste, to say the least," but that she wanted it printed "when a complete biography was written." He defends his father's judgment of Fuller by terming it a "sound and searching . . . analysis" that "told the exact truth." He is careful to be deferential to Clarke personally, but he sneers at Higginson. Inspired perhaps by his father's use of "hymen" as synonym for Ossoli, which of course Julian himself had censored, Julian refers to the *Woman's Journal* as Higginson's "female organ," in the pages of which an unmanly Higginson "has woven . . . a theory of 'married isolation' which has a sadly perfunctory twang about it." Julian ends his letter with an assessment of Fuller that is incendiary in its smug contempt: "The majority of readers will, I think, not be inconsolable that poor Margaret Fuller has at last taken her place with the numberless other dismal frauds who fill the limbo of human pretension and failure."[52]

Higginson returned the insult. In an unsigned review of the biography for the February issue of the *Atlantic,* Higginson challenges the very worth of Julian's service to his father's memory. Alluding to the savage custom of a son's killing off a father who has "outlived his usefulness" by knocking "him on the head," he compares it favorably to the more savage modern custom of sons performing the *"post mortem"* in biographies. "After Hawthorne," he warns, "who is safe?" He then ridicules Julian for showing "that he loves his father as himself" in that Julian included "a liberal share of his own autobiography." Questioning Julian's own manhood, Higginson dismisses Julian's literary career while suggesting that Julian is something of a mother's boy: "It is a great thing to know that Mr. Julian Hawthorne, whose previous writings have never given marked indications of any very refined sensibilities, really becomes tender, and almost poetic, whenever he speaks of his mother."[53] As a biographer, Julian approaches his material with "little shifting, not much method, and, it is needless to say, the most utter and heroic disregard of the sensibilities of any living person." And the special point that Higginson wished to bring out in this review to discredit Julian was that Julian was extraordinarily petty in omitting any reference to James T. Fields's valuable role in Hawthorne's career: "Of all the pettiness of Mr. Julian Hawthorne's book, there is none so petty as this omission."[54]

Through much of the review, Higginson repeats the points he made in "Wedded Isolation," but he sharpens his censure of the Hawthornes and their marriage. Earlier, he had written that "both Mr. and Mrs. Hawthorne came to each other from a life of seclusion; he had led it by peculiarity of nurture, she through illness; and when they were united, they simply admitted each other to that seclusion, leaving the world almost as far off as before." Now, he writes that "Hawthorne came to his wife from a morbidly recluse existence; she came to him from a sick-room. From the moment of contact they clung to each other, but it is hard to resist the conclusion that they helped each other do without mankind outside." To defend Hawthorne, Julian had escalated his assault on Fuller. To defend Fuller, Higginson seems more than willing to do the same to Hawthorne. Cut off from mankind by the "duplex selfishness" of "wedded isolation," Hawthorne was so gullible, asserts Higginson, that he "was apt to swallow the whole story that any informant told him," and he was particularly susceptible to being "taken in" by Mozier's gossip because Hawthorne "seems rarely to have met an intellectual woman outside of his own and his wife's family." Higginson then resurrects the image of the "morbid" Hawthorne by bluntly questioning the health of his mind. Careful to praise Hawthorne's "penetrating glimpses of the world" in his art, Higginson states that in a world not "transmuted" by art "the truth is that . . . he . . . saw most of its details through a glass, darkly; his mental processes were unsteady and fragmentary, however brilliant." [55]

Julian's first letter of response to his critics on 2 January had been written too early to respond to James Freeman Clarke's 1 January defense of Fuller. But his second response on 16 January would answer James Freeman Clarke and two critical letters in the 9 January issue of the *Transcript,* one signed by C. P. Cranch and one unsigned.

Clarke's letter was among the most conciliatory exchanges in the feud. Claiming that the publication of the notebook entry has "surprised and grieved the friends of Hawthorne no less than those of the woman that he criticises," Clarke declares "the comments false in themselves, and unworthy of the writer." As his sister before him, Clarke concentrates on defending Fuller through citation of the "facts" regarding her marriage. To counter the credibility accorded Hawthorne's "insight," he quotes extensively praises of Fuller from other eminent persons—Emerson, Hedge, Greeley, and Carlyle. And, significantly, he challenges the wholly negative picture of the Hawthornes' relationship with Fuller as painted in the biography. Clarke, in fact, suggests that the relationship was cordial, quoting as proof a letter obtained from the Fuller family and written by Sophia to Margaret. The letter informs her that Sophia and Nathaniel had decided the night before to be married and that Nathaniel had immediately suggested that Margaret could stay with them when she visited Concord. Puzzled as to how Hawthorne could later write an indictment of Margaret in his notebook, he accepts the solution offered by a friend that Hawthorne used his notebook to record "hints and suggestions . . . for future imaginative characters," that the notebooks do not represent "his final judgments on persons," and that "Hawthorne is unfortunate, as other writers before him have been unfortunate, in the publication, after death, by injudicious friends, of what is an injury to their reputation."[56]

If James Freeman Clarke's defense is among the least belligerent in tone, C. P. Cranch's 9 January letter is among the most. Clarke is conciliatory because he believed that the public's faith in both literary idols could be salvaged, but Cranch is angry precisely because he fears the public will insist on unflawed idols, preferring to believe Fuller a fraud rather than Hawthorne capable of any failure of insight, much less of cruel misjudgment. Angered that Hawthorne would write such an indictment of Fuller and that Julian would endorse it "with such unnecessary animosity," Cranch is even more appalled that the passage would be reprinted in the newspapers and "not only not censured, but applauded as a masterly portrait of the distinguished woman thus libelled." Hawthorne's "distinguished name may prevail in giving it weight with some classes of readers," Cranch jeers, but, fearing that the damage to Fuller's reputation may be permanent if Hawthorne's "insight" is not assaulted, Cranch claims that he cannot "find a fit adjective" to describe the notebook passage. The ones he does find are among the most potent used in the feud: "a virulent paragraph," "leprous distillments which Mr. Mosier [sic] poured into his ear," "a gross and merciless libel," "a string of ill-natured comments and manifest falsehoods." Unable to account for Hawthorne's turning on an old friend, he does venture a motive for Julian's inclusion of the passage and his promotion of its views—"the wider sale that it would give to his book."[57]

On 16 January, Julian responded. Apparently Julian felt it unwise to attack the eminent Clarke family, exempting James Freeman, like Sarah, from insult. He does not exercise a similar restraint with Cranch. "As for Mr. C. P. Cranch," he says, "I remember him in Rome as an amiable and inoffensive gentleman with an entertaining talent for ventriloquism." His "ventriloquism" is again being exercised, he implies, in merely echoing his friends, presenting only "the fact of his indignation, but not . . . anything else." Hypocritically—in light of his just-displayed propensity for sarcasm and ridicule—Julian accuses Cranch of masking a "weak" case by resorting "to the familiar device of abusing the plaintiff's attorney" through Cranch's suggestion that he would "have created this discussion" in hopes of promoting the sales of the biography, a charge he admits he cannot disprove, a charge for which, in fact, he provides evidence in his next public counterattack.[58]

To answer James Freeman Clarke, Julian dismisses the testimony of Fuller's friends cited by Clarke as being typical of eulogisms that "gloss over defects, and . . . magnify virtues." He also attempts to use Clarke's evidence on Fuller's behalf against her. He seizes on a statement Clarke had cited from Emerson about Fuller to show that Fuller was a self-righteous fraud, a "Pharisee." To illustrate Fuller's absolute integrity and commitment to truth, Emerson had written, and Clarke had quoted, the following: "Margaret . . . suffered no vice to insult her presence, but called the offender to instant account when the law of right or beauty was violated. . . . Others might abet a crime by silence, if they pleased; she chose to clear herself of all complicity, by calling the act by its name." Julian judges this statement "as expressing a more ugly side of Margaret's character than does anything said by Hawthorne": "Surely none of the Pharisees who were denounced by the Founder of the religion which Mr. Clarke preaches could have deserved a worse characterization than that."[59]

Julian concludes his letter by appropriating to his cause his father's "generally conceded" reputation for "deep and peculiar insight into human nature." Against such authority, those challenging Julian's and his father's reading of Fuller's life have little credibility, for, as he says, they "were never suspected of insight till now." Julian asserts his intransigence. "Not one word has been said by anybody," he proclaims, "that demands the least modification of Hawthorne's analysis; nor is there any such word to say."[60]

The next word, however, had already been written. On 10 January, Margaret's nephew, Frederick T. Fuller, published the most thorough defense of Margaret to be written during the exchange, and Julian would respond to it on 5 February in his third and final counterassault. Citing copiously from Margaret's unpublished journals and letters, Fuller argues that Margaret's relationship with Nathaniel and Sophia was cordial, even intimate, and that Nathaniel's attitude toward Margaret as it appears fourteen years after his last contact with her can be explained only by some unknown "wound" that Margaret may have "inflicted . . . unconsciously." The notebook passage, Fuller argues, is only further evidence of Hawthorne's vindictiveness, the "lengths Hawthorne could go when moved by a pique which would seem small to most men." Hawthorne's dislike of Margaret is not a surprise to Fuller, for he and "those who loved her" have long been convinced that Hawthorne modeled Zenobia after Margaret and Coverdale after himself.[61]

The larger, political implications of Hawthorne's attack on Margaret emerge in Fuller's dismissal of the notebook entry as the verbal equivalent of a "political cartoon," which "under the inspiration of party hate," maliciously distorts the truth. Julian's motives for publishing the passage, he says, may generously be "ascribed to no other cause than that he is not one to spoil a sensation to save a friend." Or even an aunt. For Julian, Fuller observes, showed no compunction in casting "more than one grievous imputation" upon Elizabeth Peabody, and "since he does not spare his own family, I can hardly in reason complain that he does not regard less binding ties."[62]

Fuller concludes his article with an anecdote contrasting a statue of Medea with a painting of Judas's betrayal of Jesus, linking Hawthorne with both the pagan vengeance of Medea and the perfidy of Judas, and identifying Margaret with the forgivingness of Jesus. Had Hawthorne been "under the impulse of motives such as Margaret would have wished to waken in him," whatever "wounded feeling" Margaret may have given him would have been transformed into "a pity and forgiveness such as I believe Margaret herself would feel toward the 'brother' who has so cruelly judged and rejected her." In the spirit of that forgiveness, Fuller closes with a conciliatory gesture, stating his hope that he has not seemed "to belittle Hawthorne's genius" because "our American heroes and saints are not so many that we can afford to turn iconoclasts."[63]

The public schism between Hawthorne and Fuller, as promoted by Julian and attacked by the Fuller faithful, had become so sensational that reviews of Julian's biography soon became reviews of the feud. Newspapers not only reprinted excerpts from various letters appearing in rival publications but began to keep score. On 11 January, for instance, the *Springfield Republican* reviewed Frederick Fuller's defense, recommending the *Literary World* article to its readers, and judged that Fuller had shown "the falsity of Hawthorne's charges" and had put "him in a really despicable position, as a revenger of petty piques and wounded vanities." Noting, however, that Fuller himself "attacks" in "matters entirely irrelevant to the discussion of Margaret and her husband," the writer reminds Fuller of his closing sentiments by uttering a common refrain heard throughout the controversy, the lament that cultural idols cannot be left alone to rest in the peace of idealizing memory: "This is one of the miseries of biographies of the present fashion, they are so exhaustive, so indiscreet and so wanton in their use of matter that their publication awakens hard feelings on every hand, and gives rise to recriminations until the fame of the dead is beclouded and fouled by offense."[64]

On 5 February, Julian spoke his final word in the controversy, and it was anything but conciliatory. In addition to the now customary personal attacks on Fuller's defenders, Julian broadens his attack on Fuller as a moral hypocrite and intensifies his representation of his father and himself as moral crusaders. Lending credence to Cranch's earlier charge, he admits that he knew that by including the Fuller passage in the biography he would incite scandal; he hoped, in fact, that it would "be noticed" because though "Margaret Fuller was in herself . . . of very slight importance . . . she represents a large and still surviving class, the existence of which is deleterious to civilization and discreditable to human nature." That class, whose demise is hastened through such exposure, is "the class which is inspired with the old Pharisaic spirit . . . which says, 'I am holier than thou.'" Coveting "personal merit in the sight of God," apostates to "the profound truth of human brotherhood," these "'respectable people,'" as they are "technically known," must have their "absurd and degrading pretensions" exposed.[65]

Thus, to challenge the representation of Fuller as the "symbol" of "high womanhood," Julian represents her as the "symbol" of an aristocracy of "high moral hypocrisy" in a democracy founded on fallibility. To those who have criticized him for violating propriety in publishing the notebook passage, Julian argues that "it has been the curse" of "the many-headed beast of mankind" because of "cowardice" to "have striven to hide our frailties, first from one another, and finally from ourselves," that "until the highest of us has confessed himself morally indistinguishable from the lowest, the first step in man's spiritual emancipation is yet to take." As he works to depict his father and himself as righteous and courageous exposers of moral hypocrisy, he urges, with no trace of irony, "Let us not try to make heroes of ourselves or of one another," for "to say that we are good, is to say that we are God."[66]

As his father had exposed Fuller, so Julian would expose Fuller's supporters. Of these "wounded" defenders of Margaret Fuller, Julian ridicules Frederick Fuller with sarcastic pity in a metaphor that must have been suggested by his own precarious fortune as the son of an illustrious father. Julian cannot bring himself, he says, to "blame" the nephew of the "Doll Stuffed with Straw" who was able to shine "prosperously in her reflected glory" as long "as the inner secret of the Doll's existence remained unrevealed" but whose situation is now worse than that of the Doll's, "appalling" even, once that "sawdust" has been exposed and emptied. Julian's malevolent pugnacity at this stage in the controversy is even directed at George William Curtis, who had praised the biography in the February issue of *Harper's Monthly* in one of the rare reviews during the heat of the controversy that did not even mention Margaret Fuller. Praising the biography for presenting a "clear perception" of Hawthorne's "moral and intellectual character" and being in every way "worthy of its illustrative subject," Curtis nevertheless becomes the target for Julian's ridicule for having written the following: "If it dispels some illusions as to Hawthorne's uniform amiability toward his contemporaries, and sometimes shows him in an unpleasant light with relation to those whose hospitality he enjoyed, it leaves us in no doubt as to the general symmetry of his character." [67]

For this slight apostasy to the memory of his father, Julian reveals the degree to which he would make the controversy a question of endorsing unquestioningly the character and judgment of one literary "idol" over the other. Charging Curtis with speaking "charitably . . . on the side of Margaret Fuller's defenders," Julian pays homage to Curtis's "honorable and useful life" before belittling it: "Why should he compel us to remember that the graceful 'Howadji,' who as Miss Fuller's contemporary, was a gushing and sentimental youth, ready to make an idol if he could not find one ready made? If his opinion of Miss Fuller now is the same that it was then, it is worth just as much—and no more." Given the hagiography of *Nathaniel Hawthorne and His Wife* and the malevolent contempt with which he holds those who would blaspheme his father's memory by challenging his judgment of Fuller, Julian's defense of his and his father's right to destroy Fuller through "exposure" is almost comically ironic in its own hypocrisy. It will also be prophetically ironic in 1913 when Julian is imprisoned for a year for trading upon his father's name in a fraudulent scheme to sell worthless stock in a mining venture. [68]

Despite—indeed, because of—Julian's best efforts to present himself and his father as heroically committed to a righteous antiheroism, Julian managed to persuade others that the idol of his own remaking in *Nathaniel Hawthorne and His Wife* had a few disturbing cracks of its own. Five days after his letter in the *Boston Evening Transcript,* the *Transcript* ran three letters responding to Julian, each expressing dismay that Julian was succeeding only in diminishing their former esteem for his father. [69]

Christopher Cranch, in his second letter in the controversy, observes that Julian's "little sermon on self-righteousness" and "the splenetic moralism in these notes from his father's journal might easily be construed as falling under that very head." But Julian, he says, is incapable of seeing that because "he is so blinded to the truth by love and reverence for his father that he thinks all his judgments were infallible." Unfortunately, as Cranch laments, "hundreds of readers" now "feel a genuine sorrow and indignation (on Hawthorne's account)" that Julian published the notebook passage and "are beginning to feel that they must make large discount of their former esteem of this author." "The main effect of the extract and of [Julian's] warm endorsement of it must be not to injure Madame Ossoli," he asserts, "but only the author and the abettor of the libel."

The two letters following Cranch's illustrate the immediate damage done to Hawthorne's reputation. W. C. Burrage writes of his former worship of Hawthorne's works, his tours of Hawthorne settings in Salem and Rome, and says that he was "inexpressibly shocked" to read the "bitter, uncalled-for blows, resurrected from the dead to slander the dead, by the bad judgment of the living." He can only wish that Julian had allowed "this flaw, this unkind side" of his father to remain hidden and not caused such "unnecessary pain to . . . lovers of Hawthorne." The third letter, unsigned, accuses Julian of slandering his father's name by publishing the notebook passage. The slander is even more disturbing in light of Julian's success in portraying his father as soundly conventional and domestic. Caught in the contradiction between domestic ideology's sacramentalization of privacy and its evangelical promotion, the writer condemns the publication of Nathaniel and Sophia's love letters as "sacrilege" yet extols as "unsurpassed" their "revelation of sincerity and sweetness" and of Hawthorne's being "tender and true in his domestic life." It is an image, however, that "makes more striking and distressing the inexplicable passages from the Roman journals, passages which in a moment distort the whole transcription of Hawthorne's character."

After some three months of public acrimony, the feud ended.[70] But we are still living with its legacy. Despite the claims of Fuller's defenders to the contrary, Hawthorne's status as a "classic" American author was not diminished by the scandal. Hawthorne's reputation of course continued to grow, and he became even more securely institutionalized in the American canon. Adopting Julian's account of the domestic bliss of the Hawthorne marriage as an article of faith that seemed supported by Hawthorne's apparent disdain for Fuller and the feminism she symbolized, both prefeminist and feminist critics, as Nina Baym remarked in 1982, have for antithetical political purposes misread Hawthorne in the same way, the way that Julian had first shown them—as an antifeminist. In order to recognize with Baym that "the question of women is the determining motive in Hawthorne's works" and that Hawthorne condemns rather than endorses the sexual politics of his male characters, recent critics such as Larry J. Reynolds, Joel Pfister, and especially T. Walter Herbert have first had to deconstruct the monument of a uniformly blissful Hawthorne marriage that Julian had memorialized and to reconstruct the "morbid" romancer brooding over his own complicity in man's sins against women.[71] Not yet recovered, however, from Julian's construction of a uniformly antagonistic relationship is the depth of Hawthorne's complex personal and fictional engagement with the Fuller who claimed in her journal to enjoy in Hawthorne's "still companionship" a "mutual visionary life" with one who "was more like a brother" to her "than any man before."[72]

If Hawthorne's reputation continued to rise until recently in the antifeminist direction Julian had chartered for it, Fuller's reputation also fell in the direction he had driven it. Largely out of print after 1884, Fuller would be briefly resurrected in 1903 in D. Appleton's publication of the *Love-Letters of Margaret Fuller, 1845–46*. Marketing *The Private Life of the Sultan* and *The Private Life of the Queen* (Victoria) on the back cover of their edition of Fuller's letters to the unscrupulous George Nathan, D. Appleton seemed to confirm that the Fuller who had once been the "golden image" of "high womanhood" for her pioneering work as an American literary critic, social activist, and feminist was now Julian's Fuller, the Fuller who claimed public interest only as a scandal-tainted woman whose forceful intellect had masked the greater power of those passions that would eventually betray her in Rome. On those occasions, until recently, when she was taken seriously in literary history, she was marginalized as a supporting player in narratives about her canonized superiors—a *Whetstone of Genius,* as Mason Wade's 1940 subtitle defined this now "strange, misty figure" in the first major biography of Fuller since Higginson's in 1884. When Wade published selections from Fuller's writings in 1941, it marked the first time since the *Love-Letters* that Fuller had been allowed to speak again for herself.[73]

Lost to the world in 1850 and to literary culture in 1884, the life and works of Fuller have gradually been restored during the five decades since Wade's biography by a group of scholars who have dedicated themselves to the mission of recovering what Thoreau could not find and Julian could not forever discredit. Working within a progressivism whose triumph Julian sought to retard, they have, in fact, resurrected Fuller's reputation on the very site that Julian had buried it. If Hawthorne read Fuller's Roman experience as a "total collapse" of her moral and literary powers and Julian read it as the inevitable unmasking of the "dismal fraud" of her feminism, recent critics have read her Roman "transgressions" as the triumph of her sexual, political, and literary life. For Bell Gale Chevigny in the late 1970s, Fuller's movement from New England to New York to Rome paralleled a "centrifugal" movement of feminist liberation from the constrictions of New England and the abstractions of Transcendentalism to the sexual freedom and political activism of Rome. The subtitle of Paula Blanchard's still standard biography, *From Transcendentalism to Revolution* (1979) announces its similar reading of her life, and Larry J. Reynolds's *European Revolutions and the American Literary Renaissance* (1988) identifies Fuller as the only voice among her long-canonized male peers to embrace the European revolutions as a fulfillment rather than a threat to the democratic promise of America.[74] Reynolds further argues that rather than suffering a "total collapse" in her literary as well as moral life, as Hawthorne had decided, Fuller in fact reached the height of her literary powers in Rome, the force of her rhetoric wedded to the immediacy of the historical moment in her firsthand accounts of the revolution.[75]

If the radical turn of Fuller's personal and political life in Rome and her martyrdom at the hands of a patriarchal culture now served to authorize her canonization as a precursor to contemporary feminist and social activism, the "dense theoretical cast" of her Transcendentalist years, according to Christina Zwarg in 1989, has nevertheless caused her to be marginalized among the heroines of the feminist movement itself. Zwarg, however, would reposition her in the forefront of the movement. For Zwarg, Fuller's movement from a feminism initiated in her "reading" to "a theory of history as an act of reading" is valuable precisely because it can serve as a model for Anglo-American feminists confronting in poststructuralism "a move away from . . . empirically based feminism." Fuller authorizes an American feminist embrace of foreign theory that, as it turns out, is not really foreign, for Fuller "anticipates the theoretical turns of European feminism and helps to show how the American feminists now turning to this European frame are in many ways returning to their own theoretical legacy." Complementing Zwarg's efforts to redeem Fuller's earliest work for an American feminist movement in transition, Jeffrey Steele's 1987 exploration of the "psychological mythmaking" of Fuller's Transcendentalist work demonstrates that far from being the product of a socially disengaged romanticism it is "an explosive effort to free the psychological and social images of woman from inhibiting patriarchal assumptions."[76]

Redeemed first on the very transgressive grounds that Julian had "disgraced" her, Fuller now reclaims a canonical position in our literary and cultural history. Her reentry into the canon, however, is not so much a creation of the politics of our reading as it is a restoration, a resurrection by politics from an oblivion imposed by politics, imposed in my account by Julian's residualist intervention in an earlier literary culture that was just as much driven as ours by ideological interests, that was just as passionate as we have been in recovering, re-creating, and defending those whose lives and works we would make represent the embodiment of our values and the fulfillment of our aspirations. When we resurrect or bury the dead in the process of rewriting literary history, we all enlist in Thoreau's mission. But the mission does not end, for what we recover can only be what we imagine we have lost and what we believe we now need.

"This Mutual Visionary Life"

The Hawthorne-Fuller Friendship

Henry James illustrates as well as anyone the collapse of Fuller's literary reputation in the late nineteenth century. In the first thirty years after her death, Margaret Fuller had become a "legend" for Henry James and his culture, but by 1903 she had become, in his words, "the unquestionably haunting Margaret-ghost," the extraordinary woman consumed by the "wolf" of Rome in the "underplot" of a marriage that made "explanation difficult." Of Fuller the "legend," James could find it possible in 1879 to praise "some of her writing" as having "extreme beauty" and "all of it . . . real interest," but by 1903 he would proclaim that the "Margaret-ghost" had "left nothing behind her, her written utterance being naught." Fuller was still the subject of talk, but according to James, every hope she had had of being taken seriously as an intellectual had been, for a time, lost: her life fed the impulse of her culture's desire to create mythic narratives about cultural heroes while her work went unread and out of print. James evoked the "ghost" of Fuller in the name of the "New England Corinne," the "moral *improvisatrice*." Even for one of her last surviving friends and archdefenders, Julia Ward Howe, Fuller had become by 1903 a "name to conjure with" as "the inspired Pythoness" and "Sibyl" who had once "in a vision walked, rapt, inspired . . . with a message to deliver, whose import she could not know." The "ghost" of her "name" now stood "guard" at "the entrance of the enlarged domain of womanhood." Despite Howe's elevation of Fuller to an archangel in a feminist heaven, Howe, like James, dismisses Fuller the writer; the "literary material which she left behind," Howe asserts, is but "small in dimension." Howe's very comments introduce the *Love-Letters of Margaret Fuller, 1845–1846*. The last of Fuller's writings to be published for the next thirty-eight years, the *Love-Letters* seemed to support both James's and Howe's, and indeed the entire literary establishment's, dismissal of Fuller's importance as a writer just as it so obviously confirmed that the debate about the "failed" passions of her romantic life had become, since 1884, the center of her cultural interest.[1]

Thus, though Fuller's works would remain out of print, her life would be resurrected briefly in the 1920s during the flush of enthusiasm for Freudian theory. Katherine Anthony's *Margaret Fuller: A Psychological Biography* (1920) represents Fuller in the embodiment of the passionate woman whose sexuality terrified a repressive New England. During this decade of intellectual and literary reassessment of genteel Victorian culture, V. L. Parrington in his *Main Currents in American Thought* (1927) would appropriate Anthony's Freudian Fuller and define Fuller's place in the newly emerging canon, not as a writer but as the "epitome" of "emotional" romanticism whose "rich paganism" was wasted on a repressive New England. "No sharper criticism could be leveled at New England," he would claim, "than that it could do no better with such material, lent it by the gods." Yet despite his ostensible defense of this "victim of sex," Parrington himself uses the "material" of her life to victimize her further. Dismissing Fuller as "not a scholar like Theodore Parker, not a thinker like Thoreau, not an artist like Emerson," Parrington characterizes her as "a ferment of troubled aspirations" and "of disastrous frustrations" whose "emotions were forever embroiling her intellect." Though he would assign the blame for her difficulties on her repressive era, the hysterical female of Parrington's representation (one whose life, he speculates, would "have been much less tragic" had she "married early" and "turned" her "excessive energy . . . into domestic channels") "left" nothing "quite adequate to explain her contemporary reputation," for as a writer she was "in no sense an artist, scarcely a competent craftsman" and thus "wrote nothing that bears the mark of high distinction either in thought or style."[2]

Ignoring her contribution to American feminism and social criticism and dismissing with contempt her literary efforts, Parrington locates her primary cultural significance in the confirmation of the Freudian tragic narrative of frustrated passion in a repressive society. A "wonder and riddle" to her repressed New England contemporaries, Fuller is useful to literary history, Parrington suggests, as a means of exposing the latent Puritanism of her securely canonized friends, especially Hawthorne. Unaware of or simply ignoring the intimacy of the Hawthorne-Fuller friendship that Frederick Fuller had briefly exposed in his aunt's unpublished journals, Parrington takes as a given the reductive animosity that Julian had attributed to the

Hawthorne-Fuller friendship. But he reinterprets that animosity within the context of his own age of Freud and flappers. If Julian's Hawthorne is the courageous moral defender of the conventionally domestic and the manly denouncer of the fraud of feminism, Parrington's Hawthorne can accept a "sexless feminism," a "radical feminism in the abstract," but not the "frank avowal of sex" that confronted him in the "concrete." Fuller's "rich paganism," Parrington states, "disturbed" a Hawthorne "restrained by certain Puritan inhibitions" and "ruffled his instinctive squeamishness." Parrington thus transforms Hawthorne's allegory of Fuller's fall by reassigning to Hawthorne the role of hypocritical prude whose residualist Calvinism cannot be refined away. Three years later, Margaret Bell's biography of Fuller would essentially second Parrington's interpretation, explaining Hawthorne's "antipathy" toward Fuller as being driven by "some deep repression," speculating that "he may possibly have been more attracted" to her "than he knew." [3]

Parrington's inversion of Hawthorne's Fuller allegory of course reinterprets the relationship by reassigning to Hawthorne the role of tragic victim of inescapable inner limitations, but it does not redefine the relationship. Though complicated by Freudian insights, Parrington's interpretation of the relationship between Hawthorne and Fuller is still founded on the assumption of an unquestioned antagonism—still founded, that is, on Julian's terms. With at times considerable variations, the pattern of Parrington's reassessment of the Hawthorne-Fuller relationship will hold for both Hawthorne and Fuller partisans. Not even the most committed of Hawthorne's defenders will adopt Julian's reverent endorsement of Hawthorne's "insights" into Fuller, and Fuller partisans will often assail Hawthorne's character and motives more critically than Parrington, but all, to varying degrees, will accept the essential antagonism at the heart of Julian's re-creation of the relationship.

If Parrington established the pattern for reinterpreting without redefining the relationship, Mason Wade provided the list of explanations from which later scholars would draw their particular choices to identify the sources of Hawthorne's animosity. Providing one of the most comprehensive and insightful analyses of the relationship to date, Wade argued in 1940, as Fuller defenders had in 1884–85, that the Hawthorne-Fuller relationship had once been amicable, that in fact Hawthorne and Fuller ironically had much in common, but he accepts Julian's characterization of Hawthorne's essential antagonism during the later years, explaining Hawthorne's animosity as having multiple possible sources—his "dislike of consciously intellectual women"; his recoil from Fuller's passionate nature because of his own "shyness, reticence, and shrinking fascination with sexual matters"; his professional jealousy of "the fame which came so much more easily and earlier to her than it did to him"; his resentment of "the admiration that his Sophia paid the Sibyl of the Conversations"; and his mental decline during his last "dark years." Hawthorne's relationship with Fuller was sufficiently complicated to lend credence to each and all of Wade's possible explanations for Hawthorne's sudden eruption in 1858 over Mozier's gossip, but Wade's assumption of a souring in the once amicable relationship during Hawthorne's later years oversimplifies the troubled fascination that the "riddle" of Fuller had always been for Hawthorne.[4]

After Anthony, Bell, Parrington, and Wade had all suggested in their sympathetic treatments of Fuller that Hawthorne's patriarchal animosity toward her was founded either on envy or on repressed sexual attraction, Randall Stewart in his highly regarded 1948 Hawthorne biography countered this reemergence of the "dark" Hawthorne by resurrecting Julian's Hawthorne— the conventional, happy husband. Of the early years of their apparent friendship, Stewart writes: "Hawthorne could enjoy Margaret's company and ideas without feeling, as some moderns have supposed, a sexual interest: such a supposition is incompatible with his marital happiness."[5] Here, Stewart identifies the problem, bluntly. If Hawthorne was at all attracted to Fuller, then his marriage could not have been the uniformly blissful, conventionally domestic relationship that Julian had so persuasively promoted. Hawthorne's animosity toward Fuller was simply a necessary premise for reaching the conclusion that Julian had first put forth. The premise was both personal and ideological. For Hawthorne to be attracted to Fuller would require that he also be attracted, in some measure at least, to her feminist ideas. Hawthorne's animosity toward Fuller was thus an essential premise to sustain both antifeminist and, until recently, feminist readings of Hawthorne, both of which, as Nina Baym has persuasively argued, interpreted Hawthorne as a conservative writer with a profound dislike for strong, independent women. In an antifeminist Hawthorne, contemporary conservatives appropriated a literary classic as an authority for their prejudices, and feminists found "the sort of patriarchal mind-set" they expected to find "in writings by men."[6]

According to Hawthorne biographer Arlin Turner, for example, Hawthorne "recoiled" from "the excessive admiration" that Sophia initially had for Fuller, worked assiduously if subtly to undermine that admiration, and succeeded once Fuller became more and more "dedicated to the cause of women's rights." Thus, in Turner's narrative of the Hawthorne-Fuller relationship, Hawthorne perceives Sophia's admiration for Fuller as a potentially disruptive force in their marriage, which he is able to neutralize once Sophia can see, for herself, where heroines such as Fuller would lead her. Though Fuller scholars also assume that Fuller represented a threat to Hawthorne, in their accounts Hawthorne did not fear her influence on Sophia so much as he feared it upon himself. For Blanchard, Hawthorne, as his marriage proved, preferred the "'safe' woman" who is "pallid, pure, and a little stupid," and found the "intellect plus erotic passion and will" of such women as Fuller "dangerous . . . because she represents what the author would like to suppress in himself." Along similar lines, but even more bluntly, Allen claims that Hawthorne preferred the submissive dependence of a Sophia "for long-term relationships" but "recognized Margaret's sexuality and passionate nature, responded to it, and was terrified of it and of his own passionate sexuality, actual or potential." Thus, to both "the Puritan and the male supremacist in him," Fuller "was the enemy, to be attacked unmercifully."[7]

In a major breakthrough in Hawthorne studies, Nina Baym asserted that readers of Hawthorne's life and works, regardless of their gender politics, had been mistaking the messenger for the message, that in fact what appeared to be Hawthorne's antifeminism was instead Hawthorne's condemnation of antifeminists. "The ability to accept woman—either as the 'other' or as a part of the self—becomes in his writing a test of man's wholeness," she asserted, and it was a test that most of his male characters failed and failed miserably.[8] The tradition of a Hawthorne-Fuller antagonism, however, had become so deeply entrenched that even Baym did not challenge "such *facts* of biography as Hawthorne's intense dislike of Margaret Fuller" (my emphasis).[9] By not reassessing the Hawthorne-Fuller relationship, Baym created a problem for herself. In order to explain how Hawthorne could be antagonistic toward the greatest feminist he ever knew, and knew well, and yet insist that his "prevailing attitude toward feminist ideas, in all four major romances, is strongly sympathetic," Baym made three rather bold moves, two in the same sentence. First, she separated Hawthorne's attitudes toward Fuller and feminism, and then she rejoined them, but only to imply that Hawthorne was a more loyal feminist than Fuller: "Hawthorne's dislike for Margaret Fuller has been confused with a general dislike for the feminist movement; but his response to Fuller was a personal reaction that had nothing to do with her views and a good deal to do with his suspicion (perhaps right, perhaps wrong) that she was not sincere in them."[10] With the Hawthorne-Fuller antagonism still intact, Fuller disqualified as the figure haunting Hawthorne's depiction of such "good women" as Zenobia and Miriam, and with no one else in Hawthorne's life available as a "muse," Baym must then argue that "in neither the short works or the long romances are these figures mimetic so much as they are signifiers of valuable traits—ideals, to use Hawthorne's language, dressed up in the garments of the real."[11]

Baym's penetrating insights into Hawthorne's engagement with the feminine within himself have paved the way for some of the most provocative recent work on Hawthorne, the work of such scholars as Gloria Erlich, Leland S. Person Jr., Evan Carton, Larry J. Reynolds, Robert K. Martin, Joel Pfister, and T. Walter Herbert. Each of them, however, has had to contend with the biographical problem that Baym avoided rather than confronted when she made Hawthorne a highly autobiographical writer who would nevertheless turn ironically to the abstract for inspiration when he created his most vital women characters. For Erlich, the masculine-feminine models and sexual tensions within the family serve to account for Hawthorne's gender ambivalences. For Person, Hawthorne finds his power as an artist once he discovers in his relationship with Sophia the liberating power of the feminine that his art can both release and contain. Evan Carton finds Hawthorne's engagement with the feminine commencing with his fathering of a daughter. Robert K. Martin locates the source of Hawthorne's masculine-feminine tensions in his identification with the "dangerous liminal space" between "the world of both men and women," an "unacknowledged, or at least denied, desire for intimate male companionship." For Reynolds, Pfister, and Herbert, Fuller is reintroduced to play a part, at least, in provoking Hawthorne to reexamine the grounds on which he had established his own relationship with Sophia and on which, by extension, he inscribed the men and women in his works. They do not, however, reexamine Hawthorne's relationship with Fuller. The tradition of an antagonistic Hawthorne-Fuller relationship still obscures the depth with which Fuller's brief presence in Hawthorne's life penetrated his imagination.[12]

This chapter examines Hawthorne's troubled fascination with Fuller by reexamining their relationship as it is represented by Hawthorne and Fuller in their letters and journals. I argue that Julian's simplistic redefinition of that relationship has obscured their intimate, if short-lived, friendship and concealed much of his father's ambivalent admiration for Fuller, an admiration that, in his allegorical representations of her, becomes an obsession with the personal and ideological provocation that Fuller inspired in him.

Hawthorne first met Fuller in the fall of 1839 and last saw her in the fall of 1844. These five years, of course, are among the most crucial in Hawthorne's life. In 1839 he had only recently emerged from the anonymity of his Salem study with the publication of *Twice-Told Tales,* and he had just become engaged to Sophia, initiating at once both his public entry into the literary world and his private engagement with the sexual. During this period, he would struggle to find his place in both worlds. By the end of 1844 he had been married two and a half years, had had his first child, and had completed many of the tales for *Mosses*—including the "Egotism or the Bosom Serpent," "The Birth-mark," and "Rappaccini's Daughter." He was still struggling to find a means of securing his status as a professional writer. And he was still struggling within himself, as increasingly evidenced in his tales, to come to terms with his obsessive desire to define, and thus control, the feminine, a desire that is so clearly manifest in the courtship letters to Sophia that he began writing soon after he and Sophia met Fuller in October 1839. Hawthorne first writes of Fuller within the rhetorical context of these letters; it is a context that must be examined, as Person has shown us, if we are to understand not only his initial relationship with Fuller but also his early explorations of his own power to employ writing as a means of re-creating woman within, as Marlon Ross terms it, the "contours of masculine desire."[13]

Person's groundbreaking study of Hawthorne's love letters to Sophia makes essentially the same points that I make about their importance to the study of Hawthorne's sexual and romantic awakening, of his negotiation with conflicting images of the feminine, and of his later creative impulses, but we reach opposite conclusions because we assign different motives and consequences. Person reads the letters basically as Hawthorne's successful attempt to locate his identity in Sophia's, and I read them as his successful attempt to redefine Sophia's in his.[14] Hawthorne's later, more obsessive and conscience-stricken explorations of that same power over women will fuel the intensity of his great romances as he reflects in guilt and despair over his sterile success in defining his wife and their relationship and as he simultaneously struggles with the "riddle" of Fuller, the woman who insists on defining herself and who challenges his power to contain her in the scripts that he writes her life to be. In his intimate friendship with Fuller, Hawthorne will encounter a woman who not only resists such male "magnetism" as Hawthorne will exert on Sophia but who exerts a power over Hawthorne's imagination that he will struggle with much of his life.

Within a month after her marriage to Hawthorne, Sophia would reassure her worried mother that her "Adam," her "crown of Perfection," the same man who would seven months later write "The Birth-mark," "loves power as little as any mortal I ever knew" and thus "it is never a question of private will between us, but of absolute right." The Peabodys, of course, had reason to worry. In another fourteen years, Sophia would write proudly to her sister Elizabeth of her willing submersion within the character and will of her husband, proclaiming that a "flower preserved in celestial ichor in immortal bloom & fragrance . . . would be a faint emblem of my being in my husband," that, in fact, "as the years develop my soul & faculties, I am better conscious of the pure amber in which I find myself imbedded—of such a golden purity that every thing is glorified as I look through it."[15] The process by which Hawthorne induced Sophia to imbed herself within the pure amber of his vision began with the courtship letters. If Sophia resisted Hawthorne's initial attempts to re-create her in the image of his desire, we will never know, for Hawthorne insured that posterity could read their early love only as he wrote it, know only the maiden Sophia preserved in the "golden purity" of his letters: preparing to leave for the consulate in Liverpool, Hawthorne records in his notebook that in addition to "heaps of old letters and papers," he burned "hundreds of Sophia's maiden letters—the world has no more such; and now they are all ashes." In triumph, he adds, "What a trustful guardian of secret matters fire is! What should we do without Fire and Death?" Having destroyed all evidence of the Sophia that she might have once imagined herself to be in her relationship with him, Hawthorne, in the very next entry, links fire, death, and the violence of his manipulative love. He writes: "Cupid, in these latter times, has probably laid aside his bow and arrows; and uses fire-arms—a pistol—perhaps a revolver" (8:552).[16]

We have then, as he intended, only Hawthorne's version of their love. In her study of nineteenth-century love letters, Karen Lystra contends that in reaction to the public constrictions of Victorian culture individuals turned to the intimacies of romantic love to discover and express their "true" selves.[17] The intimacy of Hawthorne's letters to Sophia during their courtship would seem to confirm Lystra's thesis, for nowhere else can we find Hawthorne seemingly so willing to break the silence of his legendary reserve.[18] What the letters reveal is not in any sense, of course, the transparently "true" self of Hawthorne but the "self" that he would represent himself to be and allow her to love and the "self" that he would construct to love and have her become.[19]

Not content with the woman he has found, Hawthorne, like Pygmalion, constructs an ideal for the Sophia that is not—the spiritualized "Dove"—which he sets in opposition to the Sophia Peabody that is—the "naughty" Sophia. The Pygmalion myth, contends Susan Gubar, is the very paradigm of a "male creativity" that seeks to reverse the biological "humiliation" of woman's ability to create man by employing art to re-create woman in the image of his own desire; the living "art object" of the female has "like Pygmalion's ivory girl . . . no name or identity or voice of her own." For Person, Hawthorne creates his greatest art when he surrenders himself to a Pygmalion-like creative process, but for Person, Hawthorne is not a Pygmalion who seeks "creative and possessive power over a woman through his art" but one who as an "agent or medium" enables "a woman's self-creation . . . through him." A closer examination of Hawthorne's letters, however, reveals that Hawthorne himself is often quite disturbed by the very "possessive power" that he attempts to exercise, as a Pygmalion, over Sophia.[20]

Hawthorne himself is very conscious of the self-generated origins of the artifice of his "Dove." His "Dove" is the "likeness," he tells Sophia, "that has haunted the dreams of poets, ever since the world began," but though she "has flitted shadowlike away from all other mortals," he alone has found his "dream . . . become the reality of all realities" in the "Poem" that is his "Dove" (15:382), and he will allow "nothing," he tells her, to disturb "the preconceived idea of you in my mind" (15:379), for "without the idea of you" he does not know what he should "do in this weary world" (15:399).

In a letter written early in their engagement, 26 May 1839, Hawthorne delineates for Sophia the terms of their relationship by defining the role that he is assigning her in his life. She is to be, as he addresses the letter, *"Mine own self,"* the self-created spirit that, absent from her, he summons from within his heart when "thinking of you," the "Dove" that "flits lightly" through his "musings," allowing him to "feel as if my being were dissolved, and the *idea of you* were diffused throughout it" (15:316; my emphases). She is and must be, in other words, "imbedded" within Hawthorne's spirit, assuming the role of his "awe" inspiring "angel" that converts his "love into religion" (15:317), for as he tells her in a later letter, she had been given to him "to be the salvation of my soul" (15:330). Submerging her spirit within his, losing her very self to save the self that she in turn becomes, she must silence the voice that she has lost. Hawthorne is blunt: "It is singular, too, that this awe (or whatever it be) does not prevent me from feeling that it is I who have the charge of you, and that my Dove is to follow my guidance and do my bidding. Am I not very bold to say this? And will not you rebel? Oh no; because I possess this power only so far as I love you. My love gives me the right, and your love consents to it" (15:317). As Herbert has argued, by granting Sophia moral superiority, Hawthorne placed himself at a disadvantage that he could correct only by asserting his superiority in matters of the world and claiming his role as her master tutor, to whom she was thus expected to defer silently in all earthly matters. Whether, or to what extent, Sophia rebelled at this time, we cannot know.[21] But the remainder of the letter suggests strongly that Hawthorne himself rebelled, condemning in his dreams the self that would so nakedly assert its power to subsume another within its "own self."

Immediately after writing this passage, Hawthorne writes of falling asleep and dreaming of sleeping naked for a year in a field, the bedclothes that covered him becoming in his dream his pallet on the grass. Awakening in his dream, he finds that the grass that his bedclothes had covered "had been burnt—one square place, exactly the size of the bed clothes" but that "fresh" pieces of "grass and herbage" had been "scattered over this burnt space." He instructs his Dove to "interpret this," but in an illustration of the power he had just claimed as his prerogative, he commands her not to "draw any sombre omens from it" (15:317–18). The interpretative caution is perhaps a warning in disguise, but if Sophia's later insistence on avoiding the implications of Hawthorne's disturbing fictions is any indication, she missed the warning and accepted faithfully the limits he imposes here on interpreting the text of his character. The dream, of course, is rich with meanings that Hawthorne has placed off limits to Sophia, but Hawthorne teases Sophia with the possibilities: "What was the fire that blasted the spot of earth which I occupied, while the grass flourished all around?—and what comfort am I to draw from the fresh herbage amid the burnt space?" He believes that she, as the "Dove," "mingle[s] with my dreams, but take[s] care to flit away just before I awake" (15:318). The dream, of course, was about his Dove, about the demonic desire to make the dream of the dreamlike Dove a reality. The burnt grass covered by the bedclothes displaces the burnt self that the bedclothes covered during the dream. In other words, Hawthorne in his sleep condemns as demonic the Mephistophelian self who has just proposed that Sophia surrender her identity to the soul of the woman that he creates and owns in his heart, the self-generated "Dove." The living woman, represented by the "grass" and "herbage," would be sacrificed and scattered over the burnt shape of Hawthorne's condemned self as an ironic consecration of the "unholy" space that he has just proposed she occupy.

A decade later Hawthorne is to name himself "Ethan Brand" and transform the dream into a tale, but only months later, in October 1839, the month in which Hawthorne would meet Fuller, he is to appropriate Icarus as the model of his self-damnation. In what he calls a "foolish flight of fantasy," he writes to his "Ownest Dove" of his fears that his Dove will turn "naughty" and fly from the "home in his deepest heart" to the home that she says she longs for "in the gladsome air" (15:350–51). Attempting to re-possess his vision, he would "do his best to fly in pursuit of the faithless Dove; and for that purpose would ascend to the top-mast of a salt-ship, and leap desperately into the air, and fall down head-foremost upon the deck, and break his neck." "Engraven on his tombstone" would be the warning he has just allegorized but does not heed: "Mate not thyself with a Dove, unless thou hast wings to fly" (15:351).

The Icarus fantasy represents multiple anxieties besetting Hawthorne. He has created from the "air" of his imaginative desire an ideal for Sophia to incarnate "within his heart," but in envisioning the flight of that ideal, he imagines his own betrayal of that vision through his failure to maintain it within "his deepest heart"—his fear, as he expresses it later, "that my Dove had been only a dream and a vision and . . . had vanished into unlocality and nothingness" (15:461). It will be a nightmare that he will relive in his life and reimagine in the same images in *Blithedale* and *The Marble Faun*. In the folly of his doomed "flight," he acknowledges, of course, that he can never really possess the Dove. As a self-created ideal of unobtainable desire, the Dove promises him a love that he cannot have, a love, in fact, that will de-stroy him if he attempts (as he has and will) the impossible and tries to make it his own. By placing the impossible burden of his own salvation on a self-generated ideal of love, creating, as he would say of Fuller, his own "re-deemer," he has made it his damnation (14:157).[22] The fantasy also allego-rizes Hawthorne's fears that Sophia, for her part, will rebel, turn "faithless" and "naughty," refusing to accept "her home in his deepest heart" as his Dove. To a great extent, the fantasy functions within the context of the let-ters as part of his campaign to intimidate Sophia into accepting his transfor-mation of her as his "Ownest Dove." He can "sport with the idea" only because, he tells her pointedly, "you will never fly away from me" (15:351).

Three weeks after he writes of the flight of the "naughty Dove," Haw-thorne reclaims the loyalty of the ideal by reassigning the possibility of resis-tance and flight to "naughty Sophie Hawthorne" (15:357). Hereafter in the letters, Hawthorne will oppose the perfection of the "Dove" to the imperfec-tion of "naughty Sophie," reminding her of the ideal in which he has invested his love, the ideal she has yet to become but, he suggests insistently through contrast, she must strive to be. Writing from his apartment in Boston on 23 October 1839, he first introduces the three selves of their love in seeming playfulness but suggests the subtraction he would employ to transform the trinity into the unity of "Mine Own Self": "And now if my Dove were here, she and that naughty Sophie Hawthorne, how happy we all three—two—

one—(How many are there of us?)—how happy might we be!" (15:357). He would unite with the Dove in "sweet sleep," imagining the "pictorial magnificence and heavenly love" of the dream that she prepares for him to "enter," where he will "find himself in the midst of her enchantments." Though his Dove would question the right of Sophie Hawthorne to "share our nuptial couch," he would insist that "like it or no, that naughty little person must share our pillow" (15:357), and presumably enter with him into the dream of the Dove. Unlike his "Ownest Dove," Sophie Hawthorne not only resists his control but "has bewitched him" with her unmanageability, at one moment united with his Dove and dedicated to his salvation and at another, unpredictably, the rebellious "Sophie" taking on "airs," asserting her independence: "Sometimes, while your husband conceives himself to be holding his Dove in his arms, low and behold! there is the arch face of Sophie Hawthorne peeping up at him. And again, in the very midst of Sophie Hawthorne's airs, while he is meditating what sort of chastisement would suit her misdemeanors, all of a sudden he becomes conscious of his Dove, with her wings folded upon his heart to keep it warm " (15:358). Could he "combine the characteristics of Sophie Hawthorne and my Dove," he tells her pointedly, he would have "the very perfection of her race," the "heart" finding "all it yearns for, in such a woman" (15:358). Yet in the next day's addition to the same letter, he alludes again to the antagonism of the duality, referring to an unexplained "delightful scene . . . between Sophie Hawthorne and my Dove, when the former rebelled so stoutly against Destiny, and the latter, with such meek mournfulness, submitted" (15:359). Raising the question of which he loves "the best," Hawthorne claims to love both "equally," yet immediately casts doubt on this claim by asserting that he has "reason to apprehend more trouble with Sophie Hawthorne than with my Dove" (15:359).

Though he will periodically claim to respect the "rebel" in "naughty Sophie," he will consistently contrast his absolute union with the "idea" of Sophia in her personification as the Dove to his conflict with the Sophia who fails to live up to his conceptions. Contemplating, for instance, the possibility of his love entering "those inward regions" to read what "never can be expressed in written or spoken words," Hawthorne asserts that "the Dove can do it, even if Sophie Hawthorne fail," for the Dove is, after all, the ideal of the Other that has become himself: "How I should delight to see an epistle from myself to Sophie Hawthorne, written by my Dove!—or to my Dove, Sophie Hawthorne being the amanuensis!" (15:388). "Imbedded" within his heart's home as the Dove, Sophia would indeed become little more than the "amanuensis" of, as she claimed later to her sister Elizabeth, Hawthorne's "golden purity." As an extension of his own spirit, for instance, he writes to the Dove as to himself in a 3 January 1840 letter, telling his Dove to give "naughty Sophie Hawthorne" the message "that I still entreat her to allow my Dove to kiss her cheek," hoping that in accepting the "kiss" of his spirit "her spirit is beginning to be tamed" (15:399). The "tamed" and the "untamed," the "Strophe and Antistrophe," as he refers to the two in a 21 January 1840 letter, elicit two types of loves that he claims are one love, "infinitely intensified" because "they share it together." Despite his reassurance, he leaves no doubt in Sophia's mind that his love for the two is decidedly different. He claims that the "perfect and angelic nature" of the Dove "awaken[s] infinite tenderness" in him because she has an "inalienable and unquestionable right" to his love, but he asserts that he is "forced to love" the "naughty Sophie Hawthorne" with his "wayward heart." It is Sophie's "office," he instructs her, "to cheer and sustain" his Dove, her duty, that is, to become the Dove (15:400). In a later letter, adopting his customary guise of the playful lover, Hawthorne makes his preference for the Dove clear: "Mine own Dove, how unhappy art thou to be linked with such a mate!— to be bound up in the same volume with her!—and me unhappy, too, to be forced to keep such a turbulent little rebel in my inmost heart! Dost thou not think she might be persuaded to withdraw herself, quietly, and take up her residence somewhere else?" (15:471).

If it is "naughty Sophie's" "office" to "sustain" the Dove and be "tamed" by the kiss of the Dove's spirit, it is Hawthorne's "office," he asserts, to "tame" the Dove. Exerting the "power" that he had declared to be the "right" of his love and the "consent" of hers (15:317), he claims the role, he tells the Dove, of "interpreter between the world and yourself—one who should sometimes set you right, not in the abstract (for there you are never wrong) but relatively to human and earthly matters" (15:375). Conceding her superiority "in immortal reality," he claims the right to provide her "guidance and instruction" among the "flitting shadows" of the world—his chief "instruction" in this letter being not to "grieve your husband's spirit, when he essays to do his office" (15:375). As "interpreter" for the Dove, Hawthorne in effect is claiming what he has created, the right to the "voice" of the Dove, for it, as he was to say of her body, "belongs wholly to me" (15:464).

No where does he "instruct" the Dove so severely as when he perceives a threat to his control over her. When Sophia turned to hypnotism for possible relief from her headaches, Hawthorne confronted in the mysteries of the magnetist not only a rival to his power over the Dove but also a mirror image of himself as manipulator, interpreter. Hawthorne condemns magnetism with an anger that barely conceals his desperate possessiveness and that suggests his own horror at confronting, in the crude replication of magnetism, the power he had gained over the self of another:

> I am unwilling that a power should be exercised on thee. . . . If I possessed such a power over thee, I should not dare to exercise it; nor can I consent to its being exercised by another. Supposing that this power arises from the transfusion of one spirit into another, it seems to me that the sacredness of an individual is violated by it; there would be an intrusion into thy holy of holies—and the intruder would not be thy husband! Canst thou think, without a shrinking of thy soul, of any human being coming into closer communion with thee than I may?—than either nature or my own sense of right would permit me? *I* cannot. And, dearest, thou must remember, too, that thou art now a part of me, and that by surrendering thyself to the influence of his magnetic lady, thou surrenderest more than thine own moral and spiritual being—allowing that the influence *is* a moral and spiritual one. (15:588)

In the days before their marriage, as they postponed the ceremony waiting for Sophia to recover from illness, Sophia apparently ignored Hawthorne's previous guidance and again submitted herself to another treatment of magnetism. The image of Sophia controlled by another struck Hawthorne again with terror. He wrote to her of awakening from sleep "in an absolute quake" after a night of being "haunted with ghastly dreams" of her "being magnetized" (15:634). If Hawthorne was to imagine his failure to mate with his ideal of woman as his reenactment of the folly of Icarus, he was to dream of his success as a nightmare of the "magnetized" woman who has "surrendered" her "moral and spiritual being" to the power of the "magnetist"— "naughty Sophie" finally submissive to the power of his desire, tamed, imbedded within the ideal of the Dove. It would be a nightmare he would agonize over again and again within the concealed confessions of his self-condemning fictions of male egotists "violating" the "holiest of holies" of their women.

In the intimacy of his friendship with Margaret Fuller, Hawthorne encountered a woman who challenged the sort of male magnetism he had exerted over Sophia and would condemn in himself. Committed to the process of continuously redefining herself according to her own ideal and of urging other women to do the same, she would make of herself, as Hawthorne was later to say, her "own Redeemer." In his letters Hawthorne was to imagine Sophia as the "Strophe and Antistrophe," the submissive "Dove" and the rebellious, "naughty Sophie," but once he had succeeded in submerging the latter into the former, in his fiction he was to explore the psychic costs to both Sophia and himself of his "mating with a Dove" and to confess and condemn his attraction to the Dove's "Antistrophe," no longer embodied in the now-tamed "naughty Sophie," but in Margaret Fuller.[23] Not only did Fuller come to represent for Hawthorne the embodiment of feminine resistance to the type of personal and cultural male magnetism that Hawthorne employed to reorder and master Sophia's character, but she also came to represent both the seductively attractive and intimidatingly repellent poles of the magnetic force that such a woman could have on others. The documentary evidence left to us is admittedly scant, but what we do have suggests that during the short period of their friendship, Hawthorne established an intimacy with Fuller that, Sophia excepted, he established with no other woman. After they last saw each other in the fall of 1844, he began in his fiction to puzzle over his ambivalent attraction to this woman who represented everything he had systematically suppressed in his wife, to master, in other words, the "riddle" of her character and their relationship and to come to terms with the very sources of his need to master it.

When Hawthorne first met Fuller in October 1839, she was preparing to initiate the two ventures that would confirm her growing reputation as one of the leading intellectuals and certainly the most provocative woman in America: the editorship of the *Dial* during its first two years and the subscription series of organized intellectual discussions among the wives and daughters of the New England intellectual elite, the "Conversations," which were to be so successful that they were held every winter from 1840 through 1844. The year before, she had decided to give up the one vocation that was then open to women of intellectual talent, school teaching, had moved her family to Boston, been invited by Emerson to be among the very few women who attended meetings of the Transcendentalist Club, and begun what she hoped would be her masterpiece, a biography of Goethe, whose chief champion in America she had become. Though she would never complete the biography, in May 1839 she had published her translation of Eckermann's *Conversations with Goethe in the Last Years of His Life* as volume 4 of George Ripley's Specimens of Foreign Standard Literature series, and in 1842, for Elizabeth Peabody's press, she had also published her translation of the correspondence of Bettina to Günderode. As editor of the *Dial* during its first two years, she would write essays on the arts and literary criticism (including reviews of Hawthorne's *Grandfather's Chair* and *Twice-Told Tales*). In July 1843 she would also write for *Dial* the feminist essay that she (and Elizabeth Hoar) had urged Emerson in 1838 to write, Fuller at the time prodding him to the task by proclaiming that "women are Slaves."[24] The lengthy essay with the awkward title "The Great Lawsuit: Man versus Men. Woman versus Women" would later be revised and expanded in late 1844 into *Woman in the Nineteenth Century*. Turning over the editorship of the *Dial* to Emerson in 1842, Fuller traveled to the upper Midwest frontier in 1843 and published in the following year *Summer on the Lakes, 1843*.

During their five-year friendship, then, both Fuller and Hawthorne were emerging from relative obscurity to national preeminence as American writers, and both were struggling to make literature their sole means of support. Each was single when they met but Fuller, as the head of her family, was attempting to support her mother and younger brothers, while Hawthorne was struggling to acquire the means to marry Sophia. By the time she departed from the Boston-Concord literary scene in the fall of 1844 to assume the position of literary critic and social commentator for Horace Greeley's *New-York Daily Tribune*, she had established during these five years of her friendship with Hawthorne a literary reputation that clearly exceeded that of Hawthorne's, and unlike him, she had found a way to support herself and her family by her writing.

As both were entering the literary world and struggling to secure a living there, they were also confronting crises in their personal lives, both attempting to define the terms of an ideal relationship that would give them the emotional salvation they sought. While Hawthorne was at work on defining love as a religion with an idealized Sophia transformed into his savior, haunted in the process by misgivings about the implications of his purposes and methods, Fuller was confronting in the passionate intensity of her relationships the torment of inextricably interwoven, ambivalent longings of both friend and lover. Fueling "the intensity of her friendships with both sexes," according to Fuller biographer Paula Blanchard, was her early effort in life "to sublimate her sexual feelings" and accept "the denial of marriage and motherhood" as "the price demanded for a female intellect as flamboyant as . . . [hers]," but her sublimation was shallow enough to trouble her consciously.[25] By 1839 she had apparently allowed her friendship with Sam Ward to develop into love only to find that he had become engaged to Anna Barker, with whom Fuller had shared for years a devoted, passionate friendship. Their engagement and marriage the following year troubled Fuller greatly, as did, for a time, the emotional undertow of her increasingly intense and ambivalent relationship with Emerson.[26] By 1841 "the queen of a parliament of love," as Emerson was to describe her role within her "broad web of relations," was to write, "Once I was all intellect; now I am almost all feeling. Nature vindicates her rights, and I feel all Italy glowing beneath the Saxon crust. This cannot last long; I shall burn to ashes if all this smoulders here much longer."[27]

The Fuller that Hawthorne would come to know seemed to her most intimate friends to possess the "magnetic" power over others that Hawthorne deplored, yet in his relationship with Sophia, cultivated himself. After her death, Fuller's friends would speak in awe of the spell that Fuller's power of personality had exerted over them, representing her in the image of the female magnetist that she had often represented herself to be. Most of them written within months of her death, these accounts memorialize hyperbolically perhaps, but the consistency in which Fuller is represented as a woman of mesmeric power attests, at the very least, to her power to inspire potent memories in the very images she had fashioned for herself.[28] James Freeman Clarke, for instance, claimed that she "possessed, in a greater degree than any person I ever knew, the power of so magnetizing others, when she wished, by the power of her mind, that they would lay open to her all the secrets of their nature" as she sought "to understand the inward springs of thought and action in their souls." It was a power that granted her the ability to exert the "profoundest influence on individual souls," which she used, he says, to urge them to "aspire to something higher, better, holier, than they had now attained."[29] In a militant language suggesting the initial resistance of individuals to Fuller's passionate assault on their intimacy (the very language that Coverdale will use to describe Zenobia) Sarah Freeman Clarke wrote:

> She broke her lance upon your shield. Encountering her glance, something like an electric shock was felt. Her eye pierced through your disguises. Your outworks fell before her first assault, and you were at her mercy. . . . Though she spoke rudely searching words, and told you startling truths, though she broke down your little shams and defenses, you felt exhilarated by the compliment of being found out, and even that she had cared to find you out. I think this was what attracted or bound us to her. . . . Many of us recoiled from her at first; we feared her too powerful dominion over us, but as she was powerful, so she was tender; as she was exacting, she was generous. She demanded our best, and she gave us her best. To be with her was the most powerful stimulus, intellectual and moral.[30]

Similarly, William Henry Channing would write:

> I know not how otherwise to describe her subtle charm, than by saying that she was at once a clairvoyante and a magnetizer. She read another's bosom-secret, and she imparted of her own force. She interpreted the cipher in the talisman of one's destiny, that he had tried in vain to spell alone; by sympathy

she brought out the invisible characters traced by experience on his heart; and in the mirror of her conscience he might see the image of his very self, as dwarfed in actual appearance, or developed after the divine ideal.[31]

Employing the militant language used by Sarah Clarke but employing it perhaps as a means of absolving himself somewhat from his role in initiating his well-known ambivalent intimacy with Fuller, Emerson would publicly describe how Fuller initially "repelled" him as well as others, men thinking that "she carried too many guns" and women not liking one "who despised them" for their weakness, but he describes himself as finding it "impossible long to hold out against such urgent assault." "Persons," he says, "were her game, specially, if marked by fortune, or character, or success. . . . Indeed, they fell in her way." Through her magnetic power, he claims, she "had drawn to her every superior young man or young woman she had met"; she "knew . . . what necessity to lead in every circle, belonged of right to her," and, as he says, she was "the queen" of the brilliant circle of her friends.[32] The brilliant circle that became known as the Transcendentalists, Emerson wrote in his notebook in the late 1860s, was but a collection of diverse individuals with similar intellectual interests who "were only held together" by their bond of friendship with Fuller: "Margaret with her radiant genius & fiery heat," he says, "was the real centre that drew so many & so various individuals to a seeming union."[33]

In his friendship with Fuller, Hawthorne thus confronted a woman who, by these accounts, possessed the power to penetrate into the deepest regions of her friends' most private selves and establish an intimacy they could share with few others. Indeed, in his private notebooks, Emerson in two blunt words perhaps best characterized the experience of being Fuller's friend: "Total intimacy."[34] Hawthorne did, in fact, develop such an intimacy with Fuller, but if Fuller exerted any magnetism over Hawthorne, it was the magnetism of his own complex attraction to her as one of those extraordinarily rare friends with whom this notoriously reserved man could be intimate. We may judge just how rare such friends were in Hawthorne's life by an entry he made in his notebook late in life. Distressed in 1858 over his inability to converse with a female acquaintance, Hawthorne examined his failure and concluded that for him, "there must first be a close and unembarrassed contiguity with my companion, or I cannot say one real word." He then wrote: "I doubt whether I have ever really talked with half a dozen persons in my life, either men or women" (14:178). Of those half a dozen persons, we may surmise that at least two of them were Sophia and Horatio Bridge. From her many private conversations with Hawthorne on often highly per-

sonal matters, Fuller would have been a third. Given the animosity traditionally associated with Hawthorne's attitudes toward Fuller, such "a close and
unembarrassed contiguity" between Hawthorne and Fuller may be initially
difficult even to imagine, but Hawthorne's attraction to Fuller had many
sources.

For one, Fuller had intelligence, wit, humor, spontaneity, and passion.
She was one of the best-educated woman in America and one of the most
engaging. Her often-proclaimed brilliance as an entertaining and provoca-
tively insightful conversationalist was matched by her power to listen and
sympathize with a compassion whose depths, combined with her frankness
about her own life, encouraged her friends to feel comfortable enough to
engage in similar self-revelations. Hawthorne thus found in Fuller not only
an engaging and entertaining friend but also a friend whose intensely intimate self-revelations and profound compassion for others both modeled and
encouraged the trust that Hawthorne needed to be similarly open. Besides
sharing similar professional interests and difficulties, during the early 1840s
both were exploring similar issues in their own lives, namely, the relationships between men and women in friendship and in marriage and the dual
nature of the masculine and feminine within man and woman. These were
topics that Hawthorne would be encouraged to discuss with Fuller because
of Fuller's closeness to both Sophia and him, of her initial faith and continuing interest in the possibility that their marriage was an extraordinary union
capable of transcending the boundaries of conventional marriages, and of
her open acknowledgment of her admiration for what she perceived as Hawthorne's rare combination of "manliness" and of a rare "feminine" power of
insight into women.

Hawthorne was also attracted to Fuller, I believe, because in her diverse
resemblances to his older sister Elizabeth, she came to fulfill, after his marriage, the role Elizabeth could no longer play in his life. By marrying Sophia,
Hawthorne built a barrier between himself and Elizabeth that would never
be really overcome. She never quite forgave Hawthorne for marrying Sophia, and her lifelong coldness toward Sophia in turn strained Hawthorne's
relationship with her.[35]

Gloria Erlich believes that after leaving his family, Hawthorne "longed
for and idealized his mother's and Louisa's compliance and Ebe's intellectual
stimulation" and satisfied his need for "uncritical acceptance" in his marriage
to Sophia.[36] Sophia indeed provided the uncritical acceptance that Hawthorne, like his Hollingsworth, longed for, but her compliance was so complete and her acceptance so uncritical that she could not satisfactorily fill

the place of Elizabeth in Hawthorne's life. Fuller could and did. In Fuller, Hawthorne encountered a woman every bit as intelligent, well-educated, witty, and talented as Elizabeth. Often bedridden like Sophia with migraine headaches and facing the same cultural and professional obstacles that Elizabeth and Sophia faced as talented women of superior intelligence, Fuller became what the two others could have become but did not. Hawthorne had to have admired that. Importantly, like Elizabeth and Sophia, she sympathized completely with Hawthorne's art and gave him her full faith in his powers and potential as an artist. Like Elizabeth but very unlike Sophia, Fuller's faith in Hawthorne was not uncritical. She read him better than Sophia could. To her praise of what he had done, she always insisted that he could and must do better, and in her sympathetic readings of his work and his life, she identified exactly in which direction Hawthorne must move artistically. As it happens, her criticism of his flaws anticipates and parallels his own criticism, and the direction that his work takes once they become friends will be the direction she encouraged and, in fact, enabled him to take. Fuller promoted Hawthorne's career not only as a friend but as a powerful literary critic. As both friend and critic, Fuller, more than anyone else, became the "ideal reader" Hawthorne first discusses in 1844 in "Rappaccini's Daughter."

We know very little about the early years of Hawthorne's relationship with Fuller, and the evidence we do have—Hawthorne's courtship letters to Sophia—is intricately related to the rhetorical context of those letters, related, that is, to Hawthorne's representations of self and of the Dove he would have Sophia become. Hawthorne first mentions Fuller in a 5 December 1839 letter to Sophia, less than a month and a half after he had met her, saying that he had been "invited to dine at Mr. Bancroft's yesterday, with Miss Margaret Fuller; but Providence had given me some business to do; for which I was very thankful" (15:382). Taken out of context first by Sophia in *Passages from the American Notebooks* (15:383 n. 3) and later by others, the sentence has been used by Hawthorne critics as evidence of his dislike of Fuller in particular and of feminists in general. Of course, it could just as well be read as revealing Hawthorne's dislike of his political patron, George Bancroft, who awarded Hawthorne his lucrative post at the Boston Custom House at the urging of Sophia's influential sister Elizabeth Peabody. Within the context of several other such messages to Sophia, however, it does reveal that he would establish limits to his participation in her world, for in engaging himself to Sophia, Hawthorne had found himself immediately thrust into the tightly knit social-intellectual circle of Boston, whose advance guard would make their camp for a time in Elizabeth Peabody's bookstore. As Hawthorne was riddled by doubt and initially reluctant to enter publicly the literary arena by collecting his tales under his name, so he was reluctant at first to engage himself socially with those whose influence he had already come to need.

The world that Hawthorne would occupy, he tells Sophia in these early courtship letters, is the world that he would have her join: Hawthorne consistently represents himself to Sophia as finding his only reality away from the Boston Custom House and in the seclusion of his apartment, where he can indulge himself, he tells her, in "reveries" about her (15:380). When Sophia encourages him to participate in her world, as she did the week before he wrote about the Bancroft-Fuller dinner when she offered him tickets to a series of Emerson lectures, he tells her to give the tickets to someone else, for as he bluntly informs her, "My evenings are very precious to me; and some of them are unavoidably thrown away in paying or receiving visits" (15:380). In the world of his "reveries," Sophia becomes his Dove, but in Sophia's world, he becomes her dependent. In an 18 December letter, thirteen days after the Fuller statement, he writes in mock desperation about another Bancroft invitation, this time to dine at Dr. Channing's: "What is to be done? Anything, rather than go. I never will venture into company, unless I can put myself under the protection of Sophie Hawthorne—she, I am sure, will take care that no harm comes to me. Or my Dove might take me 'under her wing'" (15:389).

Fuller is not mentioned again in the letters until January 1841, the second winter of Fuller's successful series of Conversations. After resigning from the Boston Custom House with a substantial savings and before investing it in the Brook Farm experiment, Hawthorne visited Salem for a week in January, writing to Sophia on 13 January. In this letter he responds to Sophia's apparent complaint in one of her letters to an attack of headache brought on by a dream of an "Arabian execution" (15:511). Having just described his world without his Dove as "but the semblance of life . . . a vision, but without any spirituality," he blames her headache on his absence from her dreams: "Thou shouldst have dreamed of thy husband's breast," he instructs her, "and then thou wouldst have awaked with a very delicious thrill in thy heart, and no pain in thy head" (15:511). In mock worry, he then implies that in "naughty Sophie's" world, represented by Fuller and the women attending the Conversations, his Dove's illness will only grow worse: "And what wilt thou do to-day, persecuted little Dove, when thy abiding-place will be a Babel of talkers? Would that Miss Margaret Fuller might lose her tongue!—or my Dove her ears, and so be left wholly to her husband's golden silence!" (15:511). The very intent of Fuller's Conversations was to enable women to discover their voices by providing a forum that encouraged them to engage in serious intellectual discussion, but in a perfect union of Sophia with the Dove in Hawthorne's heart, "naughty Sophie's" assertion of self, her voice, would, by necessity, have to be silenced and her ears deafened to any voice that would lure her from her home in "her husband's golden silence."

Of course, Hawthorne writes the passage in the tone of a light-hearted lover's jest, the tone that he adopts for virtually all the "naughty Sophie" passages in the letters. Hawthorne's intent, however, seems serious, and when he truly feels his power over Sophia threatened, as he does when she allows herself to be magnetized, his tone is anything but light hearted. He, in fact, changes tone immediately after the Fuller passage, defending "his golden silence" as the wordless perfection of the spiritualized love he shares with his Dove-wife, the Dove that he claims, later in the letter, he "worships," for she is his "type of womanly perfection" (15:513): "Dearest wife, I truly think that we could dispense with audible speech, and yet never feel the want of an interpreter between our spirits. We have soared into a region where we talk together in a language that can have no earthly echo. Articulate words are a harsh clamor and dissonance. When man arrives at his highest perfection, he will again be dumb!—for I suppose he was dumb at the Creation, and must perform an entire circle in order to return to that blessed state" (15:511–12). Hawthorne's references to Fuller in this letter have been read, of course, as evidence of his disdain for her, but in the context of his ongoing campaign to subsume Sophia within his idealization of the Dove, Hawthorne seems merely to be employing Fuller as "naughty Sophie's" surrogate and the Dove's foil, saying little, if anything, about Fuller personally.

In fact, there is every reason to believe that Hawthorne's relationship with Fuller during this period was close, a friendship founded not only on their relationships with Sophia but on their common professional interests. By this time, both Fuller and Hawthorne had grown ever more dependent professionally and financially on the social-literary world headquartered at Elizabeth Peabody's bookstore. Elizabeth hosted the Conversations, then Fuller's primary source of income, printed the *Dial*, and published Fuller's second book. Having helped Hawthorne obtain the Boston Custom House position, Elizabeth Peabody worked to promote his career, republishing in 1839 his most popular tale, "The Gentle Boy," with a frontispiece illustration by Sophia, and launching him on what they hoped would be a lucrative venture in writing stories for children, printing in November 1840, *Grandfather's Chair,* the first of three children's books Hawthorne would write for Elizabeth's press. When Hawthorne wrote the 13 January letter, he expected at any moment publication of the second volume of the series, *Famous Old People,* and in fact expresses in the letter some irritation at its delay (15:513).

That very month, Fuller had joined Peabody in the effort to promote Hawthorne, writing a positive review of *Grandfather's Chair* for the *Dial,* the first of three reviews of the author she will proclaim in 1846 as "the best writer of the day" in her otherwise highly critical essay "American Literature, Its Position in the Present." Fuller's strategy in the review is to praise Hawthorne's "perfect success" in "this new direction of his powers," while helping him avoid earning a reputation as a writer for children. Praising "this gifted author" for "employing his pen to raise the tone of children's literature," Fuller, nevertheless, places her emphasis on encouraging the public to attend more closely to his serious fiction. To a public raised on Scott's Waverley novels, she proclaims: "No one of all our imaginative writers has indicated a genius at once so fine and rich, and especially with a power so peculiar in making present the past scenes in our own history." Specifically, she praises "Endicott and his Men" [sic] from the 1838 *Token* as being superior to anything in *Grandfather's Chair.* Hawthorne will remember this commendation of "Endicott" and associate Fuller with the story. Though she praises his decision to continue writing for children, alluding to the new volume in the series due out that month, she praises the "delicate satire" of his serious work and ends the review by "demanding" of Hawthorne that he "write again to the older and sadder, and steep them in the deep well of his sweet, humorsome musings." This review will be only the first of Fuller's efforts to encourage Hawthorne to develop the promise of his "peculiar" powers. Her implicit message to Hawthorne is that he must continue with his serious work despite the temptation to meet the demands of the publishing market for children.[37]

The "delicate satire" that Fuller identified as a distinguishing characteristic of Hawthorne's work is employed at her expense in the next letters in which Hawthorne mentions her. Writing to Sophia ("Ownest love") immediately after his arrival at Brook Farm during an April snowstorm, Hawthorne creates a comic narrative of himself as a novice farmer learning to master the labor of the farm, his most daunting challenge being milking the cows. The seemingly good-natured humor of his satire—of himself and Fuller—masks the darker implications of this fable of male mastery. Identifying the most "fractious" of the cows as "a Transcendental heifer, belonging to Miss Margaret Fuller," one "apt to kick over a milk-pail," and thus resembling "her mistress," Hawthorne, "the unregenerated man" shivering within him, prays that he will be assigned "the kindliest cow in the herd—otherwise he will perform his duty with fear and trembling" (15:526–27). In an addition to the letter on the following day, he informs Sophia that, true to the character he perceived, "Miss Fuller's cow hooks the other cows, and has made herself ruler of the herd, and behaves in a very tyrannical manner" (15:528). Two days later, he tells her that he "has milked a cow!!!" and that the other cows have rebelled "against the usurpation of Miss Fuller's cow," and now, presumably beset by her own fear and trembling, "she is compelled to take refuge" under his protection, "keeping [so] close to him" while he tried to work that "he found it necessary to give her two or three gentle pats with a shovel": "But still she preferred to trust herself to my tender mercies, rather than venture among the horns of the herd. She is not an amiable cow; but she has a very intelligent face, and seems to be of a reflective cast of character. I doubt not that she will soon perceive the expediency of being on good terms with the rest of the sisterhood" (15:531).

One is tempted not to make too much of this, to do, as Arlin Turner does in his biography, simply to present it as exemplifying "his usual playful spirit," something "Sophia would of course know how to read," or to read it as Edwin Haviland Miller does, as a successful attempt "to reduce Fuller to size" in the admiring eyes of Sophia. Of course, it is meant to be, or to seem, "playful," and it clearly seeks to "reduce Fuller to size" as a potential rival to Hawthorne's powers as the Dove's earthly "interpreter," but within the context of Hawthorne's letters to Sophia, it functions similarly in its seriousness of intent to the "naughty Sophie" passages, something that Sophia would by now indeed know how to read. If "naughty Sophie" is the "fractious" earthly woman of will who resists Hawthorne's spiritualized idealization of her as his Dove, then in the barnyard reductiveness of a satiric fable, "naughty Sophie" finds her equivalent in the "Transcendental heifer" who rebels against man's desire to master her sexuality for his own needs, to "milk" her.[38]

Such a reading of Hawthorne's witty fable is consistent with his repeated use of seemingly light-hearted humor as a rhetorical strategy in his letters to Sophia. Like the "Transcendental heifer" passage, each of the "naughty Sophie" passages makes light of Hawthorne's determination to master the troublesome "naughty Sophie" through his transformation of her into the gentle "Dove." The humor functions, however, as a means of making the seriousness of Hawthorne's message palatable not only to a possibly resistant Sophia but also to a conscience-stricken Hawthorne; through humor, in other words, he avoids a confrontation with and over his intent. The message to Sophia in this barnyard fable of Fuller is essentially that of the "naughty Sophie" passages, but it is the first such passage in the letters in which Hawthorne represents himself as mastering another woman of will, the first real substitute, in other words, for "naughty Sophie." It will not be the last.

By 1842 it is clear from letters and journals that both Hawthorne's and Sophia's friendship with Fuller had become more intimate. Hawthorne, of course, had had numerous opportunities in 1841 to develop his relationship with Fuller during her frequent visits to Brook Farm. By February 1842, in a letter to Sophia, he refers to Fuller for the first time, as he will for the rest of his life, as simply "Margaret," a first-name intimacy exceedingly rare in Hawthorne's letters. The letter clearly suggests that Fuller had indeed become one of his most trusted friends. Writing from Salem, Hawthorne attempts to explain to Sophia why he cannot bring himself to follow her "parting injunction" (15:611)—to tell his mother and sisters of the marriage that they had planned, and delayed, for years. After explaining the "tacit law" of his family never to speak "our deepest heart-concernments," he excuses his own difficulties in taking "my heart in my hand" and showing "it to them" by arguing that even when he speaks most intimately of Sophia, he finds that he has not "*really* spoken of thee" (15:611–12). Deploying the dichotomy of Sophia as "other" and as "self," the very dichotomy that founds "naughty Sophie" and the "Dove," Hawthorne claims that when he has attempted to speak of her "the idea in my mind was apart from thee—it embraced nothing of thine inner and essential self" that lies "in my deepest, deepest heart" but was merely "an outward and faintly-traced shadow that I summoned up, to perform thy part" (15:612). To emphasize just how impossible it would be to speak of the *real* Sophia to his family, he admits that he has been unable to speak of her "inner and essential self" even with those with whom he feels most free to speak, "So that thy sister Mary, or Mrs. Ripley, or even Margaret, were deceived, and fancied that I was talking about thee." These are, he tells her, the "persons from whom, if from any, I might expect true sympathy in regard to thee" (15:612). With the series of names ending with "or even Margaret," he suggests that Sophia as well as he would expect his intimacy with Fuller to allow him, as with no one else, to express the deepest conceptions of his love.

Hawthorne, of course, could not bring himself to tell his mother and sisters of the planned June wedding until mere weeks before the ceremony—"execution," he termed it when he wrote of it to his sister Louisa

(15:636, 639). But on 10 May, when he and Sophia finally set the date after having visited Concord to inspect the Manse, they decided they could finally inform their friends, and on the very next day, perhaps the first of their friends to be told of their plans was Fuller. Writing to Fuller that they had decided to marry and had chosen June for their wedding, Sophia suggests that Hawthorne's decision to choose Concord for their home had been influenced by their friendship with her and the fact that she made frequent, extended visits to Concord: "Mr. Hawthorne, last evening, in the midst of his emotions so deep and absorbing, after deciding, said that Margaret can now, when she visits Mr. Emerson, spend part of the time with us." If Hawthorne "recoiled from the excessive admiration" that Sophia held for Fuller, as biographer Arlin Turner has concluded, then Hawthorne's statement here (which Turner does not quote) is more than a little problematic, for at the very moment that he makes one of the most momentous and emotionally absorbing decisions of his life, Hawthorne thinks immediately of sharing the home of his honeymoon with another woman and of sharing her with Emerson.[39] And he does this at a moment when Sophia's admiration for Fuller as well as for Emerson had reached perhaps its highest pitch. Demonstrating the "enthusiastic attachment" that Emerson described in those who had come under Fuller's "powerful magnetism," Sophia included in the same letter a sonnet she had written to Fuller, "To the Priestess of the Temple not made with hands," which concludes: "Behold! I reverent stand before thy shrine / In recognition of thy words divine."[40]

Fuller's admiration for Hawthorne is only slightly more restrained than that of Sophia's for Fuller. Responding to Sophia's letter, Fuller bestows upon Hawthorne high praise indeed, for she seems to perceive in Hawthorne's balance of feminine sensitivity and undemonstrative masculine force that rare equilibrium between the feminine and masculine selves that she would famously term in *Woman in the Nineteenth Century* as the "great radical dualism" of human nature. "Great happiness" awaits Sophia, Fuller predicts, for "if ever I saw a man who combined delicate tenderness to understand the heart of a woman, with quiet depth and manliness enough to satisfy her, it is Mr. Hawthorne."[41] Fuller had long recognized a "delicate tenderness" in Hawthorne, before, in fact, she met him, for when she read the anonymously published "Gentle Boy" eight years before this, she was so impressed that she wrote in a letter: "It is marked by so much grace and delicacy of feeling, that I am very desirous to know the author, whom I take to be a woman."[42] Though Fuller here extols Hawthorne's ability to understand and satisfy "a woman," and praises the quality of Sophia's love for Hawthorne ("wise and pure and religious" and promising "a pure and rational happiness"), she omits any specific observations about Hawthorne's love for Sophia. However, in a passage that may have been influenced by the relationship that she, but not Lidian, shared with Emerson, she at once both raises and then casts doubts on the possibility that Sophia and Hawthorne may develop a love that encompasses an intellectual friendship, a love that she will later praise in "The Great Lawsuit" and *Woman in the Nineteenth Century* as being essential to a marriage of equality: "How simple and rational, too, seems your plan of life. You will be separated only by your several pursuits and just enough daily to freshen the founts of thought and feeling; to one who cannot think of love merely in the heart, or even in the common destiny of two souls, but as necessarily comprehending intellectual friendship, too, it seems the happiest lot imaginable that lies before you. But, if it should not be so, if unexpected griefs or perils should arise, I know that mutual love and heavenly trust will gleam brightly through the dark." To explain the source of her faith and her doubt, Fuller then adds a passage that, together with her review of *Twice-Told Tales* in July, may have lingered in Hawthorne's mind when Fuller left for New York in the autumn of 1844 and he began, almost immediately, to write "Rappaccini's Daughter": "I do not *demand* the earnest of a future happiness to all believing souls. I wish to temper the mind to believe, without prematurely craving *sight,* but it is sweet when here and there some little spots of garden ground reveal the flowers that deck our natural Eden,—sweet when some characters can bear fruit without the aid of the knife, and the first scene of that age-long drama in which each child of God must act to find himself is plainly to be deciphered, and its cadences harmonious to the ear."[43] A few weeks later, Fuller again employed a metaphor that recalls this reference to Edenic fruit when she described the pleasure that Emerson would have in acquiring Hawthorne as one of his "new colonists": "You will find him more *mellow* than most fruits at your board," she wrote Emerson, "and of distinct flavor too."[44]

The "distinct flavor" of the "mellow" fruit of Hawthorne's character, his "delicate tenderness" and "quiet depth and manliness"—Fuller was clearly intrigued by the man. But judging from her July 1842 review of Hawthorne's reissue of *Twice-Told Tales,* she was impatient with both the writer and the man for not disturbing his "quiet" depths, for not engaging in the "age-long drama . . . to find himself." She both praises and condemns the tales not for the success that she willingly grants them, but for "a great reserve of thought and strength never yet at all brought forward." The masculine "quiet depth and manliness" and the feminine "delicate tenderness" that

Fuller attributed to Hawthorne's character find their metaphoric parallels in the sexual suggestiveness of "a noble tree" and "a wood-embosomed lake:" "Like gleams of light on a noble tree which stands untouched and self-sufficing in its fulness of foliage on a distant hill-slope,—like slight ripples wrinkling the smooth surface, but never stirring the quiet depths of a wood-embosomed lake, these tales distantly indicate the bent of the author's mind, and the very frankness with which they impart to us slight outward details and habits shows how little yet is told." Terming the "invention" of his "imaginative pieces" a "phantom or shadow, rather than a real growth," Fuller describes his characters with a metaphor Hawthorne himself uses in "The Custom-House" for the same purpose: "The men and women, too, flicker large and unsubstantial, like 'shadows from the evening firelight,' seen 'upon the parlor wall.'" "This frigidity and thinness," she claims, "bespeaks a want of deeper experiences, for which no talent at observation, no sympathies, however ready and delicate, can compensate." These "deeper experiences" will come should Hawthorne "ever hear a voice that truly calls upon his solitude to ope his study door." Then the "genius" of his life will be "fully roused to its work, and initiated into its own life, so as to paint with blood-warm colors."[45]

Published in the month of Hawthorne's marriage, Fuller's review is provocative in its suggestiveness. While her earlier review of *Grandfather's Chair* had encouraged Hawthorne to commit himself to his serious work without being sidetracked by his skill in tapping into the children's literature market, this review clearly suggests that his serious work has yet to develop its promise because of his hesitancy to engage his passions in "deeper experiences," the "frigidity and thinness" of his characters being but a "shadow" of his personal failure. Emphasizing throughout the promise of his characters as well as his talent, Fuller suggests that he will develop his potential only if he encounters someone who will engage his passions, break the silence of this "quiet depth" in "a voice that truly calls upon his solitude," that (to convert her passive into the active) "fully rouses" him to his "work" by "initiating" him "into his own life" so that, "blood-warm" himself, he can then "paint with blood-warm colors." Read in conjunction with her letter to Sophia, the review may explain why Fuller analyzed Sophia's "wise and pure and religious" love for Hawthorne but not his for her, why she wrote not of Hawthorne's "understanding" of Sophia, as accomplishment, but of his ability, as unrealized potential, "to understand the heart of a woman" and "satisfy her," why she stressed also not the *"sight"* of "a future happiness" but her "wish to temper the mind to believe" in it. The review would suggest that Fuller believed that Sophia had not yet "roused" Hawthorne's "genius," not been the "voice" that could truly penetrate his solitude and supply his "want of deeper experiences." But then, written on the eve of their marriage, the review may reflect Fuller's fantasy that a sexually active, passionate Sophia would soon ignite Hawthorne's potential, emblazon his as yet cold genius. The erotic subtext of Fuller's metaphors would certainly suggest that she saw a sexual connection between Hawthorne's needs as a man and his as yet unrealized potential as an artist. If he would save himself from the passionless monologue of that solitude Fuller so often condemned in Emerson, Hawthorne must initiate a dialogue with this voice of the feminine Other, the voice just outside his study door.

For Hawthorne, the review may have seemed a penetrating intuition on Fuller's part of the deeper experiences that he had withheld from his fiction and from Sophia. For despite his apparent intimacy with Sophia in his letters and his claims of finding salvation through Sophia's love, Hawthorne had explicitly refused to disclose the self that had not been transformed by her love. Explaining why he cannot tell his mother and sisters of the approaching wedding, Hawthorne blames the "tacit law" of his family's "strange reserve" that prohibits them from speaking of their "deepest heart-concernments" (15:611), but toward the close of the letter, he informs her, in effect, that he shall observe that "tacit law" in their relationship. Though the Dove's "sunshine falls continually" into "infinite depths," he tells her, it is, he implies, blocked by "a cloudy veil" that "stretches over the abyss of my nature." He denies that his refusal to open that region of the self to her originates in "a love of secrecy and darkness," but he insists that it will remain in "secrecy and darkness" unless she proves herself insightful enough to discover it for herself: "I am glad that God sees through my heart; and if any angel has power to penetrate into it, he is welcome to know everything that is there. Yes; and so may any mortal, who is capable of full sympathy, and therefore worthy to come into my depths. But he must find his own way there. I can neither guide him nor enlighten him" (15:612).

When—immediately after her most searching criticism—Fuller abruptly ends the review with the statement that "we wait new missives from the same hand," she challenges Hawthorne to meet the demands of her criticism, to engage in a dialogue with the voice that truly calls upon him, the voice that he may hear in the deeper experiences of marriage or the voice that he hears in this review.

The evidence suggests that to a surprising extent Hawthorne accepted Fuller's challenge. At first in person and later in fiction, Hawthorne engaged in an intimate dialogue with the woman who called him forth, this woman who had the magnetic ability, say all who knew her, to penetrate by sympathy and insight into a person's most private self. On 17 August 1842, less than two months after the Hawthorne marriage, Fuller arrived in Concord for a monthlong stay at Emerson's house. Her journal entries during that visit record her uneasy attempts to navigate her ambivalent relationships with Emerson and her brother-in-law Ellery Channing, who were drawn to her for the intellectual friendship they could not establish with their wives but who found that friendship fraught with vaguely sexual tensions. Two years had passed since Fuller had found to her disappointment that Emerson would be unable to establish the depth of intimacy she had sought from him, but though she states that her "expectations" of him "are moderate now," they literally and figuratively, as she says, "stop at all our old places," rehashing their old debates of love and marriage during their moonlight walks down well-worn paths. The debates merely strengthened Fuller's impatience with the bloodless self-sufficiency of the Emerson she described in the journal as having "little sympathy with mere life," who "does not seem to see the plants grow, merely that he may rejoice in their energy."[46]

If Fuller during this stay struggles to accept her perception of the limits of Emerson's capacity for intimacy and for wedding the passionate to the intellectual life, she explores the potential for "delicate tenderness" and "depth and manliness" she had seen in Hawthorne and rejoices in his willingness to meet her challenge of a deeper, more intimate friendship. Fuller's contrast between the two men is implicit in her description of moonlight walks with them, Emerson on the nineteenth and Hawthorne on the twentieth. Walking with Emerson by the banks of the moonlit Concord, Fuller records Emerson's inability to respond emotionally and aesthetically to the beauty of the scene:

> Looking at the moon in the river he said the same thing as in his letter, how each twinkling light breaking there summons to demand the whole secret, and how "promising, promising nature never fulfils what she thus gives us a right to expect." I said I never could meet him here, the beauty does not stimulate me to ask *why?*, and press to the centre, I was satisfied for the moment, full as if my existence was filled out, for nature had said the very word that was lying in my heart. Then we had an excellent talk: We agreed that my god was love, his truth.[47]

The next day, 20 August, Fuller visited the Hawthornes for the first time at the Manse and comments that "it was very pleasant." Fuller, however, is noticeably silent in her journal about her impression of the newlyweds and says nothing about their conversation during the visit. Sophia, in fact, is not even mentioned. Fuller's interest is clearly focused on Hawthorne and his confessions to her of the changes wrought on him by his initiation into the life of marriage and sexual passion. Fuller's description of Hawthorne's reaction to that moment in his life as well as that moment of their conversation contrasts sharply with her description of her previous night's disappointment as Hawthorne reveals the capacity she ascribed to herself, to feel "as if my existence was filled out": "H. walked home with me: we stopped some time to look at the moon; she was struggling with clouds. H said he should be much more willing to die than two months ago, for he had had some real possession in life, but still he never wished to leave this earth: it was beautiful enough. He expressed, as he always does, many fine perceptions. I like to hear the lightest thing he says."[48]

In life Hawthorne could reserve exclusive right to narrate his courtship of Sophia by burning her letters, expressing in the underlying rage of the act, as Edwin Haviland Miller and T. Walter Herbert have observed, the ritualistic end of the romance, but in death Sophia could exact her revenge by editing his notebooks.[49] Hawthorne's description of Fuller's visit and their walk in the moonlight on 20 August—if he wrote one at all—was destroyed when two and three-fourths pages of the journal entry that follows Sophia's comments on the events of 19 August were torn out (8:780), presumably by Sophia. However, from Sophia's account in her 22 August letter to her mother of Fuller's first visit to the Manse, it is clear that Hawthorne, by choosing Concord, indeed looked forward to the opportunities it would afford for entertaining Fuller in his home. Never quoted in full by biographers, Sophia's description of Fuller's visit suggests the extent to which both Hawthornes honored her friendship and courted her sympathy. Sophia wrote her mother that Fuller surprised them at an intimate moment. Hearing footsteps, she writes, "I sprang from my husband's embrace, and found Queen Margaret." Instead of being embarrassed or irritated by the intrusion, as partial quotations of the passages have suggested, Sophia says that they "were delighted," particularly Hawthorne: "She came in so beautifully, as Mr. Hawthorne truly said, and he looked full of gleaming welcome." Indeed, Hawthorne and Sophia welcomed her as though she were a queen:

> We put her into the easiest chair, for she was pale & weary, & disrobed her of shawl & bonnet, & prevailed upon her to stay to tea. It was tea-time, & I gave her tea in one of the exquisite french cups—like a little urn (you know which—) & she returned the favor by distilling into our ears Sydnean showers of discourse— She was like the moon, radiant & gentle. Then I took her up

into my chambers & she was charmed & thought that Aurora was the finest idea. She admired all the house, & then we returned to the hall & sat & saw the moon rise while she sung of little Waldo, till the dampness sent us back to the parlor. There we made her lie down on the couch. Presently the roll of chariot wheels was heard in our avenue, & Louisa Hawthorne arrived. My husband went home with dear Margaret, while I welcomed & gave tea to Louisa.[50]

Leaving Sophia to entertain his sister, Hawthorne walked Fuller back to Emerson's house. Hawthorne seems to have responded to the beauties of the moonlight and the free intimacy of their conversation no less enthusiastically than did Fuller. He told Sophia that he had seen "the superbest display of moonlit clouds" while "coming back" from Emerson's. In one of the highest compliments that Hawthorne could pay another person—and rarely, if ever, did—he also reported that "he had a most beautiful walk with her, & she expressed the fulness of her sympathy with him in a very satisfactory way."[51]

The intimacy of their conversation on Saturday during their moonlight walk is continued on Sunday in a long afternoon alone in the woods of Sleepy Hollow. Fuller had left a book at the Hawthornes, and Hawthorne, leaving Sophia alone once more to entertain Louisa, walks through the woods to Emerson's house to see Fuller again and return her book. In the long notebook entry describing that afternoon, Hawthorne breaks the passage into two parts, his walk to Emerson's house evocatively narrated as a solitary journey through the impediments of a dark forest alive with beauty and forebodings of death and his walk back to his own house and waiting wife suggestively narrated as postponed by his long, intimate encounter with Fuller in the woods.

In the first part Hawthorne evokes faint allusions to book 1 of *The Faerie Queene*, *Pilgrim's Progress*, and "Young Goodman Brown" as he describes himself getting off the "nearest way" and losing himself in the "dense and sombre" shades of the oak and pine "forest" between his Edenic home and Emerson's, at one point finding himself so entangled in bushes and underbrush that he personifies his tormentors: "Always when I founder into the midst of a tract of bushes, which cross and intertwine themselves about my legs, and brush my face, and seize hold of my clothes with a multitudinous gripe—always, in such a difficulty, I feel as if it were almost as well to lie down and die in rage and despair, as to go one step further." He next records intruding upon the solitude of "a company of crows" who were "holding their sabbath in the tops of some trees." Feeling like one "who should unawares disturb an assembly of worshippers," Hawthorne sets up his later ridicule of Emerson in the passage by playing with the irony that despite "their gravity of mien and black attire," they have "no real pretensions to religion" and are "certainly thieves and probably infidels" whose pagan "voices" on this Sabbath are "in admirable accordance with the influences of the quiet, sunny, warm, yet autumnal afternoon" (8:340–41).

For Hawthorne it is a pagan afternoon, an afternoon poignant with beauty in the shadow of death. The subtle coolness amid the heat of the breezes "thrills" Hawthorne with the first signs of "the breath of autumn," "pensive autumn," and he gives himself up to the "deliciously sweet and sad" feeling that comes with recognition "of the year's decay." As in the night before when he thinks of death at the moment of his acknowledgment that he has achieved his greatest "possession in life," so he perceives that the glorious beauty of the flowers he describes so lovingly derives in part from their impending death, their "glow" of "pensive autumn," their "gentle sadness amid their pomp." The summer of his long-awaited marriage is passing, and his awareness of its beauty is darkened by his perception of its end: "Alas, for the summer! The grass is still verdant on the hills and in the vallies; the foliage of the trees is as dense as ever, and as green; the flowers are abundant along the margin of the river, and in the hedge-rows, and deep among the woods; the days, too, are as fervid as they were a month ago—and yet, in every breath of wind, and in every beam of sunshine, there is an autumnal influence." Describing the "audible stillness" of "the song of the crickets," the bright "Golden Rod," and the "gorgeous cardinals," Hawthorne immerses himself in a sensuous experience of the passing moment (8:342).

The narrative of his journey through the woods to Emerson's house— beginning in frustration and anger and slowly transforming itself into a reflective, melancholic sensuousness—has been building toward the climatic scene in which Hawthorne finds, unexpectedly, what he has sought—Fuller. On his way back from Emerson's house, he encounters Fuller alone in the woods and decides to postpone his return home to pass the afternoon with her. Hawthorne's pleasure is evident: "After leaving the book at Mr. Emerson's, I returned through the woods, and entering Sleepy Hollow, I perceived a lady reclining near the path which bends along its verge. It was Margaret herself" (8:342). Hawthorne's narration of the scene is subtly suggestive; like the "infidel" crows who only seem to worship the Sabbath, like the beauty of nature on that summer afternoon shadowed for the perceptive by autumnal decay, the scene Hawthorne narrates about himself and Fuller maintains the innocence of their intimate friendship while suggesting its sources in the undercurrents of an unacknowledged attraction. Hawthorne's tension locates itself in his anxious awareness of Fuller's "reclining" body and of his body's proximity to hers. Self-conscious of their postures and their isolation in the woods, his desire for an uninterrupted moment alone with her finds its expression in a nervous narrative emphasis on those who threaten to intrude upon their solitude:

> She had been there the whole afternoon, meditating or reading; for she had a book in her hand, with some strange title which I did not understand and have forgotten. She said that nobody had broken her solitude, and was just giving utterance to a theory that no inhabitant of Concord ever visited Sleepy Hollow, when we saw a whole group of people entering the sacred precincts. Most of them followed a path that led them remote from us; but an old man passed near us, and smiled to see Margaret lying on the ground, and me sitting by her side. He made some remark about the beauty of the afternoon, and withdrew himself into the shadow of the wood. (8:342–43)

The old man's smile at the position of their bodies, his forgettable piece of small talk, his quick withdrawal "into the shadow of the wood"—all suggest Hawthorne's own perception of the romantic tableau of the scene and his irritation with the old man's violation of the "sacred precincts" of their intimacy, his failure, in other words, to perceive immediately, as the rest of the group of people apparently did, that they were a couple that wanted to be left alone.

Immediately after describing the old man's awkward retreat, Hawthorne, finally alone with Fuller, reports that they immediately began a long and wide-ranging conversation: "Then we talked about Autumn—and about the pleasures of getting lost in the woods—and about the crows, whose voices Margaret had heard—and about the experiences of early childhood, whose influence remains upon the character after the recollection of them has passed away—and about the sight of mountains from a distance, and the view from their summits—and about other matters of high and low philosophy" (8:343). Under the spell of the moment, Hawthorne forgets the rage that he had felt earlier in getting "off the nearest way" to Emerson's and entangled in the underbrush. Losing one's self in the pathless forest, as Hester will later propose to Dimmesdale, now has, with Fuller, a "pleasure" that Hawthorne had just denied.[52]

The nature of the wide-ranging topics of their conversation that Hawthorne reports suggests that both shared sympathetically the pleasure of indulging in the "deliciously sweet and sad" pensiveness inspired by autumn's advent, conversing reflectively on the interconnections between the "high" and the "low," the present and the past, childhood and mountains in the distance, and then in the present perceived from the autumnal summit of approaching middle age. The order in which Hawthorne lists the topics also suggests that Hawthorne initiated the conversation, since they speak first of his observations about autumn and his experiences with getting lost in the woods and seeing the crows, and the second half of the list—their confessions of childhood experiences and their lifelong influences, the romantic sublimity of mountain summits and grand perspectives, "high and low philosophy"—suggests that the conversation, which had begun with topics of an immediate but not intimate nature, became more confessional and reflective as it progressed. The rhetorical decision to list specifically the diverse topics of their conversation in rapid, almost breathless, order and ending it with the indeterminant prolificacy of "and about other matters of high and low philosophy" conveys the delight that Hawthorne experienced in the conversation, the excitement of finding himself free enough with Fuller to speak unreservedly on any topic. Given the romantic evocativeness of Hawthorne's narrative framing of the conversation, the "excitement" conveyed by the effect of the listing of topics so diverse suggests nothing so much as the early, enthusiastic explorations by two friends of the range and depth of their newly discovered capacity for mutual sympathy and intimacy. In *Blithedale*, Hawthorne will have Coverdale describe such a moment. Wandering through the woods, "threading through the more distant windings of the track," as Hawthorne had been that day, and looking "for some side-aisle" in the woods that, he says, "should admit me into the innermost sanctuary of this green cathedral," he compares encountering such openings to "human acquaintanceship," when "a casual opening sometimes lets us, all of a sudden, into the long-sought intimacy of a mysterious heart" (3:90).

In listing the topics of their conversation, Hawthorne conceals the intimacy of the conversation in the very act of revealing it, for he does not, of course, disclose anything they actually said. The most telling revelation is Hawthorne's disclosure that they discussed the subtle influences on their characters of long-forgotten experiences in early childhood. For both Hawthorne and Fuller, the topic would entail perhaps some of the most painful possibilities of self-disclosure. If Fuller's autobiographical accounts of her childhood and adolescence may serve as a guide, the topic would suggest that she likely discussed the poisonous effects that her father's oppressively rigorous intellectual training had on her, the isolation her uniqueness imposed on her. And Hawthorne's letters to Sophia and the arrival just the night before of his sister Louisa, whom he had now twice abandoned to

Sophia's hospitality in order to be with Fuller, would suggest that he may have discussed his own sense of isolation and dislocation and the "strange reserve" so characteristic of his family. At some point during her visit, on this day or another, Hawthorne is likely to have discussed with Fuller her review of *Twice-Told Tales* and her comment that the self-imposed inhibitions of his solitude or lack of "deeper experiences" had led to the "frigidity" of his characters. Whether he did or not, it is clear that in his discussion of his most private feelings of love and death with Fuller on the night before and in his account of his moment alone with Fuller in Sleepy Hollow he had in effect met the implied challenge to greater self-disclosure and intimacy that Fuller's review had issued, and he had discovered, as he reported vaguely to Sophia the night before, that Fuller "expressed the fulness of her sympathy with him in a very satisfactory way."

This much is certain. With the exception of his letters to Sophia—and, I would argue, his fiction—the entire passage describing his afternoon in the woods with Fuller represents the most intimate moment Hawthorne ever chose to record of his experiences with a woman.

The spell of the moment was broken by another "intruder," one not so perceptive, Hawthorne seems to imply, as the old man, but one just as unwelcome: "In the midst of our talk, we heard footsteps above us, on the high bank; and while the intruder was still hidden among the trees, he called to Margaret, of whom he had gotten a glimpse. Then he emerged from the green shade; and behold, it was Mr. Emerson, who, in spite of his clerical consecration, had found no better way of spending the Sabbath than to ramble among the woods" (8:343). Hawthorne's narrative suggests subtly that Emerson was covert in his approach, almost skulking in his unseemly curiosity about the couple below him, for he was not "hidden by the trees" but "hidden among the trees," not calling to a Margaret "whom he had recognized" but "of whom he had gotten a glimpse," and finally, not rambling "in the woods" but, again, "among the woods." Hawthorne's irritation at the intrusion expresses itself in his ridicule of the "clerical consecration" that Emerson had not renounced yet ceased to practice and evokes an inevitable comparison with the "infidel" crows who only appear to be religiously "grave" and only seemed to have been worshiping in the woods.

Another, more telling, contrast is evoked in the juxtaposition of his own account of his sensuously concrete yet reflectively pensive response to nature that afternoon with his account of Emerson's abstractly, and slightly ridiculous, literary response: "He appeared to have had a pleasant time; for he said that there were Muses in the woods to-day, and whispers to be heard in the breezes" (8:343). Hawthorne and Fuller heard crows, Emerson heard Muses. Like Fuller, Hawthorne had recently expressed impatience with Emerson's bloodless abstractions, writing in his notebook just six days before a trenchant contrast between Emerson and the farmer Mr. Hosmer: "It would be amusing to draw a parallel between him and his admirer, Mr. Emerson— the mystic, stretching his hand out of cloud-land, in vain search for something real; and the man of sturdy sense, all whose ideas seem to be dug out of his mind, hard and substantial, as he digs potatoes, beets, carrots, and turnips, out of the earth. Mr. Emerson is a great searcher for facts; but they seem to melt away and become unsubstantial in his grasp " (8:336).[53] The sympathetic alliance of Hawthorne and Fuller in their physical and emotional response to that autumn-haunted summer afternoon is broken by Emerson, who "had nothing better to do" than to intrude insensitively upon a day that he could not understand and, by implication, upon a couple whose desire for privacy he could not appreciate. The spell broken, "Mr. Emerson" takes "Margaret" away from him, and Hawthorne returns from the enchantment of an afternoon in the woods conversing of "high and low philosophy" with Fuller to the diminutive domestic pleasures of "tea" with his "little wife" (8:343).[54] Hawthorne closes his account of his Sunday afternoon with Fuller by describing his enchantment with the moon, repeating the themes that Fuller had recorded of his conversation on the previous night but adding the haunting image of plunging into the deathlike "sky" of the moon-reflecting river: "Last evening there was the most beautiful moonlight that ever hallowed this earthly world; and when I went to bathe in the river, which was as calm as death, it seemed like plunging down into the sky. But I had rather be on earth than ever in the seventh Heaven, just now" (8:344).

Though Fuller recorded in lengthy detail journal entries of intimate, even painfully revelatory, conversations with Emerson, his wife, Lidian, and Ellery Channing during her stay, her comment on her afternoon with Hawthorne in Sleepy Hollow when read in light of Hawthorne's suggestive narrative is perhaps more provocative in its implications than any of her other journal entries. She wrote, simply: "What a happy, happy day, all clear light. I cannot write about it."[55]

Four days later Hawthorne was to write the letter that, with the exception of the infamous notebook passage, was to be cited as primary evidence that Hawthorne recoiled from the aggressiveness of Fuller. Aware of Fuller's intimacy with the Hawthornes, Ellery Channing had asked Fuller to inquire of the Hawthornes if they would be willing to take in Ellery and Ellen as boarders. After discussing the matter with Sophia, who had originally talked with

Fuller about it and had somewhat favored the proposal before writing to Fuller to decline, Hawthorne himself wrote a lengthy letter to Fuller explaining why he did not think the arrangement would be suitable for either party, the most often quoted excerpt from this letter being, "Had it been proposed to Adam and Eve to receive two angels into their Paradise, as *boarders,* I doubt whether they would have been altogether pleased to consent" (15:646). Julian first published the letter in *Nathaniel Hawthorne and His Wife,* and as with the journal entry condemning Fuller, Julian influenced future readings of the letter by establishing its interpretive frame. Introducing "Miss Fuller" as a woman so "clever" that "most people stood in some awe," Julian presents his father as an exception, as a man who was her match in cleverness and had the courage to put her in her place. Julian ends his quotation of the letter by suggesting that Fuller had been so intimidated by the letter that she was reduced to silence and the Channings to disappointment: "This finished the episode; Miss Fuller, if she felt any dissatisfaction, not thinking it advisable to express any, and the Channings resigning themselves to finding quarters elsewhere." Biographers since then have read the letter through Julian's frame, condemning Fuller for her gall and praising Hawthorne for his diplomatic mastery of the situation.[56]

The letter is indeed diplomatic in the care that Hawthorne takes in explaining at length his several reasons for declining the proposal, but rather than revealing his displeasure at Fuller, the attention that Hawthorne gave to the letter reveals the extraordinary respect that Hawthorne had for Fuller, his concern that their relationship not be affected by his refusal of the proposal, and as a sign of their intimacy, his extraordinary ease in speaking openly with her. In fact, this letter is the longest, most intimate description of his married life that he would ever write—except for the one he would write in his next letter to Fuller. That Hawthorne replied at all is itself an indication of his respect for Fuller and his concern that she not be offended by their refusal, for Fuller had mentioned the proposal originally to Sophia, and Sophia had already declined in a separate letter.[57] Often ignored by critics but illustrated by the letter itself, as well as by accounts of their meetings in the summer of 1842 and of 1844, is Hawthorne's admission to Fuller in the closing paragraph that "there is nobody to whom I would more willingly speak my mind, because I can be certain of being thoroughly understood" (15:648). For Hawthorne, that is a startling, boldly unqualified assertion. As his love letters to Sophia and every one of his future prefaces attest, his highest hope as both a man and an artist was to establish just such a degree of "understanding" between himself and another, a "fulness of sympathy" that he had acknowledged in Fuller just five days before. Ignored as well are the simple signs of an obvious friendship—the very fact that he addresses the letter "Dear Margaret," an intimacy of address extraordinarily rare for Hawthorne, and the very fact that instead of simply closing with "Sincerely," he closes, given the context, with the more emphatically reassuring, "Sincerely your friend" (15:648).

Fuller's proposal and the Hawthornes' reaction to it did not damage the relationship between Hawthorne and Fuller, as is generally contended. In fact, the record of Fuller's visit for the remainder of 1842 and her visit during the summer of 1844 suggest that Hawthorne's friendship with Fuller continued to deepen. On Sunday, 4 September 1842, for instance, Hawthorne and Fuller had another long, private conversation. As Hawthorne is writing in his journal of Sophia's attending church that day alone and of his attitude toward observing the Sabbath, he breaks off in midsentence because of the arrival of two visitors—Fuller and Sam Ward. On 8 September, Sophia completes the journal page by describing the visit. Though she begins by regretting that Hawthorne never completed the sentence because of the interruption, a statement often quoted as evidence of Fuller's "intrusiveness," Sophia clearly welcomes Fuller's visit, which is often ignored.[58] Sophia's description of the visit, however, reveals that during the visit Hawthorne and Fuller seemed to give each other exclusive attention, leaving Sophia with the task of entertaining Ward:

> Those visitors who interrupted my dear husband in the above sentence, (O that they had come later) were Margaret & Mr Sam Ward. We had an exceedingly pleasant visit from them. Mr Ward was greatly delighted with the house & its environs. He seemed to think Boston could not afford so charming a drawing room as our quaint old parlor & that it could not be persuaded to imitate it in its present degenerate taste. We went down the orchard to the river's banks, & my husband & Mr W. laid down upon the grass while Margaret & I sat on rocks. Margaret was very brilliant & while she talked to my husband, Mr. Ward addressed himself to me, whom he apparently thought a kind of enchanted mortal, in an earthly Elysium. . . . Margaret at last invited me to take him into the house & shew him the outlived furniture, while she remained with my dearest husband.[59]

Since Ward had already seen part of the house and had not at the time requested to see the remainder, nor had been invited to, Fuller's invitation that Sophia take Ward back to the house while she and Hawthorne remained by the river may have been prompted by her desire to speak alone with Hawthorne. What she discussed with him, we will never know. As happened to the journal record of the day of Fuller's last visit to the Manse, the six pages immediately following Sophia's account of the visit were cut out (8:783). The three missing leaves, of course, may have given Hawthorne's reflections on the visit and his conversation with Fuller. Fuller's journal entry for the day does not record the conversation either, but it does suggest that Fuller may have confided in Hawthorne about her complex and painful relationship with Sam Ward and his wife, Anna Barker, both of whom Fuller had once, in her way, loved. Fuller records that it was "one of the finest days." She "enjoyed being with S. more than I have since he was married," for "he spoke straight from his mind, without reference to others or his position." Ward, like Hawthorne, talked to Fuller about death and about recent "pitched battles" within himself and seemed "all lovely, a glancing bird, a sunbeam" as long as he was "out in the field" with Fuller, but, she records, as "soon as we got into the Hawthorne's house, he seemed too fine for the place, & with a touch of the petit maitre once more."[60] Disappointed in Ward "once more," this time for his condescension to her friends, Fuller directed her exclusive attention to Hawthorne, leaving Sophia to Ward, and, once alone, she may have recounted her day to Hawthorne and confided in him. Interestingly, though Fuller resents the condescension she perceives in Ward toward her friends, Sophia imagines Ward as thinking her an "enchanted mortal, in an earthly Elysium" married to "a kingly man" who was "far surpassing all he had anticipated, for who can prefigure him?"[61] In addition to being Ward's friend, Fuller was simply more alert than Sophia to the darker nuances of character—as her perceptive reading of the source of Hawthorne's literary "frigidity" demonstrates.

Fuller's stay at Concord ended on 25 September, but before leaving she briefly records another visit on the twenty-first with the Hawthornes, this time an invitation to dine with them. After dinner, she notes that they all three took a short boat trip up the Concord. The closeness of Hawthorne's relationship with Fuller after the supposed "offense" of her proposal to board the Channings is evident not only in the dinner invitation itself but also in the assurance with which Hawthorne presumes Fuller's sympathy in ridiculing Fuller's hostess, Lidian Emerson: "Hawthorne expressed his surprise at having met Lidian out at noon day, said it seemed scarce credible you could meet such a person by the light of the sun." Hawthorne's presumption was well founded, as it turns out and as he probably knew to begin with, based on their many conversations, for Fuller aligns herself immediately with him by judging Lidian's extravagant grief over the death that year of little Waldo as being melodramatically hypocritical: "She does look very ghostly now as she glides about in her black dress, and long black veil. . . .

I feel that her child is far more to her in imagination than he ever was in reality."[62]

Fuller's intimacy with the Hawthornes was apparently well known, even among Hawthorne's friends, for when Hawthorne's Brook Farm friend Charles Newcomb desired also to board at the Manse, he did not write Hawthorne himself but instead talked Fuller into doing it. Assuming the playfully defensive tone of a friend placing another friend in an awkward situation, Fuller opens her 16 January 1843 letter by making light of the awkwardness of her own situation as the apparent agent of potential marital discord: "You must not think I have any black design against your domestic peace—Neither am I the agent of any secret tribunal of the dagger and Cord. Nor am I commissioned by the malice of some baffled lover to make you wretched." Fuller, of course, is responding with hyperbolic humor to Hawthorne's earlier contention that even an "angel," much less Ellery and Ellen Channing, would be unwelcome in Adam and Eve's Paradise, but it is perhaps relevatory of the powerful undercurrent of their relationship that, defensively, she imagines, only to disavow, Hawthorne's anxiety that she would employ her intimacy with Hawthorne insidiously against his marriage, motivated, perhaps, by the jealousy of the hypothetical "baffled lover." Assuming the very role that Hawthorne had insisted he must fill in his relationship with the "gentle" Dove, Fuller writes that she is but an "interpreter" of "gentle souls" who turn to her because she "can bear hearing the cold cruel word No, better than any soul now living," assuring Hawthorne—the "serenest and most resolute man," she flatters him—that "these propositions are none of mine." She, in fact, invites him to decline, telling him that both she and Newcomb expect it and that he need not feel obligated to state his reasons, for she will "divine them." Rather than a lengthy explanation of his reasons for declining Newcomb's proposal, she asks him instead to tell her how he and Sophia spend their days and whether he thinks of her. She is curious if the promise of an "intellectual friendship" that she had told Sophia was possible in this marriage between a writer and an artist had been fulfilled, and she assumes that Hawthorne would be willing to trust her with the intimate details of his life: "I should like much to hear something about yourselves, whether ther[e] is writing, or drawing or modelling in what room you pass the short, dark days, and long bright evenings of Jan[uar]y, what the Genius loci says whether through voice of ghost, or rat, or winter wind, or kettle singing symphony to the happy duet, and whether, by any chance, you sometimes give a thought to your friend."[63]

As a response, on 1 February 1843 Hawthorne sent Fuller his second intimate account of his marriage and his life at the Manse. In that letter he resumes the conversation he had established with Fuller about his relationship with Sophia and the effects marriage has had on their lives. These conversations, among others of course, particularly those with Emerson, were crucial in helping Fuller to conceptualize alternative forms of marriage that allowed for greater equality and individual development for women, a concern that will figure prominently in her writing of "The Great Lawsuit" in the spring. These same conversations were also crucial to the concerns that Hawthorne would increasingly make the subject of his most profound fictions.

Addressing the letter to "Dear Margaret," he indeed declines the Newcomb proposal, saying it was impossible "for a reason at present undeveloped, but which, I trust, time will bring to light," an allusion to the recently discovered pregnancy, which Sophia would soon miscarry. As he did in his earlier letter, Hawthorne acknowledges Fuller's extraordinary ability to understand him, a distinction he accords to no one else but the Dove in all his letters, but before that acknowledgment he seems to allude to her assurance of not having any "black design" upon his "domestic peace" by denying—in a phrase that, interestingly, is suggestive of moral transgressions rather than social infractions—that he has never considered her capable of "wishing any thing that ought not to be!": "So here is a second negative. How strange, when I should be so glad to do everything that you had the slightest wish for me to do, and when you are so incapable of wishing any thing that ought not to be! Whether or no you bear a negative more easily than other people, I certainly find it easier to give you one; because you do not peep at matters through a narrow chink, but can take my view as perfectly as your own" (15:670).

The proposal dealt with, Hawthorne proceeds to give Fuller an account of his state of mind. As she had requested, he speaks of his writing, telling her that the pressures of contributing monthly to periodicals keeps him "writing without any period at all," but he says nothing specifically of Sophia's "drawing or modelling." Though he claims he cannot find "anything to tell of or describe" that would not reduce the "delicate pungency" of their lives to "a very common-place residuum," his description of their continual "advances" in happiness emphasizes their isolation from the world and their daily isolation from each other, an emphasis that perhaps arises from his anticipation, with Sophia's pregnancy, of the baby that will bring that "selfish" solitude to an end: "I do suppose that nobody ever lived, in one sense, quite so selfish a life as we do. Not a footstep, except our own, comes up the avenue for weeks and weeks; and we let the world alone as much as the world does us. During the greater part of the day, we are separately engaged at our respective avocations; but we meet in my study in the evening." Though he claims that their moments together "spread over all the time that we are apart" and leave them with the sense that they are "in each other's society a good deal more than we are," his "wonder" at Sophia's ability "to dispense with all society but mine" implicitly acknowledges an anxiety that the solitude of his society is not or will not be enough.[64] Of his own state of mind, Hawthorne describes "the circle" of his life since marriage as having "come round," bringing "back many of my school-day enjoyments," such as skating, which he now experiences with "a deeper pleasure," tasting them with "a sort of epicurism" possible for one who is "boy and man together" (15:670–71). Later in the year, he was to write to Evert Duyckinck that the "reality" he has found in marriage "looks very much like some of my old dreams" (16:9). His "old dreams" as a boy had been of a return to his Edenic days in Raymond, Maine, and a life spent in isolation from the world with his mother and sisters (15:117,119); at that moment in Concord, at least, he seems, as "boy and man together," to satisfy that longing with Sophia, whom he brags of keeping "tranquil as a summer-sunset" (15:671).

Or so he presents himself to Fuller. Of course, at the very moment that he writes to Fuller he anticipates the arrival of a baby that will end forever not only his "boyhood" but his exclusive hold over Sophia's attention and love. As a boy, "like the body of the mother to the child," Larry J. Reynolds has written, "nature constituted his reality and the son felt no sense of separation from her, until the intrusion of a father figure, his Uncle Robert Manning."[65] As a man, he will, with heavy irony, be the father who will drive himself as boy from this second paradise and from perfect possession of this second woman. At the moment that he writes to Fuller, he is also writing a damnation of his resentment and rage in the preemptive fantasy of abortion that is "The Birth-mark."[66] Though Hawthorne might be willing to provide Fuller a more intimate description of his marriage than he would provide to anyone else, he could continue the conversation on love and marriage— could speak the truth, or the whole and darker side of the truth at least— only in fiction.

Hawthorne closes by telling Fuller that Sophia wants to read the letter but notes pointedly that he would not allow her because he has "too much regard for her to consent," presumably because of the atrocious handwriting, for which he has just apologized, but perhaps also because of his desire to maintain a sense of exclusivity in his increasingly independent friendship with Fuller. He and Sophia "may let the world alone as the world does" them, but Fuller is welcome to join them in the solitude of their Eden. Hawthorne closes the letter by insisting, as he had to Sophia on the night they decided on Concord as their home, that Fuller spend "a proportionable part of the time at our house" when she next comes for a visit to Concord, whether it be "for a month, or a week, or a day" (15:672). He signs the letter "Your friend."

Fuller was not able to accept Hawthorne's invitation until the summer of 1844. During the year and a half that elapsed, Fuller had published in July 1843 "The Great Lawsuit: Man *versus* Men. Woman *versus* Women," the lengthy essay advocating a revision in male-female relationships that she would expand in the fall of 1844 into *Woman in the Nineteenth Century,* and she had toured the Midwest frontier and published her account of the trip in *Summer on the Lakes, 1843.* Arriving at the Manse on 9 July 1844, Fuller spent the first ten days of her visit to Concord with the Hawthornes, whose household now included the four-month-old Una, and she visited frequently with them during the remainder of the summer and fall. Because of Julian's influence, scholars have speculated that, in addition to Fuller's proposals that the Hawthornes take on boarders, Fuller's increasing feminism drove a wedge between her and the Hawthornes.[67] Just the opposite seems to have happened. Judging from Fuller's recently published journal of her stay with the Hawthornes during the summer of 1844—one year *after* the publication of "The Great Lawsuit"—their relationship became even more intimate. In fact, editorial decisions made by Fuller or by her friend William Clarke during an apparent recopying of the original journal entries, together with mysteriously missing pages in the journal, suggest that her relationship with Hawthorne may have been even more intimate than the record that we do have. As with Hawthorne's notebooks for 1842, these editorial deletions frequently occur at crucial junctures during or immediately after descriptions of her encounters with Hawthorne.[68] Though Sophia left accounts of Una's and Fuller's immediate affection for each other, this time Hawthorne did not record in his notebooks any of his private moments with Fuller, perhaps, as Edwin Haviland Miller speculates, because "he had Sophia looking over his shoulder."[69] These moments of the summer and fall of 1844 will be the last that Fuller and Hawthorne will share as friends, for after last seeing Hawthorne in September, Fuller moved to New York to become a literary and social critic for Greeley's *New-York Daily Tribune* and, as far as we know, she and Hawthorne never met again.

When Fuller arrived in Concord in July, both she and Hawthorne were

attempting to adjust to emotional upheavals in their lives. The "selfish" solitude of Hawthorne's marriage had finally been broken, of course, by the
arrival of Una, and Hawthorne, as most new fathers, was in the midst of
adjusting not only to his immense responsibilities as a parent but also to the
end of the "boyhood pleasures" he claims he had relived in the early days of
his marriage.[70] Though Sophia would remain "imbedded" within the pure
"amber" of her husband and never admit to not worshiping him as a verita-
ble god, Hawthorne had now to share his position in Sophia's pantheon with
a child. During the first six months after Una's birth, in fact, Hawthorne had
to sleep alone, for Sophia slept in a separate bedroom with the baby.[71]

Fuller was struggling to overcome a mysterious crisis that had given her,
as she says, "much pain in the month of May."[72] Citing the frequency and
consistency in her letters and poems of images "that depict her experiencing
an analogous process of pregnancy and birth," Jeffrey Steele speculates that
the crisis that led during the summer and fall of 1844 to Fuller's most prolific
and mature period as a poet originated primarily over the deep "wound"
resulting from the simultaneous "pregnancies of Fuller's sister Ellen, Hawthorne's wife Sophia, and Emerson's wife Lydia." Martha L. Berg and Alice
De V. Perry, editors of the recently published Fuller journal for the summer
and fall of 1844, argue instead that Fuller had fallen in love with young William Clarke, brother of James Freeman and Sarah Clarke, whom she had
met during her trip to the upper Midwest in the summer of 1843. By May
1844, Berg and Perry surmise, the promise of that relationship had soured,
and Fuller's journal, particularly before she arrived at the Hawthornes', records her anguished attempts to recover from the experience.[73] On June 27,
for instance, Fuller writes: "I am not fitted to be loved & it pains me to have
close dealings with those who do not love, to whom my feelings are
'strange.' Kindness & esteem are very well. I am willing to receive & bestow
them, but these, alone are not worth feelings such as mine, & I wish I may
make no more mistakes, but keep chaste for mine own people. I have got
beyond what gave me so much pain in the month of May, but I will never
seem right, I fear." Only five days before arriving at the Hawthornes, Fuller
finds that she has not "got beyond" the pain; she writes despairingly: "O I
need some help. No I need a full a godlike embrace from some sufficient
love."[74] Fuller's journal account of her stay in Concord describes her "close
dealings" with those who do "love" her, her "own people" who do not feel
that her feelings are "strange," chiefly, of course, Emerson and Hawthorne.
When Hawthorne in "The Old Manse" alludes to Fuller's stay at his home,
he describes her as a woman "on whose feminine nature had been imposed

the heavy gift of intellectual power, such as a strong man might have staggered under, and with it the necessity to act upon the world," and includes
her as one of those three "weary and world-worn" friends "who came within
our magic circle" where he was able "to throw the spell of a tranquil spirit"
over them and give them "rest" (10:29).

Hawthorne and Una—not Emerson and certainly not Sophia, who is
rarely mentioned—are the centers of Fuller's attention in the summer of
1844. Though still drawn to Emerson, by 1844 Fuller is more resigned to,
than impatient with, Emerson's incapacity for passionate intimacy. Hearing
him read a draft of his essay "Experience" (tentatively entitled "Life") only
two days after her arrival and only one day after the birth of his son Edward,
Fuller remarks "how beautiful, and full and grand" it is before condemning
it and its author for the frigidity of its vision: "Nothing but Truth in the
Universe, no love, and no various realities. Yet how foolish with me to be
grieved at him for showing towards me what exists toward all. Then we
talked. He showed me a page from his journal which made me rather
ashamed of ever exacting more. But lure me not again too near thee, fair
Greek, I must keep steadily in mind what you really are."[75] Just as she had
subtly characterized Hawthorne as an alternative to Emerson in her journal
of 1842, Fuller seems to turn from Emerson to Hawthorne for the emotionally sympathetic understanding that she needs during this crucial period,
and Hawthorne, attempting himself to adjust to his altered relations with
Sophia, apparently responds. The record that Fuller has left us of those summer days and nights alone with Hawthorne—helping him baby-sit Una,
boating on the Concord, walking through the woods of Sleepy Hollow—
clearly suggests, as Hawthorne represented it, that Fuller found comfort
with Hawthorne as her host and companion.

Fuller and Hawthorne had much time to be alone together, for Sophia
took on the task of nursing not only Una but Fuller's newly born niece,
Margaret Fuller "Greta" Channing.[76] On Saturday night, 13 July, four days
after her arrival, Fuller records her first private conversation at the Manse:
"On the rock in the orchard. It was very dark, the breeze whispering in the
trees above our heads, a few stars palely gleaming. We talked of dreams &
W. [Waldo] told the nature of his. He was a little eager & sentimental tonight, but I shall not forget the conscious subtle smile with which he looked
up as he said, 'I seem so at times from sympathy, but I am not really so.'"[77]
This entry, as several others that concern Hawthorne or Emerson, was apparently edited by Fuller, for not only is a blank space (suggesting an omission) left between "I shall not forget the" and "conscious," but the entry

itself, at the top of the page, is preceded by the row of "Xs" across the bottom of the previous page, a signifier that journal editors Berg and De V. Perry believe Fuller or possibly William Clarke "introduced" into the text to mark omissions when recopying the original for circulation among friends.[78] The omission in this case eliminates whatever Fuller may have written between the first line of the day's entry, "Playing with the beautiful Una, reading," and the passage that she kept on "dreams."

In two other places the row of "Xs" suggests the omission of entire conversations with Hawthorne. On 24 July, for instance, Fuller, who was now staying with her sister Ellen, spent the day at the Manse, having brought gifts for Hawthorne and Una but not Sophia. She writes: "I went up to the H's with some *new potatoes* for H. & a rattle for Una: Armed with these dignified presents I found as kind a welcome as shawls & silks would have purchased from an Eastern Pacha. H. walked home with me beneath the lovely trembling—X X X X." Two days earlier after dining with the Hawthornes and playing with Una, Fuller records: "Walked home with H. the long Sleepy Hollow way. Through the X X X [bottom of page] X X X X X [top of next page] our intercourse could never be perfect." The three "Xs" at the bottom of one page and the five "Xs" at the top of the next suggest that Fuller wished to denote the omission of the entire conversation, not just the final sentence on one page and the first sentence on the next. Whatever was discussed, it is clear that Fuller's disappointment in the imperfection of her intercourse with Hawthorne is linked in her mind in some way with romantic disappointments. Immediately after the edited reference to her conversation with Hawthorne, she writes: "At present, it skills not, I am able to take the superior views of life, and my place in it: but I know the deep yearnings of the heart & the bafflings of time will again be felt, & then I shall long for some dear hand to hold. But I shall never forget that my curse is nothing compared with that of those who have entered into those relations but not made them real: who only *seem* husbands, wives, & friends. H. was saying as much the other evening."[79]

Fuller's recognition that her "intercourse" with Hawthorne "could never be perfect," suggests, I believe, her recognition that the romantic tension in their friendship could never be resolved or realized fully. That Fuller and Hawthorne would discuss the nature of friendships and marriages made "real" is, of course, revelatory of the intimacy of their friendship. Not only were friendship and marriage the recurring topics of disagreement over the years between Fuller and Emerson in their private conversations, but it seems clear that Hawthorne and Fuller had been discussing the failure of

Emerson to form truly intimate relations with his wife as well as with his friends. The passage further suggests that Fuller and Hawthorne had discussed their own friendship and perhaps the Hawthorne marriage as being founded on "real" rather than "seeming" relations and had used Emerson as their foil.

Fuller's pleasure in Hawthorne's company and her longing to develop their friendship to an even deeper level of intimacy than the "brotherly" relationship she will later describe it as being is evident in a couple of passages that were not deleted from the journal. On 18 July, for instance, Fuller writes of lying on a rock in the Hawthorne orchard, giving herself up to the sensuous summer afternoon—"lustrous warm, delicious happy, tender, gently stooping clouds"—listening to sounds of farmers making hay, children splashing in the river, the dancing master's "shriek and scrape" on the fiddle, the discord "harmonized by the golden fulness of light on the river on the trees, on the fields," caring "not where it lay" for "it loved and laughed on all." Into this sensuously picturesque scene she introduces Hawthorne: "H. came down about six and we went out on the river & staid till after sunset. We talked a great deal this time. I love him much & love to be with him in this sweet tender homely scene. But I should like too, to be with him on the bold ocean shore." [80] The Hawthorne "in this sweet homely scene" is the husband, the father, the friend—the "mild, deep and large" man that she had described having a "most pleasant communion" with five days before when Sophia had left Fuller alone with Hawthorne and Una, the man whom she had originally described to Sophia as having the "delicate tenderness to understand the heart of a woman." [81] The Hawthorne that she desires "to be with . . . on the bold ocean shore" suggests the man that she could not find in Emerson, the "mellow" Hawthorne of passionate potentiality, of "quiet depth and manliness enough to satisfy the heart of a woman." Fuller's desire "to be with him on the bold ocean shore" may be read, in a sense, as a more explicit prescription for the "deeper experiences" that she had claimed two years before that Hawthorne needed in order to become the "genius . . . fully roused" to his "work."

Fuller's "most pleasant communion" with Hawthorne had an immediate impact on her. In June and early July, Fuller filled her journal with descriptions of her emotional and physical agonies, her despair over the need that she cannot quite suppress for "a full a godlike embrace from some sufficient love," but after only nine days at the Old Manse, Fuller finds herself somewhat surprised to report that she "can scarcely remember" the pain of "all the thoughts that stung me so," for now her "blood flows gently" and "nei-

ther head or heart aches." [82] By the last week in July, pondering her relationship with Hawthorne after a five-hour moonlight boat ride alone with him
on 26 July, Fuller attempts to define the man who was capable of providing
her a "sufficient love," and she places Hawthorne at the apex of the triangle
of men in her life:

> Last night in the boat I could not help thinking each has something—more
> all. With Waldo how impossible to enjoy this still companionship, this mutual
> visionary life. With William even: with whom I have for moments & hours
> been so happy could I ever depend on his being *at leisure [sic]*, to live thus;
> certainly for ages I could not. But then H. has not the deep polished intellect
> of the one or the pure & passionate beauty of the other. He has his own
> powers: I seem to want them all. [83]

As she had done on 21 August 1842 after spending the afternoon in Sleepy
Hollow with Hawthorne, Fuller concludes the entry with the statement that
she "cannot write about it," but what she does write about that night on the
Concord with Hawthorne suggests that the "mutual visionary life" that she
found in Hawthorne's "still companionship" may have been complicated by
a more romantic attraction:

> I got to the Parsonage about 5 & we went out in the boat immediately. But
> the wind being against us made it too hard work for the boatman & soft
> clouds overspreading the whole sky it seemed that we should have no moon
> back, so we did not go quite to Fairhaven, but stopped about half a mile this
> side & went on shore to walk. But soon the moon rose in great beauty above
> a wood & we went to the boat again. We floated carelessly running ashore
> every now & then, and reached home a little after ten. O it is a sweet dream
> in memory, yet I regretted afterward that I had been led to talk so much. Had
> we floated silently, the captives of the scene, it would have been more entirely
> separate from the past. Now there are associations with these hours they can-
> not be remembered alone. The night was *so* beautiful, too, after we came in!
> I cannot write about it, but two poems occurred to me. I shall write them out
> so soon as I am able. [84]

The morning after her experience with Hawthorne, Emerson seems
more inadequate than ever; Fuller writes: "I have just been in to see Waldo
a few minutes. Sweet child.—Great Sage—Undeveloped Man!" It is not the
first time in the journal that Fuller juxtaposes Emerson's inadequacies with
Hawthorne's "own powers." The paragraph immediately preceding Fuller's
account of visiting Hawthorne on 24 July with gifts for him and Una and of
walking home with him "beneath the lovely trembling—X X X X" in fact
ridicules Emerson more mercilessly than Hawthorne was ever to do:
"Waldo came in & talked his transcendental fatalism a little. Then went
away, declaring he should not come again till he was less stupid. I had as lief

he would sit here and not say a word, but it would be impossible to make him understand *that*."[85]

After the long entry describing her 26 July boat ride with Hawthorne, Fuller does not write again in her journal until 30 July, this time to describe the effect of her disappointment in not being able to take another boat ride with Hawthorne: "Evening at the Parsonage but Mr. Bradford was there and wanted to go with H. in the boat. So I staid by myself in the avenue or went up the hill opposite with Leo [Hawthorne's St. Bernard]. playing Mephisto. to the Goethean life & then late I went into the orchard & lay on the rock looking up to the sky through the old twisted broken trees.—I am not happy tonight & ugly memories shed their bitter in the cup, but it was a beautiful, a spirit haunted night." This is not the first time Fuller suggests a connection between her relationship with Hawthorne and her emotional or physical well-being. After her heavily edited description of the 22 July walk home with Hawthorne through "the long Sleepy Hollow way," which left her with the impression that their "intercourse could never be perfect" and that she would soon "long for some dear hand to hold," she begins the next day's entry simply: "My head aches today, I can scarce do anything." Two days later, on the morning after bringing gifts to Hawthorne and Una and walking home again at night with Hawthorne "beneath the lovely trembling— X X X X X," Fuller suggests that she is recuperating from her recent crisis—sleeping late, the mind not wanting "to be waked" because "the body needs a long lullaby": "Nestling stilly, long wing feathers grow again."[86]

In her final journal entry on Hawthorne before leaving Concord in August, Fuller records her "sadness" that Una will not be quite the baby she is now, but as she thinks of the changes wrought by time on Una, she also thinks of the possibilities of future development in her relationship with Hawthorne. Describing yet another walk through the woods with Hawthorne, she first recounts the experience in an implicitly suggestive narrative. She then adds a coda that explicitly negates the suggestiveness by attributing to Hawthorne, if not quite to herself, the presently innocent nature of their intimacy and its potentiality for even greater depth: "Walk with H. in the woods long paths, dark and mystical. We went far & it was quite dark when we returned: we lost the path & I got wet in the long grass & had much scrambling. Yet this was pleasant too in its way though I reached home quite 'beat out' & went straight to bed with burning headache as I did last night. I feel more like a sister to H. or rather more that he might be a brother to me than ever with any man before. Yet with him it is though sweet, not deep kindred, at least, not deep yet."[87]

Fuller's temptation, but refusal, to define her feelings toward Hawthorne as "sisterly" while asserting his "brotherly" role with her may have been added to the description of this walk as a result of the conversation she had with Sophia two days before, the only conversation in fact that she records in her journal as having had with Sophia during her entire stay. Toward the end of the journal, on 14 October, nearly a month after she had taken leave of Emerson and Hawthorne before departing for New York, Fuller records that "visions came to haunt" her, and she exclaims: "O let the past be quite past. Help me my Angel to an increasing delicacy of conscience and a stricter honor." The cryptic conversation that Fuller recorded of Sophia's conversation and her reaction to it may have contributed not only to her attempt to define Hawthorne's relationship to her as being "brotherly" but also to the haunting, conscience-stricken visions of her past. On 31 July Fuller writes: "Sophia told me a truth for which I thank her: she seemed nobly. 'Each Orpheus must to the depths descend.' I walked home with H. through the woods. The skies were sighing & veiling their lids, & began to weep almost as soon as I was housed. . . . I have been writing a little note to Sophia about the truth. I will think prayerfully of it. I am very unwell, thanks to moonlight damps of last night, I suppose." [88]

Whatever was said between Sophia and Fuller on 31 July, Fuller's friendship with the Hawthornes did not seem to be affected. Returning to Concord on 21 September after an absence of almost two months, Fuller records having tea with the Hawthornes and walking home with Hawthorne beneath the "very bright, cold moonlight." She had already begun expanding "The Great Lawsuit" into *Woman in the Nineteenth Century* and had returned to Concord apparently to discuss with Emerson and Hawthorne the offer she had received from Horace Greeley, for she writes, "Both W. & H. think the N. Y. plan of great promise, which I did not expect." [89]

She left Concord the next day, and in the two-month interval between Concord and New York, she was busily at work transforming "The Great Lawsuit" into *Woman in the Nineteenth Century*. She had entered the Hawthorne household in July having yet to recover from a debilitating emotional crisis, but she was able to leave Concord ready to make the biggest personal and professional move of her life, ready to enter, as it turns out, the most productive and important phases of her literary career. In the last contact that we know about, the Hawthornes wrote a now-lost letter to her concerning *Woman in the Nineteenth Century*. Whatever they said, it certainly did not dampen Fuller's enthusiasm for their friendship. In her 22 May 1845 response to the Hawthornes' letter, she seems clearly to have cherished the memory of the summer at the Manse and continued apparently to look forward to a deepening of her kinship with Hawthorne. She wrote that she hoped "to see you once more at the dear old house, with the green fields and lazy river and have, perhaps, sweet hours [ ] of last summer [ ] [i]f things work well, I hope to come. Una alone will be changed, yet still I think the same. Farewell, dear friends, now, for this is only meant as a hasty sign of affection."[90] Her plans did not work out. She never saw Hawthorne again, and we have no evidence that they corresponded. But she did not forget her friend. In New York she continued to promote Hawthorne's career through her personal contacts and through her power as a widely read literary critic.

Hawthorne certainly did not forget her. Though he would never again walk the woods of Concord with her, his conversations with her did not end. Fuller did much more to promote Hawthorne's literary career than simply praise him every time she reviewed his work. She probably never realized it, but more than anyone or anything, she seems responsible for unsettling Hawthorne's fiction, for enabling him to "paint" with "blood-warm colors." After the summer of 1844, Hawthorne, like Fuller, also embarked on the greatest phase of his literary career. It began less than one month after she left Concord. It began the moment Hawthorne initiated a new conversation with her, the literary conversation that is "Rappaccini's Daughter."

"Rappaccini's Daughter" and the Voice of Beatrice

> I will compare the attempt to escape him to the hopeless race that men sometimes run with memory, or their own hearts, or their moral selves. . . . I will be self-contemplative, as Nature bids me, and make him the picture or visible type of what I muse upon, that my mind may not wander so vaguely as heretofore, chasing its own shadow through a chaos and catching only the monsters that abide there.
>
> NATHANIEL HAWTHORNE, "MONSIEUR DU MIROIR"

Any entrance into Rappaccini's garden leaves us fraught with the humbling suspicion that we are following perilously in Giovanni's footsteps, carrying with us our own vial of interpretative poison.[1] This is as Hawthorne would have it, for this is as Hawthorne experienced it. Struggling to complete the tale he had begun sometime in mid-October 1844, Hawthorne read the unfinished manuscript to Sophia: "But how is it to end?" she asked him, when he laid down the paper. "Is Beatrice to be a demon or an angel?" "I have no idea!" was Hawthorne's reply, spoken with some emotion.[2] Hawthorne, in fact, ended the tale by condemning the very desire to conclude it, to fix himself to an "idea" that in the falsity of its reductive certainty would unravel the "riddle" of Beatrice.[3] But then he began the tale for that very purpose, for the "riddle" of Beatrice had become for Hawthorne inseparably bound, as he writes of Giovanni, with the "mystery which he deemed the riddle of his own existence" (10:110). The sources of the baffling complexity of the tale, I contend, originate in the very complexity of Hawthorne's at-

traction to and fear of Emerson's influence and of the even more "lurid intermixture" of emotions that Margaret Fuller had aroused in Hawthorne
(10:105).

Echoes of Milton and Dante in "Rappaccini's Daughter" are impossible
to miss. But the tale is much more than simply a Rappaccini-like "commixture" of Milton's Adam meeting Dante's Beatrice in Hawthorne's translation
of "the new Eden" into "the present world" (10:96). His narrator raises that
possibility perhaps because he would prefer that we keep our interpretative
eyes fixed there, focused on the distant, on the tale's intertextual negotiations
between those classic texts. "New" and "present," however, should hold
our attention. The new Eden for Hawthorne was Emerson's Concord, and
the feminine voice that spoke most alluringly and dangerously in that
Emersonian-mediated garden was the voice of Emerson's protégée, Fuller.[4]
Hawthorne's adoption of Dante's "Beatrice" rather than Adam's "Eve" for
the name of the heroine of this new Eden suggests that Hawthorne's playful
masquerade as merely the translator of the tale is much less playful and
much more revealing than he perhaps would want his public to know. In
something akin to a Dimmesdale-like concealed confession, Hawthorne, in
effect, may be acknowledging to that "individual" or "isolated clique" (10:91)
capable of reading him that he is broadly translating for his own purposes
Emerson's own translation the year before of Dante's *Vita Nuova,* the passionate narrative and poetic account by Dante of the pain and rapture of his love
for the unapproachable Beatrice. Emerson translated the *Vita Nuova* at the
height of his admiration for Fuller, who had also talked often of translating
it. As Robert D. Richardson Jr. has observed, Emerson clearly associated
Fuller with Beatrice.[5]

About the time that he translated Dante, Emerson wrote an amazing
panegyric on Fuller. Others had disappointed him, but "this child inspires
always more faith in her," he wrote with paternalistic pride. "She rose before
me at times into heroical & godlike regions, and I could remember no superior women, but thought of Ceres, Minerva, Proserpine, and the august
ideal forms of the Foreworld." That one of his "august ideal forms" included
Dante's Beatrice is made explicit two paragraphs later when he wishes that
Fuller's "golden moments" of "magnanimity" could be "fitly narrated," for
though he claims that Dante's "'Nuova Vita' is almost unique," he admits
that he has "called" her "imperfect record" of one such moment in her life
a "Nuovissima Vita."[6] Hawthorne was certainly one of those to whom Emerson compared Fuller with such "august ideal forms" as a Proserpine or a
Beatrice, for in the same month as Emerson's journal entry, Hawthorne re-

corded in his own journal a visit from Emerson during which Emerson "apotheosized" Fuller "as the greatest woman . . . of ancient or modern times, and the one figure in the world worth considering" (8:371). Hawthorne certainly thought Fuller and his relationship with her and with Emerson worth considering. For the narrative form that Emerson had sought in order to capture Fuller's near mythic but elusive effect on others, Hawthorne found in Emerson's translation a means for translating his own private experience into public art. He also found, through Emerson, a model in Dante for the kind of writer that, beginning with "Rappaccini's Daughter," he would increasingly become. "Dante's praise," Emerson had claimed in the essay "The Poet," "is that he dared to write his autobiography in colossal cipher, or into universality." Indeed, Dante's *Vita Nuova* is a work of art about art and its intimate but veiled origins in the life of the artist. Dante writes about Dante the lover who becomes Dante the poet in order to confess his love in poems that he hoped would both conceal the object of his love from the public and yet reveal it to the unapproachable woman who has unknowingly inspired in him both torment and ecstasy. If Giovanni resembles Dante's tormented-ecstatic lover and if the untouchable Beatrice Rappaccini resembles Dante's unapproachable Beatrice, then Hawthorne, the translator of his foreign self, Aubépine, assumes the role of Dante the writer writing about Dante the lover who translates his inexpressible love into the language of an art that is both public and private, readable and unreadable.

Beginning the tale within weeks of his last walk with Fuller in the woods of Concord and during the very month that her mentor and his friend and rival, Emerson, published his second series of essays, Hawthorne "translates" his troubling relationship with them both into the "picture or visible types" of the tale—attempting through art, as his narrator in "Monsieur du Miroir" proclaims, to contain the "chaos" of his "musings" and through the concealed confessions of allegory to confront the "monsters that abide there." The tale thus performs its subject; it is a riddle of a riddle, a translation that requires translation. The prefatory "Writings of Aubépine" suggests as much. Hawthorne invites us with self-deprecatory humor to read through the thin fiction of his self-presentation, to "translate" it; for "Aubépine," we read "Hawthorne," for "translator," we read "author." In another sense, however, Hawthorne took up the transparent mask of translator because in transmuting life into art he had attempted in a very real sense to translate the language of his experience into the language of art. With Giovanni as his "visible type," Hawthorne is the "author" of the life that as writer he translates into his tale. As Hawthorne himself attempts to find in art a language that will allow him to read the meaning of his own experience, he translates that private text into a public text that approximates but does not equal its original, a text that we can and yet cannot read. Compelled to read the "riddle" of Fuller's character and his troublingly ambivalent relationship with her, detesting his very need to do so, and compelled also to conceal the very confession that is the tale, Hawthorne images in the mirror of Giovanni not only his reflection but ours. The tale performs his agony. We read the secondary language of the translator's tale, but in taking seriously Hawthorne's playful invitation to become translators ourselves, we are challenged to have the depth that Giovanni lacked, the faith to believe that we hear another, truer language, the first language of the tale's primary source.

The preface introduces both the private and the public texts and provides for the "individual" whom he claims as his audience an interpretative entrance into Rappaccini's garden. The "individual or possibly isolated clique" capable of reading the tale is and is not a self-deprecatory appeal to his readers' aesthetic and class vanities. Beneath the public text of Hawthorne's apology for his art is his solicitude of, literally, an individual reader, for in addition to writing his own version of Emerson's translation of Dante and appropriating Dante's artistic enterprise, the private text is something of a response to the challenges issued by Margaret Fuller in her July 1842 review of *Twice-Told Tales*. Of his "imaginative pieces," Fuller had written:

> The invention is not clearly woven, far from being all compact, and seems a phantom or shadow, rather than a real growth. The men and women, too, flicker large and unsubstantial, like "shadows from the evening firelight," seen "upon the parlor wall." But this would be otherwise, probably, were the genius fully roused to its work, and initiated into its own life, so as to paint with blood-warm colors. This frigidity and thinness of design usually bespeaks a want of deeper experiences, for which no talent at observation, no sympathies, however ready and delicate, can compensate. We wait new missives from the same hand.[7]

Hawthorne's review of Aubépine's work not only acknowledges most of the same points of criticism but also employs similar phrasing. Hawthorne will implicitly address Aubépine's "want of deeper experiences" in his treatment of Giovanni, but here he seems explicitly to address Fuller's criticism of his failure to "paint with blood-warm colors"—of his shadowy characters' "frigidity and thinness"—by instead blaming "an inveterate love of allegory" for making Aubépine "apt to invest his plots and characters with the aspect of scenery and people in the clouds and steal away the human warmth out of his conceptions" (10:91–92). In phrases that parallel Fuller's challenge to his contentment with imparting but "slight outward details and habits" that suggest "how little yet is told" and with providing an "invention" that "is not clearly woven" or "a real growth," Hawthorne writes that Aubépine "contents himself with a very slight embroidery of outward manners,—the faintest possible counterfeit of real life" (10:92). Occasionally Aubépine provides just enough "pathos and tenderness" or "humor" to "make us feel as if . . . we were yet within the limits of our native earth" (10:92), but these compensations of "observation" and of "sympathy," as Fuller argued, were not enough. Hawthorne must live "deeper experiences" and create a passionate art out of a passionate life. To do that, he must abandon his solitude and risk responding to "a voice that truly calls" upon him.[8]

If through paraphrase his preface, his very first preface, seems to acknowledge that he had heard Fuller's voice, his restatement of her criticism and his assumption of the role of translator and American promoter of a continental author seem acts of literary ventriloquism, registering his voice in her key, for Fuller had become widely recognized for her translations and her unfinished biography, and in general, her championship of Goethe. She also had long waged an American critical campaign on behalf of German and French romantics, in particular courageously defending against popular prejudice Madame de Staël and George Sand. In identifying Aubépine's literary predicament as being "too popular" for the "spiritual or metaphysical requisitions" of the Transcendentalists as well as "too refined" for "the intellect and sympathies of the multitude" (10:91), Hawthorne also aligns himself with Fuller. Though credited by Emerson with being the one person responsible for whatever unity the Transcendentalists had as a group, Fuller had become over the years as dissatisfied with Emerson's passionless abstractions as had Hawthorne.[9]

During the preceding summer, her private journal had registered again and again her impatience with Emerson's "cold" intellectualizations, juxtaposed most often by her expressions of contentment in Hawthorne's "still companionship" and their "mutual visionary life."[10] When she arrived in New York, in fact, she selected the October publication of Emerson's *Essays: Second Series* (which she had read in July while staying with the Hawthornes) as the topic of her first review for the *New-York Daily Tribune*. Published on 7 December 1844 (the same month that "Rappaccini's Daughter" appeared in the *Democratic Review*), Fuller's lengthy review lavishes much praise on Emerson but frankly concludes that because he had been "chilled by the critical intellect," he was incomplete as a man and as a writer: "We miss what we expect in the work of the great poet, or the great philosopher, the liberal air of all the zones: the glow, uniform yet various in tint, which is given to a body by free circulation of the heart's blood from the hour of birth. Here is, undoubtedly, the man of ideas, but we want the ideal man also; want the heart and genius of human life to interpret it, and here our satisfaction is not so perfect."[11] Dissatisfied with "the petty intellectualities, cant, and bloodless theory" of her friends in Boston, as she had stated to Emerson in a 17 August 1843 letter from Chicago, she found herself with "no place . . . to live," for she was equally unsettled by the "merely instinctive existence" of the frontier multitude in the Midwest, which, as she said, "silenced" her.[12] Writing "Rappaccini's Daughter" as Fuller moved to New York and began settling into her job as a newspaper columnist and critic, Hawthorne (though he and Emerson had encouraged her to accept the position) would have every reason to anticipate that her work, like his, would be "too refined" for her audience of New York newspaper readers and "too popular" for Emerson and his circle.

Within the private text of "The Writings of Aubépine," Hawthorne addresses Fuller in a language that she, at least, would be able to read. Positioning himself with her in the readerless space of an ideological and literary isolation, Hawthorne encodes her intimate identification with the tale that follows even as he seems to distance himself from it. As she was the "author" of the critique of Hawthorne's art that he "translated" into his own critique of Aubépine's, so she will be, with Hawthorne, the original "coauthor" of the experience that he presents as translation. Performing its subject, this passionate tale "paints with blood-warm colors" the passionate response of a man to a "voice" that calls upon him to forsake his wary "solitude" for "deeper experiences." In responding to that voice, Hawthorne is responding to his own voice as well as Fuller's, for Fuller challenges him to examine his own attraction to and fear of the deeper experiences of a dialogue with a feminine nature that both promises release from and yet threatens the self-sufficiency of his male solitude. As often noted, the notorious shift in point of view in the tale (the sudden emergence of the narrative "voice" condemning Giovanni and defending Beatrice) is largely responsible for the complexity of the tale, but this complexity, as I hope to demonstrate, originates in Hawthorne's own extraordinarily complex conversation with those "voices" within himself that spoke most clearly in his dialogue with Fuller and Emerson. Less than two years later, as Larry J. Reynolds has demonstrated of "The Old Manse," Hawthorne continued this dialogue with Emerson, attempting there, as he did here, earlier, in "Rappaccini's Daughter," to interrupt the monologue of the self-sufficient masculine individualist who reads all nature as self by engaging in an intimate dialogue with a feminine Other who promises release from the self, freedom from the walls of Rappaccini's garden.[13] It is an Other whose voice Hawthorne recognizes in Fuller's, whose voice Hawthorne makes his own.

Much of the narrative form and thematic tensions of Hawthorne's tale seems to respond to Fuller's voice and echo her own figurative language, but determining the precise degree of intertextual appropriation is difficult. Hawthorne and Fuller both drew upon a romantic discourse in which nature imagery commonly melded with biblical and Miltonic allusions. Nevertheless, the parallels are striking. In Fuller's 4 June 1842 letter to Sophia, for instance, Fuller reacts to Sophia's announcement of her impending marriage to Hawthorne by praising Hawthorne profusely ("if ever I saw a man who combined delicate tenderness to understand the heart of a woman, with quiet depth and manliness enough to satisfy her, it is Mr Hawthorne") and by expressing her belief that their marriage offered the unique opportunity for love to develop into its rarest of forms, "intellectual friendship." She then raises the possibility that they will fail to achieve this level of intimacy but insists that she is confident that despite potential problems "mutual love and heavenly trust will gleam brightly through the dark." She defends this faith by writing: "I do not *demand* the earnest of a future happiness to all believing souls. I wish to temper the mind to believe, without prematurely craving *sight,* but it is sweet when here and there some little spots of garden ground reveal the flowers that deck our natural Eden,—sweet when some characters can bear fruit without the aid of the knife, and the first scene of that age-long drama in which each child of God must act to find himself is plainly to be deciphered, and its cadences harmonious to the ear."[14]

"Rappaccini's Daughter" may be read as Hawthorne's transformation of Fuller's sensory, organic, and biblical figures for her affirmation of faith in Hawthorne and Sophia's happiness into the narrative and thematic figures of his betrayal of that faith. Entering the unnatural Eden of the new Adam whose intervention through the "aid of" the cold intellect's "knife" has transformed the "sweet" flowers of nature into "poisons" intended to heal but capable, possibly, of harm, Giovanni re-presents, as "visible type," Hawthorne's own anxious entrance into the seductively influential and un-natural Eden of Emerson's Transcendentalized Nature—into, that is, as he says in "The Old Manse," the "wonderful magnetism" of Emerson's Concord, where "the light revealed objects unseen before," where "uncertain, troubled, earnest wanderers" sought his truth but too often saw its opposite in their own delusions, "night-birds" envisioned as "fowls of angelic feather" (10:30–31). As Hawthorne in "The Old Manse" aligns Emerson's protégée Fuller with best friends Franklin Pierce and Horatio Bridge under the opposing influence of his own "magic circle" in Concord, where he heals their "weary and world-worn spirits" through the "spell" of his own "tranquil spirit" (10:29), so Giovanni would save Beatrice from Rappaccini's poison by having her imbibe his antidote. Giovanni thus engages himself in the "age-long drama" of male rivalry for possession of a woman that he both loves and loathes. It is a drama that he says holds the "riddle of his existence" because he hopes that the torment of the "lurid intermixture" of emotions that is his confused but obsessive desire for her will end when he possesses the ability to define, with certainty, her mystery. Hermeneutically and biblically, he must "know" her to have her. However, because Giovanni, in Fuller's words, *does* "*demand* the earnest of a future happiness" by "prematurely craving *sight*," because, in other words, he fails to be a "believing soul" and accept from her lips the truth that she has to offer to him, nothing is "plainly to be deciphered." Nothing, that is, except that in failing to heed Beatrice's voice, he does not "find" her but himself in its "cadences," no longer so "harmonious to the ear" because they name the "poison" within his own "thwarted nature."

So close are several of the significant details in this tale to Fuller's own statements in her personal papers that it is likely that Fuller repeated many of these observations to Hawthorne during their numerous private conversations. Hawthorne's representation of those under Emerson's influence and patronage as plants cultivated in Emerson's garden parallels, for instance, Fuller's own image of Emerson. In a 23 June 1842 letter to Emerson: "The new colonists will be with you soon. Your community seems to grow. I think you must take pleasure in Hawthorne when you know him. You will find him more *mellow* than most fruits at your board, and of distinct flavor too." Hawthorne's allegorical use of the insidious fragrance emanating from Rappaccini's garden closely parallels Fuller's conception of the powerful and potentially destructive nature of Emerson's influence on her as an intoxicating odor impossible to breathe for long. Concluding a stay at Emerson's in September 1842, Fuller observes in her journal: "I ought to go away now these last days I have been fairly intoxicated with his mind. I am not in full possession of my own. I feel faint in the presence of too strong a fragrance." [15] In "The Old Manse" Hawthorne echoes Fuller's line in describing Emerson's influence: "But it was impossible to dwell in his vicinity, without inhaling, more or less, the mountain-atmosphere of his lofty thought, which, in the brains of some people, wrought a singular giddiness—new truth being as heady as new wine" (10:31). The "magic circle" of his "tranquil spirit," into which, Hawthorne says in "The Old Manse" he drew Fuller, Bridges, and Pierce, was also claimed by Fuller, who acknowledges "some magic about me which draws other spirits into my circle whether I will or they will or no."[16] Giovanni assigns a similar power to Beatrice when he describes being "irrevocably within her sphere" and compelled to "obey the law that whirled him onward, in ever-lessening circles" toward her (10:109). And, finally, Giovanni's initial description of his surprising ease in conversing with Beatrice as making him feel "like a brother" (10:113) repeats Fuller's own characterization in her 1844 journal of Hawthorne as being "more . . . a brother" to her "than ever . . . any man before."[17]

More generally, but importantly, Fuller's unpublished "Autobiographical Romance," and her exploration of a feminist symbolism in her flower sketches for the *Dial*, "The Magnolia of Lake Pontchartrain" (1841) and "Yuca Filamentosa" (1842) suggested to Hawthorne an allegorical figure for Fuller of Fuller's own choosing. Noted for wearing a flower in her hair, Fuller had long associated the feminine side of her nature with flowers and her mother's garden.[18] Her 1840 autobiographical sketch of her youth significantly allies the masculine influence of her father's harsh insistence on her intellectual development with the stern rational virtues of heroic, imperial Rome but counters that influence with the artistic world of Greece and the feminine world of her mother, linked figuratively in Fuller's imagination with the beauty of her mother's garden and the nurturing love she bestowed on it.[19] While the sketch was not published during Fuller's lifetime, Fuller in talks with Hawthorne may have employed this figurative opposition to locate the continuing influence of her childhood on her life. The influence of childhood on their adult lives was the most personal subject Hawthorne listed of the many and varied topics of his conversation with Fuller in the woods of Sleepy Hollow on 21 August 1842. The influence of Fuller's father is clearly on Hawthorne's mind when of all the possible descriptive statements he could have made to identify Fuller in "The Old Manse," he thinks of her as one "on whose feminine nature had been *imposed* the heavy gift of intellectual *power,* such as a strong man might have staggered under, and with it the necessity to act upon the world" (10:29; my emphases).

As Joel Pfister has noted, Hawthorne's tale appropriates the oppositions of the father's oppressive intellectual cultivation of his daughter against the mother's cultivation of her flowers.[20] "I kissed them," Fuller says of her mother's flowers. "I pressed them to my bosom with passionate emotions, such as I have never dared to express to any human being" and "an ambition swelled my heart to be as beautiful, as perfect as they." Compare Fuller's statement with the following passage describing Beatrice: "She bent towards the magnificent plant, and opened her arms as if to embrace it. 'Yes, my sister, my splendor, it shall be Beatrice's task to nurse and serve thee; and thou shalt reward her with thy kisses and perfumed breath, which to her is as the breath of life!'" (10:97). But for Fuller, as for Beatrice, her father's intervention in her "natural" development caused "much of life" to be "devoured in the bud." Fuller cannot be "as perfect as they," for "living and blooming" in their "unchecked law," her mother's flowers can never know "the blights, the distortions, which beset the human being and which at such hours it would seem that no glories of free agency could ever repay!"[21] Had Hawthorne not been friends with Fuller and held intimate conversations with her, had he not had possible access to her unpublished account of her childhood, he would have had access to Fuller's positive account of her father's influence on her extraordinary intellectual development in Fuller's thinly veiled autobiographical account of Miranda in "The Great Lawsuit."

Fuller introduces the brief story of Miranda's development to illustrate her point "that the restraints upon the sex were insuperable only to those who think them so, or who noisily strive to break them." With "a strong electric nature, which repelled those who did not belong to her, and attracted those who did," Miranda was educated—given "the keys to the wonders of the universe"—by a father who believed "in the equality of the sexes" and held "no sentimental reverence for woman." As a consequence, Miranda developed a "sense of self-dependence" and a "mind [that] was often the leading one, always effective."[22] Fuller does not discuss Miranda's mother nor the influence of her lack of influence; her absence in the brief tale, like that of Beatrice's mother, is not even explicitly noted. As the contrast between her "Autobiographical Romance" and her tale of Miranda makes evident, Fuller clearly had ambivalent feelings about her father's influence on her development, an ambivalence that is not merely the result of her rhetorical need in "The Great Lawsuit" to stress the benefits of giving girls a rigorous childhood education. Hawthorne's portrayal of the relationship between Dr. Rappaccini and his daughter—his good intentions and his damaging influence, Beatrice's love for him but her disapproval of his experiments—is equally ambivalent.

Even if Hawthorne had not seen Fuller often with flowers in her hair and heard her discourse on the special symbolism of flowers, "The Magnolia of Lake Pontchartrain" and "Yuca Filamentosa" alone would have been sufficient to establish for Hawthorne Fuller's identification of the feminine with the flower. In Jeffrey Steele's insightful analysis of Fuller's attempts at "psychological mythmaking," Fuller's flower sketches figure prominently in his account of Fuller's search for myths and symbols that explore "the psychological dimensions of a female being forced to withdraw from heterosexual society and to rely upon her own resources." Shaken by Sam Ward's marriage to Anna Barker and disappointed in Emerson's inability to meet her in a friendship on her own terms, Fuller, according to Steele, expresses in these sketches "the female power drawing" her "outside the orbit of male domination," specifically the domination, he argues convincingly, of Emerson.[23] In both sketches, Fuller endows the flower with the mythic beauty and creative force of the feminine, powers that the male featured in each sketch fails to comprehend and thus rejects. Unable to find himself "in other forms of nature," the male narrator of "The Magnolia of Lake Pontchartrain" admits to having retreated into the "centre of [his] being" where he "found all being"; that is man's problem, Fuller's feminine voice, the Magnolia, proclaims. Imprisoned within the masculine self and imprisoning all with him, man can only "recombine the lines and colors of his own existence." To transcend the self, to be truly creative, man must experience the feminine power of "the queen and guardian of the flowers," but that power cannot be known, she tells him, "till thou art it . . . till thou has passed through it." Ending "The Magnolia of Pontchartrain" with the declaration that cultivation of the "secret powers" of the feminine requires that a woman "take a step inward" and "become a vestal priestess" capable of "purer" and "deeper thought," Fuller suggests that, as things now stand, she may gain the power of a feminine self-sufficiency only by withdrawing from a world defined by the self-reflections of the masculine self and entering the province of "the queen and guardian of the flowers." The ending, as Steele argues, describes the "need to accept female existence on its own terms," an acceptance that will come for women only when men could "listen to and acknowledge the validity of their insights as women."[24]

In "Yuca Filamentosa," Fuller's identification with the yuca flower is clearly personal. Fond of reminding herself and others—including Hawthorne—that "Margaret" means "pearl," Fuller praises the pearl and the opal as the moon's "gems" and proclaims the night-blooming yuca as the moon's flower. Engendering the calm, lonely moon as a feminine power bestowing a loving beauty on earth, Fuller clearly identifies herself with the mystery of the yuca, which blooms by brooding "on her own heart" and the moon, but which withers under the "unsparing scrutiny" of the rational, masculine sun, becoming "dull, awkward, sallow in its loneliness." Inspired by the beauty and meaning of the yuca, the speaker solicits the appreciation of her male friend Alcemon, who rather expectedly proves to be as dull to the moon's influence as the yuca is to the sun's. Fuller's application of the flower's symbolism to her life is direct: "Fate! let me never murmur more. . . . Remember the Yuca; wait and trust; and either Sun or Moon, according to thy fidelity, will bring thee to love and to know."[25]

"Rappaccini's Daughter" acknowledges the challenge of Fuller's feminist claim to a separate realm of knowledge by employing in parallel fashion, by translating, Fuller's appropriation of the flower and moon as feminist symbols for woman's access to a beauty and a power—a knowledge—that transcends reliance on the "stern scrutiny" of the rational light of the masculine sun. Giovanni first observes Beatrice tending her garden in twilight; as "night was already closing in," Beatrice and flower seem one as Beatrice proclaims sisterhood with the purple blossoms that she passionately embraces as her source of "the breath of life" (10:96–97). Giovanni and Rappaccini, as men, are both drawn to and repelled by the intriguing beauty and frightening power of the feminine; the flower's "breath of life" for Beatrice becomes for them "the breath of death." Under the influence of the moon, Giovanni is drawn to the power of the feminine, receptive enough to recognize its symbolism—"flower and maiden were different, and yet the same"—but too fearful to embrace its meaning—rejecting flower and girl as "fraught with some strange peril in either shape." Under the complete influence of the masculine sun, which as the tale puts it, brings "every thing within the limits of ordinary experience," Giovanni finds that by taking "a most rational view of the whole matter" he can no longer recognize, much less embrace or repel, the "mysteries" that had been so "fertile" in his night dreams (10:98).

Hawthorne thus faithfully parallels Fuller's symbolism of moon-flower-feminine consciousness to stand for a passionate, intuitive, feminine way of knowing whose beauty and power "wither"—become unrecognized and unacknowledged—under the "stern scrutiny" of a masculine, rational sun. There is, of course, a twist here. Both the purple blossoms and Beatrice herself have been transformed by the rational, scientific mind of Dr. Rappaccini into creations of extraordinary beauty and possible peril. The natural, creative forces that Fuller's symbolism celebrated are redefined through male consciousness, contained and transformed—by Rappaccini in his garden and by Giovanni in his mind—into the unnatural and destructive. Fearing these creative forces in nature and woman, Rappaccini imposes an artificial hybridization of the natural and the unnatural on flower and daughter, imprisoning them within the walls of a private Eden where he can tend and scrutinize but never touch. In Rappaccini's garden, the "secret powers" of the "'Mothers,'" as Fuller called feminine creative force, have been so suppressed by the father's intervention that, in the very absence of any allusion to the absence of the mother, Beatrice becomes literally her father's creation.[26]

What Rappaccini does physically, Giovanni does mentally. Like the "two trees" of seemingly "alien race" described by Hawthorne in "The Old Manse," Rappaccini and Giovanni are united "in an inextricable twine" like the marriage of the "hemlock and the maple" by the grape vine that "enrich[es] them with a purple offspring, of which neither is the parent" (10:23). Giovanni's own "lurid intermixture of emotions" is projected onto a "hybridized" Beatrice, angel and demon, both being the feminine made unnatural by man's imposition of a meaning to contain the mysteries he cannot confront without first naming. Though not examined by Nina Auerbach, "Rappaccini's Daughter" illustrates her thesis that the nineteenth-century male's preoccupation with mythic representations of women as angels or demons arose in an age of religious doubt as vehicles for spiritual transfiguration, celebrating "the secrecy and spiritual ambiguity of woman's ascribed powers" even as it sought to suppress them: "The social restrictions that crippled women's lives, the physical weaknesses wished on them," she argues, "were fearful attempts to exorcise a mysterious power."[27]

Another Fuller sketch for the *Dial,* "Leila," celebrates this mysterious power in the embodiment of a goddess with the feminine powers celebrated in Fuller's flower sketches. Here, too, Fuller identified personally with her mythic personification of the feminine. Emerson recalls in the *Memoirs* Fuller once explaining her attraction to the name "Leila": "When I first met with the name Leila . . . I knew, from the very look and sound, it was mine; I knew that it meant night,—night, which brings out stars, as sorrow brings out truths." In Fuller's sketch, Leila represents the awful powers of "all the elemental powers of nature," of a creativity that when embraced "showers down . . . balm and blessing," instantly creates flowers and "rivers of bliss," and (in the very imagery of Hawthorne's tale but in an opposing way) transforms "prison walls" into "Edens." When rejected, she can seem demonic, subversive. Confronting her, men "shrink from the overflow of the infinite," become "baffled" and "angry" in their inability to reduce her to "a form" to "clasp to the living breast." In the end, they proclaim her "mad, because they felt she made them so."[28]

As Fuller's sketch and Auerbach's cultural mythography suggest, "Rappaccini's Daughter" self-reflectively narrates the contemporary cultural process by which man is attracted to and appalled by a feminine power whose mystery and energy he feels compelled to contain, whose "Eden" he must enclose in the "prison walls" of a home-restricted, artificial, Edenic garden or of a rigid, knowable category—angel or demon. Feeling himself "within the influence of an unintelligible power by the communication which he had opened with Beatrice," Giovanni reacts as Fuller had claimed. He finds "her rich beauty" a "madness to him," a "wild offspring of both love and horror." To contain the "fierce and subtle poison within him," he can think only of flight or suppression. Unwilling or unable to escape her, he considers redefining her "extraordinary being" within a "familiar and daylight view" that would bring her "rigidly and systematically within the limits of ordinary experience" (10:105). The angelic or the demonic—the Beatrice of Dante who redeems man or the Beatrice Cenci who avenges man's brutal dominion—both serve as rigid categories subordinating the threatening power of the extraordinary and unintelligible to the reassuring dominion of cultural constructs of ordinary experience.

Fuller's and Emerson's presence in the tale are by no means limited to Hawthorne's dialogue with Fuller's texts. Hawthorne enacts the "bloodwarm" tale of his anxiety over Emerson's influence and over his own ambivalent feelings for Fuller through the complex tension of epistemological and gender allegiances demanded by conflicting senses—Emerson's vision and Fuller's voice. The conflict is most succinctly stated when Giovanni asks Beatrice if, as a counter to "idle rumors," he can trust what he has seen of her with his own eyes (10:111). But not trusting what he has seen, he quickly renegotiates the basis on which he will define Beatrice's nature by urging her, with vague sexual suggestiveness, to have him "believe nothing save what comes from your own lips" (10:111–12). Beatrice in turn demands that Giovanni "forget whatever" he "may have fancied" regarding her and, significantly, restates Giovanni's request to limit his contact to the truth of her lips' voice, not touch: "If true to the outward senses, still it may be false in its essence; but the *words* of Beatrice Rappaccini's lips are true from the depths of the heart outward. Those you may believe" (10:112; my emphasis). Giovanni does not, of course, believe. Like Rappaccini himself, he is wedded not merely to "sight" but to "vision," the idealist vision that reads nature as symbol and, as this tale demonstrates, sees not deep realities but shallow delusions. Appropriating Emerson's language as well as thought, Giovanni announces early on that Rappaccini's garden "would serve . . . as a symbolic language to keep him in communion with Nature" (10:98). Deeper than the irony of his misreading of the symbolism of Beatrice's nature is his very desire to read her nature as symbolic, for as this tale suggests, the desire to read the physical for the symbolic arises from the desire to gain power over a nature that one actually fears having communion with. The symbolic language of the eye imposes meaning through the pronouncements of an interpretative monologue, but the language of the voice converses in the unending dialogue of a human communion. Displaying Aubépine's "inveterate love of allegory," the tale performs the very symbolic act that it condemns; but at the same time that it enacts Hawthorne's own desire to gain power over the very natures that he fears, it gives voice to his self-condemnation and it engages in the kind of dialogue with Fuller that Giovanni silences with Beatrice.[29]

As Hawthorne said in "The Old Manse" of those under the influence of Emerson's "light," those who gaze into, much less enter, Rappaccini's garden are apt to see "objects unseen before" (10:31). Under the influence of Emerson's "wonderful magnetism," they not only see but also become themselves "objects unseen before"—"hobgoblins of flesh and blood" (10:30). Hawthorne's observations on Emerson and his influence on his followers in "The Old Manse" are themselves translations of his earlier statements on Emerson encoded within the symbolic world of Rappaccini's garden; indeed, as Reynolds has argued, Hawthorne's anxiety over Emerson's influence shapes Hawthorne's self-representations throughout "The Old Manse," just as it had earlier found expression in Rappaccini's characterization.[30] Rappaccini produces a new Eden of strangely beautiful but unnatural shrubs and flowers that represent the perversion not only of vegetative but of human nature that results from "a look as deep as Nature, but without Nature's warmth of love" (10:107). Rappaccini's garden is oddly described as being "*peopled* with plants and herbs," which "all had their individual virtues, known to the scientific mind that fostered them" because these plants were equated in Hawthorne's mind to those he will later designate as Emerson's "hobgoblins" (10:95; my emphasis). Like Emerson, an idealist with noble intentions, Rappaccini creates and cultivates unnaturally beautiful and possibly poisonous plants (and a daughter-protégée) just as Emerson cultivates brilliant but possibly deluded insights and followers. If the "transparent eyeball" of Emerson was able to read through the symbols of the seen to the unseen, to "translate" Nature, so Rappaccini studies "every shrub . . . as if he was looking into their inmost nature, making observations in regard to their creative energy" (10:95–96).

Human nature, however, is the real interest of Rappaccini's experimental studies, as Giovanni suspects of Rappaccini and Hawthorne fears of Emerson. As Rappaccini trained his penetrating vision on his plants to know and "foster" their "individual virtues" and "their creative energy," so he seems to train his gaze on Giovanni, fixing "his eyes upon Giovanni with an intentness that seemed to bring out whatever was within him worthy of notice" (10:106–7). His desire to penetrate and cultivate the essence of a person's individual virtues, however, serves a coldly intellectual and spiritual, rather than human, love. That is why he observes rather than touches, why he arms himself with gloves and a mask to avoid contact with his own creations. Just as Emerson claimed to see the divine within the individual and to claim in "Self-Reliance" that the individual's obligation to the truth and to his own spiritual integrity took precedence over all other relations, including those of family, so Rappaccini is said to be willing to "sacrifice human life, his own among the rest, or whatever else was dearest to him, for the sake of adding so much as a grain of mustard seed to the great heap of his accumulated knowledge" (10:99–100). Dr. Rappaccini's lack of warmth, of course, was the most common complaint made by and about Emerson. "Souls never touch," Emerson writes in "Experience," and when Fuller read a draft of that essay in the summer of 1844 while staying with Hawthorne, she condemned Emerson's vision of life as one might imagine Beatrice condemning her father's: "How beautiful, and full and grand. But oh, how cold. Nothing but Truth in the Universe, no love, and no various realities." [31]

It is Baglioni, of course, who charges that Rappaccini is willing to sacrifice life for knowledge. According to conventional judgment, Baglioni is not to be trusted because, less brilliant than Rappaccini but just as driven as he is to possess Giovanni's allegiance, he is motivated by professional and personal envy of Rappaccini. Hawthorne, however, employs Baglioni as a spokesman for one side of himself and for Emerson's conventional critics. On the one hand, Baglioni expresses Hawthorne's (and Fuller's) own critique of Emerson's cold idealism and of his anxieties about Emerson's ability and perhaps desire to obtain power and influence over his followers. On the other, Baglioni also speaks for the conservative academic and theological establishment, epitomized in Emerson's case by Andrews Norton. In Baglioni's view, Rappaccini's experiments in "healing" man are as poisonous as, from Norton's point of view, Emerson's prescription for man's spiritual redemption residing in recognition of his own divinity. It is in this role that Baglioni functions as an actor as well as spokesman in the tale. He competes for Giovanni's allegiance, offering only his own brand of poison as antidote—his conservative skepticism and his "idle rumors" (10:111)—for Rappaccini's idealism and for Giovanni's "faith" in Beatrice's goodness. His skepticism and his fear that Beatrice, as an intellectual woman, threatens his position in the world bespeak his role as spokesman for a conventionality that often proved attractive to Hawthorne; indeed, as the friend of Giovanni's father, Baglioni in effect speaks for the conservative tradition of Hawthorne's forefathers against the radical threats to that tradition represented by Emerson's "new" hybrid of Christian theology and secular philosophy and by Fuller's threatening feminism. Within the context of the tale, however, Hawthorne rejects Baglioni and all he represents as being perhaps more poisonous than Rappaccini's cold idealism. Rappaccini sees with the intellect and the spirit, but Baglioni sees only with the eyes. Beatrice alone speaks for the intellect, the spirit, *and* the heart.

Our eyes, like Giovanni's, are apt to deceive us. For all of the critical commentary on Beatrice's beauty, we seldom notice that it is her voice and her voice alone that Hawthorne locates as the source of her beauty and her truth. Beatrice warns Giovanni against the truth that he thinks he has seen—literally, like Baglioni, or symbolically, like Rappaccini: "If true to the outward senses, still it may be false in its essence." For the deceptions of vision, she offers the truths of the heart's voice: "But the words of Beatrice Rappaccini's lips are true from the depths of the heart outward" (10:112). Though Giovanni will eventually ignore Beatrice's advice, he is attracted to Beatrice first by her voice, not by her physical beauty. He hears before he sees her, and her voice is "as rich as a tropical sunset," making him "think of deep hues of purple or crimson and of perfumes heavily delectable" (10:96–97). Like the fountain in the center of the garden, this "rich voice" is later described as coming "forth . . . like a gush of music" (10:104). Rich, purple, crimson, perfumed, musical— again and again in the tale descriptions of Beatrice's voice suggest that the "essence" of her beauty, her passion, and her truth reside in "the words" that come "from the depths" of her "heart." To underline this emphasis, Hawthorne does not single out any other feature of Beatrice for specific description; in fact, one effect of the symbolism of Giovanni's tormenting fear that her body is poisonous, "ugly," is to suggest that the "Oriental sunshine" of Beatrice's physical beauty arises solely from her spirit, not her features, paralleled in the tale's symbolism by the pure water of the fountain gushing from a shattered urn.[32] Having initially characterized her physical beauty as coming from the effect of her spirit on her appearance—her "life, health, and energy" (10:97)—and having later characterized her, based on the impression left by their conversations, as being, surprisingly, "human" and "endowed with all gentle and feminine qualities," Giovanni finds that "whatever had looked ugly" in "her physical and moral system" had come to seem "beautiful" (10:114). This "confidence" that Giovanni places in Beatrice is "founded," as the narrator points out, on "something truer and more real than what we can see with the eyes and touch with the finger," identified as "the necessary force" of Beatrice's "high attributes," which are capable of overcoming, at least temporarily, Giovanni's incapacity for "any deep and generous faith" (10:120).

In the power of Beatrice's voice to enchant Giovanni with the beauty of her spirit, with the words coming from the depths of her heart, Fuller's physical presence, never itself characterized by contemporaries as being conventionally beautiful, is translated into the tale. Famous for her series of organized intellectual discussions for the women of Boston, the Conversations, and praised by all contemporaries for the brilliance of her talk, Fuller, in opposition to Emerson's rhetoric of vision, employed and advocated a rhetoric of conversation as the way to truth. When she warned Hawthorne that no mere "talents of observation" can compensate for "deeper experiences," that to be "fully roused to its work" the "genius" of the artist who would read humanity rightly must listen "to a voice that truly calls upon his solitude to ope his study door," Fuller was prescribing to Hawthorne the communion of dialogue rather than the solitude of the observer's eye and the monologue of its pronouncements.[33]

Hawthorne's tale allegorizes these opposing rhetorics, endorsing Fuller's as it condemns Emerson's. In self-imposed isolation from an academy that, judging by Baglioni, is so complacent and insecure that it is not receptive to a dialogue with the new and innovative, Rappaccini listens only to his own voice and follows his monomaniacal vision to its unnatural end. The power of the uncompromising will of the individualist who has forsaken the subordinations of self that dialogue requires is employed, ironically and perhaps inevitably, to exert power over others. Desiring to give his daughter the "marvelous gift" of the power of the perfectly invulnerable individualist, he must subordinate her entirely to his will so that she may subordinate others. By repelling—by destroying, in fact—all human contact, he makes her immune to such violations of the self as Giovanni inflicts upon her in the first and only social relationship she is allowed to have. Literally and figuratively, however, Beatrice prefers Giovanni's poison to her father's. Before his coming, her need for human contact and dialogue had been expressed in her personification of the flowers as sisterly companions who responded to her speech and embrace. Once Giovanni establishes a dialogue with her, her

need for him is fulfilled in speech, not touch, and Giovanni's happiest moments are those in which he listens to her voice rather than to the interior
voices that torment him with the desire and fear of her touch. Fuller's recommendation to Hawthorne that he listen to that "voice which truly calls
upon his solitude to ope his study door" finds its dramatic parallel within
the tale: with the "rich sweetness of her tones," Beatrice sends up her voice
to "float around" Giovanni "in his chamber and echo and reverberate
throughout his heart"—calling him out to talk with her in the garden,
where, under the influence of their dialogue, he frees himself momentarily
from the fear-induced delusions that he speaks to himself in the interior
monologues of his own solitude (10:115).

Fuller's prescription for Hawthorne in 1842 was stated even more
strongly in 1844 as a damning diagnosis of Emerson's deficiencies. Emerson's
attempt to read the "symbolic language of Nature" chilled him, she asserted,
because he "did not lie along the ground long enough to hear the secret
whispers of our parent life." He did not touch nor hear what he observed;
thus, he in turn could not be touched by what he saw nor participate in a
dialogue with any but his own voice. As Fuller wrote in a mischievously
erotic metaphor, he needed to "be thrown by conflicts on the lap of mother
earth, to see if he would not rise again with added powers."[34] The conflict
between Emerson and Fuller, between intellect's vision and communion's
voice, is perhaps best illustrated by Fuller's account of a 19 August 1842 walk
with Emerson:

> In the evening I took a walk with W. Looking at the moon in the river he said
> the same thing as in his letter, how each twinkling light breaking there sum-
> mons to demand the whole secret, and how "promising, promising nature
> never fulfils what she thus gives us a right to expect." I said I never could meet
> him here, the beauty does not stimulate me to ask *why?* [her emphasis], and
> press to the centre, I was satisfied for the moment, full as if my existence was
> filled out, for nature had *said the very word that was lying in my heart.* Then we
> had an excellent talk: We agreed that *my god was love, his truth* [my em-
> phases].[35]

The very next day Fuller walked with Hawthorne on another moonlit
night and recorded that Hawthorne, like her, embraced, rather than questioned, the moon and the beauty that it bestowed on earth, expressing to
her his own sense of a fulfilled existence in his wish never "to leave this
earth: it was beautiful enough." In contrast to her dissatisfaction with Emerson's frigid intellectualizations, Fuller writes glowingly of her conversation
with Hawthorne, stating that he "expressed, as he always does, many fine

perceptions," and concluding, "I like to hear the lightest thing he says."[36] Such juxtapositions are frequent in Fuller's journals of 1842 and 1844 as Fuller begins to accept the permanence of Emerson's incompleteness and begins to develop an increasingly intimate friendship with Hawthorne.

Hawthorne's friendship with Fuller is at the very narrative heart of the private text that Hawthorne translates into the relationship between Giovanni and Beatrice. As Giovanni first comes under Beatrice's influence after moving "out of his native sphere" into the "gloomy" house bordering Rappaccini's garden (10:93), so Hawthorne, who had known Fuller since 1839, did not begin to establish a deeply personal and independent friendship with Fuller until 1842 when he moved into Emerson's former home and began to have extensive conversations with Fuller, usually alone, in walks through the woods and boat rides on the Concord. The deepening of that friendship and the revelation, to Hawthorne, of previously unsuspected dimensions in Fuller's character—including her dissatisfaction with Emerson and Emersonian idealism—are imaged in Giovanni's hearing and seeing Beatrice at a distance, even briefly conversing with her from the height of his window, before his entrance into the garden exposes him to "the effect of her character" and he is able to perceive her "so human and so maidenlike qualities" (10:113). The "intimate familiarity" established by Beatrice once Giovanni is alone with her immediately dispels the "hues of terror" in which Giovanni's imagination "had *idealized*" her when he saw her only in her seemingly unnatural, poisonousness relationship with her "sisterly" flowers (10:113; my emphasis).

Beatrice's ability to vanquish by the force of her character Giovanni's fears parallels a recurrent theme of friends' recollections of Fuller's uncanny ability to win over those who had initially feared or were repelled by her forceful personality, intimidating intellect, and outspoken feminism. Giovanni's initial perception of Beatrice suggests something of Hawthorne's own early reservations about Fuller. Prior to 1842 Hawthorne's relationship with Fuller had been largely mediated by her closer friendship with Sophia, who had idolized her, as did many of her friends, as a feminist "priestess." As his letters on Fuller's "Transcendental heifer" suggest, to some extent Hawthorne had perceived Fuller's aggressive feminism and friendship with Sophia as a threat to his attempts to transform a self-reliant "naughty Sophie" into a dependent, feminized "Dove." Fuller was the woman Sophia was not meant to be. Educated by a driven father since early childhood, Fuller far exceeded the expectations set for even the brightest of boys and found herself painfully alienated from her peers because of it. As her own father had planned, Fuller became what Rappaccini had intended for Beatrice—the extraordinary woman who not only avoided but challenged "the condition of a weak woman" (10:127). "Imposed" on her "feminine nature," says Hawthorne in "The Old Manse," was her father's "heavy gift of intellectual power" (10:29), and if Hawthorne, as Reynolds has argued, perceived Emerson "as a father figure who has separated the narrator, or Hawthorne, from a maternal, pre-Oedipal reality" in "The Old Manse" through his powerfully infectious vision of Nature, then Hawthorne first drew upon that perception in "Rappaccini's Daughter."[37]

As a formidable influence on Fuller, Hawthorne suggests, Emerson took up where Fuller's biological father had left off, assuming the paternal role of Fuller's intellectual mentor whose effect on Fuller was to further alienate her from "the limits of ordinary experience" by having her "imbibe," in Baglioni's words, the poison of "erroneous ideas" (10:99). Hawthorne's resentment of Emerson's influence on Fuller provides the subtext for the 8 April 1843 notebook entry in which Hawthorne, for Sophia's benefit, mocks Emerson's paternalistic pride in Fuller and his patronizing assumption of his ability to grade her intellectual and personal development: "He seemed fullest of Margaret Fuller, who, he says, has risen perceptibly into a higher state, since their last meeting. He apotheosized her as the greatest woman, I believe, of ancient or modern times, and the one figure in the world worth considering. (There rings the supper-bell)" (8:371).[38] As Hawthorne had discovered though, Fuller, like Beatrice, had "risen perceptibly into a higher state" by resisting the paternal, by voicing the need to embrace a passionate, feminine nature as a maternal antidote to the father's coldly intellectual vision of an idealized nature and an invulnerable but alienating self-reliance. In "The Old Manse" Hawthorne locates Fuller within his "magic circle" rather than within the sphere of Emerson's "wonderful magnetism" because, among other reasons, he identified Fuller's resistance to Emerson's paternal influence as aligned with his own. To the Emersonian-like male spokesman in "The Magnolia of Lake Pontchartrain" who claims that he found the "secret of peace" by retreating into the "centre" of his "being" where he found "all being," where "from one point" he "can draw all lines," the Fuller-like female spokesman, the Magnolia, reminds him that "man never creates, he only recombines the lines and colors of his own existence." There is "but one paternal power," she rebukes his self-deification; in nature those who would be creative must seek to find themselves in the feminine force that men have variously named "fairy," "goddess," "angel," the force that Fuller names "the queen and guardian of all the flowers." All the "secret powers" are "feminine," she tells him; all are "'Mothers.'"[39]

In the allegorical terms of the tale, Emerson's Nature is Rappaccini's garden, where Emerson's mediation of nature becomes Rappaccini's horticultural "commixtures" and "adulteries"—nature no longer "the production . . . of God's making, but the monstrous offspring of man's depraved fancy, glowing with only an evil mockery of beauty" (10:110). Written less than two months after Hawthorne's arrival in Concord, Hawthorne's 21 August 1842 notebook passage described in the previous chapter faintly suggests the intellectual and spiritual dangers Hawthorne imagined in any movement toward Emerson's powerful influence; journeying toward Emerson's house through the woods, he "misses" the "nearest way," "wanders," becomes entangled in the underbrush, and is consumed by his own "rage and despair." Exploiting the allegorical suggestiveness of that passage, Hawthorne may have translated his entry into Concord and Emerson's sphere of influence into the allegory of Giovanni's first entry into Rappaccini's garden. As Hawthorne "could scarcely force a passage through" the bushes "which cross and intertwine themselves" about his legs, so Giovanni's first step into Rappaccini's garden requires "forcing himself through the entanglement of a shrub that wreathed its tendrils over the hidden entrance" (10:109).[40] Instead of the "Golden-Rod, and the gorgeous Cardinals, all the most glorious flowers of the year" (8:342), which Hawthorne had seen while wandering in Sleepy Hollow that day, Giovanni sees in Rappaccini's garden plants whose "gorgeousness seemed fierce, passionate, and even unnatural," plants personified, "commixtures" of nature and of the transforming power of man's desire: "There was hardly an individual shrub which a wanderer, straying by himself through a forest, would not have been startled to find growing wild, as if an unearthly face had glared at him out of the thicket" (10:110).

As Hawthorne had been drawn to Emerson's house to see Fuller and return her book, so Giovanni enters Rappaccini's garden intent on seeing Beatrice. Neither Hawthorne nor Giovanni finds exactly what he expected. Hawthorne did not meet Fuller at Emerson's house, but to his surprise, he finds her in the forest. The narrative of that moment registers the excitement of the discovery. Alone, they explore the seemingly endless grounds of their sympathetic interests—until, that is, the spell of their intimacy is broken by Emerson's intrusion. Giovanni also unexpectedly discovers that Beatrice, despite his own impressions and Baglioni's rumors, is not "in" her father's house intellectually, not "deeply skilled" in her "father's science" and willingly associated with the garden of his "commixtures," for, like himself, she recoils from her father's experiments on nature and finds that many of her father's flowers, as she readily admits, "shock and offend me when they meet my eye" (10:111). As "her spirit gushed out before him like a fresh rill" in the "pure delight" of her "communion" with him, Giovanni also discovers that though capable of the "queenlike haughtiness" so frequently ascribed to Fuller, Beatrice was at heart "so human and maidenlike," so "endowed with all gentle and feminine qualities," that "she was worthiest to be worshipped" rather than feared (10:113–14).

Hawthorne's evident excitement in conversing with Fuller so unreservedly on that late summer afternoon is inscribed in Giovanni's intoxication with Beatrice's speech, which seems to create "a fragrance in the atmosphere" that Giovanni first fears before gazing through her eyes "into her transparent soul" and deciding that the "strange richness" that "embalmed her words" was created not by her father's poisonous influence but by "steeping them in her heart" (10:112). The topics of their conversation also parallel the general nature and sequence of topics discussed by Hawthorne and Fuller. As Hawthorne and Fuller spoke first of the coming autumn and of their day in the woods, then the more personal topics of their childhoods and the permanent influence of those years, and finally the shifting perspectives of mountains from a distance and from the summit and other topics of "high and low philosophy," so Beatrice is said to talk to Giovanni first of "matters as simple as the daylight or summer clouds," then of his "distant home, his friends, his mother, and his sisters," and then finally "thoughts, too, from a deep source, and fantasies of a gemlike brilliancy" (10:200). Just as Emerson had been characterized as an "intruder," who, "in the midst of their talk," Hawthorne and Fuller hear stalking the bank above them "hidden among the trees," so Rappaccini is discovered by Giovanni to have been lurking "within the shadow of the entrance" and "watching the scene, he knew not how long" (10:114).

Of that 21 August 1842 afternoon alone with Hawthorne, Fuller would comment in her journal, "What a happy, happy day, all clear light. I cannot write about it." Two years later, just weeks before accepting Greeley's offer of a position on the *New-York Daily Tribune,* she wrote that she had come to cherish her friendship with Hawthorne as one of the most intimate in her life and that she expected that friendship to continue deepening: "Walk with H. in the woods long paths, dark and mystical. We went far & it was quite dark when we returned: we lost the path & I got wet in the long grass & had much scrambling. . . . I feel more like a sister to H. or rather more that he might be a brother to me than ever with any man before. Yet with him it is though sweet, not deep kindred, at least, not deep yet."[41] Though this would prove to be Fuller's most definitive characterization of her relationship with Hawthorne, Fuller's hesitation to admit to feeling a "sisterly" relationship with Hawthorne and her expectation of a deepening in their seemingly extraordinary kinship suggests continuing ambiguities and potentialities in their relationship that she still could not quite define.

Hawthorne would acknowledge the "brotherly" nature of his friendship with Fuller in Giovanni's surprise during that first meeting that "he could be conversing with Beatrice like a brother" (10:113) and in Beatrice's later "confidence" in Giovanni's friendship being "as unreserved as if they had been playmates from early infancy" (10:115). But he would also acknowledge in Giovanni's betrayal of Beatrice that though Fuller, like Beatrice, was "the more admirable by so much as she was the more unique" (10:114), he was not himself sufficiently unique as a man to keep from betraying the faith that Fuller had placed in him and their relationship. Finding himself under "the influence of an unintelligible power" in an ambiguous relationship with the most extraordinary American woman of her day, Hawthorne, through Giovanni and the narrator, explores his compulsion to redefine Fuller's uniqueness and his troubling relationship to her within the intelligible terms of conventional cultural constructs for the mystery of woman's body and spirit—demon or angel. By translating Fuller's person and texts into his own voice, Hawthorne with self-conscious irony attempts to reassert control over the troubling ambiguities of Fuller's character and of their relationship by allegorizing his condemnation of his compulsion to allegorize her.

As the subtle narrative framing and tone of his account of the afternoon of 21 August 1842 suggest and as his characterization of Giovanni makes explicit, Hawthorne recognized within himself a sexual tension in his relationship with Fuller that threatened the "brotherly" nature on which their relationship was founded and depended. As with Hawthorne and Fuller's relationship, the "intimate familiarity" of Giovanni and Beatrice's friendship is established and maintained through conversation, not touch, but Giovanni's "shallowness of feeling and insincerity of character" make him incapable of sustaining the uniqueness of such a relationship with a woman without bringing it "within the limits of ordinary experience," those limits of course being man's ordinary sexualization of his relationship with a woman. Giovanni may experience the uniqueness of such an "intimate familiarity" a "feminine nature" whose "holy and passionate outgush" of "the heart" envelops "him in a religious calm," but ultimately he cannot understand it nor accept it without betraying it (10:121–22). Giovanni may indeed hear her heart's truth, but he reads her body as the symbol of his own revulsion at the monstrosity of an obsession whose self-generated origins he cannot claim. As Nina Baym has so persuasively argued, Giovanni, like many of Hawthorne's male characters after 1842, is "revolted" by Beatrice's body to the same extent that he is "obsessed, possessed" by it. The "thwarted nature" of Hawthorne's male characters, Baym claims, is Hawthorne's indictment of the unnaturalness of that "part of the [male] psyche that repudiates human sexuality," that mutilates, in order to deny, woman's sexuality.[42] Baym, I think, is certainly right in the main, but I argue that in this tale, at least with Giovanni, Hawthorne is equally troubled by man's inability to relate to woman in any other way than a sexualized one. Giovanni and Beatrice's relationship originates with and depends on his attending to her unique voice rather than gazing at her body and reading it as the text of her character. Beatrice admits Giovanni into her heart, and Giovanni experiences through their conversations "the golden crown of enchantment" that is his "intimate familiarity" with Beatrice (10:114–15). But he cannot comprehend, much less sustain, such an intimate friendship without wishing to violate the very physical barriers that make it possible:

> By all appreciable signs, they loved; they had looked love with eyes that conveyed the holy secret from the depths of one soul into the depths of the other, as if it were too sacred to be whispered by the way; they had even spoken love in those gushes of passion when their spirits darted forth in articulated breath like tongues of long hidden flame; and yet there had been no seal of lips, no clasp of hands, nor any slightest caress such as love claims and hallows. He had never touched one of the gleaming ringlets of her hair; her garment—so marked was the physical barrier between them—had never been waved against him by a breeze. On the few occasions when Giovanni had seemed tempted to overstep the limit, Beatrice grew so sad, so stern, and withal wore such a look of desolate separation, shuddering at itself, that not a spoken word was requisite to repel him. (10:115–16)

Beatrice's claim that she "dreamed only to love" Giovanni for "a little time" and desired only a union of his "image in mine heart" challenges the limits that we have set for "ordinary experience" in a post-Freudian age (10:125). In an otherwise penetrating article condemning the antifeminist poison of the male characters in the tale, Richard Brenzo has suggested, for instance, that Giovanni's "insight" into the sexual nature of his relationship with Beatrice exceeds Beatrice's own awareness of the source of her "deepest feelings" for him.[43] To make this suggestion, however, Brenzo, like Giovanni, must trust his own "fancy" and distrust "the words of Beatrice Rappaccini's lips." For Beatrice, however, the only love possible between her and Giovanni is the union of hearts in dialogue "as unreserved as if they had been playmates from early infancy" (10:115), the union of a "brotherly" relationship between a man and a woman in a love that is "truer and more real than what we can see with the eyes and touch with the finger" (10:120). Such a love is intimate friendship, the intellectual friendship that Fuller had described to Sophia as the highest form of love.[44]

In such a friendship between a man and a woman the body can be indeed poisonous to the relationship. Hawthorne and Fuller, I contend, experienced such a friendship, but in recognizing a sexual dimension in his response to Fuller, Hawthorne recognized the poison of his own thwarted nature, his own fancies about the prohibited body of Fuller, the body that, if touched, would have proved poisonous not only to his relationship with Fuller but also, of course, to his relationship with Sophia. Hawthorne also recognized, however, that such a response was but a measure of his own shallowness, an ordinary reassertion of masculine power over an intimacy that he both craved and feared. Such a response would also align him with Emerson, he with his "magic circle" redeeming a "weary and world-worn" Fuller (as he describes her in "The Old Manse" [10:29]) from Emerson's sphere of "wonderful magnetism," just as Giovanni in opposing Rappaccini's malignant control discovers the poison at the source of his own desire to redeem Beatrice, to bring her within his own power. Giovanni's desperate attempt to assert a sexual power over Beatrice, however, originates in his panic over his loss of power.[45] Appalled at Beatrice's grip on his imagination, Giovanni literally attempts to silence her voice and defuse the potency of her mystery by making her body the receptacle of his desire and revulsion, his angel and his demon: "Let us join our lips in one kiss of unutterable hatred, and so die!" (10:124).

Yet Hawthorne's very recognition and condemnation of this competitive masculine desire for interpretative and physical power over the feminine realigns him with Fuller, for in the texts of Fuller's work, Hawthorne had been challenged to reexamine his impulse to read the text of woman's power in her body. He had read the very terms he would use to condemn both Giovanni and Rappaccini in Fuller's "Magnolia of Lake Pontchartrain." In this work, Fuller had explained man's uncomprehending attraction to the feminine Other as a desire to lose oneself within its creative force, a force that nevertheless inspires masculine fear and rejection precisely because it can be known only through the abrogation of masculine power and the loss of self.

Having experienced the power of "the queen and guardian of the flowers," the feminine Magnolia explains to the male narrator:

> Of this being I cannot speak to thee in any language now possible betwixt us. For this is a being of another order from thee, an order whose presence thou mayest feel, nay, approach step by step, but which cannot be known till thou art it, nor seen nor spoken of till thou hast passed through it.
>
> Suffice it to say, that it is not such a being as men love to paint, a fairy,—like them, only lesser and more exquisite than they, a goddess, larger and of statelier proportion, an angel,—like still, only with an added power. Man never creates, he only recombines the lines and colors of his own existence. . . . Like all such beings she was feminine. All the secret powers are 'Mothers.' There is but one paternal power.[46]

Fairy, goddess, angel—Hawthorne, of course, could have added "Dove" to the list. In "Rappaccini's Daughter" he does add "demon," as he added "naughty Sophie" to his courtship letters, for he recognized that in constraining the power of the feminine in the self-shaped reflection of a "thwarted nature" redeemed in the image of an "angelic" woman, man also imagined the horror of his failure to subsume the resistant female Other in the shape of a demonic woman. The demonization of the resistant woman is thus but another self-shaped reflection, a reverse image of the angelic woman whose origins the demonic woman shares—both arising from man's horror at the threat to self that intimacy with the feminine entails when man finds himself, like Giovanni, "irrevocably within her sphere."

Hawthorne could not tell Sophia whether Beatrice was to be an angel or demon because he could not tell her that Beatrice was neither and that he was both—that both solutions to the riddle of her existence were solutions to the riddle of his own existence. Nor could he explain to her how the "naughty Sophie" she had been and the "Dove" she had become were translations of his own desire to redeem a self that, as he had once been willing to suggest to her, was but "an unspiritual shadow" struggling "vainly to catch hold of something real," finding himself a "reality" only through his definition of her (15:511).[47] And he certainly could not tell her, of course, that in reading Fuller's texts and in attempting to read Fuller's character and their ambivalent friendship he had found himself once again drawn into the role of a male "interpreter" of feminine mystery (see 15:375). This time, however, he confronted the mystery of a woman who seemed extraordinary enough not only to resist the angelic and demonic interpretations of "ordinary experience" but also to understand as he did the origins of man's desire to suppress a feminine power that he both craves and fears through masculine translations of the feminine into cultural constructs no less constraining than the walls of Rappaccini's poisonous Eden.

Drawn to the feminine power in nature and allied with Fuller against the paternal mediations of Emerson, Hawthorne nevertheless found that Fuller posed a threat to him in a way that Emerson did not, for by the example of her life, the insight of her texts, and the attraction she held for him, she called into question the very terms by which Hawthorne had defined his relationship with Sophia and challenged him to an intimacy that those very terms had served to deflect. As a "feminine nature" still struggling, as he suggests in "The Old Manse" (10:29), with the burdens imposed on her in childhood by her intellectually ambitious father, she also challenged the new father of a baby girl to ponder the consequences of his own inclination to enforce masculine desire through patriarchal power.[48] His first reaction to Una's birth, after all, had been to brag to his best friend that he preferred having had a daughter rather than a son because "there is something so especially piquant in having helped to create a future woman" (16:25).

Fuller's friendship with Hawthorne, however, was as enabling as it was threatening, for she provoked him, through person and text, to recognize in the complicity of his own thwarted nature the ordinary experience by which men poison the lives of women and destroy in fear their hope of any real intimacy with them. Nina Baym, I think, is right in identifying this as Hawthorne's big theme and in locating its ascendancy to obsessive self-reflection during the Old Manse period.[49] To one degree or another Hawthorne would reenter Rappaccini's garden again and again after 1844 as he continued to meditate on the personal and cultural challenge of Fuller's life and its implications for his own. Against Fuller, Hawthorne continued both to assert and to critique cultural constructions of the masculine and the feminine, constructions on which Hawthorne had uneasily staked his marriage and his manhood.

Angel or demon? Demon or angel? *Rapire*—to rape, to enchant. *Rappacinàre*—to reconcile, to make peace. Rappaccini. Hawthorne would continue his struggle to translate it.

Nina Baym complained as late as 1984 that antifeminist and feminist readings of Hawthorne shared the same assumptions and drew the same conclusions, one to praise and the other to condemn. Identifying hers as a minority voice, Baym proposed that Hawthorne's tales indict the very masculine prejudices that they dramatize. My reading of "Rappaccini's Daughter" is allied with Baym's vision of Hawthorne's purposes. Most cultural readings of mid-nineteenth century texts make much of the power of the domestic ideal in shaping literary and lived representations of women. What is often under-estimated, however, is the cultural power of those resistant to that ideology, those engaged in shaping what Raymond Williams termed an "emergent" ideology. That Hawthorne was to some degree allied with those engaged in that resistance is supported by an examination of the specific audience for which "Rappaccini's Daughter" was written and the context in which it was published.[50]

Known for its politics—literary and national—the *United States Magazine and Democratic Review* was firmly committed to giving women a voice both in society and in its pages. Six months before the publication of "Rappaccini's Daughter," for instance, the *Democratic Review* ran an unsigned essay entitled "The Legal Wrongs of Women," which called for a complete revision of a legal and social system that sanctioned the slavery of all women, a system kept in place by "those who cannot indulge" their "love of power . . . on a great scale" and therefore must "be content with its utmost possible exercise in a limited sphere." Lest there be any doubt about the position of the maga-zine, an editorial note is printed at the foot of the first page of the essay: "The present Article on its own face avows itself as the production of a female pen; but we will not let the occasion pass without adding to it a more emphatic expression of our full approval and adoption of its views, than would be contained in its mere insertion in our pages without note or comment." In that same issue, in an article entitled "Female Novelists," W. A. Jones, after reviewing major women writers, asserts that "women write for women" but that "there is a race of masculine writers, with feminine delicacy of mind, who ought to be added to the list of novelists for a lady's reading." To the list of such writers as Rousseau, Sterne, and Goethe, Jones adds three Ameri-cans—Irving, Dana, and Hawthorne. Hawthorne (contributor of six tales that year to the *Democratic Review*) receives his strongest endorsement. The *Democratic Review*, in fact, lived up to its commitment to women's issues and to its solicitude of women readers by granting an extraordinary amount of space to women writers. The September issue featured five signed pieces written by women, including works by Elizabeth Barrett and Lydia Maria Child. Hawthorne's audience for "Rappaccini's Daughter" would thus have been more alert than many a twentieth-century scholar to the gender values being endorsed in the tale.[51]

When Hawthorne included "Rappaccini's Daughter" in *Mosses from an Old Manse*, he carefully selected its first readers—his critical audience. As copies of *Mosses from an Old Manse* rolled off the press, Hawthorne wrote Duyckinck a letter listing ten names to whom he wished copies to be sent.

Fuller's name topped the list (16:158)! As the critic for the *Dial,* Fuller had embraced Hawthorne's career early on and had helped secure his status within the literary community whose axis centered in Boston-Concord. He now looked to her to help do the same for him in New York. And she did. For in many respects, their careers were following parallel paths. Publishing *Mosses* in 1846 in Duyckinck's Library of American Books series for the New York firm of Wiley and Putnam and anticipating a nationwide audience, Hawthorne would seek in "The Old Manse" to create a distinctive literary identity independent of associations with Emerson and the notoriety of Concord-centered idealism.

When Fuller first moved to New York in late 1844, she too had taken the opportunity in her first New York review to reposition herself publicly against Emerson's passionless idealism and, as Hawthorne said in "The Old Manse," to commit the "heavy gift of [her] intellectual power . . . to act upon the world" (10:29). Among the least-recognized of her projects was her commitment to enlarge Hawthorne's national reputation using her own expanded critical forum in both her *New-York Tribune* column and in *Papers on Literature and Art,* her own 1846 volume in Duyckinck's series. To encourage her efforts, Hawthorne did more than simply ensure that she received the first advance copies of his book. As he had done in the "Writings of Aubépine," he invited Fuller's attention not only by making an unmistakable and flattering allusion to her as being among his most intimate friends within his "magic circle" at Concord but also by ending "The Old Manse" with a seeming reinscription of Fuller's 1842 criticism of his work as his own self-judgment ("fitful sketches with so little external life about them," "so reserved," "never . . . expressing satisfactorily the thoughts which they profess to image" [10:34]) and by responding directly, if privately, to the "solitary voice" he had just claimed as his own, the voice that had "called upon him to ope his study door."[52] To the "circle of friends" that he claimed to be his "limited number of readers" (10:34), Hawthorne—who had only paragraphs before claimed to have admitted his readers only to "the green sward, but just within the cavern's mouth" of his life (10:32)—now follows Fuller's advice in her own metaphorical terms by welcoming the reader as his "guest" into the privacy of his "study" (10:34–35), where, by the invitation of implication if not by frank admission, the reader, guided by the manuscripts, may wander deeper into the "cavern," beyond at least the entrance provided by "The Old Manse."

How far Fuller wandered into the "cavern" we cannot know with any certainty, for she did not leave an account of her private response to the

"Writings of Aubépine," "Rappaccini's Daughter," or "The Old Manse." But in her public role as critic, she promoted him as never before, asserting in "American Literature; Its Position in the Present," an 1846 essay written especially for *Papers on Literature and Art,* that Hawthorne was "the best writer of the day."[53] In her lengthy front-page review of *Mosses* for the 22 June 1846 *New-York Daily Tribune,* Fuller characterizes Hawthorne's genius as so obvious to the discerning reader that anything she or any other critic can say would be either "superfluous or impertinent." Her duty as a critic, she implies, is that of a publicist, for despite Hawthorne's "standard reputation" among discerning readers, Fuller claims that Hawthorne "has not been very widely read" because of his previous publishers; with her own New York firm of Wiley and Putnam, however, he "will have a chance to collect all his own public about him, and that be felt as a presence which before was only a rumor." Fuller's review serves to improve Hawthorne's chance to enlarge his readership on his own terms not only by profuse praise of his best work but also by publicly endorsing through firsthand authority the "admirable good sense" of "The Old Manse," his "record of objects and influences" in Concord, a gesture that, together with her praise for the "wit" and "wisdom" of "The Celestial Rail-road," reaffirms her alliance with Hawthorne in their common critique of Emerson.[54]

Her review, however, does intimate that she may have read Hawthorne as he intended. Fuller revisits her former criticism of Hawthorne in a diction that suggests a perceptive reading of "The Birth-mark" and "Rappaccini's Daughter." While Hawthorne is to be praised for his "pensive sense of the spiritual or demoniacal influences that haunt the palpable life and common walks of men," she regrets that "at this stage of his mind's life" he has laid, like Aylmer, "no more decisive hand upon the apparition," though she "had hoped that we should see, no more as in a glass darkly, but face to face." Responding perhaps to Hawthorne's reading of her through Giovanni's reading of Beatrice, Fuller then asserts that "Hawthorne intimates and suggests, but he does not lay bare the mysteries of our being." When she does directly confront both "The Birth-mark" and "Rappaccini's Daughter," what she does not say in this public promotion of Hawthorne is as telling as what she does say. Praising the tales for embodying "truths of profound importance," Fuller restricts herself to extolling in Georgiana and Beatrice the one quality that would redeem the tales for her readers and, perhaps, for her—"the loveliest ideal of love and the beauty of feminine purity, (by which we mean no mere acts or abstinences, but perfect single truth felt and done in gentleness) which is its root." Of the men who violate their love and purity, Fuller remains conspicuously silent. Fuller ends her review with a public acknowledgment of the power that Hawthorne had claimed for his "tranquil" spirit, the power that he had said, and that she now confirms, brought her within his "magic circle": "And now, beside the full, calm yet romantic stream of his mind, we will rest. It has refreshment for the weary, islets of fascination no less than dark recesses and shadows for the imaginative, pure reflections for the pure of heart and eye, and, like the Concord he so well describes, many exquisite lilies for him who knows how to get at them."[55] If in her review Fuller draws the public's attention only to the "good and beautiful results," the pure "white pond-lilies" in "The Birth-mark" and "Rappaccini's Daughter," she draws Hawthorne's attention—both here and in her profuse praise of "Young Goodman Brown," "The Artist of the Beautiful," and "Roger Malvin's Burial"—to her receptive reading of Hawthorne's less than pure "yellow water-lilies."

A few months after writing this review, Fuller left for Europe. Expecting her return after the fall of the revolutionary forces in Rome, with a presumably illegitimate baby in her arms, Hawthorne reinitiates his dialogue with Fuller in the autumn of 1849. He could not know it at the time, of course, but the wreck of the *Elizabeth* would prevent Fuller from telling him whether finally, in Hester, he had placed his "hands on the apparition" and laid "bare the mysteries" of her being.

"Speak Thou for Me!"

The "Strange Earnestness" of *The Scarlet Letter*

You speak, my friend, with a strange earnestness.
ROGER TO ARTHUR IN *The Scarlet Letter*

Many fine arguments have been made that would locate the creative origins of *The Scarlet Letter* in Hawthorne's personal crises in the summer of 1849—the scandal over his "decapitation" at the Custom House and the greater personal crisis of his mother's death.[1] As influential as these events may have been to the impetus to write again and as much as they may have influenced the narrative, they do not allow or answer a crucial question about the origins of the narrative. Why write about adultery? Specifically on the consequences of an adulterous moment seven years in the past? And why meditate on the "motives and modes of passion that influence" the characters in the narrative to such a degree that Sophia would be astonished by, even resentful of, the fury with which Hawthorne worked (1:33)?[2]

The source studies that find the romance's narrative origins in Hawthorne's meditation on New England history, particularly on Anne Hutchinson, fail also to account for the passion with which Hawthorne wrote.[3] Can we really read the romance as the profound but detached artistic product of a purely historical imagination? Hawthorne could not. When he read, or "tried to read," the just-completed manuscript to Sophia, as he confessed to himself years later in his journal, he found himself so moved by his own words during the final scenes that, like the voice of Arthur in its metaphorical effect on Hester, his own "voice swelled and heaved as if I were tossed up and down on an ocean, as it subsided after a storm." "I was in a very nervous state, then," he reminds himself, "having gone through a great diversity and severity of emotion, for many months past. I think I have never overcome my own adamant in any other instance."[4] Hawthorne would fail to mention his own reaction in a letter written the next day to his friend Horatio Bridge, but he does report proudly that Sophia, after the reading, had gone to bed with "a grievous headache," the effect, he implies, of the work's power (16:311).[5] Given his later, private account of the unbearable emotion with which he read, we may well suspect that Sophia's headache was brought on not only by what Hawthorne wrote of Arthur and Hester but also by what Sophia inferred from the passion with which he wrote it and read it. As Herbert has so thoroughly demonstrated, however, Sophia consistently and resolutely avoided facing disturbing truths, suppressing any suggestion that Hawthorne was not her altogether happy Apollo.[6] When her less-worshipful sister Elizabeth passed along approvingly the observation that Hawthorne in writing *The Scarlet Letter* had "purified himself by casting out a legion of devils into imaginary beings," Sophia insisted vehemently that "it was a work of the imagination wholly & no personal experience, as you well know."[7] Was Hawthorne's romance the creation of the sympathetic artist's imaginative identification with sin and guilt, as Sophia would have it, or was it, like Arthur's passionate sermons, another author's concealed confession? Elizabeth, as Sophia reminded her, did not know; however, she could infer what Sophia would never admit. Perhaps the moral of *The Scarlet Letter* is, in fact, the moral the narrator says it is: "Be true! Be true! Be true! Show freely to the world, if not your worst, yet some trait whereby the worst may be inferred!" (1:260).

What is often overlooked in Hawthorne's famous image of himself as romancer in a moonlit, coal-fired familiar room "glancing at the looking-glass" and recording the meeting of the "Actual and Imaginary" (1:35–36) is what is not directly revealed but may be seen—what may be, that is, inferred. Hawthorne directs our attention to the "neutral territory" that lies "deep within" the "haunted verge" of the mirror, but if we shift our focus from the margins of the glass to its anything-but-neutral center we may see a face staring into the mirror's margins at the "ghosts" that, once transformed by the light of his imagination, no longer "affrighten" him, a face staring also into the mirror's center, at his own face, transformed also, ghostly too in the light (1:36). It is this face that will not be seen in the mirror nor recognized behind the "veil" by "most of his schoolmates and lifemates," those who think they are closest to him but who understand him less than the "one heart and mind of perfect sympathy," the "kind and apprehensive, though not the closest friend" who will listen to him and in recognizing his voice as the voice speaking "of the circumstances that lie around" them and "even of himself" will be the "genial consciousness" that will enable him to "complete his circle of existence by bringing him into communion with" the "divided segment" of his "own nature" (1:3–4).

The self-riven Arthur in the romance speaks as does this author of the romance.[8] The "strange earnestness" of Arthur's concealed confessions finds also only "one heart and mind of perfect sympathy" capable of recognizing that what sounds like the voice of an imaginary self, a persona conceived in the desire for rhetorical effect, is, in fact, his actual voice being true, as openly as he finds possible, to his own nature. Perhaps we join the interpretative community of Arthur's congregation—of Hawthorne's "schoolmates and lifemates"—when we read as mere rhetorical pose Hawthorne's claim that "thoughts are frozen and utterance benumbed" unless he has a "true relation" with that audience of "one heart and mind of perfect sympathy" (1:4). Perhaps the pose is not, after all, a pose. With his first chapters at press and his final three chapters yet to be written, Hawthorne concluded the romance by imagining in Arthur's triumphant eloquence the irony of his own anticipated success with the impending publication of his "scarlet letter" to the world, its title page garishly blazoned like Hester's breast with Arthur's concealed sign of his own guilt, guilt self-inscribed beneath the cover of his clothing but exposed and finally read on the body of Arthur within the body of the book. A member of the "priesthood" of literature— as he had named himself recently in a letter to Longfellow (16:270–71)— Hawthorne makes Arthur's Election Day sermon a metaphor for the "passion and pathos," the power and purpose, of his own art (1:243).[9]

Arthur speaks two messages to two audiences. Those near him in the congregation hear the "grosser medium" of Arthur's words, the meaning that "clogs" the "spiritual sense" (1:243). At a distance, outside the walls of Arthur's church, Hester, the second audience, the audience of "one mind and heart of perfect sympathy," listens "with such intentness" and "so intimately" that she hears the personal message within the sermon, the sermon's "spiritual sense," the "profound and continual undertone" of "the complaint of a human heart, sorrow-laden, perchance guilty, telling its secret, whether of guilt or sorrow, to the great heart of mankind; beseeching its sympathy or forgiveness,—at every moment—in each accent" (1:243– 44). "Guilt or sorrow," "sympathy or forgiveness"—even if we hear the confessional undertone sustaining the sermon's or the romance's power, we may, like Arthur's auditors, like witnesses to his final evasive confession on the scaffold, interpret the brand of the "red-hot iron," the "burning heat" of the "scarlet letter" on Hawthorne's own breast, when he takes it up, as the mark of the author's passionate sorrow and sympathy (1:32). Or we may, like "the one mind and heart of perfect sympathy," like Hester of Arthur, interpret Hawthorne's "shudder," his "involuntary" failure to hold the burning letter long to his breast, as the sign of his own identification with the scarlet letter, of his own guilt, which he, like Arthur, cannot show freely to the world. We may note as well that just as Arthur did not achieve his greatest artistic power until he burned the first draft of his Election Day sermon and transformed his anguish into a passionate, public oration that did and did not reveal its creative origins in the self, so Hawthorne could not "warm" exclusively at the "intellectual forge" of his "imagination" the "figures" of his tale until he entered the coal-fired, moonlit "familiar room" of the actual and confronted in its heat and light the "neutral territory" of the real transformed by the imaginary, until he confronted, that is, the "ghosts" in the mirror (1:34–36).

1

Speak thou for me!
HESTER TO ARTHUR IN *The Scarlet Letter*

In Hawthorne's authorial fiction, the "ghosts" of the real speak through the imaginative voice of Hawthorne as "editor" of a briefer tale based on an actual event already once-told by a former surveyor with antiquarian and literary interests—by, in other words, something of the "ghost" of Hawthorne himself. As editor, Hawthorne acknowledges that he has expanded imaginatively on "the modes and motives of the passions" of the brief original but declares that "the authenticity of the outline" of the event remains true to its unedited origins (1:33). In "Rappaccini's Daughter," Hawthorne had adopted the persona of "translator" as a veil for his transformation of private experience into public art. As it anticipates the characters and themes of *The Scarlet Letter*, "Rappaccini's Daughter" attempts to work out "the riddle" that Beatrice holds for Giovanni's "existence." In *The Scarlet Letter* Hawthorne adopts the persona of editor for identical purposes—to examine a "riddle," as he claims, that he "saw little hope of solving," except perhaps through art (1:31). It is the riddle, of course, of Hester's character and Arthur's obsession. As editor, he may transform the original text of the tale through extensive revision while disavowing personal responsibility for its now-edited origins. He may claim to be its writer but not its author. Because he presents himself to us behind the veil of editor, we dismiss, as Arthur's congregation did his confessions, Hawthorne's pose as a transparently rhetorical fiction. Of course he is its author. But he is its author in the deepest, most personal sense, and that is why he must also be its editor, why he must revise the original narrative, retaining while concealing its origins, saying but not saying. As Hawthorne brought the romance to a close, he summoned Arthur to the pulpit and the scaffold to make his confession. He seems to summon himself as well. Providing one highly edited autobiographical account of the origins of *The Scarlet Letter* in "The Custom-House," in the confessional subtext of Arthur's sermon, Hawthorne closes the romance by providing a revelatory metaphor for the deeply personal origins and power of his art, the letter to be heard in the "undertone" of the literal letter of his words, the letter to be seen on the scaffold, beneath the cover of and inscribed on the very body of its progenitor. But the revelation continues. At the most crucial—and currently the most critically contested point—Hawthorne must account for Hester's future without Arthur, and he does so by becoming, in fact, the editor rather than the author of the tale. In so doing, he provides us with an essential revelation of part of the tale's origins and of his role as both its author and its editor.

Quite simply, Hawthorne did not author Hester's fate. Margaret Fuller did. In 1843, almost seven years before Hawthorne wrote the ending to *The Scarlet Letter*, Fuller had boldly praised and yet condemned George Sand in "The Great Lawsuit" in the terms that Hawthorne would have his narrator employ to judge Hester both in the chapter "Another View of Hester" and in the penultimate paragraph of the romance.[10] Sand, Fuller wrote, was "rich in genius, of most tender sympathies, and capable of high virtue and a chastened harmony," but she suffered the fate of many such women, women who "ought not to find themselves by birth in a place so narrow, that in breaking bonds they become outlaws," who because they cannot find "much room in the world" for themselves "run their heads wildly against its laws."[11] Fuller then concludes as Hawthorne would conclude:

> Women like Sand will speak now, and cannot be silenced; their characters and their eloquence alike foretell an era when such as they shall easier learn to lead true lives. But though such forebode, not such shall be the parents of it. Those who would reform the world must show that they do not speak in the heat of wild impulse; their lives must be unstained by passionate error; they must be severe lawgivers to themselves. As to their transgressions and opinions, it may be observed, that the resolve of Eloisa to be only the mistress of Abelard, was that of one who saw the contract of marriage as a seal of degradation. Wherever abuses of this sort are seen, the timid will suffer, the bold

protest. But society is in the right to outlaw them till she has revised her law, and she must be taught to do so, by one who speaks with authority, not in anger and haste.[12]

So said Margaret Fuller—when, as Hawthorne commented on Hester, she "had vainly imagined that she herself might be the destined prophetess" (1:263). As Hawthorne wrote the last paragraphs in early February 1850, he anticipated Margaret Fuller's imminent return of "her own free will" (1:263) from the failures of a "hardly accomplished revolution" (1:43) in Italy to a still puritanical New England, where, in the end, as Hester had at the beginning, she and her presumably illegitimate baby, Angelo, would have to confront public censure and humiliation.[13] She would also have to face what Hester did not. As Hawthorne envisions Fuller's ordeal on the scaffold of public opinion in nineteenth-century New England, he reminds us repeatedly and pointedly during his description of Hester's ordeal two centuries before of the greater cruelty that Hester would have faced in a New England of "our days" (1:50)—the "heartlessness" of becoming "only a theme for jest" (1:56)—of suffering only "mocking infamy and ridicule" (1:50). Almost nine years later, eight after Fuller's death, Hawthorne would claim that it would be from such "ridicule" that "Providence" had been "kind" in saving Fuller (14:156–57).

In February 1850, however, Hawthorne would anticipate Fuller's return by imagining the possibility, and perhaps even advocating, a different reception for Fuller, one in which, as he says of Hester, "the scarlet letter" had "ceased to be a stigma which attracted the world's scorn and bitterness" and had become, through the sympathetic agency of the romance itself, "a type of something to be sorrowed over, and looked upon with awe, yet with reverence too" (1:263). He imagined her returning, as Hester did, to resume her work as counselor to wronged women, living long enough to read her words on Sand restated as the ironic prophecy of her own inability, by her own standards, to become the "destined prophetess."[14] And yet confronting women's questions as to "why they were so wretched," she would continue to teach them to identify the sources of their sorrow not in their "sin" nor their "shame" but in the very unjust, very "unsure" nature of "the whole relation between men and women" (1:263). "Destined prophetess" or not, she would continue, as Richard Millington has recently argued, to prophesy, and her prophecy would continue to subvert rather than reconfirm the patriarchal culture that had condemned her and made wretched other women.[15]

If the "office" of the scarlet letter, as Sacvan Bercovitch has claimed, is to subdue Hester to a gradualist liberal consensus, to have her accept that subjugation freely, and to have her counsel other women to do the same, it fails.[16] For she comes back to New England unrepentantly not only to counsel others to reject the very cultural values that condemn them but also, defiantly, to be near the site of her memories and of the body of the very person she had at one time, despite her suffering, refused to leave. She will join him finally in the same cemetery, and though their society will not allow even their "dust" to "mingle," they, finally, will be united through inscription, through the scarlet letter, their now common legend on the tombstone, in the romance (1:264). It should be noted that the "old and sunken" grave (1:264) of the man who had once gained "the very proudest eminence of superiority" for prophesying "a high and glorious destiny for the newly gathered people of the Lord" (1:249) is unmarked—apparently forgotten, that is—until it is conjoined by the grave of the woman who prophesied that these "newly gathered people of the Lord" needed to learn a "new truth" about the "whole relation between men and women" (1:263) before they could, in effect, merit their "high and glorious destiny."

Because no one has fully recognized that Hawthorne speaks for and about Fuller at the close of the romance, the irony of the ending has gone largely unappreciated.[17] He closes the romance as he began it, by writing of Hester's fate two centuries before from the double perspective of her time and his. Hester's words in the seventeenth century are Fuller's words in the nineteenth century. Nothing has changed. "Heaven's own time" has clearly not come, not for women. But then, "heaven's own time" had not come for the "newly gathered people of the Lord" in New England and America. Their "high and glorious destiny" had not arrived, largely because, as Fuller herself had written in "The Great Lawsuit," the chosen people of America, like the Jews "when Moses was leading them to the promised land," had done everything that "inherited depravity could, to hinder the promise of heaven from its fulfillment," the "cross" having been planted in America "only to be blasphemed by cruelty and fraud"—to "the red man, the black man," and, as she later makes abundantly clear, to all women.[18]

Two centuries after Hawthorne would have a fraudulent Arthur elevate himself temporarily to his culture's highest eminence by envisioning a "high and glorious destiny" for America, Fuller would deplore the proliferation in her own age of such "'word heroes' . . . word-Christs" as Hawthorne's Arthur, protesting that because "never were lungs so puffed with the wind of declamation, on moral and religious subjects, as now," she feels "tempted to implore" them "to remember that hypocrisy is the most hopeless as well as the meanest of crimes, and that those must surely be polluted by it, who do not keep a little of all this morality and religion for private use." She would look back on the "ages of failure" in American history to achieve "freedom and equality" for women as well as for "the red man, the black man" and yet still be able to maintain that though it might be "given to eternity to fulfill . . . this country is as surely destined to elucidate a great moral law, as Europe was to promote the mental culture of man."[19] Arthur's prophecy and Hester's intersect in Fuller's.

The ending of *The Scarlet Letter* originates where it had begun—with Fuller—and with Hawthorne's renewed confrontation with the riddle of her character and of their relationship. Fuller has for some time, of course, been linked loosely with Hawthorne's Hester. First to argue persuasively for Fuller as a model for Hester, Francis E. Kearns noted the parallels between Fuller's and Hester's lives as mothers of illegitimate children who are or become linked with the non-English aristocracy, as social reformers and feminists, as counselors to women, and as nurses to the dying. Reynolds explored the link in more depth, arguing that, more than that of any of the other suggested models for Hester, Fuller's life "served" Hawthorne "most provokingly" for both personal and ideological reasons, Fuller and Hester representing in Hawthorne's mind "the figures of Liberty and Eve," the "ideas of revolution and temptation, which lie at the heart of the novel." As "Eve," Reynolds suggests, Fuller during her intimate friendship with Hawthorne at Concord had unwittingly become the object of Hawthorne's sexual interest. Hawthorne's "guilt and anger" over his own "attraction to her" provide the best explanation, argues Reynolds, for the motivation behind Hawthorne's sudden, inexplicable denunciation of Fuller in 1858 when he heard gossip about her relationship with Ossoli. As "Liberty," Fuller, "a female revolutionary trying to overthrow the world's most prominent political-religious leader," merged with "Eve" in Hawthorne's mind to represent "a freethinking temptress who had almost subverted his right-minded thoughts and feelings." More recently, Sacvan Bercovitch has built on Reynolds's original exploration of Hawthorne's conservative reaction to European revolutions and has expanded that context to include Hawthorne's anxieties about potential revolutions within the home and within the nation prompted by radical advocates of women's rights and abolitionism. Though he does not explore the subject in any depth, Bercovitch follows Reynolds by endorsing the view that Fuller provided the model for Hester as the embodiment of many of Hawthorne's concerns.[20]

I contend that Fuller figured much more deeply in Hawthorne's imagination before and during the writing of *The Scarlet Letter* than anyone has suspected. In all the aforementioned studies, Fuller is cited as the model for the socially and sexually threatening Hester that the narrator of *The Scarlet Letter* condemns. I argue, however, that Fuller informs Hawthorne's total conception of Hester, the Hester who inspires Hawthorne's sympathetic admiration and respect as well as his fears and guilt. Hawthorne did not simply decide suddenly in September 1849 to retrieve a character from "Endicott and the Red Cross," write a romance about a seventeenth-century Puritan mother of an illegitimate baby, and then draw upon his friend's life to flesh out his characterization of Hester's radical potential. Fuller was at the heart of Hawthorne's very conception of Hester. Through Hester, Hawthorne, on one level at least, continues his now-distant dialogue with Fuller and attempts to represent, if not actually to solve, the riddle of Fuller and their relationship.

2

Hawthorne began *The Scarlet Letter* seven years and one month after that fateful afternoon in the woods of Sleepy Hollow with Fuller, the moment when their friendship intensified into an ambivalent intimacy that would haunt Hawthorne for years, the very moment he had puzzled over in his representation of Giovanni's first encounter with Beatrice in Rappaccini's garden. In the seven years that had passed since that moment, in the five years since confronting it in "Rappaccini's Daughter," much had changed for both Hawthorne and Fuller. Their world then had been Emerson's Edenic garden in Concord; seven years later they each found themselves, though a continent apart, in a troubling world of personal crises and political strife, in a world where the garden, it seemed, for all of its own shadows, had now become a fully dark forest.

While Hawthorne fought a very public and humiliating battle during the late spring and summer to retain his position in the Salem Custom House, a position he had gained by following fellow Democrats in their brief return to power and had lost to the resurgence of a Whig party led by Zachary Taylor, Fuller fought a grander and more dangerous political battle on behalf of the revolutionary republican government of Rome, besieged during June and early July by French troops fighting to restore an overthrown Papacy and foreign hegemony.[21] She had publicly and privately committed herself entirely to the battle. Having written as a correspondent for the *New-York Daily Tribune* firsthand accounts celebrating the inception of the revolution, Fuller risked her life to remain in the city during the nightly French artillery bombardment and the daily fighting to describe to America those "sad but glorious days" when the republican forces fought a desperate battle to save a doomed revolution that had become, in Fuller's proud words, "now radical" in its determination to bring republican government to all of Italy, to make "the idea," "the destiny of our own great nation," the destiny of all Europe.[22] As a participant, she aided the wounded at the hospital on Tiber Island and described the terrible mutilations of the young. Though sickened by the suffering and the destruction, she nevertheless took on the persona of prophetess of Liberty defiantly chronicling the tragic victory of "tyranny" over "democracy," presenting herself as being more than willing to be a martyr to the good cause if it would "transport" her soul "to some sphere where Virtue and Love are not tyrannized over by egotism and brute force."[23] Watching the young die, describing a pair of skeletal legs that "protruded from a bank of one barricade," imagining her own death as republican martyr, Fuller in Rome, like Hawthorne in Salem beside his mother's sickbed, confronted the terrors of death during July 1849 as neither of them had before.[24]

By the end of the summer both of them, in suffering devastating political and personal losses, would confront extraordinarily uncertain futures. In mid-July, Fuller by military edict would be ordered to leave her adopted home in Rome. She went first to Rieti, the mountain town where she had left her baby in the care of a wet nurse, finding him near death from malnutrition. By October she found temporary sanctuary in Florence, uncertain for a time whether to return to America. In early September, Hawthorne, recovering from his "brain fever" after his mother's death and his firing from the Custom House, would also begin the search for another home, an exile from Salem looking to be a "citizen of somewhere else" (1:44).[25] Both faced poverty with no certain prospects for any immediate relief. Fuller would place her hopes on completing and publishing the history of the Italian revolution that she had announced as early as December 1848.[26] She would finish it in Florence, claim it as her masterpiece, and apparently, lose it at sea during the shipwreck that cost her life. Placing his own hopes on writing, Hawthorne would follow Fuller's way but not her course. Both would write histories, but histories of different kinds. If she could be said to be following in autobiographically based history what Hawthorne called the "wiser effort" of diffusing "thought and imagination through the opaque substance of to-day" in order to find "the true and indestructible value" within a troubled world (1:37), Hawthorne chose the ghostly light of a historical romance of the seventeenth century to illuminate the "opaque substance" of his and Fuller's past, present, and anticipated future.

As Reynolds has noted, Hawthorne began his historical romance less than two weeks after learning in early September through Caroline Sturgis Tappan that Fuller had become the mother of an apparently illegitimate baby.[27] Hawthorne reacted to this final shock of an unsettling summer by writing his "scarlet letter" to and about Fuller and himself. Fuller inspired not only the subject and the character but also the private audience for Hawthorne's "confidential depths of revelation" (1:3). Hawthorne acknowledged that Fuller possessed the sympathetic power to understand him, an admission that as far as we can tell he made to no one else, including Sophia. Following the lead of his earlier response to Fuller in his first published preface, "Writings of Aubépine"—in which he had represented his audience as an "individual or possibly isolated clique"—Hawthorne again presents himself as addressing "only and exclusively" an audience of a single friend, "the one heart and mind of perfect sympathy" who will listen to his "talk" of the "circumstances that lie around us" as he searched in dialogue, by the act of writing, for "the divided segment" of his own being in the natures of Arthur, Roger, and Hester, hoping to "complete his circle of existence by bringing" himself "into communion with it" (1:3–4). He seems to attempt, in other words, to solve once again what Giovanni had called "the riddle of his own existence," the riddle that he had located in "the mystery" of Beatrice—"the riddle" that Fuller had become and as late as 1858 still remained.

3

Under the appellation of Roger Chillingworth, the reader will remember, was hidden another name, which its former wearer had resolved should never more be spoken.
                    The Scarlet Letter

The figure of the branded woman condemned and scorned by Puritan society, punished by the humiliation of wearing the scarlet A, was first introduced, of course, in the 1837 tale "Endicott and the Red Cross." When Fuller wrote her first review of Hawthorne in 1841 to praise *Grandfather's Chair* yet to urge him to continue to draw from his "deep well" for "the older and sadder," of all the tales Hawthorne had written, "Endicott and the Red Cross" was the one tale Fuller singled out as representing the "power so peculiar" to his "genius."[28] Hawthorne, as I have argued, gave Fuller's reviews his most serious attention. As Hawthorne began "Rappaccini's Daughter" in October 1844, meditating deeply on his relationship with Fuller, translating in part her review of *Twice-Told Tales* into his translator's preface, he thought of her earlier review and the tale she had praised and he considered another narrative in which he could confront and yet conceal his relationship with Fuller. On 13 October, seven years after he had first created her, he suddenly recalls in his notebook, and without further comment, the woman, the letter, and the sin that he later would not describe or name: "The life of a woman, who, by the old colony law, was condemned always to wear the letter A, sewed on her garment, in token of her having committed adultery" (8:254). Written earlier on the same day, another entry reveals him meditating with a Giovanni-like self-contempt on the nature of his enterprise in "Rappaccini's Daughter." As he considers the origins of an author's works in his life, he expresses his disgust at those writers, like Byron, who too transparently, too artlessly reveal to the public their innermost lives, who "serve up their own hearts, duly spiced, and with brain-sauce out of their own heads, as a repast for the public" (8:253).[29] Rather than deter him from an autobiographical impulse, his disgust worked to strengthen his determination to conceal the fundamental confessional nature of his work from all but the most sympathetic.

Months before beginning *The Scarlet Letter,* before he hears gossip of scandal, we find Hawthorne again thinking of Endicott and his own family's role in the cruel persecution of a woman, not an adulteress but the outspoken Quaker radical Ann Coleman. Published in May 1849 in Elizabeth Peabody's *Aesthetic Papers,* positioned as the lead piece in a trilogy of politically critical articles—S. H. Perkins's "Abuse of Representative Government" and Henry David Thoreau's "Resistance to Civil Government"—Hawthorne's "Mainstreet," in itself and in the setting that Peabody gave it within *Aesthetic Papers,* suggests that Hawthorne's sympathetic portrait of Ann Coleman's "bold" denunciation of "established authority, . . . the priest and his steeple-house" may have been informed by his sympathetic reading of Fuller's increasingly outspoken defense of the Roman revolutionary republicans.[30] Coleman's "wild, shrill voice" denouncing established, intolerant authority "appalls" those in authority and provokes them to brutal suppression precisely because of the revolutionary effect of her words on the people, the "living truth" that she told, which seemed, "for the first time," to have "forced its way through the crust of habit" and "reached their hearts and awakened them to life."[31]

If in the spring Fuller's outspoken support of the revolution in Rome and her withering criticism of an America that had betrayed its "nobler spirit" informed Hawthorne's depiction of Ann Coleman, by the fall Fuller's status as an apparently unwed mother led Hawthorne once again at a crucial moment to associate Fuller with the woman condemned by the letter A. Drawing, I believe, upon Thoreau's doctrine of the radical power of passive individual resistance, Hawthorne would combine both figures in Hester. She would greet humiliating persecution not with a "wild, shrill" cry of condemnation but with a defiant silence. Her silence, however, is not assent, for in her bold speculation and counsel to women she is not the meek, submissive figure of pity Hawthorne had envisioned in 1837.

What Hawthorne had heard in 1849 about Fuller's infant son, Angelo, or his father, the Marquis Giovanni Angelo Ossoli, we do not know. We do know, of course, that he chose to model Hester's child after his own.[32] But in choosing the name "Pearl" for Una's fictional counterpart, Hawthorne provides yet another suggestion of Fuller's intimate involvement in *The Scarlet Letter*. Hawthorne first mentions the possibility of naming a character "Pearl" in a long, undated passage in his notebook between entries dated 1 June 1842 and 27 July 1844: "Pearl—the English of Margaret—a pretty name for a girl in a story" (8:242). Written during the period in which Hawthorne's friendship with Fuller was at its most intense, the notation on the origins of the name "Margaret" was almost certainly inspired by his conversations with Fuller, for she habitually informed others of her name's meaning and was fond of meditating on the implications its symbolism held for her life.[33] The association between Fuller, Una, and the character Pearl, however, was deeper in Hawthorne's mind than merely comparable names. The extraordinarily close relationship that Fuller and Una established with each other between July and late September 1844—between Una's fifth and seventh months—created an association between the two in Hawthorne's mind that would not only inform his characterization of Hester and Pearl but also subtly influence his characterization of the Fuller-like Miriam in 1858–59, when the first collapse of Una's physical and mental health struck terror in his heart at the very moment that he was writing of Fuller's own "collapse."[34]

The intimate relationship between Una and Fuller established during this brief period in Una's life could not be widely known until the 1991 publication of Fuller's 1844 journal. Previously, the only published description of Fuller with Una had been Sophia's comment in the Hawthornes' joint notebook quoted in Arlin Turner's 1980 biography. In that description, Sophia emphasized Una's uncanny ability to recognize and admire genius in others. She describes Una at first staring at Fuller "with earnest and even frowning brow" because she recognized that she was in the presence of "a complex being, rich and magnificent, but difficult to comprehend and of a peculiar kind, perhaps unique." Once Fuller took her in her arms, however, the frown quickly disappeared. Una "smiled approvingly" once she had comprehended "her greatness and real sweetness and love" and then "trusted in her wholly," remaining "with full content by the hour" in Fuller's arms. Without access to Fuller's 1844 journal, Turner quotes that passage as evidence of Sophia's "continuing, half-playful argument" about Fuller with Hawthorne and, in Turner's animus toward Fuller, even goes so far as to speculate that Sophia "perhaps concocted" the story "to prove that a child could discern Margaret's virtue." [35]

Fuller's 1844 journal leaves no doubt that the relationship between Fuller and Una was indeed extraordinary. Fuller's visit to Concord in July 1844 was occasioned in large part by the births of two children and the expected birth of a third. Fulfilling the expectation that Hawthorne had expressed when he and Sophia had selected Concord for their first home, Fuller arrived in Concord to be the houseguest of the Hawthornes and visit with them and their firstborn, Una. She also came to visit with her sister, Ellen, her brother-in-law, Ellery, and their recent firstborn, her niece and namesake, Margaret "Greta" Channing. When Fuller arrived at the Hawthornes, Lidian Emerson was also just days away from delivering her second son, Edward Waldo Emerson. Between their many walks through the night woods and their boat rides on the Concord, Hawthorne was to see Fuller with babies in her arms frequently during her monthlong visit, particularly Una. In fact, during her stay with the Hawthornes, she and Hawthorne would spend much of the day together baby-sitting Una while Sophia was away at the Channings serving as Greta's wet nurse, Ellen having proven incapable of nursing the baby herself. [36] Whatever preternaturally perceptive and trusting relationship Una may have felt toward Fuller in Sophia's eyes, clearly, in Fuller's eyes at least, there was a powerful and reciprocal bond with Una, whom she described on the day she first met her as "a most beautiful child," her beauty being both "noble and harmonious," both "strong" and "sweet." [37] Nine days later she recounts an early evening walk with Hawthorne by the river and comments that "I love him much, & love to be with him in this sweet tender homely scene" though "I should like too, to be with him on the bold ocean shore"; she then describes the "homely scene" that took place on their return and of a bond between herself and Una that Fuller narrates as being stronger—at least on this night—than that of parent and child:

> When we came back Una was lying on the sofa all undrest. She acted like a little wild thing towards me, leaning towards me, stretching out her arms whenever I turned. Her mother tried to attract her attention, in vain, her

father took my place, she looked on him and smiled, but discontinued this gesture, the moment I came she resumed it. She has daily become more attached to me; she often kisses me in her way, or nestles her head in my bosom. But her prettiest and most marked way with me is to lean her forehead upon mine. As she does this she looks into my eyes, & I into hers. This act gives me singular pleasure: it is described in no initiation. I never saw any body prompted to do it as a caress. It indicates I think great purity of relation.[38]

Fuller then considers the "treasury of sweet pictures of this child" that she has stored in her "mind" and concludes: "Never was lovelier or nobler little creature! Next to little Waldo I love her better than any child I ever saw." In this often troubled summer, her relationship with Una, as well as with Una's father, seemed to bring Fuller what peace she was to find. That night, after spending the early evening with Hawthorne and then with Una, Fuller describes going out into the night and lying "in the avenue for hours, looking up at the stars." As "the trees whispered," she records, "How happy, even pure I felt!—"[39]

The bond Fuller felt with Una exceeded that with her niece, of whom she writes, "this child interests but does not attach me yet." Though she would describe Emerson's three-year-old daughter Edith as "like a seraph" with a "poetic and tender" smile, she worried that she was "too frail a beauty for this world," inferior to Una, whose "noble and harmonious beauty seems as strong as sweet, as if she might stay here always."[40]

Spending her last full day in Concord with the Hawthornes before returning to Cambridge, Fuller records that her regret in having to depart is centered on Una and Hawthorne: "O it is sad that I shall see Una no more in this stage of her beauty. When I *do* see her again she will be quite another child." The emphasis that Fuller placed on "do" suggests, of course, her determination to reestablish the bond with Una, even if she is "quite another child." In the same journal entry Fuller expressed a similar determination to reestablish and deepen an already intimate relationship with Hawthorne. Describing getting lost in the forest's "long paths, dark and mystical" with Hawthorne and concluding that she felt with Hawthorne that he "might be a brother" to her more than she had ever felt "with any man before," she writes, "Yet with him it is though sweet, not deep kindred, at least, not deep yet."[41]

As she began revising "The Great Lawsuit" that fall, Fuller paid tribute to Una and to Hawthorne by expanding her conception of the development of the individual and of the possibilities of intellectual and spiritual union in marriage to include the enormous influence of parenthood in marriages based on equality. In her journal, Fuller had written on 18 July that Una was "the child of a [blank space in manuscript] holy and equal marriage" and that she would "have a good chance for freedom and happiness in the quiet wisdom of her father, the obedient goodness of her mother."[42] In her revision of "The Great Lawsuit," she adds the following paragraph to *Woman in the Nineteenth Century* immediately after her discussion of friendship between men and women and before her discussion of four types of marriages; it would be Fuller's single greatest revision in her conception of marriage:

> What deep communion, what real intercourse is implied by the sharing [of] the joys and cares of parentage, when any degree of equality is admitted between the parties! It is true that, in a majority of instances, the man looks upon his wife as an adopted child, and places her to the other children in the relation of nurse or governess, rather than of parent. Her influence with them is sure, but she misses the education which should enlighten that influence, by being thus treated. It is the order of nature that children should complete the education, moral and mental, of parents, by making them think what is needed for the best culture of human beings, and conquer all faults and impulses that interfere with their giving this to these dear objects, who represent the world to them. Father and mother should assist one another to learn what is required for this sublime priesthood of nature. But, for this, a religious recognition of equality is required.[43]

When Hawthorne heard that Fuller had become a mother herself and he looked into the "tarnished mirror" of memory to re-create her story and his story in that of the woman bearing the letter A and of her unconfessed lover, the "ghosts" that he would see in that "familiar room" would appear as they did five years before. Hawthorne saw his child in Fuller's arms, and as Sophia recognized and as Fuller claimed, he witnessed the extraordinary bond Fuller established with Una during the very summer in which his own relationship with Fuller reached its greatest intimacy. In reconceiving his own child as Hester's child and Margaret's namesake, Hawthorne unites Margaret and Una in "Pearl" and suggests the depth of his sympathetic identification with Hester as Pearl's "other," "actual" parent. By so doing, he also strengthens the confessional implications of his decision to name Pearl's father the "imaginary" Arthur and then to edit the presence of that hidden presence of himself as the child's "actual" father, yet leave a trace of his method of concealment by selecting a last name that comments on the "dim" figure of the author in the first name—Arthur Dimmesdale.

The Scarlet Letter would have the "Actual" and the "Imaginary" meet on many such levels. It is a historical romance of New England set in the remote past of another revolution across the Atlantic, 1642 through 1649, the seven-year span of Hester and Arthur's union, separation, and then reunion, and it is also, it seems, Hawthorne's meditation on his own recent past, on the seven years between 1842 and 1849, between that moment in the woods of Sleepy Hollow in August 1842 when he discovered, through conversation, that his friendship with Fuller was capable of, and indeed had already developed into, a deeper intimacy, and that moment when, as he anticipated, Fuller would return from the European revolutions, with baby in arms, to confront public scorn and ridicule but also, of course, to confront him after a five-year absence from his life. He, like all her friends, would have to discover the grounds on which he could respond to the new challenge that Fuller posed to their friendship and their values.

His response, to himself and to Fuller, is to write the "scarlet letter" for which he at once and on several levels both claims and disclaims authorship through the "edited" narrative of Hester, Arthur, Pearl, and Roger. He fathered the imaginary child "Pearl" in Una, named her after the "Margaret" whose life and character authored Hester, and at once both exposed and concealed her paternity by naming her father "Arthur." If such covert creative strategies reveal Hawthorne meditating on the implications of the "motives and modes of passion" that drew him into an intimate friendship with Fuller seven years in the past, his decision to name Hester's injured and injuring husband and interrogator Roger Chillingworth reveals him employing a similar strategy in his meditation on his present and future relationship, as both a man and an artist, with Fuller.

"Chillingworth" appropriately names, as many have noted, Hawthorne's own disgust with the cold interrogation of the heart, the penetration and mastery of self and other that is the center of Hawthorne's own creative obsessions. "Prynne" is the name that Roger would conceal. But Hawthorne also conceals Roger's association with "Prynne." In its obscure way, "Prynne" may be as appropriately descriptive as are the names "Dimmesdale" and "Chillingworth." As has been noted, but rarely, Hawthorne named Roger after his historical contemporary William Prynne (1600–1669).[44] The historical Prynne was a Presbyterian lawyer and writer whose criticism of the king in 1634 and Bishop Laud in 1637 led him to be imprisoned, stripped of his Oxford degree, disbarred, disfigured by the cutting off first of his ear lobes and then their stumps, and most notably for Hawthorne's purposes, branded on both his cheeks with S. L. for "seditious libeler," which he in turn transformed into a badge of honor, as Hester was to do with her letter, by reinterpreting it, the brand becoming for him *Stigmata Laudis,* the brutal signature of his enemy Laud. Prynne's claim to martyrdom at the hands of state and church tyranny, however, was dissipated by his later betrayal of fellow Presbyterians. Once he was elected to the House of Commons, he accused the Commonwealth government of moral laxity, joined the king's side, and later became in fact the champion of the state and church that he had once opposed, writing *Vindication of Ecclesiastical Jurisdiction of the English Kings* (1666–70). Of particular thematic importance for his namesake's function in *The Scarlet Letter* is the fact that he originally earned the displeasure of Charles I, whose wife was something of an amateur actress, by writing *Histrio-Mastix* (1633), an attack on makeup, long hair, and primarily lewd entertainment, particularly plays, in which he indexed the names of actresses under the heading "notorious whores." Prynne was also renowned for his vindictiveness, particularly in the persecution of his old enemy, Laud. He tampered with witnesses, personally searched Laud's rooms, rifled through his pockets, published Laud's private diary in mutilated form, and prior to his trial, wrote an account of Laud's "crimes" entitled "Hidden Works of Darkness Brought to Public Light." Most importantly, for our concerns at least, he is also noted for attacking John Milton's ideas on divorce and for provoking Milton to answer him in *Colasterion* and to allude to him contemptuously in *Means to Remove Hirelings* as a "hot querist for tithes . . . a fierce reformer once, now rankled by a contrary heat."[45]

Hawthorne's identification of Roger "Chillingworth" Prynne with William Prynne and of both with that part of himself he felt compelled to condemn within the concealed scaffold of his art is, to say the least, complex. Like his historical counterpart branded by the scarlet scar tissue of the letters S. L., the fictional Prynne sees himself—through both his false marriage to Hester and his current relationship with her as cuckold—as being equally branded by her S. L., her scarlet letter A. In a powerfully ironic dramatization of the historical Prynne's equation of stage actresses with "notorious whores," the long-absent fictional Prynne's first glimpse of Hester on his return is the one he obtains by joining the audience to watch Hester's defiant performance of her shame on the public stage that is the scaffold. Though he was unable to expose himself—to hold metaphorically the letter to his own chest, as Hawthorne also claims to have been unable to do—he, like Hawthorne, is compelled to interrogate Hester and Arthur, to penetrate to the "motives and modes" of their "passion" and to violate, in order to expose, the sanctity of the self. Within Hawthorne's fictional world, Prynne thus "authors" the action in the same way and for the same motives that Hawthorne authors the tale. To do so, both must become, like William

Prynne, "seditious libelers" who betray themselves as they betray others. When Prynne takes on the false identity of "Chillingworth" so that he may "seditiously" expose Arthur's tormented self while claiming in the role of detached anatomist and physician of the heart that he would cure Arthur by provoking him to a damning confession, he but practices the same "arts of deception" as Hawthorne.[46] He dramatizes within the tale Hawthorne's act of writing the tale and becomes the living embodiment of Hawthorne's contempt for the very origins of his art in the brutal dissection and assiduously concealed exposure of the self, the self betrayed. The scarlet scar of the historical Prynne and the brand appropriate for that part of Hawthorne masquerading in the fictional Prynne's false identity as "Chillingworth" is indeed S.L.—the "seditious libeler" who, like that other part of Hawthorne invested in Arthur, would be known for the esteem accorded to the triumph born of his greatest confession and deception—*The Scarlet Letter.*

Hawthorne, I suspect, selected the name "Prynne" for at least two other reasons—Prynne's betrayal of his political principles and former allies and, more importantly, Prynne's opposition to Milton's views of marriage. In both cases, Hawthorne's identification of Chillingworth with Prynne and in turn Hawthorne's identification of a part of himself with Chillingworth reveal Hawthorne, once again, expressing contempt for his own deceptions and betrayals. In both cases, also, we find Hawthorne meditating on Fuller and the meaning of their past and present relationship.

Hawthorne, of course, presented himself in "The Custom-House" as a somewhat sanguine political martyr to a brutal government, a "decapitated surveyor," a contemporary of the other victims of injustice and intolerance portrayed in "Main-street," which, we must remember, he still planned at the time that he wrote "The Custom-House" to include among the tales to be published with *The Scarlet Letter.* But while Fuller metaphorically exposed herself in the summer of 1849 to the "guillotine" of a once-revolutionary French government now crushing its fellow republican revolutionaries in Italy, Hawthorne fought with all his might to retain his position within the government.[47] Influenced by his other radical friend, Thoreau, Hawthorne would almost paraphrase "Resistance to Civil Government" to condemn his own loss of self, of "proper strength," in leaning "on the mighty arm of the Republic," and he would have us believe that, while he in fact clung desperately to the office, he had already begun—before the ax fell—to consider leaving the Custom House in order to preserve what remained of his self-reliant manhood (1:38). A part of Hawthorne did, in fact, see himself as betrayed and publicly humiliated, another martyr to the brute force of state power, a power that in "The Custom-House" he insists he did not use when he controlled the "guillotine." He did sympathetically identify with the political losses and personal scandal of Fuller, and he expressed that sympathy in the narrator's admiration for the proud defiance of Hester on the scaffold. But a part of him also acknowledged his hypocrisy and confronted his own betrayal of himself and his friends.[48] If he positions his narrator and his reader alongside Hester on the scaffold, he also positions Arthur Dimmesdale above and Roger Prynne below. One carries out his duties to the state in judging her, and one stands with the multitude in condemning her. Both should stand with her and speak on her behalf, but both betray her with silence, a silence that one asks her to break in order to expose him and that one signals her to keep in order to conceal him.

In the more transparently veiled autobiography of "The Custom-House," Hawthorne would present his betrayal as a sign "of a system naturally well balanced" (1:25). Temporarily at least, he could abandon his stimulating friends in Concord—as well as nature, books, literature, and "a gift, a faculty," all "imaginative delight"—and join without a "murmur" the "living dead" old men and the soulless inspector and be the better for what he admits is a "corrupt" and "corrupting" service to the state (1:25–26). As long as he did not live too long as someone "other than . . . [he] had been," he could "recall" and thus redeem his truer self (1:26). Informed by Thoreau's classification of those who serve the state, Hawthorne could indict in the barely living old men and the soulless inspector those who serve the state only with their bodies and are, as Thoreau wrote, on a "level with wood and earth and stones . . . [and] horses and dogs." He could include himself, at least temporarily, with those who serve chiefly with their minds but not their consciences and are, in Thoreau's words, thus "as likely to serve the devil, without *intending* it, as God." And he could seek redemption by realigning himself with and writing in defense of Thoreau's "heroes, patriots, martyrs, reformers" who are "commonly treated as enemies" by the state because they serve it by resisting it "with their consciences."[49] He would write first "Main-street" and then, recalling his old self and his old friend, who was now truly something of an "enemy" to the old order of state and domestic politics, he would write *The Scarlet Letter.*

The intersection between state and domestic politics, of course, is marriage, and Hawthorne's selection of "Prynne" is especially appropriate in that the historical Prynne's attack on Milton's views of marriage and divorce are parallel to the two conceptions of marriage that, as T. Walter Herbert has so persuasively argued, are at issue in *The Scarlet Letter.*[50] Milton had argued that marriage consisted of a sacred bond of love between a man and a woman in the eyes of God, that it was instituted by God as a union of spirits meant to prevent or remedy the solitude of the self, and that once this bond had ceased to exist the marriage had ended. The state simply recognizes—in marriage or in divorce—what the couple and God have already recognized. For Milton, the single civil cause then recognized for divorce—adultery—was the "last and meanest" cause, in fact "a perverse injury" to God's intent for marriage, for adultery destroyed only those unions that were based not on an intellectual and spiritual bond but on "a sublunary and bestial burning, which frugal diet, without marriage, would easily satisfy." Milton condemns Protestants for having rejected Catholicism's elevation of marriage to a sacrament only to make it an "idol" with which they "invest . . . such an awful sanctity and give it such adamantine chains to bind with, as if it were to be worshipped like some Indian deity, when it can confer no blessing upon us, but works more and more to our misery."[51] The historical Prynne's objection to Milton may be heard in Roger "Chillingworth" Prynne's insistence on his legal—rather than emotional or sacred—claim to Hester: "Thou and thine, Hester Prynne, belong to me" (1:76). He makes this claim, of course, immediately after admitting that her "wrong" to him had been the consequence of his original "betrayal" of her into a loveless marriage.[52] Hester's claim to Arthur that their relationship "had a consecration of its own" (1:195) suggests that she seeks to redefine marriage, as Milton did, as a sacred bond established by love, not civil contract. She may sever the bonds of a false marriage by breaking her civil obligation to "belong" to Prynne, but she remains faithful to the higher "consecration" of her "marriage" to Arthur, except, significantly, when she allows Prynne's claim to a civil right over her to persuade her to keep his identity secret. Hester's crime against the state and against official morality, of course, is that she broke the vows of her civil marriage.

When Hawthorne edited the passage from Margaret Fuller's "Great Lawsuit" and *Woman in the Nineteenth Century* to write Hester's fate, he prophesied that the "angel and the apostle of the coming revelation" of the new order between men and women will not be stained by "sin" and "shame" but will show "how sacred love should make us happy" (1:263). Because "sacred love" is usually taken to mean "married love," critics have read that phrase to be Hawthorne's resolution of his ambiguity toward Hester. Under the terms of the mid-nineteenth century's discourse on the religious sanctity of marriage, he decides, finally, to condemn her, just as Fuller, the source of and for whom that passage was written, had argued that, despite "the contract of marriage" being often "a seal of degradation" that "the timid will suffer" and "the bold protest," "society is in the right to outlaw them till she has revised her law," which she "must be taught to do . . . by one who speaks with authority, not in anger and haste."[53] Hawthorne's "resolution" of his ambiguity, however, may just as well be read as his final, ironic gesture toward Hester, and through her to Fuller, if we complicate, as both he and Fuller did, the often disjunctive relationship between "marriage" and "sacred love."

Hawthorne was drawn to the acrimonious marriage debate between Prynne and Milton in the seventeenth century because it provided an appropriate historical parallel for the dialogue he and Fuller, and indeed the entire Concord circle, had once had over the nature of marriage, a dialogue that informed Fuller's views of marriage and celibacy in "The Great Lawsuit" and *Woman in the Nineteenth Century,* and a dialogue that Hawthorne reinitiates in *The Scarlet Letter.*[54] In the conversations that took place in Concord, Hawthorne and Fuller both held essentially Miltonic views of marriage as a sacred union. Emerson, however, represented the views of Prynne. In this, and in other ways, Hawthorne recalls for reexamination the triangular tensions in Concord between himself, Fuller, and Emerson that he had earlier "translated" into Rappaccini's garden.

Hester's justification of her union with Arthur as having a "consecration of its own" that supersedes civil recognition follows to its inevitable end the argument that Hawthorne and Fuller had both made for marriage. A full three years before Hawthorne and Sophia signed the civil contract in a public ceremony, Hawthorne had "consecrated" his relationship with Sophia as a "marriage" that, as he explained to her, "God himself has joined," for they had established "a bond between our Souls, infinitely stronger than any external rite" (15:329). Throughout his courtship letters to Sophia over the next three years, he refers to himself as her "husband" and to her, his Dove, as his "wife." Indeed, much of the tension in Hawthorne's premarital "marriage" talk in those letters arises from his anxiety that a resistant, "naughty Sophie" threatened to disrupt the idealized union he had created between them when he cast her in the role of his redemptive "Dove." We also know that long before he and Sophia actually married and moved to Concord he had attempted to describe to Fuller, if not his own family, the intimacy of his relationship with Sophia (15:612). Though Hawthorne had complained to Sophia that he could not describe satisfactorily their bond to others, "not even Margaret," Fuller seems to have understood him rather well.

In her reply to Sophia's announcement that she and Hawthorne were finally to be married formally, Fuller expresses her faith in Sophia's ability to maintain precisely the kind of love Hawthorne had long insisted his Dove had given him in their "marriage," a love that Fuller describes as "wise and pure and religious." Fuller had also become convinced through their many conversations that Hawthorne possessed a unique balance of the masculine and feminine that made him capable of responding to and sustaining such a love: "I think there will be great happiness," she predicted to Sophia, "for if ever I saw a man who combined delicate tenderness to understand the heart of a woman, with quiet depth and manliness enough to satisfy her, it is Mr Hawthorne." Though Sophia's love for Hawthorne was "wise, pure, and religious," she imagines them capable of an even higher form of union—an "intellectual friendship" of two artists that surpasses "love merely in the heart" or even "the common destiny of two souls."[55] When Hawthorne and Sophia finally moved to Concord, Hawthorne found, at least initially, that they had come to represent, in his mind as well as Fuller's, an alternative Eden to the one proposed by Emerson's vision of self-reliant individualism.[56]

For several years Fuller and Emerson had skirmished over the nature and possibilities of friendship and marriage. Voiced often in an emotionally charged undertone, their debate centered on whether the self-sovereign individual could ever really unite intimately with another soul. Fuller had insisted that such unions were possible, and Emerson had been equally insistent that they were not. Fuller records in her journal on 1 September 1842, for instance, an afternoon walk with Emerson in which the subject of marriage was once again discussed. First observing that Emerson "has little sympathy with mere life," Fuller illustrates her point by summarizing Emerson's views on marriage:

> We got to talking, as we almost always do, on Man and Woman, and Marriage.—W. took his usual ground. Love is only phenomenal, a contrivance of nature, in her circular motion. Man, in proportion as he is completely unfolded is man and woman by turns. The soul knows nothing of marriage, in the sense of a permanent union between two personal existences. The soul is married to each new thought as it enters into it. If this thought puts on the form of man or woman[,] if it last you seventy years, what then? There is but one love, that for the Soul of all Souls, let it put on what cunning disguises it will, still at last you find yourself lonely,—*the Soul.* There seems to be no end to these conversations.[57]

And indeed there was no end. Eight days later, Emerson entered Fuller's bedroom to read what he had written in his journal about marriage, and their debate began again, but Emerson was, as Fuller phrased it, "nowise convinced." But Fuller would not drop the subject either. Reading through his journals later, she quotes two of Emerson's statements about marriage and then vows that she "shall write to him about it." One of the statements illustrates clearly just how far apart his views of marriage were from Fuller's and Hawthorne's and just how close they are to "Chillingworth" Prynne's: "Is it not enough that souls should meet in a law, in a thought, obey the same love, demonstrate the same idea. These alone are the nuptials of minds[.] I marry you for better, not for worse, I marry impersonally."[58] As Fuller challenged Emerson's attempt to ground his unhappiness in philosophy, she had to contend with the consequences in Emerson's "mere life." Lidian's great unhappiness and her jealousy of Fuller's intimacy with Emerson erupted one night at the dinner table in an embarrassing scene. Lidian's problem, Fuller wrote, was that she still hoped Emerson's "character" would one day "alter" and he would "be capable of an intimate union." By now, however, Fuller had come to know better. Her "expectations" of a more intimate friendship with Emerson were "moderate now," she had written soon after arriving for her stay at the Emersons' that summer.[59]

In Hawthorne, however, her expectations at this time were clearly on the ascendent. Fuller began to see in Hawthorne the possibility of establishing the type of intimate friendship she had sought with Emerson. In contrast to Emerson, Hawthorne seemed capable of responding to nature, marriage, and friendship with an intelligence warmed by a depth and quiet passion impossible to Emerson. On Saturday night, 20 August 1842, the day before their afternoon-long conversation in the woods of Sleepy Hollow, Fuller describes Hawthorne during their walk taking in the beauty of the moon and responding to the moment by speaking to her of his marriage, telling her that he "should be much more willing to die than two months ago, for he had had some real possession in life, but still he never wished to leave this earth: it was beautiful enough." Hawthorne, Fuller then writes, "expressed, as he always does, many fine perceptions. I like to hear the lightest thing he says!"[60]

During the winter after that summer, as Reynolds has observed, Fuller continued her debate with Emerson on marriage by writing "The Great Lawsuit," attempting, as she had noted in a letter to Emerson in the fall, to prove "that permanent marriage cannot interfere with the soul's destiny."[61] Fuller's conception of marriage is informed by her contrasting conversations and experience with Emerson and Hawthorne and is framed within the terms of the Milton and Prynne debate, namely, "whether earthly marriage is to be a union of souls, or merely a contract of convenience and utility."[62] Of the four types of marriage she identifies in "The Great Lawsuit," her opinion of Emerson's second marriage shapes her description of the lowest type, a practical, civil marriage between a provider and a housekeeper who feel for each other merely a "mutual esteem" and "mutual dependence."[63] Sophia's "wise, pure, and religious" love and Hawthorne's capacity to develop an "intellectual friendship" with a woman provide Fuller with an example of a marriage that seems capable of reaching its highest and fullest potential as the fourth type of marriage—a "religious" marriage of a man and a woman on a "pilgrimage towards a common shrine," a marriage that incorporates all other types, including the marriage of "intellectual companionship" just below it on Fuller's scale.[64]

As the friendship between Fuller and Hawthorne deepened during the summer of 1844, they resumed their dialogue over the relationship between men and women in friendship and in marriage just as, only weeks later, Fuller was to resume her dialogue with the public over these same issues in revising "The Great Lawsuit" into *Woman in the Nineteenth Century*. After one of her many walks alone with Hawthorne through Sleepy Hollow, Fuller considers her "place" in life and finds that though she is able to take a "superior" view of it, she knows that "the deep yearnings of the heart & the bafflings of time will again be felt, & then I shall long for some dear hand to hold." She quells the impulse to self-pity, however, by recalling a recent conversation with Hawthorne: "But I shall never forget that my curse is nothing compared with that of those who have entered into those relations but not made them real: who only *seem* husbands, wives, & friends. H. was saying as much the other evening."[65] Fuller does not identify Emerson as the subject of her and Hawthorne's condemnation of the false spouse and friend, but when Emerson later read that passage as he was preparing Fuller's *Memoirs,* he clearly considered himself the topic of their talk and did what he could to obscure that fact.[66]

In a sense, Hawthorne continues that very conversation in *The Scarlet Letter,* and he, like Emerson, does what he can to obscure that fact. As Fuller's paraphrase and endorsement of Hawthorne's statement seems to imply, both she and Hawthorne considered not only Emerson's marriage with Lidian as a false union but also his friendship with them as less "real" than the friendship they had "entered into."

In "Chillingworth" Prynne, Hawthorne would embody a segment of his being that he despised, but he would also shape Prynne's character, to a great extent, in the image of the Emerson he had come to see not only as his rival in friendship with Fuller but also as the embodiment of that part of himself that, in the name of his own masculine self-sufficiency, resisted making his "relations" with the feminine "real." In Prynne's alias, "Chilling-worth" is the husband, friend, and philosopher that Emerson had come to seem to both Fuller and Hawthorne, the man whose vision of life (in an essay called, at the time, in fact, "Life") Fuller had condemned in 1844 as being "beautiful, and full and grand" yet "oh, how cold." "Nothing but Truth in the Universe, no love, and no various realities." In a statement that Hester could have easily made of Chillingworth, Fuller then rebukes herself for hav-ing been "foolish . . . to be grieved at him for showing towards" her "what exists toward all," and reminds herself that she must never again trust him, as Lidian still did, to be capable of making a relationship "real": "But lure me not again too near thee, fair Greek, I must keep steadily in mind what you are." In his scholarly solitude and justification for the claims of the un-checked self, in his unorthodox study of nature, in his "seeming" friendship, and of course, in his failure to seek, much less form, a "sacred" union in his marriage, Emerson's "ghost" in Hawthorne's past inhabits his imaginative vision of Chillingworth.[67]

4

> He knew not whether it were a woman or a shadow. It may be, that his path-way through life was haunted thus, by a spectre that had stolen out from among his thoughts.
> ARTHUR ON SEEING HESTER IN THE FOREST, AGAIN, IN *The Scarlet Letter*

As he did in October 1844, when he searched for the narrative vehicle that became "Rappaccini's Daughter," in September 1849, with Fuller and baby in "pleasant" Italy (to use Hester's adjective), Hawthorne followed a symmetrical logic of narrative deception in recalling the woman branded by the stigma of the letter A. The woods of Concord had become the garden of Italy in "Rappaccini's Daughter," and now the garden of a decidedly "un-pleasant," revolution-torn Italy would become the forests of the New World during the time (1642–49) of another upheaval across the seas, a time parallel two hundred years ago to the upheaval in the lives of both Fuller and Haw-thorne. Traces of Hawthorne's method explain, for instance, why his narra-tor would think of Hester and her infant on the scaffold in terms of an Ital-ianate, Catholic Madonna confronting the severity of a paternalistic Puritan morality—a reversal of Protestant Fuller's predicament at the time in Rome but appropriate to the likely perception of Fuller on her return from Italy with her child and her Italian-Catholic husband—why also he would consis-tently allude to the man who was her secret lover as a "priest" associated with the imagery of Catholicism rather than as a "minister."[68] If and when Fuller and her baby, Angelo, stepped off the ship from Italy, as Hester and Pearl stepped into the light from the seclusion of prison, she too would have to confront the ancestors of Hester's judges. She would have to explain what marriage had served to "consecrate" the conception of that child, and she would be expected to name the father.

She would have to confront as well the two men who, in Hawthorne's mind, had once been closest to her and rivals for her intimacy, the two men who would no longer be imagined as the mentor-father Dr. Rappaccini and the faithless friend Giovanni, but—given the revelation of Fuller's bold sexuality—imagined as the manipulative and loveless husband Chillingworth and the guilt-obsessed, self-absorbed lover Dimmesdale. The garden becomes the forest where Beatrice—still pure if not virginal—becomes Hester meeting her Arthur.

Hawthorne, in effect, rewrites "Rappaccini's Daughter" as *The Scarlet Letter*. Inspector Pue's brief tale, as Hawthorne claimed, is indeed edited and expanded. As he did in "Rappaccini's Daughter," Hawthorne revisits that afternoon in the woods of Sleepy Hollow when his and Fuller's relationship had deepened into intimate friendship.[69] In a tale of adultery in which the adulterous moment does not happen, in which in fact the very act is not named, Hawthorne imagines having realized a relationship with Fuller that did not happen, a relationship that his guilt-haunted imagination will not permit him to confront except in its moralized aftermath, in a retrospective art. Seven years had passed, and Hawthorne and Fuller had long been separated. But just as Hawthorne imagines that he will soon have to confront Fuller again and meet her this time as a sexually experienced, scandal-tainted mother with child, so Hawthorne describes in the "tarnished mirror" of his imagination Arthur and Hester's moment in the forest as a reunion of "ghosts" in which both confront in the "mirror" of each other and themselves the forces within their natures that had led them to this moment in their lives: "Each a ghost, and awe-stricken at the other ghost! They were awe-stricken likewise at themselves; because the crisis flung back to them their consciousness, and revealed to each heart its history and experience, as life never does, except at such breathless epochs. The soul beheld its features in the mirror of the passing moment" (1:190).

What they, and we, see are two very different natures, but they are, essentially, the same two natures we saw in Beatrice and Giovanni. Once again, Hawthorne stages a confrontation between man's desire to submit to the force of a liberating, feminine nature and his perversion of that desire through fear and suppression—in himself and in "human law." As Giovanni with Beatrice, Arthur discovers the poison of Hester's love not within her, but within his own "unsacred" desire for, and fear of, her forbidden body and the "wild, heathen Nature of the forest" and "Love, whether newly born or aroused," which have come to be represented by her body (1:203). If it is within Hester's nature to "consecrate" herself to a kind of "sacred love" that would endure seven years of silence and ignominy and yet draw her back to his side even after his death, it is not within Arthur's nature. His love is compounded by the kind of "lurid intermixture" of emotions that erupt in the solitude of his study even as he attempts to flay them into suppression, the same emotions he finds wickedly liberated during his walk back to town after his second encounter with Hester in the forest. Nature, his nature, does not blossom into beauty nor express itself as a transforming, life-giving love of the self for the Other, the very "sacred love" that God, according to Milton, had made possible in the marriage of one soul to another as a means of liberating us from the pangs of solitude. Arthur's love, on the contrary, more nearly resembles what Milton terms "a sublunary and bestial burning," which Arthur cannot "chasten," as Milton claims he should be able to do.[70] As with Giovanni, Arthur's passion, once it is no longer directed at suppressing the despised self, is directed at others, expressing itself in the desire to use its cruel power to infect others with a share of its misery, and infect them, revealingly, by a brutal candor rather than by covert confession. Significantly, Arthur resists this temptation and remains silent. For Arthur, such passion must indeed be contained within the walls of his heart and "subjugated by human law," though ironically it is from such containments that his passion was originally perverted. Only in the act of writing and of speaking as an artist of the pulpit does he find a culturally sanctioned means to contain and yet to liberate his desire—both for abject confession and for power.

In Arthur's "shattered and subdued" spirit and in his dependency on Hester's bold courage to speak and act upon his own desires, Hawthorne complicates the confrontation between the masculine and feminine here and elsewhere in the romance by reversing the roles—Arthur in a conventionally "feminine" role and Hester in a conventionally "masculine" one. The implications of such a reversal gain greater significance if read within the context of another topic of dialogue among the Concord group—the fluidity of gender. In their ongoing conversation about the nature of marriage and friendship and about the development of the self-reliant individual, Emerson and Fuller had agreed that the fully realized individual crossed, at some level, the boundaries of gender. For Fuller, the ideal to be strived for was a harmony of both masculine and feminine qualities, a balance, as noted in her letter to Sophia, that she thought Hawthorne approached. One of the most famous passages of "The Great Lawsuit" originates from these conversations. Fuller writes that "male and female represent the two sides of the great radical dualism," each "perpetually passing into one another" so that "there is no wholly masculine man, no purely feminine woman." In *Woman in the Nineteenth Century*, she identifies the characteristics of this "radical dualism" as "Energy and Harmony, Power and Beauty, Intellect and Love," the first of each pair being traditionally associated with the masculine, the second of each with the feminine.[71]

In the seven years prior to her reunion with Arthur in the forest, in order to endure, Hester has had to suppress the feminine in her life, if not in her art. Once in the forest again with Arthur and giving herself up to the liberating influence of "Nature" and "Love," Hester undergoes a transformation that seems to bring each of the three pairs of masculine and feminine traits into equilibrium, finding, for a moment, what Fuller described as most rare, and fleeting, "perfect harmony in human nature."[72] Transformed by love, "her sex, her youth, and whole richness of her beauty, came back" (1:202). She is once again beautiful in a conventionally feminine way, but in confronting the ruin of Arthur and the possibility of transforming present misery into future happiness, she loses none of the masculine qualities that have sustained her—her energy, power, and intellect. At that moment of harmony within Hester's nature, when she reclaims the feminine that she has suppressed, "all at once, as with a sudden smile of heaven," a sympathetic Nature seems resurrected. Sunlight "floods" shadows, green leaves "gladden," and dying leaves "transmute" into gold (1:202–3). The generative, feminine principle of passion and beauty in Nature that Fuller had celebrated in her flower sketches and that Beatrice had embodied for Giovanni transforms both Hester and the forest, but not Arthur. For Arthur, for the male narrator, and for the patriarchal order they represent, the feminine power of the natural world of the forest and of its human expression in love inspires both desire and terror.[73] If Hester is resurrected by such a power, Arthur experiences it as a "wild, free atmosphere of an unredeemed, unchristianized, lawless region" that must be "subjugated by human law," the "human" law, of course, of the men who make it (1:201, 203). Before the interview, Arthur had deployed his increasingly depleting "masculinity," not to endure, much less overcome, his own shame, but to exacerbate it. Possessing little if any of Fuller's six traits of gender during much of the interview with Hester, Arthur, in his walk back home and in his study that night, is also transformed, but instead of a harmony of the masculine and feminine, he finds himself once again "a man," but a man in whom the masculine traits of energy, power, and intellect express themselves in a passion untempered by feminine "love, beauty, harmony." It is a violent, potentially destructive passion that is ignited not by his desire for nor submission to the feminine power that transformed Hester but by his fear of it.[74] Ironically, though Arthur and the narrator himself may fear the "wild, heathen Nature" associated with Hester's love, as Giovanni feared Beatrice's "poison," the destructive power at work here, as in "Rappaccini's Daughter," is not feminine, but masculine.

And that power is encoded in a "human law" that mystifies its gendered origins. As Michael J. Colacurcio has demonstrated, Hawthorne rewrites New England history to make this very point, deliberately creating a historical anachronism by making Bellingham, as governor, the chief legal authority enforcing Hester's punishment. Hawthorne has Governor Bellingham, as the highest representative of civil authority and "human law," punish Hester for a sexual offense similar to one he had committed—taking to himself a wife without the benefit of an official marriage ceremony and doing so with impunity, if not without some scandal.[75]

Thus, in order to return to town, where Nature has indeed been subjugated by law, such law at least as represented by Bellingham, Hester must destroy the equilibrium attained in the forest. She must once again suppress the feminine and take on the decidedly masculine. And she must take it on through an act of physical suppression—pinning back her luxuriant hair beneath her cap, pinning back the badge of masculine judgment on her breast.

If Hawthorne would have Hester find in her masculine nature the strength and courage to endure her estrangement from society and from Arthur, he would also associate her bold and increasingly radical speculation with the imbalance she must maintain between the masculine and feminine. She who had "once been woman, and ceased to be so" in order to survive had suppressed her "tenderness," her "passion," and her "feeling" and turned to "thought," the "world's law" becoming "no law for her mind" (1:164). The "shame, despair, solitude" of her position "had made her strong, but taught her much amiss" (1:199).

While it may certainly seem that Hawthorne is clearly condemning Hester's, and indirectly Fuller's, bold feminism, he is actually in accord here with Fuller. Almost a decade before he had met Fuller or formed his first truly intimate relationship with a woman, with Sophia, Hawthorne, then twenty-six and struggling in obscurity as a writer, had used the introduction to his unsigned biographical sketch "Mrs. Hutchinson" for the *Salem Gazette* to express his resentment against critics who were encouraging "a girlish feebleness to the tottering infancy of our literature" by praising too uncritically the work of a growing number of women writers. Such critics, he charged, labor under a misplaced "courtesy" and "a false liberality, which mistakes the strong division-lines of Nature for arbitrary distinctions."[76] The "strong division-lines of Nature" so uncomplicatedly distinct to the sexually naive twenty-six-year-old were considerably less distinct or uncomplicated to the sexually experienced forty-five-year-old who in the two decades since writing that subordinate clause had married, fathered a daughter, become intimate friends with the leading feminist of the day, and spent much of the 1840s participating—as a man and as a writer—in the debate reexamining the relations between the sexes.[77] By 1849 Hawthorne could join Fuller in condemning cultural constructions of gender that provide women, according to Fuller, "a place so narrow, that, in breaking bonds, they become outlaws." Confined to the claustrophobic sphere of the "strong-division lines" of a "Nature" defined by human law and society, such gifted, intelligent women as the Fuller-like feminist in Hawthorne's "Christmas Banquet" (1844), find that "in the world," as opposed to the home, there is "nothing to achieve, nothing to enjoy, and nothing even to suffer." She, like all such women, finds her "unemployed energy" thrown back on itself, driving her "to the verge of madness by dark broodings over the wrongs of her sex, and its exclusion from a proper field of action" (10:303). Were society to provide such women with sufficient "room in the world" to develop fully their masculine and feminine natures, as Fuller says, with George Sand and Mary Wollstonecraft as her examples, "they would not," according to Fuller, "run their heads so wildly against the walls, but prize their shelter rather." "George Sand smokes, wears male attire, wishes to be addressed as Mon frère," Fuller had written in "The Great Lawsuit," but "perhaps, if she found those who were as brothers indeed, she would not care whether she were brother or sister." As Hester was to do in transforming the sign of the scarlet letter to read "Able" and "Angel," such women as Sand and Wollstonecraft, even without such "room," eventually "find their way, at last, to light and air" though "the world will not take off the brand it has set upon them."[78]

Fuller's plea in "The Great Lawsuit" and *Woman in the Nineteenth Century* is for the "fair and suitable position" for women that Hester sought, and it was for a "position" that allowed women the "room" to develop the full potential of their natures, masculine and feminine, without suppressing either. For Fuller, as well as Hawthorne, this meant that what had come to be seen as "the very nature of the opposite sex, or its long hereditary habit, which has become like nature" had "to be essentially modified" and that women must undergo "a still mightier change" in developing the masculine half of their dual nature. In doing so, however, they risked, as in George Sand's case, the creation of another imbalance, losing "the ethereal essence wherein"—according to contemporary constructions of the feminine that both Hawthorne and to a lesser extent Fuller assented—"she has her truest life" (1:165–66). The "whole relation between men and women" needed to be established "on a surer ground of mutual happiness" (1:263), as Hawthorne has Hester say, but until that time, as Fuller wrote and Hawthorne edited for Hester, "the timid will suffer, the bold protest . . . but society is in the right to outlaw them till she has revised her law, and she must be taught to do so, by one who speaks with authority, not in anger and haste." To speak with such "authority," Fuller wrote, "those who would reform the world must show that they do not speak in the heat of wild impulse; their lives must be unstained by passionate error; they must be severe lawgivers to themselves."[79]

In 1843 Fuller had condemned both the "seal of degradation" branded on women by "the contract of marriage" and the "passionate error" of those who broke "bonds" and spoke "in the heat of wild impulse." Though Fuller would grant in "The Great Lawsuit" that "any elevation, in the view of union, is to be hailed with joy," rather than accepting the imperfections of unions in the present, she would be a "severe lawgiver" to herself in proclaiming "celibacy as the great fact of the time . . . from which no vow, no arrangement, can at present save a thinking mind." Fuller concludes "The Great Lawsuit," in fact, by speculating that given the present state of marriage and woman's subjugation to her husband, the "prophetess" who would "vindicate" the "birthright for all women" might have to speak as a virgin.[80] Though Hawthorne's penultimate paragraph in *The Scarlet Letter* edits and redeploys Fuller's earlier passage on George Sand and Mary Wollstonecraft, this final passage in Fuller's essay informs much of Hawthorne's response to Fuller in his depiction of Hester:

> A profound thinker has said "no married woman can represent the female world, for she belongs to her husband. The idea of woman must be represented by a virgin."
>
> But that is the very fault of marriage, and of the present relation between the sexes, that the woman does belong to the man, instead of forming a whole

with him. Were it otherwise there would be no such limitation to the thought.

Woman, self-centred, would never be absorbed by any relation; it would be only an experience to her as to man. It is a vulgar error that love, *a* love to woman is her whole existence; she also is born for Truth and Love in their universal energy. Would she but assume her inheritance, Mary would not be the only Virgin Mother. Not Manzoni alone would celebrate in his wife the virgin mind with the maternal wisdom and conjugal affections. The soul is ever young, ever virgin.

And will not she soon appear? The woman who shall vindicate their birthright for all women; who shall teach what to claim, and how to use what they obtain? Shall not her name be for her era Victoria, for her country and her life Virginia? Yet predictions are rash; she herself must teach us to give her the fitting name.[81]

The fitting name that Hawthorne would have his Madonna-like heroine give to her vision of the "destined prophetess" of "Love and Truth," and a new truth about love itself, would be the prophetess not of a "chaste" but of a "sacred love." Fuller was not to be the "virginal" prophetess that she had once "vainly imagined herself to be," for she had turned to the chaste life, as Hester had chosen it after 1642, not as an ideal, but as a temporary alternative to the present "seal of degradation" imposed on women by "the contract of marriage." Like Hester, like Hawthorne, Fuller all along had acknowledged that not all marriages were based on "sacred love" and that "sacred love" itself, as Hawthorne had explained to Sophia and as Hester would explain to Arthur, had a "consecration all its own" that superseded the "external rites" of civil marriage. The "sacred love that *should* make us happy" is, as Fuller defined it, a marriage of the masculine and feminine within the self and between a man and a woman, a marriage in which the woman does not "belong to the man" but forms "a whole with him."

Chastity is indeed after 1642 the "fact of the time" for Roger and Arthur as well as Hester, but in each case, the chaste life must be maintained by an isolation that splits the self by prohibiting a union—within or without—between masculine and feminine, man and woman. In each, the masculine subjugates the feminine, and in each that willful suppression destroys what could have been redeemed. For Hawthorne, men without women and women without men reinstate within the individual the very masculine subjugation of the feminine that chastity seeks to avoid in marriage.

If in Hester's time, and in Fuller and Hawthorne's, such a love found itself in conflict with the "long hereditary habit" of gender constructions that had come to seem "like nature" and in conflict all too often as well with the sacramentalization of the civil contract of marriage, such a love could be safely expressed only in an edited language that translated the actual into the imaginary, creating an art in which Hawthorne could confront the ghosts of the past in a room where they no longer "affrighten," give them speech again, say again differently what had already been said, and say also what had not and could not be said in any other language.

"Silken Bands" and "Iron Fetters"

Fuller at Fire Island, Hawthorne at Lenox

The bands, that were silken once, are apt to become iron
fetters, when we desire to shake them off. Our souls, after
all, are not our own. We convey a property in them to
those with whom we associate, but to what extent can
never be known, until we feel the tug, the agony, of our
abortive effort to resume an exclusive sway over ourselves.
Thus, in all the weeks of my absence, my thoughts continually reverted back, brooding over the by-gone months, and
bringing up incidents that seemed hardly to have left a trace
of themselves, in the passage. I spent painful hours in recalling these trifles, and rendering them more misty and unsubstantial than at first, by the quality of speculative musing,
thus kneaded in with them. Hollingsworth, Zenobia, Priscilla! These three had absorbed my life into themselves.

COVERDALE IN *The Blithedale Romance*

Early in *The Blithedale Romance*, Zenobia confronts Coverdale, asking him to
explain the source of his constant, intense gaze. "I seem to interest you very
much," she tells him, "and yet—or else a woman's instinct is for once deceived—I cannot reckon you as an admirer. What are you seeking to discover in me?" Because he is "surprised into the truth by the unexpectedness
of her attack," Coverdale confesses, "The mystery of your life. . . . And you
will never tell me" (3:47). Zenobia indeed does not tell him, but she does
allow him, as Beatrice did Giovanni, to "look into her eyes, as if challenging"
him "to drop a plummet-line down into the depths of her consciousness."
As Giovanni with Beatrice, so Coverdale with Zenobia—he cannot meet her
challenge. "I see nothing now," he tells her, "unless it be the face of a sprite,
laughing at me from the bottom of a deep well" (3:48).

The site of Coverdale's gaze remains fixed at the end where it had been from the first. As he concludes his tale, he directs our attention to the place where he started, the place where we discover we have been all along. The "deep well" of Zenobia's eyes is now veiled by the depths of her grave, but Coverdale has stood by that grave from the beginning, haunted every bit as much as Hollingsworth by Zenobia's ghost, still trying to fathom her mystery, still feeling the "tug, the agony" of his "abortive effort to resume an exclusive sway" over himself. But, as he has come to realize, "our souls, after all, are not our own" (3:194). A part of him lies buried in that grave.

In the winter of 1851–52, through his surrogate, his "translator," Miles Coverdale, Hawthorne still pondered in Zenobia the mystery that Fuller remained for him, but the "plummet-line" that Hawthorne would have to drop in order to penetrate that mystery could no longer be in Fuller's "eyes" but in the "deep well" of her grave at the bottom of the Atlantic Ocean. Five months after the publication of *The Scarlet Letter*, Fuller, Ossoli, and their baby drowned on the shores of the United States in the wreck of the *Elizabeth*. Fuller never had the chance to read Hawthorne's "scarlet letter" to her, but in one peculiar passage in *The Blithedale Romance*, Hawthorne covertly acknowledges Fuller's association with *The Scarlet Letter* while seeming only to pay an overt tribute to her memory as "one of the most gifted women of the age." When Priscilla brings Coverdale a nightcap that she has made him, she also brings him "a sealed letter." After she offers it to him and he does not take it, she draws it back and holds "it against her bosom, with both hands clasped over it." At precisely that moment, Coverdale is "forcibly struck" by her resemblance to Margaret Fuller—not to Fuller's "figure" nor her "features," he is careful to note, but to "her air." "Strangely enough," as Coverdale says, the letter is from Fuller, and when Coverdale tells Priscilla that she had reminded him of Fuller, Priscilla asks, "How could I possibly make myself resemble this lady, merely by holding her letter in my hand?" Coverdale admits that "it would puzzle me to explain it" and then tries to deny that there is anything to explain by dismissing the letter's role in triggering his association of her with Fuller, insisting that "it was just a coincidence—nothing more" (3:51–52). Priscilla hands Coverdale the letter, but Coverdale does not tell us its contents. Hawthorne, however, just has. The letter that Priscilla clasps to her bosom reminds Coverdale of Fuller because Hawthorne, if we follow the logic of his self-directed pun, had had another character resembling Fuller place Fuller's "letter" on her breast. *The Scarlet Letter* itself had been written on one level as something of a "letter" to Fuller, but after 19 July 1850 only Hawthorne would be left to break its seal.

If in "Rappaccini's Daughter" and *The Scarlet Letter* Hawthorne had taken great care to conceal both his and Fuller's presence, he takes little such care in *The Blithedale Romance.* From the moment of its publication to the present, readers have detected the spirit of Fuller inhabiting Zenobia's character just as easily as they have identified a significant part of Hawthorne given voice in Miles Coverdale.[1] Surely Hawthorne knew they would. But perhaps he knew they would hear another Dimmesdale-like confession, which they would once again fail to really hear. Or perhaps, if they indeed heard this time, he no longer really cared as much as he had. An examination of the context surrounding the writing of *The Blithedale Romance* helps to explain why that last possibility merits serious consideration. Among other things, such an examination explains why, in Coverdale, Hawthorne is not so much writing about what he was in danger of becoming, had he remained a bachelor, but about what in fact he had become. It also explains why Zenobia's grave marks the site of Fuller's presence in Hawthorne's discontent and guilt.

On the day after finishing the "h-ll-fired story" of *The Scarlet Letter,* Hawthorne admitted to his friend Horatio Bridge that he was physically and mentally exhausted. His health, he claimed, had not been what it once was "for many years past," and he did not believe he could "long stand such a life of bodily inactivity and mental exertion" as he had "led for the last few months." He had hidden his concerns from Sophia, he admitted, and he instructed Bridge not to allude to the matter in future letters. The past year had exhausted Hawthorne, and just at the moment when he was to receive the general acclaim that had so long eluded him, at forty-five he was feeling decidedly middle-aged, his "lack of physical vigor and energy," he said, beginning to affect his mind. Were he "anywhere else" but Salem, he was confident, he should "at once be entirely another man" (16:312).

His problems, however, were deeper than exhaustion and place. Twenty-five years after graduating from college and dedicating himself to literature, he still had not fulfilled his artistic ambitions nor had he consistently been able through his literary work to support himself, much less his growing family. He felt himself a failure. When he received a collection of five hundred dollars from George Hillard and other, unnamed friends through the mail in January 1850—only days after submitting all but the last three chapters of *The Scarlet Letter* to Fields—he described in his letter of acknowledgment the tears that had risen to his eyes at the post office. In what Edwin Haviland Miller has termed the "unusual candor" with which he reveals "the exacting creed by which he lived—and punished himself," Hawthorne then expressed a deeper sense of shame and bitterness over his plight than humility and gratitude would seem to warrant.[2] "Ill success in life is really and justly a matter of shame. I am ashamed of it, and I ought to be. The fault of a failure is attributable—in a great degree, at least—to the man who fails. I should apply this truth in judging of other men; and it behooves me not to shun its point or edge in taking it home to my own heart. Nobody has a right to live in this world, unless he be strong and able, and applies his ability to good purpose" (16:309).

The only means of retaining his "self-respect" under the circumstances, he concluded, was to employ his shame as "an incitement" to his "utmost exertions" so that he would "not need their help again" (16:309). The first of his exertions, of course, was to bring Dimmesdale to the pulpit for the moment of his greatest professional success and then to the scaffold for his long-delayed exposure of hidden ruin and failure. He would not grant Dimmesdale the "right to live in this world," but he would Hester, for despite her self-defined failure to live up to her conception of the "destined prophetess," she would be "strong and able" enough not only to endure but to be faithful to her principles and her love.

Fields, of course, had big plans for the future exertions that an exhausted and despondent Hawthorne had promised, but first Hawthorne felt he must make a complete break with Salem, for which he now had "infinite contempt" (16:329), and find a secluded place to work. Before he was able to do that, however, he had to suffer another humiliating reminder of his past failures when he had to return Sophia and his children to her family in Boston to live for a month in the transition between the move from Salem to Lenox. He could not bring himself to join them, however.[3] Instead, he visited Bridge in Portsmouth and then, once back in Boston, he took temporary bachelor's quarters in a boarding house. The painful contrast of Bridge's prosperity with his own circumstances exacerbated his despondency. "Thou didst much amiss," he wrote Sophia, "to marry a husband who cannot keep thee like a lady, as Bridge does his wife. . . . Thou hast a hard lot in life; and so have I that witness it, and can do little or nothing to help thee" (16:333–34). Despite, or perhaps because of, his sense of failure as a husband, he seemed to enjoy the release provided by his temporary separation from family tensions. Away from wife and children in his boarding room, Hawthorne frequented Parker's Tavern, visited, drank, and dined with friends, attended a rowdy theatrical performance, and wrote detailed descriptions in his notebook of his experiences and observations (8:487–509), recording all with an expansiveness that Miller attributes to his sense of freedom from Sophia's "looking over his shoulder."[4] Hawthorne would later draw liberally from this experience in writing *The Blithedale Romance*—literally in his use of note-book descriptions and more figuratively in his characterization of Cover-dale's sense of failure and inadequacy when he retreats from communal and passionate engagement to the solitude and superficial relations of his bache-lor life.

By the last week of May, he had finally escaped to that "somewhere else" he had vowed in "The Custom-House" that he would find. Of all the options he explored—including homes near such close friends as Bridge and Long-fellow—he chose to move into the little red farmhouse in Lenox and make Caroline Sturgis Tappan, Fuller's closest friend, his landlady.[5] Because the house was not yet ready, Hawthorne and family spent the first two weeks as Caroline's houseguests, with Caroline even urging the Hawthornes to make that arrangement permanent.[6]

Less than a week before the Hawthornes arrived in Lenox, Fuller, with Ossoli and son, had boarded the *Elizabeth* to begin the voyage back to America that Fuller had long contemplated and Hawthorne anticipated. Caroline had been the first to whom Fuller had confided about her baby and her liaison with Ossoli, and throughout 1849 and early 1850 Fuller had writ-ten her frequently and intimately. As the person who had most likely been the first to inform the Hawthornes of Fuller's baby during Sophia's visit with her in early September 1849, Caroline would have informed the Hawthornes of the details of Fuller's last days in Rome, her brief exile in Rieti and in Perugia, and her longer and more recent exile in Florence. Given the then rather common practice of circulating personal letters among mutual, inti-mate friends, it is also possible that Caroline shared some of Fuller's letters with the Hawthornes. They would certainly have discussed Fuller's antici-pated reception back in New England, including the visit she had promised to make to Lenox, and her professional as well as personal prospects.[7]

Early during his stay with Caroline, Hawthorne fell victim for the second time in less than a year to what Sophia described as a "tolerable nervous fever" brought on because he was "so harassed in spirit" by "brain-work and disquiet." "His eyes," she wrote, "looked like two immense spheres of troubled light" and his face "wan & shadowy." Sophia seemed clearly aware that the illness was linked to a crisis of the spirit that had left him "not so vigorous, yet as in former days, before the last year began," but she believed he would revive and she would soon "see him as in Concord." Still troubled by the episode two months later, Sophia wrote again to her mother of the illness and expanded on the explanation that Hawthorne had encouraged, reporting that he "has not recovered his pristine vigor" because he thought that it was "*Salem* which he is dragging at his ankles still." The past year had been, she wrote, "the trying year of his life, as well as of mine—I have not yet found again all my wings—neither is his tread yet again elastic."[8] The death of his mother, the personal and financial turmoil arising from the Custom House firing, the shock of scandal surrounding Fuller, the fury with which he wrote *The Scarlet Letter,* the humiliation of having his friends gather a collection on his behalf, his rejection by and bitterness against Salem, his wife and their children's return to her family, his move to Lenox—no amount of success for *The Scarlet Letter* could quite undo the damage. If Hawthorne's explosive reaction eight years later to Mozier's gossip about Fuller and Ossoli is any indication, hearing intimate details of Fuller's life in Italy from Caroline and anticipating a confrontation with her and Ossoli in the coming weeks could only have intensified Hawthorne's anxiety. He had chosen, however, and quite deliberately, to position himself and his family beside the one mutual friend that Fuller had been most intimate with and that she had promised to visit on her return. Soon, in fact, he was to refer to the little red farmhouse as "the Scarlet Letter."[9]

Less than two months after the Hawthornes moved into that "Scarlet Letter," Fuller and Ossoli were swept off the decks of the disintegrating *Elizabeth* as numerous witnesses watched helplessly from the beach. Though many of the crew had managed to swim to shore holding on to floating wreckage, they later told of Fuller's consistent refusal to accept their aid and risk the swim if it meant separating from her baby or Ossoli. Just before Ossoli and then Fuller were washed overboard by waves, a sailor grabbed Angelo, now twenty-two months old, and attempted, unsuccessfully, to swim to shore with him.

We have no record of Hawthorne's immediate reaction to Fuller's death, but we do have, in Sophia's letters, some indication of the force of the blow. In a drama of grief appropriate to the news, Caroline, without saying a word, simply placed the newspaper article in Sophia's hands. In the same 1 August letter to her mother in which she recounted Hawthorne's distress over the past year and his recent illness, Sophia describes her reaction to the death of Fuller. "I dread to speak of Margaret," she begins, and then explains: "Oh, was ever anything so tragical, so dreary, so unspeakably agonizing as the image of Margaret upon that wreck, alone, sitting with her hands upon her knees and tempestuous waves breaking over her!" The image haunted her. "But I cannot dwell upon it," she wrote. She particularly regretted that Angelino could not at least have been saved, and alluding to the year of rumors about Fuller's liaison with Ossoli, she consoled herself, as Hawthorne certainly did not, that "if they were truly bound together, as they seemed to be, I am glad they died together."[10]

The image of Fuller "with her hands upon her knees and tempestuous waves breaking over her" came straight from dramatic *New-York Daily Tribune* eyewitness accounts of Fuller's final hours. On 23 July, the *Tribune* devoted page four to the first eyewitness accounts of the wreck and to a lengthy tribute to Fuller by Greeley, who asserted, flatly, that "America has produced no woman who in mental endowments and acquirements has surpassed Margaret Fuller." He then initiated the idea for the project that would result in Clarke, Channing, and Emerson's two-volume *Memoirs of Margaret Fuller Ossoli* (1852), and, I argue, for Hawthorne's *Blithedale Romance.* Lamenting that "one so radiantly lofty in intellect, so devoted to Human Liberty and Well-being, so ready to dare and to endure for the upraising of her sex and her race, should perish from among us and leave no memento less imperfect and casual than those we now have," Greeley called for her friends and relatives "promptly and acceptably" to prepare "a Memoir with a selection from her writings." On the following day, two additional articles, again taking up most of page four, provided far greater detail of Fuller's last hours. Both quoted survivors who described Fuller's refusal to accept help because of her determination not to separate from Ossoli or her baby. One witness claimed that "she had from the first expressed a willingness to live or die with them, but not to live without them." The other told of how Fuller and Ossoli had helped quiet a hysterical passenger and had encouraged her and others to reconcile "themselves to the idea of death," Ossoli leading the group in prayer, and then all sitting "down calmly to await the parting of the vessel." This survivor also told of how Fuller "steadily refused" to attempt to save herself or trust her baby to another. Her last words, the ship's cook reported, were, "I see nothing but death before me—I shall never reach the shore." Fuller's determination to die with Ossoli and her baby may have consoled Sophia and her vision of the nobility of self-negating sacrifice in love, but for others—and I argue that Hawthorne was reluctantly and bitterly among their number—Fuller's actions suggested that her experiences over the past year and her uncertain prospects on shore had weakened her will to live. Thirty-four years later, in fact, Thomas Wentworth Higginson would feel compelled to refute the persistence of this interpretation by calling into question the veracity of the eyewitness accounts, claiming, erroneously, that they had all come from the commanding officer, who had saved himself and allowed his passengers to die.[11]

Fuller's death was shocking, national news. From 23 through 31 July, the

New-York Daily Tribune and its sister paper the *New York Weekly Tribune* devoted eleven different articles to the tragedy. During that same period the *Boston Daily Evening Transcript* ran six articles, all based on *Tribune* accounts. From August through January, tributes appeared in the *Southern Literary Messenger, Harper's New Monthly Magazine, United States Magazine and Democratic Review, National Era, New York Freeman's Journal and Catholic Register, Literary World,* and *American Register and Magazine.*[12]

If Fuller's tragic death was of such interest to the readers of New York and Boston papers and national magazines, it would have been of even greater interest to the residents and summer visitors in the Berkshires. By moving to Lenox, Hawthorne had established himself within a virtual colony and summer resort for authors and artists, the famous 5 August 1850 picnic in which Hawthorne and Melville first met being but the most spectacular of many lesser literary encounters. In such a setting, Fuller's death, the mystery surrounding her relationship to Ossoli, and the controversy over the noble or the suicidal nature of the impulses that drove Fuller to refuse to attempt to save herself—all would have been topics of immense interest and discussion. Sophia, for instance, gives some indication of those discussions in her 1 August letter to her mother as she decides that based on the manner of their deaths Fuller and Ossoli must have been "truly bound together" and that it was therefore appropriate that "they died together." The letter also provides a glimpse of the interchanges between Fuller's friends, for Sophia reports to her mother on the contents of copies of Ellery Channing's letter and Thoreau's report to Emerson, copies made by Elizabeth Hoar, sent to Caroline, and shown to Sophia.[13]

Eight years later, recalling Fuller and her death, Hawthorne would write that "there never was such a tragedy as her whole story" (14:156), but in the summer of 1850 he left no written record of his immediate reaction. We do know, however, that it was not until late in August that he found the will and the strength to write again, and even then, not with enthusiasm or ease. In a curious phrase that intimates perhaps an unconscious perception of the origins of Hawthorne's muse, Sophia wrote on 1 August to her mother that Hawthorne had yet to write much because he lacked the vigor to "seize the skirts of ideas and pin them down for further investigation." Even his notebook entries that summer, as Mellow observes, were extraordinarily perfunctory except for his unusual interest in the family's hens.[14] In a passage suggestive of the tense marital politics that Herbert finds played out covertly in the Hawthornes' journals, in July, Hawthorne—having spent much of his first months in close quarters with Sophia and the children as they put the red farmhouse in order—links the "croaking" of a hen's maternal self-absorption with the futility of "human language."[15] In the "self-important gait; the side-way turn of her head, and cock of her eye, as she pries into one and another nook, croaking all the while," the hen, looking for a place to nest, seems to believe "that the egg in question is the most important thing that has been brought to pass since the world began." "Human language," Hawthorne muses bitterly and pointedly, "is but little better than the croak and cackle of fowls," and "sometimes not so adequate" (8:294). By mid-August, however, Hawthorne reported to Fields that he was once again wrestling with that language, forcing himself "every morning (much against my will)" to shut himself up "religiously" in his study. He found, however, that he much preferred "gazing at Monument Mountain" out the window than "at the infernal sheet of paper" in front of him (16:359).

For the next year Hawthorne tried to insure that those "infernal" sheets before him did not tell another "h-ll-fired story." Hawthorne's motives in turning away from the "shadows" of *The Scarlet Letter* to the "sunshine" of *The House of the Seven Gables* and *A Wonder-Book for Girls and Boys* and then returning to them again in *The Blithedale Romance* are complex. Hawthorne, of course, was from the beginning apologetic that in writing *The Scarlet Letter* he "found it impossible to relieve the shadows of the story with so much light as I would gladly have thrown in," but as the context of that statement in his letter to Fields reveals, his concern was centered on reader reception and sales, fearing that he would "weary very many people, and disgust some." He wanted to "kill the public outright," and he feared that *The Scarlet Letter* would fail unless "relieved" by the addition of "half a dozen shorter tales" (16:307). The success of *The Scarlet Letter* proved him wrong, of course, but it contributed to another problem. Though few explicitly accused him of self-portraiture in *The Scarlet Letter*, even his friends had begun to wonder how the Hawthorne they thought they knew could write such a dark tale of adultery. Hawthorne's friend and recent benefactor George Hillard put the matter to Hawthorne succinctly in a 28 March 1850 letter:

> You are, intellectually speaking, quite a puzzle to me. How comes it that with so thoroughly healthy an organization as you have, you have such a taste for the morbid anatomy of the human heart, and such knowledge of it, too? I should fancy from your books that you were burdened with some secret sorrow; that you had some blue chamber in your soul into which you hardly dared to enter yourself; but when I see you, you give me the impression of a man as healthy as Adam was in Paradise. For my own taste, I could wish that you would dwell more in the seen, and converse more with cheerful thoughts and lightsome images, and expand into a story the spirit of the Town-pump.

But while waiting for this, let me be thankful for the weird and sad strain which breathes from the "Scarlet Letter," which I read with most absorbing interest.[16]

Having already defended Hawthorne from her sister Elizabeth's assent to the allegation that in *The Scarlet Letter* Hawthorne had "purified himself by casting out a legion of devils," Sophia found that the literary set in the Berkshires had already typed Hawthorne, in Cornelius Mathews's epithet, as "Mr. Noble Melancholy." Even with her mother she found it necessary to counter that characterization. In a 4 September 1850 letter, she seemed amazed at "how many people insist that Mr. Hawthorne is gloomy, since he is *not*." She was willing to admit that "he is pensive, perhaps—as all contemplative people must be—especially when as in him 'a great heart is the household fire of a grand intellect' (to quote his own words)," but she was insistent that his works were anything but autobiographical in origin: "He has always seemed to me, in his remote moods, like a stray Seraph, who had experienced in his own life no evil; but by the intuition of a divine intellect saw and sorrowed over all evil." His life, she assures her mother, has been absolutely "pure from the smallest taint of earthliness," and thus, his knowledge "of crime . . . is the best proof to me of the absurdity of the prevalent idea that it is necessary to go through the fiery ordeal of sin to become wise and good," a doctrine that Sophia then, as Hilda later, characterizes as a "blasphemy and the unpardonable sin" because "it is really adjuring God's voice within."[17] As far as Sophia was concerned, Hawthorne might as well have been referring to himself when he closed *The Scarlet Letter* with a description of the "angel and apostle" of "sacred love."

Perhaps Hawthorne knew by this time that nothing he could do would disabuse Sophia of such unswerving deification; nevertheless, it is impossible to calculate the burden such expectations placed on him, just as it is equally impossible to calculate the burden Sophia herself felt in sustaining her incarnation as Hawthorne's "Dove."[18] During the next year, learning in the early fall that he would become the father of a third child, Hawthorne would dutifully try to shoulder that burden as a husband and as a writer.

Fuller's death, I believe, reinforced his desire to turn from the "shadows" of "Rappaccini's Daughter" and *The Scarlet Letter*. If he wrote both works with Fuller in mind not only as his subject but also as a privately and covertly addressed reader, her death (as Emerson immediately acknowledged of himself) had robbed him of his "audience."[19] By turning away from the riddling "shadows" of Beatrice and Hester toward the simple "sunshine" of Phoebe's redemptive domesticity and the radical Holgrave's humble acquiescence to her power, Hawthorne set out to prove, as he had implicitly promised Hillard, that he was "strong and able" enough to apply "his ability to good purpose" (16:309), the good purpose, that is, of meeting the expectations of another audience—the audience literally closest to him (Sophia, who instantly pronounced *The House of the Seven Gables* as better than *The Scarlet Letter* and secured Hawthorne's immediate assent [16:386]), to that next closest (such friends as Hillard), and to the general reading public. He could also silence growing speculations about some "blue chamber" in his "soul." As he insistently claimed, if the "sunshine" of *The House of the Seven Gables* made it a better book than *The Scarlet Letter,* that was because it was "a more natural and healthy product" of his mind (16:421), the work of the *real* Hawthorne, he seemed to say. Herman Melville's remarkable tribute in "Hawthorne and His Mosses" to the "dark" Hawthorne complicated matters considerably. Though both Sophia and Hawthorne were immensely flattered by Melville's article, its appearance during the first weeks of Hawthorne's writing of *The House of the Seven Gables* would have served not only to confirm Hawthorne's concern about the growing perception of his character and work but also to stimulate his efforts to prove himself a man and a writer of "sunshine" as well as "shadows."

Hawthorne's claim that *The House of the Seven Gables* was a "more natural" product of his mind is belied by the great difficulty he reported having in its writing. Secluding himself "religiously," as he termed it with a happy precision, he wrote to Fields in early November (the month he had originally promised to complete it) that though he worked with great diligence he worked slowly. Hawthorne's claims that *The House of the Seven Gables,* in contrast to *The Scarlet Letter,* required "more care and thought" and that he had to "wait oftener for a mood" suggest that when he characterized in the same letter "writing a romance" to "careering on the utmost verge of a precipitous absurdity," he was locating the source of his resistance in his twin fears of "tumbling over" again into the "shadows" and of appearing "absurd" in the determined efforts he would have to make to avoid doing that (16:371). The "one tone" of *The Scarlet Letter* that made it easier for him, he said, "to get" his "pitch" and "go on interminably" was the "one tone" of an unconflicted, unforced purpose. Four weeks later, the book still not finished, he addressed the problem explicitly. "It darkens damnably towards the close," he wrote to Fields, "but I shall try hard to pour some setting sunshine over it" (16:376). Less than two weeks later, his difficulty in forcing the sun to shine over his tale is clearly implied in his next letter to Fields: "I have been in a Slough of Despond, for some days past—having written so fiercely that I came to a stand still." He was "bewildered," not knowing "what to do next," determined to be "quiet" until he did (16:378). Even after he had apparently finished the book in mid-January and had begun reading it to Sophia, he spent another ten days revising the concluding chapters before reading them to Sophia.[20] If the conclusion has seemed forced to generations of later readers, Sophia probably spoke for many readers of her time who found Holgrave's disavowal of radical thought and his acquiescence to Phoebe's redemptively domestic and unquestioning love a conclusion in which "the flowers of Paradise scattered over all the dark places, the sweet wall-flower scent of Phoebe's character," an ending of "unspeakable grace and beauty" that cast "upon the sterner tragedy of the commencement an ethereal light, and a dear home-loveliness and satisfaction."[21]

Even as Hawthorne struggled to force himself to "pour . . . some sunshine" over his tribute to Sophia in the character of Phoebe, he had already begun to make his appeal to the audience that he hoped to address, and placate, in *The House of the Seven Gables.* The release in November of a compilation of his previously published historical sketches for children in *True Stories from History and Biography* initiated his effort to answer questions generated by *The Scarlet Letter* about his character.[22] The success of *True Stories* confirmed at least the commercial value of Hawthorne's efforts and encouraged him to write the even more successful *Wonder-Book for Girls and Boys* immediately after *The House of the Seven Gables.* By April 1851 *True Stories* had been issued twice, with a total press run of 4,500 copies, only 500 fewer than *The Scarlet Letter* over its first six months. *The House of the Seven Gables* would exceed *The Scarlet Letter,* with 6,710 copies printed by the end of six months, 810 more copies than had been printed of *The Scarlet Letter* by August 1851, and *A Wonder-Book* would reach 4,667 copies less than two months after its release in November 1851. By comparison, *Twice-Told Tales,* released in March 1851 in a third edition with a preface by Hawthorne, would have a single press run of only 2,000 copies. Competing unsuccessfully in December 1851 with his own just-released *Wonder-Book,* Hawthorne's collection of previously uncollected tales, *The Snow-Image,* would have a first printing of only 2,425 copies, another run of 1,000 copies not needed until a full twelve months later.[23]

By the end of 1851, the message seemed clear. For a forty-seven-year-old writer who had had difficulty supporting his wife and two children and who had just fathered his third child, "dear home loveliness and satisfaction" could be counted on to pay—in praise at home and cash in the bank. These two motives for writing were indeed strong for Hawthorne, but they took second and third place, respectively, to an even greater motive. "The only sensible ends of literature," Hawthorne wrote Bridge as *The House of the Seven Gables* was being printed, "are, first, the pleasurable toil of writing, secondly, the gratification of one's family and friends, and lastly the solid cash" (16:407). As Hawthorne's "Slough of Despond" in completing *The House of the Seven Gables* and as other evidence throughout 1851 suggest, Hawthorne's attempts to satisfy the second and third "ends" had taken some of the pleasure out of the toil. In that same letter to Bridge, Hawthorne repeated what would come to seem a decidedly defensive assertion that in his opinion his new romance was "better" than *The Scarlet Letter* and at least "portions of it are as good as anything that I can hope to write." In contemplating the success of the work, however, he laments "how slowly" he has "made . . . [his] way in life" and "how much is still to be done," yet he bitterly contemplates the "bubble Reputation" he anticipates achieving, for he asserts that he will "not be one whit the happier if mine were world-wide and time-long, than I was when nobody but yourself had faith in me" (16:407). Throughout 1851 and early 1852, Hawthorne repeatedly took stock of his life and his career, and his nostalgia for a lost past betrayed his present unhappiness.

In his preface to the third edition of *Twice-Told Tales,* which was published in the same month he wrote his letter to Bridge, Hawthorne looks back longingly on his early obscurity when he had no "reasonable prospect of reputation or profit" and wrote for "nothing but the pleasure itself of composition." But then, he notes, with barely concealed bitterness, though that was "an enjoyment not at all amiss in its way, and perhaps essential to the merit of the work in hand," it did not satisfy the other two "ends" of writing. It could not "keep the chill out of a writer's heart, or the numbness out of his fingers" (9:3). Venturing to become his own critic and identifying the very weaknesses in the very bodily terms Fuller had first taught him to see in his work, Hawthorne laments that "instead of passion, there is sentiment," that "even in what purport to be pictures of actual life, we have allegory, not always so warmly dressed in its habiliments of flesh and blood." In a word, his work then suffered from "tameness" (9:5). He is, of course, right if those early tales are contrasted with such later works as "The Birth-mark," "Rappaccini's Daughter," or *The Scarlet Letter.* But the same could be said of *The House of the Seven Gables.* Written during or immediately after forcing "sunshine" into the conclusion of his latest romance, Hawthorne's concern with

the "tameness," the predominance of "sentiment" over "passion" in his earlier works intimates his present concerns about the direction his writing
was taking.

Those concerns are given greater voice nine months later in the preface
to the December 1851 publication of *The Snow-Image.* Written as a letter to
Bridge, the preface is a nostalgic tribute to the gloriousness of their youthful
friendship, to Bridge's early and critical faith in his work, and to his earlier
work as a writer. Looking backward, comparing his past talent with his present efforts, Hawthorne can find little evidence of progress to console the
labors of his middle age. These tales, he says, "come so nearly up to the
standard of the best that I can achieve now" that "the ripened autumnal fruit
tastes but little better than the early windfalls." Hawthorne's is the voice that
he will give to Coverdale beginning the very month in which this preface is
published: "It would, indeed, be mortifying to believe that the summertime
of life has passed away, without any greater progress and improvement than
is indicated here" (11:6). With his gaze fixed on that lost summer, Hawthorne consoles himself that "in youth, men are apt to write more wisely
than they really know or feel, and the remainder of life may be not idly spent
in realizing and convincing themselves of the wisdom which they uttered
long ago" (11:6). At the end of his labors on *The House of the Seven Gables,* he
wrote to his sister Elizabeth that "except for necessity" he now hated "the
thought of writing" (16:402). At the end of *A Wonder-Book,* he admitted to
his other sister, Louisa, that he had come to "abominate the sight" of a pen
(16:453). For all his exertions, he could please family and friends, he could
produce the ready cash, but he could no longer find pleasure in the toil.

Evidence also suggests that at least by the summer of 1851 the Hawthorne household in Lenox fell short of the "home loveliness" that he celebrated with his pen. The "covert sexual politics" that Herbert finds at the
heart of the Hawthorne household in 1852 journal entries is clearly evident
in 1851.[24] When Hawthorne took Una with him on a two-day visit to Melville's in mid-March, for instance, Sophia, seven months pregnant, used
much of her time alone to write a nine-page description of the household
frustrations and emotional misery she endured in Hawthorne's absence.[25]
She concludes her litany of unhappiness with one of those "groveling protestations of absolute devotion" that Herbert has argued "conceal an unvanquished will to power," a "disembodied and invisible womanly rage that provokes a disabling masculine guilt." "How thou art adored," she concludes.
"Was ever one so loved? I love thee 725 millions of times more than I ever
did at this moment."[26]

When Sophia took Una and two-month-old Rose for a two-week stay with her parents in July, Hawthorne reciprocated. Writing a special journal section entitled "Twenty Days of Julian & Little Bunny By Papa" for Sophia to read on her return (8:436–86), Hawthorne recounts with unconcealed irritation his sufferings at the hands of little Julian, who plagued him more than a "mortal father ought to endure," Hawthorne's most insistent complaint being that Julian never left his side and was "continually thrusting his word between every sentence of all my reading, and smashing every attempt at reflection into a thousand fragments" (8:454). Of "little bunny," Hawthorne admits to being "strongly tempted of the Evil One to murder him privately" or have his neighbor "drown him" (8:437). Hawthorne directed the full fury of his frustration, however, at the location, not the inhabitants, of their home in Lenox (8:439–40).

Interestingly, the one event during Sophia's absence that he describes as being thoroughly pleasant was a visit by an admirer of his works—a "rather young, comely" Quaker lady with "a pleasant smile" and "eyes that readily responded to one's thought so that it was not difficult to talk with her." Praising her for having "a singular, but yet a gentle freedom in expressing her own opinions;—an entire absence of affectation," Hawthorne concludes that hers was "the only pleasant visit I ever experienced, in my capacity as an author" (8:456–57).[27] Even more interesting and revelatory, however, is Hawthorne's account of his suppressed admiration for three women on horseback that he and Julian encountered on a walk:

> On our way home, we met three ladies on horseback, attended by a gentleman; and the little man asked me whether I thought the ladies pretty, and said that he did not. They really were rather pretty, in my opinion; but I suspect that their appearance on horseback did not suit his taste; and I agree with him that a woman is [a] monstrous and disagreeable spectacle, in such an attitude. But the old boy is very critical in matters of beauty; although I think that the real grounds of his censures usually lies in some wrong done to his sense of fitness and propriety. But this sense is sometimes conventional with him. For instance, he denied that the Quaker lady, who called on me, was pretty; and it turned out that he did not like the unaccustomed fashion of her dress, and her thees and thous. (8:482)

Julian, it seems, changed little between 1851 and 1884. In part, the passage is an indirect confession of his suppressed dissent with Sophia's conventionality—the source of little Julian's rigid sense of female propriety and the very conventionality he had so recently toiled to celebrate in Phoebe. Elusive and self-conflicted, Hawthorne at once both expresses his admiration for unconventional women, his concealment of that admiration, his pro forma assent to a conventional condemnation of that admiration, and his condemnation of that very conventionality. The pattern of revelation and suppression of these self-conflicted attitudes seems to lie at the heart of his great fictions.

As he was expected to do, however, Hawthorne adopted Sophia's strategy and dismissed his frustrations in a hymn of thanksgiving whose rhetorical excess suggests the possibility of its being something of a parody. Julian is "a sweet and lovely little boy" who is "worthy of all the love that I am capable of giving him": "Thank God! God bless him! God bless Phoebe for giving him to me! God bless her as the best wife and mother in the world! God bless Una, whom I long to see again! God bless little Rosebud! God bless me, for Phoebe's and all their sakes! No other man has so good a wife; nobody has better children. Would I were worthier of her and them!" (8:472–73).

The fatherly disaffections of a middle-aged impatience that Hawthorne attempts to dissolve here had been compounded by the birth in May of his third child, Rose. For the first time, he witnessed childbirth, forced to assist his father-in-law during the unexpected delivery in the middle of the night. Sophia deeply regretted that, for she had meant that he "should never be present at such a time."[28] The fastidious Hawthorne's idealization of Sophia as his Dove could only have reeled under the shock of the biological reality of childbirth, as Sophia knew. The birth of Rose during Hawthorne's forty-seventh year not only served to increase his awareness of the perverse effort required to sustain his idealization of the actual and his anxieties about age and finances but also may have altered, if not ended, Hawthorne and Sophia's sexual relationship. Sophia's purported statement to her sister Elizabeth that "Mr. Hawthorne's passions were under his feet" and that they had carefully planned the births of their children has led Miller to conclude that after Rose's birth Hawthorne either controlled his sexual desire or employed contemporary birth control devices.[29] Herbert, however, bluntly and perhaps rashly concludes that "the Hawthornes . . . discontinued sexual intercourse after the birth of Rose."[30] Short of a direct admission, which does not exist, we can never know. We do know, however, that despite the Hawthornes' apparently healthy sexual life during their early Old Manse days Sophia once claimed that Hawthorne "hated to be touched more than any one I ever knew," that after the birth of Una the Hawthornes slept in separate beds for six months, and that Julian slept with Sophia for his first two years.[31] After the birth of Rose, Sophia wrote to Elizabeth, just before returning home to her parents, that during the three months of her "confinement," she and Hawthorne had had a "complete separation" and that "when I was able to be down stairs, still he was separated this time," leading her to observe, strangely, that "he has but just stepped over the threshold of a hermitage—He is but just not a hermit still."[32] The separation that Sophia wrote of in early July would be extended, of course, throughout much of the remaining summer when she left Hawthorne with Julian on 28 July to visit West Newton.

Three days after the first anniversary of Fuller's death and a week before Sophia left Hawthorne a bachelor and baby-sitter for three weeks, Hawthorne announced to Fields that if his next work were a romance he meant "to put an extra touch of the devil into it." Thinking of himself, I suspect, more than his readers, he explained that he doubted "whether the public will stand two quiet books in succession, without my losing ground" (16:462). Hawthorne's concerns about his "quiet books" reflect his concerns about his life. Almost three months before his letter to Fields and shortly before the birth of Rose, Hawthorne had written Longfellow that despite being "comfortable" in Lenox and "as happy as mortal can be," he found that "sometimes my soul gets into a ferment, as it were, and becomes troublous and bubblous with too much peace and rest" (16:431). Two days after his letter to Fields, he revealed to William Pike what he had not revealed to Fields. "To put the extra touch of the devil" back into his works, he planned to "take the Community for a subject" and write about his "experiences and observations at Brook Farm" (16:465).

Immediately after Fuller's death, Hawthorne had turned from "the blue chamber" in his soul that had created a Hester and had dutifully attempted to embrace in his life and in his work the "sunshine" of a Phoebe. A year had passed, however, and as Hawthorne found it more and more difficult to suppress middle-aged discontent with his life and his work, he began to look backward—not just to his summer at Brook Farm but to what he would call in his preface to *The Snow-Image* more generally as "the summertime of life" that had "passed away" (11:6). He would stage that "summertime" at Brook Farm in 1841, but in the "theatre" of his mind he would be reenacting other summers, primarily the summer of 1844 at Concord, the summer seven years gone, the same years that Coverdale marks cryptically in the novel as the "nearly seven years of worldly life" that it had "taken" him to "hive up the bitter honey" of advice that he gives to Priscilla (3:76). That advice, significantly, had been to "let the future go" and "as for the present moment" not to expect to see in the "innermost, holiest niche" of the one she loved her "own likeness" but "a dusty image, thrust aside into a corner, and by-

and-by to be flung out-of-doors, where any foot may trample upon it" (3:76). It is the advice of a lover betrayed by abandonment, by time, or by the success of a rival.

Almost precisely at the moment that Hawthorne decided to write of his past, he announced that he could no longer endure his present. He directed his discontent, however, at the site of his home rather than at the life that he led in it. Of Lenox and its weather, he wrote in his journal "I detest it! I detest it!! I detest it!!! I hate Berkshire with my whole soul, and would joyfully see its mountains laid flat!" (8:439). As Hawthorne over the summer and fall contemplated his new romance, he first longed to return to a home by the sea.[33] He then became increasingly determined to return bodily to the place that had become the private theater of his mind. It was the place where he had once come closest to finding an Eden in marriage and in community with friends, the place where he now wished to restage in his art and then in his life his lost past—not Brook Farm, but Concord.

Hawthorne's old friend from Concord, Ellery Channing, recognized, whether he was aware of it or not, the sources of Hawthorne's longing to return to Concord. When Ellery journeyed from Concord in October 1851 to visit with his old flame, Caroline, and his friend, Hawthorne, he recorded in a 30 October 1851 letter to his wife, Ellen Fuller Channing, that Hawthorne thought "a good deal of coming to Concord, and possibly . . . buy-[ing] a place," a prospect that Ellery "would not encourage" because "he always . . . finds fault with the people among whom he settles." Ellery was probably referring to the Hawthornes' now strained relations with the Tappans, but he may have been just as concerned as Hawthorne was over the alterations he perceived in his old friend. Hawthorne "seems older, & I think he has suffered much living in this place."[34] He explained: "His ways not the ways of the world have attracted the attention of the people; his habit of not calling on people, & his having written some books have made him a lion. I do not know that he has felt this, but I think he has felt his lack of society." For Hawthorne to seclude himself in the little red farmhouse with Sophia and his three children seemed, to Ellery at least, a miserable existence: "I should think Sophia could not realize his ideal at all. She is by no means prepossessing and has not added to her beauty by time. And she has none of the means whereby elegance & refinement may be shed over the humblest apartment. Her children brought up in the worst way for visitors, by themselves, & never having been to school, have of course nothing but bad manners. They break in when not required, & are not in fact either handsome or attractive. But how could the parents help this." Ellery concluded sadly that he had "formed a very different opinion of the H's this visit from any I ever had before, and H. has greatly altered."[35]

In late November, Hawthorne made his long-contemplated move. For the winter, he and his family would occupy Horace and Mary Peabody Mann's home in West Newton while his brother-in-law fulfilled his congressional duties in Washington and Hawthorne began looking, as early as December, for a home to buy in Concord.[36] Dependent again on his wife's family for a temporary family haven, looking for a way to return to Concord, Hawthorne would immediately start, finally, his long promised return to "the Community." He would begin *The Blithedale Romance* in December, finish it in May, and return to Concord in early June.

Published in the United States just five days before the second anniversary of Fuller's death, *The Blithedale Romance* would appear four months after the publication of Emerson, Clarke, and Channing's *Memoirs of Margaret Fuller Ossoli*. Written by intimate friends, both books would pay homage to their memories of Fuller's remarkable impact on their lives. The *Memoirs* attempted through personal reminiscence, biography, and highly edited selections from Fuller's letters, journals, and published writings to meet the challenge first articulated by Greeley—to avoid "the misfortune" of having Fuller's memory perish by compiling "a selection from her writings" that "promptly and acceptably embodied" her "thoughts," while recognizing that "the best" of Fuller's "intellect and character cannot be obtained from her writings alone." Attempting to fix Fuller as a historical subject, the *Memoirs* would be immediately assailed as a historical fiction. One reviewer wrote that each of the editors "turns Miss Fuller round and round until he gets her in certain lights familiar or propitious to himself" and thus "you are provoked by the feeling that it is owing to an act of will, or of discretion, on the part of the biographers that you are not getting the actual and substantial life of the woman."[37] For Hawthorne, however, Fuller's life and character and his own unshakable fascination with her had long been a "riddle," a "fiction," whose meaning in his own most intimate history he would once again attempt to locate in the interpretative representations of romance.[38] For Fuller, life was art, and for Hawthorne, art provided the only means by which he could safely and adequately represent her life, and his life.[39] At its deepest biographical level, Hawthorne's representation of Fuller's life in Zenobia is autobiographical, but at its surface, his reincarnation of Fuller's character in Zenobia was so evident and so successful in capturing a passionate and radical vitality missing in the *Memoirs* that one earlier reviewer recommended "the study of Zenobia" as "an excellent introduction to the study" of Fuller, justifying the recommendation, in perhaps an implicit allusion to the *Memoirs,* by noting with an unwittingly prescient insight that "there are problems both in biography and in history which imagination only can solve."[40]

Hawthorne's motives in choosing to write about Fuller and his past were primarily motivated by his discontent with his life and his career, but other important factors weighed in that decision. For one, in writing so transparently of Fuller in the character of Zenobia, he knew that part of that "extra touch of the devil" that would make this book decidedly "unquiet" would be the notoriety it would attract. Fuller's preeminence as an advocate for women's rights, her heroic defense of the Italian revolution, the scandal surrounding her liaison with Ossoli and the legitimacy of her child, the sensational coverage of her tragic death, and importantly, the imminent publication of the *Memoirs* by Emerson and friends—all would work to attract a curious public to a work of "autobiographical" fiction whose most vital character would be clearly, but still uncertainly, modeled after Fuller. Hawthorne, who had read in the spring Dickens's autobiographical representation of his youth in the first-person narrative *David Copperfield,* would read *Moby-Dick* in November and begin in December his own experiment in risking a first-person narrative.

Literary history, of course, has long been fascinated with the extraordinary impact Hawthorne had on Melville, so much so, in fact, that other dimensions of Hawthorne's life at Lenox have been overshadowed by Melville's presence. Generally overlooked as well is Melville's literary influence on Hawthorne. While this is not the place to explore that influence, I venture to suggest that though Hawthorne began in the fall of 1850 to move away from the "blackness" that Melville found in his fiction and sought authorization for in his own works, Melville's personal intensity and the extraordinary passion with which he transformed and imbued his revision of his whale novel into *Moby-Dick* served to aggravate Hawthorne's discontent with the use he had recently made of his talent to redeem through justification a domesticity that distressed him. Hawthorne may have provided us an image of that creative discontent and its relationship to his life in his portrayal of Coverdale reading: "My book was of the dullest, yet had a sort of sluggish flow, like that of a stream in which your boat is as often aground as afloat. Had there been a more impetuous rush, a more absorbing passion of the narrative, I should the sooner have struggled out of its uneasy current, and have given myself up to the swell and subsidence of my thoughts. But, as it was, the torpid life of the book served as an unobtrusive accompaniment to the life within me and about me" (3:147).[41] On the boat of a book, desiring the passion of an "impetuous rush" and the "swell ... of my thoughts" but admitting that the torpidity of his life finds its reflection in his book, Coverdale, as his imagery suggests, longs for a book—and a life—that will absorb him in its passionate intensity, a book like *The Scarlet Letter,* or a book like the one Hawthorne had just read, *Moby-Dick.* We, however, will read that book by listening to his voice tell us of that moment in his life when he became incapable of writing it.

CHAPTER SEVEN

Dreaming the "Same Dream Twice"

The Ghost Story of *The Blithedale Romance*

> By long brooding over our recollections, we subtilize them
> into something akin to imaginary stuff, and hardly capable
> of being distinguished from it.
>
> COVERDALE IN *The Blithedale Romance*

> I should think it a poor and meagre nature, that is capable
> of but one set of forms, and must convert all the past into
> a dream, merely because the present happens to be unlike
> it. Why should we be content with our homely life of a few
> months past, to the exclusion of all other modes?
>
> ZENOBIA TO COVERDALE IN *The Blithedale Romance*

The Blithedale Romance is the tale of an "unquiet heart" haunted by dreams of a lost past (3:206). It is a tale of nostalgia and of mourning told by a middle-aged man who would "rather look backward ten times, than forward once," who would rather, as Priscilla cannot quite understand, "dream the same dream twice." He has survived, if Zenobia has not. He will stand by her grave and tell us all. But he will be no Ishmael, no exuberant spirit risking all to sail into the passionately sublime in chase of that "grand hooded phantom." And that, as he would be the first to admit, is precisely his problem. The future, he explains, holds only the certainty "that the good we aim at will not be attained," and even if it is it will be "something else . . . never dreamed of," something we "did not particularly want" (3:75–76). In *Blithedale*, Hawthorne, through Coverdale, will turn from the sunshine promised by the future and probe in the shadows of memory for the good that he aimed at and attained only to find that it was not what he had dreamed of. Conceived on the first anniversary of Fuller's death, written as Hawthorne negotiated a return to Concord, and completed just days before he moved back, *Blithedale* translates into romance Hawthorne's dream of the same dream twice, his attempt to recover and understand that moment in his past when the Community of Sophia, Fuller, and even Emerson seemed for a brief moment as close to an Eden as he would ever know.

Hawthorne's friend William Pike, the first to whom Hawthorne had confided his plans to write about the Community, recognized that Hawthorne in *Blithedale* was revisiting an old dream, attempting to recapture what he had lost in *The House of the Seven Gables*. In a letter to Hawthorne written just four days after the U.S. publication of *Blithedale,* Pike noted appreciatively that *Blithedale* was "more like 'The Scarlet Letter' than 'The House of Seven Gables,'" for in both, "you probe deeply,—you go down among the moody silences of the heart, and open those depths whence come motives that give complexion to actions, and make in men what are called states of mind; being conditions of mind which cannot be removed either by our own reasoning or by the reasoning of others." Pike finds *Blithedale,* like *The Scarlet Letter,* to be most penetrating as a revelation of "that class of actions and manifestations in men so inexplicable"—above all of love and "the silent, unseen, internal elements which first set the machinery in motion, which works out results so strange to those who penetrate only to a certain depth in the soul." What Pike seems to recognize about *Blithedale* is that Hawthorne is returning from the love story of *The House of the Seven Gables* to the love story of *The Scarlet Letter.* Pike was too good a friend, however, to probe Hawthorne for the origins of his power to penetrate what Pike termed "the deepest, profoundest" of "the inmost of all the emotions" once he had turned away, as Hollingsworth did not, from the love of and for a Sophia-like Phoebe and returned, in a Zenobia, to another Hester.[1]

Blithedale is a love story mourning both a love lost and a love attained.[2] In his characteristic way, Hawthorne tried to tell us this. His experiences at Brook Farm are indeed "altogether incidental to the main purpose of this Romance." Brook Farm is but the "theatre . . . where the creatures of his brain may play their phantasmagorical antics, without exposing them to too close a comparison with the actual events of real lives" (3:1). Hawthorne meant this more literally than he knew his readers would take it. Instead of choosing an actual place and publicly known experience in his past and peopling it with fictional characters, as he only seems to intend to say, he means exactly what he says. Brook Farm is the fiction, the place where he hopes that "the creatures of his brain" may be safe from being exposed "to too close a comparison" with the very "actual events of real lives" on which his mental drama is based—the recollections that he, like Coverdale, has been so "long brooding over" that he has "subtilize[d] them into something akin to imaginary stuff, and hardly capable of being distinguished from it" (3:104–5).

With Coverdale, Hawthorne represents the impossibility of ever knowing at what point the "Actual" and the "Imaginary" merge, at what point, in effect, life becomes memory's romance, or memory's romance a life. The elusiveness of event, much less meaning, that pervades the dreamlike narrative of *Blithedale* appropriately represents Hawthorne's own confrontation with the meaning of his memories and the hold that they had come to have over his life.[3] As memory returns to the past and transforms the Actual into the Imaginary, so Hawthorne chose in this fiction to veil the origins of the Imaginary in the Actual by returning to his literary past and resurrecting from "Writings of Aubépine" and "Rappaccini's Daughter" the figure of the translator as the medium through whom he will transform the romance of recollected experience into the romance of public art. Miles Coverdale— the name itself suggests the strategy.[4] It identifies him as a contemporary reincarnation of the great translator of another time, and it enacts, through approximation of both sound and meaning, the translation from the seventeenth to the nineteenth century, from one romance to another, of his literary ancestor, Arthur Dimmesdale—one "dimming," the other "covering," the same "dale" to which Hawthorne returns. As a translator, Coverdale both reveals and "covers" meaning through the inevitable distortions of translation. Transforming the original text of "actual events in real lives" in Hawthorne's experience, Coverdale creates a text that becomes in the end his own. He performs in the romance what memory has already performed in Hawthorne's mind. Coverdale's self-consciously unreliable, reconstructed recollections are Hawthorne's own translation of the workings of a mind haunted by its desire to distinguish between the Actual and the Imaginary that compose the fictions of perception and memory. Hawthorne's problem, as Coverdale states it, is this:

> It is not, I apprehend, a healthy kind of mental occupation, to devote ourselves too exclusively to the study of individual men and women. If the person under examination be one's self, the result is pretty certain to be diseased action of the heart, almost before we can snatch a second glance. Or, if we take the freedom to put a friend under our microscope, we thereby insulate

him from many of his true relations, magnify his peculiarities, inevitably tear him into parts, and, of course, patch him very clumsily together again. What wonder, then, should we be frightened by the aspect of the monster, which, after all—though we can point to every feature of his deformity in the real personage—may be said to have been created mainly by ourselves! (3:69)

The "monsters" of the mind are the "ghosts" that Hawthorne referred to in "The Custom-House." In the firelight and moon glow of romance, however, they may be reanimated in the mirror of Hawthorne's reimagining and safely confronted. There their spirits do as Hawthorne bids, and there they may be exorcised through the power of a mesmeric art.

The ghost that most haunts Hawthorne is the ghost that haunts Hollingsworth, the memory of Zenobia whose "vindictive shadow dogged the side where Priscilla was not" (3:243). "Our souls, after all, are not our own," Coverdale admits. "We convey a property in them to those with whom we associate, but to what extent can never be known, until we feel the tug, the agony, of our abortive effort to resume an exclusive sway over ourselves" (3:194). Through Coverdale, Hawthorne attempts in the telling of this tale to reclaim an exclusive sway over himself, describing his own abortive effort to exorcise Zenobia's "ghost" and "the spectral throng, so apt to steal out of an unquiet heart" (3:206). In a tale within this tale, Hawthorne allows that ghost to steal out of his own unquiet heart and speak, translating into his text the voice of the ghost of Fuller, imagining her response to his obsessive desire to unveil the mystery of a life that now lives only in memory, only in legend.

"Zenobia's Legend" serves as a counternarrative to *Blithedale*, illuminating through mimesis the origins of Hawthorne's purposes and methods even as it judges and condemns them. It is presented, in fact, as such. During an evening in which the characters of *Blithedale* have attempted to entertain themselves by pretending in *"tableaux vivants"* to act out the lives of characters in the literature that they have been reading, Zenobia interrupts the charade with a comment that could be read as a self-reflective expression of Hawthorne's own anxieties. "I am getting weary of this," she says. "Our own features, and our own figures and airs, show a little too intrusively through all the characters we assume. We have so much familiarity with one another's realities, that we cannot remove ourselves, at pleasure, into an imaginary sphere" (3:106–7). Zenobia then shows them how to remove themselves into the imaginary by proceeding to renarrate the very tale that Hawthorne, through Coverdale, has been telling in *Blithedale*. In "The Silvery Veil," her version of Coverdale's "Veiled Lady," real people who have been re-created as characters in Hawthorne's *Blithedale* will themselves be transformed into characters in Zenobia's allegory of Coverdale's translation of Hawthorne's romance of memory and desire. It is "not exactly a ghost-story," Zenobia admits, "but something so nearly like it that you shall hardly tell the difference" (3:107).

Hawthorne, through Coverdale, literally translates Fuller's voice into this countertale, which he in turn appropriates and renames in his own retelling, "The Silvery Veil" becoming his "Zenobia's Legend," this "ghost story" of her "ghost story" of his own tale. As Fuller herself often complained and as her friends sometimes too readily assented, Fuller's electric power of voice and gesture rarely retained its full force when committed to the written word.[5] Zenobia—not her "real" name, Coverdale tells us, even at Blithedale, and certainly not in *Blithedale*—also "had the gift of telling a fanciful little story, off hand, in a way that made it greatly more effective, than it was usually found to be, when she afterwards elaborated the same production with her pen" (3:107). In Coverdale's attempt to account for the power of Zenobia's speech, Hawthorne has Coverdale attribute to Zenobia conversational mannerisms idiosyncratic to Fuller and, in an explicit intertextual gesture toward his own past metaphors, suggests her identity as the original of Beatrice: "Zenobia told it, wildly and rapidly, hesitating at no extravagance, and dashing at absurdities which I am too timorous to repeat—giving it the varied emphasis of her inimitable voice, and the pictorial illustration of her mobile face, while, through it all, we caught the freshest aroma of the thoughts, as they came bubbling out of her mind" (3:107). Beatrice's voice— "aromatic," "bubbling"—once again captivates a Giovanni turned Coverdale. The "extravagance" and "absurdities" of Zenobia's tale of a man confronting the mystery of a woman whose face will reflect his own heart and be his fate, of a man betraying himself and womanhood by his obsessive desire to expose rather than embrace on faith the mystery of the feminine— these "extravagances" retell not only Hawthorne's tale of Giovanni confronting Beatrice in the garden but also the tales to which Hawthorne's "Rappaccini's Daughter" respond—Fuller's "Leila" and her flower tales, "The Magnolia of Lake Pontchartrain" and "Yuca Filamentosa." All three of those tales present in the same mythic mode as Zenobia's "Silvery Veil" an allegory of a man's confrontation with the mystery of the beauty and the creative powers of the feminine, powers that the man fails to embrace and eventually rejects because he seeks to know rationally what can only be comprehended by an unquestioning acceptance.

Gazing into the eyes of "the spirit under a mask"—Leila (Fuller's personification of the infinite feminine principle)—and confronting "boundlessness . . . depth below depth," men seek, as Coverdale had sought unsuccessfully in the "deep well" of Zenobia's eyes, a "form" that they "may clasp to the living breast," because they "are bound in sense, time, and thought"; all men but poets call "Leila mad because they felt she made them so." Given voice, Fuller's Magnolia speaks to the man in quest of this feminine power, warning him that "this is a being of another order from thee, an order whose presence thou mayest feel, nay, approach step by step, but which cannot be known till thou art it, nor seen nor spoken of till thou hast passed through it." When Zenobia's Theodore demands to know of the Veiled Lady the "mystery" that Coverdale has already admitted seeking of Zenobia, he— like Coverdale, like the man in "The Magnolia of Lake Pontchartrain"—is given the opportunity to approach that mystery and know it through an unquestioning acceptance. In Theodore's case, his acceptance must come through the kiss of faith that Giovanni would not give. He, like all the others, does not have the faith to accept without "knowing" what cannot be "known." "Secret, radiant, profound ever, and never to be known," Fuller's Magnolia describes this feminine force; though "many forms indicate . . . none declare her."[6] Like Fuller's male narrator at the end of "Magnolia," who declares that "the Magnolia left me, I left not her, but must abide forever in the thought to which the clue was found in the margin of that lake of the South," so Zenobia would have Theodore's "retribution" be "to pine, forever and ever, for another sight of that dim, mournful face—which might have been his life-long, household, fireside joy—to desire, and waste life in a feverish quest, and never meet it more!" (3:114).[7] Haunted by their failures, such men, according to Fuller, attempt to re-create that lost vision in an art that is but a mirror of their own desire. The "feminine" that haunts men, according to Fuller's Magnolia, "is not such a being as men love to paint, a fairy—like them, only lesser and more exquisite than they, a goddess, larger and of statelier proportion, an angel,—like still, only with an added power." In a sentence that could serve as a substitute for Coverdale's lengthy meditation on the "monsters" of memory or for Hawthorne's own self-critical awareness of the origins and limitations of his own art, the Magnolia then explains, "Man never creates, he only recombines the lines and colors of his own existence."[8]

When Hawthorne has Coverdale proclaim that the "daily flower" that Zenobia wears in her hair "affected my imagination" for "as long . . . as I continued to know this remarkable woman" in "very much the same way" as the "slight delirium" of his recent fever, when he identifies the flower as "a subtle expression" of her "character" and admits that it "has struck a deep root into my memory" (3:45, 15), not only is he encoding his fixation with Zenobia's sexuality, as is generally recognized, and alluding to Fuller, who frequently wore a flower in her hair, but he is also identifying Zenobia with Beatrice and both with Fuller, whose "flowers" in her mythic feminist sketches, as well as the "flower" on her body, had struck a deep root in Hawthorne's consciousness and affected his imagination. Hawthorne adopted Fuller's representation of herself with flowers and of flowers with a feminine creative force that caused "delirium" in men because he identified himself with Fuller's male seekers haunted by the mystery of the feminine.

Zenobia's "Silvery Veil" interrupts the tableaux vivants that she and the other characters have been performing from literature, specifically from Shakespeare's plays. Hawthorne's choice is not, it seems, coincidental.[9] If their characters "show a little too intrusively through all the characters" they play, Zenobia seeks to imitate Hamlet's "play within the play" for the same purposes Hamlet had—to expose the inner characters of the persons performing the charade they are living at Blithedale. That too is Hawthorne's strategy in "Zenobia's Legend" for the charade that is *Blithedale.* The tale within the tale exposes the origins and purposes of the tale that embodies it and the tales that inspired it. As Hawthorne imagines Fuller's voice in his own, so he synthesizes "Rappaccini's Daughter" with Fuller's flower tales and insets it into another retelling of the legend that Fuller had come to write in Hawthorne's memory. He has his characters performing tableaux vivants of characters from his own and Fuller's past texts, characters who themselves "assumed" the characters of "real lives" and performed as "creatures" of Hawthorne's mental theater "phantasmagorical antics" based on "actual events" (3:1). At the center of "The Silvery Veil" in the center of *Blithedale* is the author who is the object of Zenobia's allusive "ghost story" and the subject of his own, the same author who claims the detachment of being only a translator of the works of others but who translates himself into those works, Hawthorne—alias Coverdale in *Blithedale,* alias Theodore in "The Silvery Veil," alias M. de l'Aubépine in "Rappaccini's Daughter," alias "Theodore de l'Aubépine" in love letters to Sophia.[10]

Coverdale's characterization of Zenobia's "Silvery Veil" as having "no more reality" than the recognition "of one's own self" in the "candlelight image" that "peeps at us outside of a dark window-pane" (3:108) acknowledges covertly his own and Hawthorne's deeply layered identification with "Theodore." Imitating himself in the act of imitating himself, Hawthorne has Zenobia, as he had done in "Rappaccini's Daughter" and *The Scarlet Letter,* inset private conversations and translated texts within her tale to signal to that "solitary friend" in her audience the private dialogue intended beneath the public text. Transcribing a private conversation she had had earlier with Coverdale when she had demanded to know the motives of his constant gaze ("What are you seeking to discover in me?" [3:47]), she has the Veiled Lady ask Theodore, "What wouldst thou with me?" (3:112). Coverdale's answer had been, "The mystery of your life. . . . And you will never tell me" (3:47), and Theodore's answer similarly is, "Mysterious creature, . . . I would know who and what you are!" (3:112). Zenobia, however, has the Veiled Lady confirm what Coverdale had only surmised, "My lips are forbidden to betray the secret!" (3:112). But her lips would indeed "betray the secret" if he would kiss her with a kiss "in holy faith . . . with a pure and generous purpose" before attempting to lift the veil (3:113). The lips of Zenobia through the voice of the Veiled Lady to Theodore are attempting to speak the same truth to Coverdale that Beatrice claimed her lips spoke to Giovanni.[11] Theodore seeks in the Veiled Lady what Coverdale seeks in Zenobia and what Giovanni sought in Beatrice—"the mystery which he deemed the riddle of his own existence" (10:110). It is the "riddle" Hawthorne in "The Custom-House" claimed that Hester represented but that he "saw little hope of solving" (1:31), and it is the same "riddle" Hawthorne had hoped he had found "the solution" to in April 1858 as he followed the "direction" implied by Mozier's gossip in Rome about Fuller and Ossoli (14:155–56).

The "riddle" of "Zenobia's Legend" and of *Blithedale* is the mystery not of the Veiled Lady enacted by Priscilla, but of the woman whose real name Coverdale refuses to give us and of the relationships among Hollingsworth, Priscilla, and Zenobia and between Zenobia and Westervelt, relationships that Coverdale claims became the "vortex of my meditations," the "indices of the problem which it was my business to solve" (3:70, 69). The problem that Hawthorne seeks to solve through the narrative of Coverdale's vortex of memory is the problem that immediately after Fuller's death he had tried to turn away from through writing *The House of the Seven Gables.* In *Blithedale,* one year later, as he prepares to return to the Eden he thought he had found in Concord and to which he had unconvincingly consigned Holgrave and Phoebe, he confronts "the problem." Coverdale's attempt to understand the triangular relationships among Zenobia, Hollingsworth, and Priscilla is Hawthorne's attempt to represent and understand his own past relationships with Fuller and Sophia and his own present relationship with Sophia. Comparing his role to that of a chorus in a tragedy, Coverdale is that part of

Hawthorne who restages in memory the drama of his past so that he may not only judge "the whole morality of the performance" but "atone" for "the wrong" (3:97, 161). As judge, he may perhaps condemn himself and his friends with a sentence as "stern as that of Destiny itself," but it "would be given mournfully, and with undiminished love." The sentence carried out, he "would come, as if to gather up the white ashes of those who had perished at the stake, and to tell the world—the wrong being now atoned for—how much had perished there, which it had never yet known how to praise" (3:161). Dissector of character and re-creator of the "monsters" of his own mind, problem-solver, chorus, judge, executioner, and sympathetic repository and historian of the lives he condemns while atoning for—all are Coverdale, all are Hawthorne.

But Coverdale is not all of Hawthorne. If Hawthorne invested in Coverdale that part of himself who translates onto the stage of *Blithedale* the ghosts of his own unquiet heart, he imagined his own ghost inhabiting Hollingsworth. Hawthorne, however, takes pains to deflect any attempt at identification the reader might make between him and Hollingsworth. Casting Hollingsworth as a former blacksmith who has turned philanthropist with a vengeance, subordinating everything and everybody to his megalomaniacal plan to reform criminals, he seems far from being the surrogate for Hawthorne that Coverdale in part so evidently is. Yet, as Hawthorne admitted to his readers in the preface to *The Snow-Image,* written just before beginning *Blithedale,* his prefaces "hide the man," but he is to be found in "his essential traits" if one is willing to "make quite another kind of inquest, and look through the whole range of his fictitious characters, good and evil" (11:4). With Hollingsworth, Hawthorne made that inquest difficult for good reason, for in Hollingsworth, Hawthorne attempts to exorcise that part of his character that he despises. Hollingsworth, as Coverdale observed, was "two . . . men" (3:42). In one of them, Hawthorne portrays "what was best" in himself and in Coverdale, the feminine self that responds with sympathy and tenderness for others. Though Hollingworth is not "ashamed of it, as most men often are" (3:42), that part of himself is subsumed by "the intensity" of a "masculine egotism" that "centered everything in itself" (3:123). Like "millions of other despots," the other Hollingsworth "deprived woman of her very soul . . . to make it a mere incident in the great sum of man." "The heart of true womanhood," Hollingsworth proclaims, "knows where its own sphere is, and never seeks to stray beyond it!" Those women who do stray by proclaiming their right to a development independent of their relationships to men are "petticoated monstrosities." Should these "monsters" have a chance of succeeding in their goals, Hollingsworth "would call upon my own sex to use its physical force, that unmistakeable evidence of sovereignty, to scourge them back within their proper bounds!" (3:123). As Coverdale's grouping of Hollingsworth with "millions of other despots" implies, the second Hollingsworth exemplifies the brutality of "masculine egotism" at the heart of a socially constructed manhood, a manhood that is sustained by destroying what is best within a man and that makes him the monster that he fears in women. "Are you a man?" Zenobia taunts him. "No; but a monster! A cold, heartless, self-beginning and self-ending piece of mechanism." He became that "monster," Zenobia tells him, when he "stifled down" his "inmost consciousness" and did a "deadly wrong" to his "own heart" (3:218).

As Joel Pfister has shown, the term "monstrosity" became an ubiquitous feature of such contemporary antifeminist discourse as Hollingsworth's in order "to *biologize* masculine social or literary anxieties about women." Zenobia's subversive appropriation of the term to condemn Hollingsworth is devastating in that it redeploys Hollingsworth's "biologized" definition against him: he has become a "monster" for the same reason as his "petticoated monstrosities"—by suppressing the feminine within his own nature. Zenobia's indictment of Hollingsworth is premised on Fuller's well-known formulation of the fluidity of the supposed boundaries between the masculine and the feminine: "Male and female represent the two sides of the great radical dualism. But, in fact, they are perpetually passing into one another. Fluid hardens to solid, solid rushes to fluid. There is no wholly masculine man, no purely feminine woman."[12] Though "there is no perfect harmony in human nature," Fuller writes, a human being's obligation is to develop both halves of that gender dualism, to attempt a balance and reconciliation.[13] Hollingsworth destroys his humanity by suppressing the "best part" of himself, the feminine within his "own heart." Zenobia's condemnation is Coverdale's and Hawthorne's. Coverdale, in fact, indicts Hollingsworth's brutal "masculine egotism" more severely than does Zenobia, and he consistently endorses her complaints against the wrongs committed by men against women. Immediately after Hollingsworth threatens to use physical force to prevent the "petticoated monstrosities" of feminists from broadening the "proper bounds" of women, Coverdale says: "I looked at Zenobia, however, fully expecting her to resent—as I felt, by the indignant ebullition of my own blood, that she ought—this outrageous affirmation of what struck me as the intensity of masculine egotism" (3:123). Coverdale's rejection of Hollingsworth's overture to be his disciple, it should be noted, occurs in the chapter immediately following Hollingsworth's exposure of the brutal "intensity" of his "masculine egotism." Coverdale recognizes that with friends as well as lovers Hollingsworth can "give his affections . . . only to one whom he might absorb into himself" (3:167).

In Coverdale's rejection of Hollingsworth and in his endorsement of Zenobia's denunciation of the wrongs committed by men against women is Hawthorne's rejection of that part of himself that sought to absorb the "naughty" Sophia Peabody within the sainted Dove of his desire. In *Blithedale,* the Dove finds her parallel in the Veiled Lady, who as a receptacle of man's desire is literally self-less in performing his every need, the type of true womanhood that Hollingsworth seeks and finds in Priscilla, whose sole interest to Coverdale as well is "in the fancy-work with which" he "has idly decked her out" (3:100). In Hollingsworth's words, the "true woman" is always "the Sympathizer; the unreserved, unquestioning Believer; the Recognition, withheld in every other manner, but given, in pity, through woman's heart, lest man should utterly lose faith in himself; the Echo of God's own voice, pronouncing—'It is well done!'" (3:122). Such a woman as Hollingsworth desires may think she is echoing God's own voice, but that voice, of course, is the voice of her other creator and maker: man, Hollingsworth. The very "idol" of a philanthropic enterprise to which Hollingsworth has consecrated himself to as "high-priest" is but the "false deity" of self, the "spectrum of the very priest himself, projected upon the surrounding darkness" (3:70–71). In his desire to be worshiped by the "unquestioning Believer," the "true woman," Hollingsworth would make another idol to sustain the delusion masking the first.

Hawthorne assigns to Hollingsworth the former occupation of blacksmith both to obscure his own identification with Hollingsworth and to suggest it, at least to himself.[14] The "fires" that meld Coverdale with Hollingsworth and both with Hawthorne are the "fires" of Vulcan's workshop. Early on, Coverdale comments that the passionate glow of Zenobia's cheeks "made me think of Pandora, fresh from Vulcan's workshop, and full of the celestial warmth by dint of which he had tempered and moulded her" (3:24). Though the reference is not repeated, it reverberates throughout the novel as an unspoken metaphor for the retributive furies that man has unleashed on and within himself by attempting to make woman in the image of his own desire.[15] "I have hammered thought out of iron, after heating the iron in my heart" (3:68), proclaims Hollingsworth. Prominent among those iron-forged thoughts, of course, is his conception of a "true woman" as existing solely to be man's "unquestioning Believer," and in Priscilla's malleable self, he finds, as Zenobia bitterly acknowledges, "the type of womanhood, such as man has spent centuries in making it" (3:122).[16] The fires of Vulcan's work-shop serve thus to buttress the romance's framing metaphorical structure, the stage of the male mesmerist, yet those metaphorical "fires" also suggest the fragility of that structure. In the making of a Priscilla, man is also respon-sible for creating the fury of a Pandora in a Zenobia, the fury that he at-tempts to recontain through the condemnation, as Zenobia phrases it, of his "secret tribunals" (3:215).

In a sense, Hawthorne's purposes in *Blithedale* are to expose those "tribu-nals" by making *Blithedale* itself something of a public tribunal with Cover-dale as its presiding judge. In another sense, however, Hawthorne intends *Blithedale* to open Pandora's box. By having Hollingsworth be the romance's great defender of a domestic ideology that grants woman a superior spiritu-ality only so long as it worships at the altar of a masculine egotism, Haw-thorne strips away the sentimental veils that mystify the most pervasive slave institution in the land—the "hereditary bond-slavery," as Zenobia phrases it—of woman to man (3:217). By giving Zenobia a greater voice than he gave Beatrice or Hester, by allowing that voice to haunt *Blithedale* as it does the lives of its characters, to challenge at every point in fact Haw-thorne's narrator's very urge to know her mystery and contain it within a ballad's comfortable repetitions of character and moral, Hawthorne re-creates his own Pandora, translates the words of the ghost that speaks her fury in his memory.[17] "Write this ballad," Zenobia finally instructs Cover-dale. But, as Fuller had similarly advised Hawthorne in her own criticism of his work, Zenobia commands him: "Put your soul's ache into it, and turn your sympathy to good account, as other poets do, and as poets must, unless they choose to give us glittering icicles instead of lines of fire." As for the moral, she tells him it "shall be distilled into the final stanza, in a drop of bitter honey" (3:224).

When Hawthorne sat down to write Coverdale's "ballad," seven years had passed since the summer of 1844 when Hawthorne had last walked the woods of Sleepy Hollow with Fuller. The seven years that Coverdale myste-riously claims it had taken him to "hive up the bitter honey" of warning to Priscilla that the "dusty image" of ourselves will inevitably be "thrust aside into a corner" of "the innermost, holiest niche" of the hearts "where we wish to be most valued" (3:76) are the same seven years that had passed since that "mad summer" Zenobia and Hollingsworth "spent together," the summer when—as Zenobia mysteriously, bitterly claims—"the fiend" of "self" was to make "his choicest mirth" within Hollingsworth's heart when he "stifled down . . . [his] inmost consciousness" (3:218). Zenobia's indictment of Hollingsworth could well stand as Hawthorne's indictment of his own recent life and literary career. He too had stifled down his innermost consciousness in turning away from the darker implications of his attraction to Beatrice and Hester that had enabled his writing. In his "self-deception," he had imagined himself as capable of enjoying contentment in a Holgrave turned conservative, settling for the reassurance and the sunshine of a Phoebe's love in the country, and as something of a reward, discovering financial security in the process. In Hollingsworth's rejection of Zenobia for the fortune and the blindly unquestioning worship of Priscilla, Hawthorne in a sense writes a counterallegory of Holgrave and Phoebe and of the recent direction of his own life and literary career.[18] When Zenobia describes for Coverdale the marriage that awaits Hollingsworth with Priscilla and then contrasts it with the difference she could have made in his life as an equal partner, Hawthorne appropriates, with a bitterness he assigns to Zenobia, Fuller's contrasts in *Woman in the Nineteenth Century* of two marriages—the marriage of a "mutual idolatry," in which "the parties weaken and narrow one another" as "they lock the gate against all the glories of the universe, that they may live in a cell together," the woman becoming "an unlovely syren" and the man "an effeminate boy," and the marriage of an "intellectual companionship" based on equality, the type of marriage that Fuller had thought Sophia and Hawthorne capable of attaining:[19]

> After all, he has flung away what would have served him better than the poor, pale flower he kept. What can Priscilla do for him? Put passionate warmth into his heart, when it shall be chilled with frozen hopes? Strengthen his hands, when they are weary with much doing and no performance? No; but only tend towards him with a blind, instinctive love, and hang her little, puny weakness for a clog upon his arm! She cannot even give him such sympathy as is worth the name. For will he never, in many an hour of darkness, need that proud, intellectual sympathy which he might have had from me?—the sympathy that would flash light along his course, and guide as well as cheer him? Poor Hollingsworth! Where will he find it now? (3:224–25)

With Zenobia gone, Hollingsworth will not find "that proud, intellectual sympathy" he had had in Zenobia, just as Hawthorne, like Emerson, had lost his "audience" when Fuller died.[20] Zenobia was right. In her absence, Holgrave and Phoebe become Hollingsworth and Priscilla.

Zenobia's indictment of Hollingsworth, of course, will reverberate in the hollow chambers of his heart, just as her "shadow" will dog his "side where Priscilla is not," but her rephrasing of Coverdale's earlier warning to Priscilla will go, it seems, unheeded: "Methinks you have but a melancholy lot before you, sitting all alone in that wide, cheerless heart, where, for aught you know . . . the fire which you have kindled may soon go out" (3:220). "What will you do, Priscilla, when you find no spark among the ashes?" Zenobia asks, and Priscilla answers, "Die!" (3:220). But Priscilla does not. In fact, as the fire within Hollingsworth dies and his masculine egotism is deflated by habitual depression and melancholia, Priscilla thrives. In a complete reversal of the good that Hollingsworth sought and attained only to find that it was not what he wanted, he finds himself a slave to his own childish dependency on Priscilla's strength as his "protective and watchful . . . guardian," his dependency on her in other words as an "unquestioning Believer" in what he can no longer believe (3:242). Priscilla does not seek "to exorcise the demon" that haunts Hollingsworth, according to Herbert, because in her "unquestioning reverence" for him, she "cannot even see it," yet his "moral paralysis" and her ascendent power over him will endure only so long as he "does not directly acknowledge the source of his guilt and seek to reclaim his self-respect by confronting the patriarchal axioms of his psychic constitution."[21]

Hollingsworth, however, is two men. He is not all Hawthorne. The character traits that are "patched" together to make up Coverdale's "monster" of his friend Hollingsworth also contain the traits of that other man in Concord—Emerson. Part of Hawthorne's conception of Hollingsworth's character owes itself to Hawthorne's continuing effort to negotiate Emerson's influence and his own identification with the uneasy, isolated self at the heart of Emerson's self-sufficiency. In his life and in his work, Hawthorne just could not seem to escape Emerson's presence. Indeed, he might have sought it more than he ever admitted. Hawthorne biographers in general have inadequately explained the reclusive Hawthorne's pattern of seeking out a home among communities of writers and artists—Brook Farm, Concord, the Berkshires, Concord. It is curious, for instance, that in 1852 Hawthorne paid fifteen hundred dollars for Alcott's home and an adjoining nine acres so that he could settle permanently as a neighbor to Emerson, Thoreau, and Ellery Channing, and yet in 1841 when he hoped to find a means of supporting himself and his prospective bride he invested the same amount, his life savings, in Brook Farm, a venture whose communal idealism and financial uncertainty were too unstable for even Emerson and Fuller.[22] Hawthorne, of course, claimed that he was attempting to establish a place conducive to his writing and to his future marriage, a private agenda that links him to Hollingsworth's deceptive commitment to Blithedale, but as Miller observes, the fifteen hundred dollars he invested was equivalent to his yearly salary and was certainly enough, as he proved eleven years later, to purchase a home for his writing and for Sophia.[23] Perhaps we dismiss too readily the

Hawthorne speaking behind the Coverdale who, despite his constant temptation to a self-deprecatory middle-aged cynicism, defends his youthful commitment to the ideals of Blithedale: "Whatever else I may repent of . . . let it be reckoned neither among my sins nor follies, that I once had faith and force enough to form generous hopes of the world's destiny—yes!—and to do what in me lay for their accomplishment" (3:11).

Hawthorne and Sophia did not marry until they had decided upon a home, and the place they chose, of course, was at Emerson's side. As an added attraction, Hawthorne told Sophia, Fuller would be able to share her time with them when she visited Emerson in Concord. At the time, Sophia's regard for both Emerson and Fuller can only be described as an early manifestation of the hero worship she would soon direct exclusively toward Hawthorne. When he moved to Concord, Hawthorne knew Fuller well, but not Emerson. Emerson clearly courted Hawthorne's friendship and came to have a high regard for him, if not for his writing, but Hawthorne's attitudes toward Emerson are difficult to determine. True, he wrote much about Emerson in his notebooks, and little of it is flattering. But, as Reynolds has demonstrated, much of the motivation behind Hawthorne's subtle ridicule of Emerson in his notebooks was intended for Sophia's benefit—to undermine her adoration for Emerson and redirect it, exclusively, toward her husband.[24] In his public literary work, however, Hawthorne's attitudes toward Emerson are much more ambivalent. In "The Old Manse," for instance, Hawthorne seems again to ridicule Emerson's "wonderful magnetism" for attracting "hobgoblins of flesh and blood" and to portray himself as another kind of man and writer, an alternative in Concord and in the literary marketplace (10:30). However, in locating the site of his writing at the very window from which Emerson looked out upon nature as he envisioned and wrote *Nature,* in writing his own version of his attempt to establish an identity in relationship with a different kind of nature, and most importantly, in characterizing himself as possessing a power to cast his own spell over others, Hawthorne identifies himself with, as well as against, Emerson. Against Emerson's "magnetic" influence, for example, Hawthorne offered merely another kind of mesmerism: "Others could give them pleasure and amusement, or instruction—these could be picked up anywhere—but it was for me to give them rest—rest in a life of trouble. . . . What better could be done for anybody, who came within our magic circle, than to throw the spell of a tranquil spirit over him? And when it had wrought its full effect, then we dismissed him, with misty reminiscences, as if he had been dreaming of us" (10:29). He would think of Sophia, of course, as being under such a spell, but he does not mention her, though later he will explain Priscilla's attraction to Hollingsworth as being rooted in her "unconsciously seeking to rest upon his strength" (3:77). Through a transparent reference, however, he does mention Margaret Fuller (10:29). By so doing, he makes a subtle claim for the greater power of his mesmeric spirit. The power of his "spell" had brought Emerson's then most famous protégée under his influence. In Emerson, Hawthorne saw a rival and a twin.

The more deeply layered fictions of "Rappaccini's Daughter," *The Scarlet Letter,* and *The Blithedale Romance* repeat the pattern of "The Old Manse." Dr. Rappaccini and Giovanni, Chillingworth and Dimmesdale, Hollingsworth and Coverdale—each man in each pair defines himself against the other and recognizes himself in the other. Women are the objects of their rivalries and, in their desire to exert power over those women, the sources of their identities. As Reynolds has observed, "The male rivalry between the figure of Emerson and the figure of Hawthorne as 'author' forms a subtext for not only 'The Old Manse,' but also later works, where an absent woman is both the reward and the cost of male triumph."[25] Dimmesdale and Chillingworth in *The Scarlet Letter,* Coverdale and Hollingsworth in *Blithedale*—Hawthorne's repetition of the same name pairings parallels his repetition of identities, of the "patches" that create character. In *Blithedale,* Hawthorne may be the Hollingsworth who chooses Priscilla over Zenobia, but he is also the Coverdale who envies the Emerson in Hollingsworth for his power to attract a Zenobia as well as a Priscilla. The intimacy of Fuller's friendship with Hawthorne may have begun to rival her friendship with Emerson as she became more and more resigned to Emerson's "coldness" but, for her at least, it was not to develop the sort of highly charged romantic undercurrents she experienced in her friendship with Emerson. In the freedom of memory's reimagining, Hawthorne seems to write the scene that could not happen, the scene in which Zenobia, in her final moments, speaks Fuller's disappointment in Emerson and her belated understanding of the source of Hawthorne's admiration for her: "She understood the look of admiration in my face," Coverdale says, "and—Zenobia to the last—it gave her pleasure" (3:226). What she understood is then explained by her answer to the question that Coverdale cannot bring himself to ask, nor Hawthorne to write: "It is an endless pity," said she, "that I had not bethought myself of winning your heart, Mr. Coverdale, instead of Hollingsworth's. I think I should have succeeded; and many women would have deemed you the worthier conquest of the two. You are certainly much the handsomest man. But there is a fate in these things" (3:226–27). Hawthorne does not write a response for

Coverdale. But earlier, when Zenobia had admitted to him that she "had been several times on the point of making you my confidant, for lack of a better or wiser one," Coverdale had answered with a promise: "I would at least be loyal and faithful" (3:141–42). His tale, for the most part, attempts to fulfill that promise.[26]

If the Coverdale in Hawthorne condemned the Hollingsworth, the Hollingsworth in him found its double in Emerson. Hollingsworth's obsession with the criminal within man may find its parallel with Hawthorne's literary obsessions, but his belief in the power of the self to effect its own redemption finds its parallel in Emerson's secular idealism. Hollingsworth's blind projection of "a spectrum of the very priest himself . . . upon the surrounding darkness" complements Coverdale's description of Hollingsworth's "deep eyes" as beaming "kindly upon me" like "the glow of a household fire that was burning in a cave" (3:71), both suggesting Hawthorne's association of Hollingsworth with a deluded Platonic idealism that has mistaken the light of self with the light of a disinterested ideal, the shadow with the substance. "Plato" was an identity that Emerson would have suggested to Hawthorne's imagination, for it was an identification that Emerson encouraged.[27] "Minister" was another.

Emerson was no longer a minister when Hawthorne knew him and never a philanthropist, of course, but in Hollingsworth's redeployment of gospel discourse to recruit disciples to his mission, in his sense of the sacredness of that mission of "self," and, of course, in his conversion of the Indian missionary Samuel Eliot's "pulpit" in nature, not in church, for a secular sermon, Hawthorne associates Hollingsworth with Emerson's transformation from a minister preaching the gospel of a divine Christ to a lecturer ministering to the Christ-like self. Hollingsworth's aggressive pursuit of his crusade for the reformation of criminals suggests a displaced Christian militancy, and "in Emerson's Essays, the Dial, Carlyle's works, and George Sand's romances," according to Coverdale, such "pilgrims . . . crusaders" as Hollingsworth and "the brethren and sisterhood" of Blithedale find their inspiration, read their gospels (3:52). The "light" of Hollingsworth's faith complements the Christ and Platonic "fire" images with which he is associated. Despite Coverdale's many misgivings about Hollingsworth, Coverdale has "deep reverence" for Hollingsworth's capacity for faith, a reverence that is confirmed when he hears Hollingsworth's passionate prayers beyond the wall and remarks that such a pious man is "decidedly marked out by a light of transfiguration, shed upon him in the divine interview from which he passes into his daily life" (3:39–40).

Fire, light, and transfiguration are also associated with Emerson in "The Old Manse." In a passage that suggests both the fire of Plato's "Truth" and the spiritual light of Christ that attracted the multitudes to the Mount for the Sermon, Hawthorne describes Emerson's "intellectual fire" as "a beacon burning on a hill-top" to which his pilgrims journeyed, "climbing the difficult ascent" to look "forth into the surrounding obscurity, more hopefully than hitherto," because the "light" of Emerson's idealism "revealed objects unseen before," both the noble ("mountains, gleaming lakes, glimpses of a creation among the chaos") and the ignoble ("bats and owls, and the whole host of night-birds"). In a sentence that could have been easily said by Coverdale in judgment of Hollingsworth, Hawthorne says of Emerson and his effect upon his followers, "Such delusions always hover nigh, whenever a beacon-fire of truth is kindled" (10:31).

The place where Hollingsworth preaches his "treasury of golden thoughts" (3:119), is "Eliot's Pulpit," and because, as Lauren Berlant observes, it is "the place of sexual, juridical, and theological confrontation," it "is to *Blithedale* what the scaffold is to *The Scarlet Letter.*" Eliot's Pulpit is center stage in Coverdale's play of memory, the place he returns to and anoints, according to Berlant, as "the place that contains the tangle of memory and desire his narration attempts to unravel (or reconstruct)." That place, however, is in Concord, not Brook Farm. Concord was the original location of the Apostle Eliot's missionary preaching to the Indians, and it is thus, through Hollingsworth's association with Eliot in the past and Emerson in the present, the site of Hollingsworth's secular sermons.[28] For Hawthorne, however, Eliot's Pulpit represented far more than merely a geographic deception masking an allusion that would confirm Emerson's presence in Hollingsworth's conception. It was the site to which Hawthorne's thoughts, like Coverdale's, "continually reverted back, brooding . . . and bringing up incidents that seemed hardly to have left a trace of themselves, in their passage" (3:194). It was the site, however, that left its trace in the balcony-rimmed garden of Beatrice and Giovanni and the bank-enclosed dell of Hester and Arthur, the place where, as Coverdale says sometimes happens in the dense forest or in relationships, "a casual opening . . . lets us, all of a sudden, into the long-sought intimacy of a mysterious heart" (3:90).

That place was the secluded spot in Sleepy Hollow just off the pathway where Hawthorne on 21 August 1842 first experienced, unexpectedly, "the long-sought intimacy" into the "mysterious heart" of Margaret Fuller, the place just below "the high bank," where Emerson, "the intruder . . . hidden among the trees," caught a glimpse of Fuller and interrupted their afternoon-long conversation. As in the chapter "Eliot's Pulpit" in *Blithedale,* that day too was a Sabbath, and Hawthorne, for Sophia's benefit, alludes to Emerson's lapsed but lingering ministerial pretensions, for "in spite of his clerical consecration," he "had found no better way of spending the Sabbath than to ramble among the woods" (8:343). Hollingsworth would "not exactly" preach but would talk "to us, his few disciples, in a strain that rose and fell as naturally as the wind's breath among the leaves of the birch-tree" (3:119), and Emerson, having interrupted Fuller and Hawthorne's conversation, began to talk to them of the "Muses in the woods" that day, of the "whispers to be heard in the breezes" (8:343).[29] The phrase, like the moment, lingered in Hawthorne's memory. Coverdale in his "hermitage" would contemplate "tuning" his verses "to the breezy symphony" and "meditate an essay for the Dial, in which the many tongues of Nature whispered mysteries, and seemed to ask only a little stronger puff of wind, to speak out the solution of its riddle" (3:99), thus linking a paraphrase of Emerson's metaphorical "talk" that Sabbath day to the metaphor with which Hawthorne habitually thought of Fuller's hold on his imagination, "the solution" to the "riddle" that, on that day, seemed close to being spoken out. But it was not to be spoken. In Hawthorne's narrative of that afternoon with Fuller, once Emerson, the "intruder," interrupts Fuller and Hawthorne, Emerson alone speaks. Abruptly, and with a reference to marked distinctions of intimacy and attitude, Hawthorne writes that "we separated, Mr. Emerson and Margaret towards his house, and I towards mine, where my little wife was very busy getting tea" (8:343). Mr. Emerson and Margaret, Hawthorne and the "little wife"—the last sentence identifies the four figures who confront each other at the base of Eliot's Pulpit in Hawthorne's translation of memory.

In the revisionist turn of *Blithedale,* the "little wife" that Phoebe was in *The House of the Seven Gables* becomes the little "seamstress."[30] In both, Hawthorne reimagines the Sophia whose love and worship he courted and won, only to find—as Phoebe's transformation into Priscilla suggests—that "the good" that he sought and "attained" was "something else" that he had "never dreamed of, and did not particularly want," but did apparently need, and need too much (3:75–76). In the final scene of Hollingsworth in his "self-distrustful weakness" leaning close to Priscilla, haunted on his other side by the shadow of Zenobia, we have a representation of the bitter consequences of the wrong dream fulfilled, the "cell," as Fuller had termed the home of a marriage of "mutual idolatry," in which Hollingsworth has become his own inmate and warden. If it is a tableau vivant of the self-contempt with which Hawthorne judged his own recent literary mission and his relationship with

Sophia, we have in the preceding scenes of the romance a representation of that dream and of how and where it became the wrong dream.

The dream was wrong from the beginning, and Hawthorne's letters to Sophia suggest that he knew that. *Blithedale* confirms it. In Coverdale's initial characterization of the performance of the Veiled Lady as "wonderful" and in his later "horror and disgust" at the display of "the miraculous power of one human being over the will and passions of another" (3:5, 198), we have the "Strophe and Antistrophe," not of the "Dove" and "naughty Sophie" (15:400), but of Hawthorne's own opposing attitudes toward his mesmeric influence over Sophia. Hawthorne's attempts to mesmerize Sophia Peabody are evident in his courtship letters. In a 26 May 1839 letter to Sophia, one of his earliest love letters, Hawthorne displays the extremes of both attitudes. Hawthorne describes his "Dove" as a creature conjured up by his "musings," which "flits lightly" through his thoughts "as if my being were dissolved, and the idea of you were diffused throughout it" (15:316). Despite his "awe" over the angel-like Dove, his sense of having for the first time met "a spirit" who "converts" his "love into religion," he insists on absolute control over his creature of salvation: "It is singular, too that this awe (or whatever it be) does not prevent me from feeling that it is I who have the charge of you, and that my Dove is to follow my guidance and do my bidding" (15:317). The sentences that follow not only demonstrate Hawthorne's anxious awareness of the brute will to power at the heart of his demands but also illustrate his deployment of that power.

He would bid her first to accept as a condition of their love his definition of their relationship as being constituted by the command that his love may exercise over her and by the submission that her love must accept: "Am I not very bold to say this? And will not you rebel? Oh no; because I possess this power only so far as I love you. My love gives me the right, and your love consents to it" (15:317). "Since writing the above," he tells Sophia in the next paragraph, he fell asleep and dreamed of having slept for a year only to awaken in his dream to find the ground burnt black beneath his bedclothes, the blasted earth a silhouette of his body with fresh herbs and grass sprinkled over the charred space. It is a "silly dream," Hawthorne tells her, but it clearly upset him. He challenged her to interpret it but not to draw the conclusion that the dream seemed designed by guilt to draw—"sombre omens" (15:317–18).

In another "sombre omen," Hawthorne writes to his "Ownest Dove" of a daydream in which his Dove flies away from her captivity in the "home of his deepest heart" to her home in the "gladsome air," and Hawthorne imagines himself as an Icarus killing himself in his attempt to fly after her, the moral for him—"Mate not thyself with a Dove, unless thou hast wings to fly"—the moral for her—"You will never fly away from me" (15:350–51). Sophia never flew away from Hawthorne, of course, but Hawthorne, nevertheless, suffered the consequences of "mating" himself to a self-generated Dove. When he attained the dream of the Dove that he claims "God gave" to him to be "the salvation" of his "soul" (15:330), it proved, inevitably, to be "something else," not what he had "dreamed of." While Sophia did her best to transform herself into Hawthorne's dream of salvation, Hawthorne discovered not only the emptiness of that dream but also, as the somber omens of guilt had warned him, the horror of having dreamed it. In Hawthorne's famous eruption over Sophia's having allowed herself to be mesmerized (15:588–90, 634–35) and in Coverdale's "horror and disgust" at Westervelt for exploiting the power to make "human character . . . but soft wax in his hands" (3:198), Hawthorne inscribes his angry confrontation not only with a rival to his hold over Sophia, but also with an image of himself in the crude mirror of the mesmerist.

There are, of course, two mesmerists in "The Village Hall." In Westervelt, the crude reflection of the "Imaginary" competes on the stage of Hawthorne's imagination with the image of the "Actual" in Hollingsworth. Westervelt's spell over Priscilla is broken by the greater power of the spell of Hollingsworth's command, "Come!" (3:203). When Zenobia accuses Hollingsworth of betraying the best part of himself, of having ruined his own "great and rich heart," Hollingsworth—stripped of the delusions in which he has encased himself and too impotent to deny her accusations—summons the only power he has left, turns to Priscilla, and commands again, "Priscilla, . . . come!" (3:219). And once again, she does. But by doing so, she lives out Coverdale's worst fantasies of the power of the mesmerist to virtually annihilate the individual soul of his victims, a horror Coverdale illustrated earlier in the mesmerized victim's unnatural rejection of family and loved ones (3:198). She has little difficulty in choosing between her love for her sister and her love for Hollingsworth. She simply turns her back on the sister she had idolized and follows the master who now depends on the strength of her weakness, her power to worship blindly the man who can no longer worship himself. Her worship, however, will be a terrible retribution, for it will daily remind him not only of his unholy success in transforming another into the object of his desire but also of his impotence to break the terrible spell of an unmerited adoration that he must, but cannot, live up to.

If Hollingsworth is haunted by the shadow of Zenobia's ghost "on the side where Priscilla is not," he is also haunted by the living specter of the woman he desired and got and now leans closer and closer to for the reassurance that he needs but knows is but the hollow echo of a command that he cannot now cancel, a command that, like the shadow of the woman on his side, haunts him like a prophecy gone awry in proving itself right. Woman's place, he perhaps hears himself saying again, bitterly, "is at man's side. Her office, that of the Sympathizer; the unreserved, unquestioning Believer; the Recognition, withheld in every other manner, but given, in pity, through woman's heart, lest man should utterly lose faith in himself; the Echo of God's own voice, pronouncing—'It is well done!'" (3:122). It was indeed "well done." As Hollingsworth desired, Priscilla is not to be the "petticoated monstrosity" of the self-determined woman that he fears. She is to be the "monstrosity" that he made. Appalled by the blind strength of Priscilla's spellbound love, Coverdale speaks something of Hawthorne's own appalled awe over what he had wrought:

> Her engrossing love made it all clear. Hollingsworth could have no fault. That was the one principle at the centre of the universe. And the doubtful guilt or possible integrity of other people, appearances, self-evident facts, the testimony of her own senses—even Hollingsworth's self-accusation, had he volunteered it—would have weighed not the value of a mote of thistle-down, on the other side. So secure was she of his right, that she never thought of comparing it with another's wrong, but left the latter to itself. (3:220–21)

Here, as in "Rappaccini's Daughter," *The Scarlet Letter,* and tales such as "The Birth-mark" and "Ethan Brand," Hawthorne volunteers the "self-accusation" that, true to Coverdale's analysis of Priscilla, Sophia would fail to hear, much less heed.

Priscilla's ironlike love for Hollingsworth gives her character a solidity that is as appalling in its simplicity as was her former vaporous permeability. At Zenobia's funeral, Coverdale observes the effect of the last of Priscilla's many transformations. Thinking her still too weak to withstand the shock of Zenobia's death, Coverdale finds instead that though in deep grief, she possesses "a character, so simply constituted [that it] has room only for a single predominant affection. No other feeling can touch the heart's inmost core, nor do it any deadly mischief. Thus, while we see that such a being responds to every breeze, with tremulous vibration, and imagine that she must be shattered by the first rude blast, we find her retaining her equilibrium amid shocks that might have overthrown many a sturdier frame" (3:241–42). The only "possible misfortune" that could wreck Priscilla, Coverdale says, is "Hollingsworth's unkindness." With something of the determination and anxiety that Hawthorne must have felt under the burden of Sophia's unqualified worship, Coverdale then adds that "that was destined never to befall her—never yet, at least—for Priscilla has not died" (3:242).

Hawthorne's solicitude extended, I think, to the novel's close. Though he had originally ended *Blithedale* with Coverdale at Zenobia's grave and then had added, apparently at Whipple's suggestion, an appropriate punishment for Hollingsworth in depicting him years later as a broken, haunted man, Hawthorne then apparently decided to close with Coverdale's melodramatic confession of his secret love for "PRISCILLA!"[31] The impulse on Hawthorne's part to have his surrogate name her, rather than Zenobia, as the object of his unconfessed passion betrays something of a last-minute anxiety that the autobiographical implications of the romance have left him a bit too self-exposed. Naming Priscilla, rather than Zenobia, confirms, for the record, his final allegiance to the "true woman" who has triumphed over Zenobia, to another "angel and apostle of the coming revelation," to another Phoebe. Only a tone-deaf worshipper of that ideal, however, would fail to hear the parodic voice of a melodramatic self-contempt in Coverdale's confessions: "As I write it, he [the reader] will charitably suppose me to blush, and turn away my face:—I—I myself—was in love—with—PRISCILLA!" (3:247). As Millington observes, Coverdale "can only make such a confession in a way that announces its own inauthenticity."[32] "Coverdale's Confession" is Coverdale's self-inflicted punishment. It parodies Hollingsworth's original choice of women and his continuing inability, despite the ghost of Zenobia haunting him, to admit that he made the wrong choice. If Hawthorne intends to reveal anything by Coverdale's confession, it is that the unmasked narrator, for all his seeming differences, is essentially the same man as Hollingsworth, the "patch" of Hollingsworth that is free to tell us this tale. Coverdale's choice of an ending for his tale of mourning also parodies Hawthorne's endings in the two preceding romances and the choices, in life and in art, that those endings were meant to celebrate.

Coverdale may shout "PRISCILLA!" but he cannot silence the voice of the ghost whose name we have waited for him to speak, the name he will not utter, even in the end. Nor can he silence his heart. Aware that his relationships with Zenobia and Priscilla have irrevocably altered, Coverdale describes the irrepressible voice of an unquiet heart that refuses to be silenced by denial, the voice that will speak its tale of loss, of nostalgia and mourning:

> I stood on other terms than before, not only with Hollingsworth, but with
> Zenobia and Priscilla. As regarded the two latter, it was that dreamlike and
> miserable sort of change that denies you the privilege to complain, because

you can assert no positive injury, nor lay your finger on anything tangible. It is a matter which you do not see, but feel, and which, when you try to analyze it, seems to lose its very existence, and resolve itself into a sickly humor of your own. Your understanding, possibly, may put faith in this denial. But your heart will not so easily rest satisfied. It incessantly remonstrates, though, most of the time, in a bass-note, which you do not separately distinguish; but, now-and-then, with a sharp cry, importunate to be heard, and resolute to claim belief. "Things are not as they were!"—it keeps saying—"You shall not impose on me! I will never be quiet! I will throb painfully! I will be heavy, and desolate, and shiver with cold! For I, your deep heart, know when to be miserable, as once I knew when to be happy! All is changed for us! You are beloved no more!" And, were my life to be spent over again, I would invariably lend my ear to this Cassandra of the inward depths, however clamorous the music and the merriment of a more superficial region. (3:138–39)

The voice of this "Cassandra of the inward depths" is the voice of the woman who celebrated the feminine prophetic voice of Cassandra, who claimed that voice for herself, whose character in Coverdale's tragedy of memory warns that she cannot be silenced by denial or death but will haunt the heart, speak the name of the shadow "on the side where Priscilla is not," the name that Coverdale will not utter.

What cannot be said can be dreamed. And the fiction of a dream can be said with impunity in the fiction of a romance. Coverdale claims that he left Blithedale in part to escape from the "train of thoughts" that "had worn a track through my mind," but they "kept treading remorselessly to-and-fro, in their old footsteps," and "slumber left me impotent to regulate them." Of the dreams that tormented Coverdale the moment he "had quitted" his friends, the one dream he reveals to us is the most literal translation of the problem that his tale sets out to solve. It is an image—another tableau vivant—of the ghost story speaking to him in the Cassandra's voice of memory and regret: "In those [dreams] of the last night, Hollingsworth and Zenobia, standing on either side of my bed, had bent across it to exchange a kiss of passion. Priscilla, beholding this—for she seemed to be peeping in at the chamber-window—had melted gradually away, and left only the sadness of her expression in my heart. There it still lingered, after I awoke; one of those unreasonable sadnesses that you know not how to deal with, because it involves nothing for common-sense to clutch" (3:153). The dream speaks both his desire and his fear. Coverdale dreams of himself dreaming of being Hollingsworth. In his twin and opposite, Coverdale displaces and enacts his own erotic fantasies, giving Zenobia in this dream within a dream the kiss that neither he, nor Zenobia's Theodore, nor Aubépine's Giovanni would give, the kiss that the "Cassandra of the inward depths" calls for.

It would be at once both a kiss of faith and a kiss of betrayal. It would be the one "possible misfortune" of "Hollingsworth's unkindness" that would "burst all asunder" the "fragile harp-strings" of Priscilla's nerves. Without her faith in Hollingsworth, she would lose what had created her, gave her identity, existence. In Coverdale's dream, like the Cheshire cat, she would literally, gradually melt away, leaving only her "sad expression" in the air and in the heart. To sustain that worship, the truth must remain unsaid, guilt go unconfessed. Old Moodie describes the burden of shouldering Priscilla's illusions. "In all the world," Old Moodie says, "there was nothing so difficult to be endured, by those who had any dark secret to conceal, as the glance of Priscilla's timid and melancholy eyes" (3:187). The pain of guilt, however, is intensified by the counter pain of regret for not having done what even in fantasy has become the dark secret that must be concealed. Like the dream that lingers on, after leaving Blithedale, Coverdale finds that he cannot let it go:

> I had wrenched myself too suddenly out of an accustomed sphere. There was no choice now, but to bear the pang of whatever heart-strings were snapt asunder, and that illusive torment (like the ache of a limb long ago cut off) by which a past mode of life prolongs itself into the succeeding one. I was full of idle and shapeless regrets. The thought impressed itself upon me, that I had left duties unperformed. With the power, perhaps, to act in the place of destiny, and avert misfortune from my friends, I had resigned them to their fate. That cold tendency, between instinct and intellect, which made me pry with a speculative interest into people's passions and impulses, appeared to have gone far towards unhumanizing my heart. (3:154)

Unable to leave in memory the site of his regret and the ghosts that have "absorbed" his "life into themselves" (3:194), unable to speak the truth except in dreams of dreams, Coverdale speaks for Hollingsworth. As haunted as he, but not as mute, he too can shout "PRISCILLA!" to drown out the voice that accuses him. But before he does that, he can let us hear what he cannot silence. He can translate the voice of that Cassandra. He cannot name her, he has warned us, but he can give her a name, and that name is Zenobia.

The woman whose name Coverdale refuses to give us is to be known by the legend she created in her "role" as Zenobia, writer of feminist tracts and tales, and through allusion, in her role as the historical successor to the third-century Queen of Palmyra, who courageously defied but was defeated by the Roman Empire. More than just appropriate as an epithet for Zenobia's regal manner and as an allusion to the epithet "Queen Margaret" that Sophia among others applied to Fuller and that Fuller at times represented herself, "Zenobia" suggests Hawthorne's concern with Fuller's recent past in revolutionary Rome as well as her past in his memories of Brook Farm and Con-cord.[33] Further, because a popular literary tradition had developed around the historical Zenobia, the name itself presents the literary role of the char-acter Zenobia as a woman performing the literary role of a character who is herself reenacting the life of a historical figure, the play within the play of this romance presented as the drama unfolding in Hawthorne's mind.[34]

"Zenobia" veils Fuller's identity in a stage name that simultaneously though subtly exposes her identity as the actress behind the part of the part she plays, for the name suggests the role that Fuller assumed for herself during the Roman republican revolution that toppled temporarily the Ro-man Empire's successor, the Papacy. Hawthorne is not simply interpreting Fuller's radical defiance against Roman authority as having been like the historical Zenobia's. Rather, he is suggesting that Fuller self-consciously con-structed her radical identity within that historical context on representations provided by popular literary texts of historical persons whose legends, like Zenobia's, are products of those very texts. He is also suggesting that in order for the Coverdale within him to communicate the "mystery" behind the identity Zenobia will not reveal to him and he cannot quite comprehend, much less reveal to us, he is driven to doing the same.[35] For Coverdale, Zeno-bia might have been a thousand other things than what she was, but then what she was was precisely what she decided she would be. Priscilla's com-plete opposite, Zenobia insists on creative control over the self. She writes, directs, and acts the parts that she performs.

As Chevigny has recently said of Fuller's "theatricality," such perfor-mances of the self as those of Fuller and Zenobia are acts not of inauthentic-ity but rather of "resistant female expression," a "release from repression" but also a "deliberate creative act" in which "nature and character are both given and made through desiring and defiant performances." Millington says much the same about "the passionately theatrical Zenobia," finding in her characterization that "Hawthorne anticipates the ethical discovery that in-forms the late novels of Henry James," namely, that "there is a form of self-conscious performance that leads not to inauthenticity but to existence."[36] Zenobia's "mystery," in fact, is a direct consequence of her resistance to be-ing limited, as Priscilla is so easily, to the part that men write for her. Despite Coverdale's willingness to cast her in a multiplicity of roles—writer, stump oratress, feminist and radical reformer, tragic heroine, Queen Zenobia, Eve, Pandora, Cassandra-like prophetess, sorceress—she eludes him.[37] In the lan-guage of a desperate mesmerist whose subject responds to the command of only her own voice, he at one point becomes "determined to make proof if there were any spell that would exorcise her out of the part which she seemed to be acting. She should be compelled to give me a glimpse of something true; some nature, some passion, no matter whether right or wrong, provided it were real" (3:165). He misses the point. What is so "real" about Zenobia is precisely what cannot "be compelled" to display itself. As Christina Zwarg has observed of the evasiveness and contradictoriness of contemporary accounts of Fuller, "every effort to frame her in conventionality results in a destabilization of that frame" and "reads like an undecipherable text because 'she' participated in its production" by engaging "in a series of cultural negotiations" as a form of "resistance."[38]

Like the Zenobia who "transformed" herself "into a work of art" (3:164), Fuller, in her effort to explore the possibilities of identity, often conflated, self-consciously, life with art. Her friends recognized that, and recent scholars, most notably Albert J. Von Frank, have explored its implications.[39] Reynolds and Smith, in particular, have demonstrated how in Fuller's *Tribune* dispatches from Europe her "devotion to the literary often made her blur the distinction between life and art," literary texts providing genres for historical emplotment and historical events becoming textual materials for literary use. In triumph, the republican revolutions in Europe in general and Rome in particular were represented as historical "romance"—in defeat, as historical "tragedy." As narrator and actor in the historical tragedy she dramatized, Fuller, note Reynolds and Smith, increasingly "assumed the persona of Liberty in that figure's martial aspect—stoic, uncompromising, willing to shed blood if the cause demanded it."[40] Six months after the defeat of the Roman revolutionary republicans, Fuller in her final dispatch for the *Tribune* speaks in the prophetic voice of a still-undefeated Liberty turned Cassandra:

> The seeds for a vast harvest of hatreds and contempts are sown over every inch of Roman ground, nor can that malignant growth be extirpated, till the wishes of Heaven shall waft a fire that will burn down all, root and branch, and prepare the earth for an entirely new culture. The next revolution, here and elsewhere, will be radical. Not only Jesuitism must go, but the Roman Catholic religion must go. . . . Not only the Austrian, and very potentate of foreign blood, must be deposed, but every man who assumes an arbitrary lordship over fellow man, must be driven out. . . . The New Era is no longer an embryo; it is born; it begins to walk—this very year sees its first giant steps, and can no longer mistake its features. . . . At this moment all the worst men are in power, and the best betrayed and exiled. All the falsities, the abuses of the old political forms, the old social compact, seem confirmed. Yet it is not so: the struggle that is now to begin will be fearful, but even from the first hours not doubtful. . . . That advent called EMMANUEL begins to be

understood, and shall no more so foully be blasphemed. Men shall now be represented as souls, not hands and feet, and governed accordingly.[41]

Such passages as this, with their melding of the sacred and the revolutionary apocalyptic, were perhaps on Hawthorne's mind when he described the grotesque contradictions of Zenobia's corpse, knees bent in the supplication of prayer, arm and clenched hand extended "in immitigable defiance" (3:235).[42] Such passages also illustrate why Hawthorne would have Coverdale comment that Zenobia "was made . . . for a stump-oratress" (3:44). In that role, as in the passage above, given Coverdale's self-confessed "state of moral as well as bodily faint-heartedness," her "hardihood of . . . philosophy" frankly "startled" him. "She made no scruple of oversetting all human institutions, and scattering them as with a breeze from her fan," he claims, for as "a female reformer" she had "an instinctive sense of where the life lies, and is inclined to aim directly at that spot. Especially, the relation between the sexes is naturally among the earliest to attract her notice" (3:44). In that phrase, "among the earliest," Hawthorne suggests that Zenobia's radical challenge to the "bond-slavery" of woman to man is, as it was for Fuller, but the first and most immediate manifestation of an attack upon any form of arbitrary lordship of one human being over another.

As the Cassandra's voice of Liberty in defeat, Fuller's is the voice of the defiant tragic heroine prophesying history's retribution on those who would continue to seek arbitrary lordship over others. Hers is the voice heard echoed on the smaller private stage of Coverdale's tragedy in Zenobia's defiant prophecy that, despite her "dethronement," her voice, her shadow, would haunt the male despot Hollingsworth. And, indeed, Fuller does haunt the two men behind the mask of Hollingsworth, both of whom attempt to exorcise that ghost in the telling of her story, Hawthorne in *Blithedale* and Emerson in the *Memoirs* and in his private journals.[43] For both Hawthorne and Emerson the ghost of Fuller lingering in their memories assumes the form of a tragic heroine. Contemplating the title of "Margaret and Her Friends" for the *Memoirs,* Emerson admits that "that form proved impossible." The only form that could contain his conception of her and of his role as surviving witness to her life was that of a Greek tragedy: "It only remained that the narrative, like a Greek tragedy, should suppose the chorus always on the stage, sympathizing and sympathized with by the queen of the scene."[44] Coverdale's self-appointed role in Zenobia's tragedy is almost identical to the role Emerson claims. He too would represent himself as performing a part like "the Chorus in a classic play"; the chorus because it seems to be uninvolved, "seems to be set aloof from the possibility of personal concernment, and bestows the whole measure of its hope or fear, its exultation or sorrow, on the fortunes of others, between whom and itself this sympathy is the only bond" (3:97). Coverdale's construction of Zenobia as a tragic heroine and of himself as the choral voice of the drama of her fall is suggested to him by Zenobia's self-representations, for later she tells him, "I have been several times on the point of making you my confidant. . . . But you are too young to be my Father Confessor; and you would not thank me for treating you like one of those good little handmaidens, who share the bosom-secrets of a tragedy-queen!" (3:141–42). Zenobia's representation of herself as a tragic queen is itself a representation of the part in which Fuller often cast her character.[45]

Zenobia's tragedy is not played out on the battlefield of Rome, where revolutionary republicans battled the despotism of the papal government and of reactionary foreign powers, but on the battlefield of Eliot's Pulpit, where Zenobia assaults the despotism of Hollingsworth's masculine egotism. Zenobia fights Fuller's first battle—to end the arbitrary lordship of man over woman. As Fuller did, she fights for a democratic marriage of intellectual and spiritual equals against the despotic marriage of "worshipper" to "idol," "bond-slave" to "master." Hawthorne conflates Fuller's earlier ideological fight for women's rights and for a reformation of the institution of marriage with her fight, the military fight, to overthrow the worldly power of one of the oldest institutions of arbitrary lordship, the Papacy. Zenobia's battle inscribes both of Fuller's battles in the "battlefield" imagery with which Coverdale invests his tale. Coverdale, for instance, compares his intrusion into the just-completed climatic scene between Zenobia, Hollingsworth, and Priscilla as giving him the sensation that he "had come upon a battle-field, before the smoke as yet cleared away" (3:215). Rejected by Hollingsworth, Zenobia herself speaks of her defeat in martial metaphors, a representational practice that Fuller apparently inspired, if we judge by the martial figures Fuller's friends employed in their own accounts of Fuller's "conquest" of their friendships.[46] The "moral" of the "bitter" ballad that she urges Coverdale to write, she tells him should be "this:—that, in the battlefield of life, the downright stroke, that would fall only on a man's steel headpiece, is sure to light on a woman's heart, over which she wears no breastplate" (3:224). At her funeral, Coverdale again invokes his own and Zenobia's metaphor, this time in an allusion to the Roman solution for a general's defeat: "It is a wo[e]ful thought, that a woman of Zenobia's diversified capacity should have fancied herself irretrievably defeated on the broad battle-field of life, and with no refuge, save to fall on her own sword, merely be-cause Love had gone against her" (3:241).[47]

The ideological battle between Zenobia and Hollingsworth, however, is more than just ideologically parallel to Fuller's feminist challenge and meta-phorically parallel to Fuller's presence on the military battlefield of Rome. Zenobia's ideological battle, should she win it, as the republican revolution-aries of Rome initially won theirs, could become a physical battle of force in which the claim to the "sacred" as ground for male superiority is nullified by an assertion of the power of man's "arbitrary lordship," the power that the invocation of the "sacred" had been meant to mask. As happened in Rome when the once seemingly liberal Pope Pius IX lost power to the forces of emergent republicanism and regained it only through enlisting the mili-tary force of foreign allies, so Hollingsworth says that if "these petticoated monstrosities" had a chance of being victorious in their arguments for an equality of the sexes, he "would call upon my own sex to use its physical force, that unmistakeable evidence of sovereignty, to scourge them back within their proper bounds!" (3:123). Hollingsworth's "defeat" of Zenobia, the "downright stroke" that "is sure to light on a woman's heart," is reen-acted on the midnight river with symbolic literalness: Hollingsworth makes good his earlier threat against Zenobia when he pierces her drowned heart with his "pole."[48]

With Zenobia defeated on the final "battle-field" by Hollingsworth's choice of Priscilla, Hawthorne would have Zenobia blame herself for be-traying herself: "Why should he seek me? What had I to offer him? A miser-able, bruised, and battered heart, spoilt long before he met me! A life, too, hopelessly entangled with a villain's!" Zenobia will "remove from Blithe-dale" because "a woman in my position, you understand, feels scarcely at her ease among former friends." "New faces—unaccustomed looks—those only can she tolerate," she says, for "under the eyes that knew her secret," she might "mortify herself . . . with foolish notions of having sacrificed the honor of her sex, at the foot of proud, contumacious man" (3:225). Here, as in many places in the romance, Coverdale seems to translate into Zenobia's character and circumstance Hawthorne's conflation of the two Fuller ghosts haunting him, the Fuller of his memory at Concord and the Fuller of his imagination at Rome. For Hawthorne, Fuller "sacrificed the honor of her sex at the foot of" the "proud, contumacious man" the Marquis Ossoli. If the Hawthorne in Hollingsworth can be said to have chosen Priscilla over

Zenobia, Phoebe over Alice Pyncheon, "the angel and the apostle of sacred love" over Hester, he did so, like Hollingsworth, only after learning of the scandal of Fuller's liaison with Ossoli.

That scandal and Hawthorne's reaction to it, as Chevigny has argued, are inscribed in *Blithedale* through Zenobia's mysterious yet clearly sexually tainted relationship with Westervelt and through Coverdale's angry contempt for and guilty identification with Westervelt.[49] Hawthorne, of course, would have known little about Ossoli at this time, except perhaps what he learned from rumors and from Fuller's letters to Caroline Sturgis Tappan. He probably knew the most prominently mentioned details—that he fought with the republican revolutionaries, that he was a penniless member of the minor Italian nobility, that he was handsome, and that he was the father of Fuller's son. He could not know, as no one really did, whether Ossoli was legally Fuller's husband. Married or not, the relationship between Fuller and Ossoli was intimately connected with Fuller's drowning. And he certainly knew that Fuller refused to leave Ossoli's side and attempt to save herself as the *Elizabeth* broke apart—that, in other words, she had sacrificed her life, either over her love for him or over her despair at returning mortified to confront her former friends with him, the latter being the supporting text of the persistent interpretation of her death as a suicide. Sophia chose to believe that Fuller died for love. Hawthorne just could not accept that. As already suggested by Zenobia's bitterness in her final interview with Coverdale over her life being "hopelessly entangled with a villain's," Hawthorne seems to have reacted to Fuller's liaison with Ossoli and the manner of her death as a betrayal of the best he had come to know in Fuller and of the best and the worst he had come to know, and conceal, in himself.

Hawthorne translates his anger and his inordinate curiosity about Fuller's relationship with Ossoli in his characterization of Westervelt. As Oscar Cargill discovered long ago, the unusual name "Westervelt" itself unmasks Hawthorne's concern in *Blithedale* with Fuller, for "Westervelt" was the name of a Swedish sailor listed in the *New-York Tribune* among those who drowned along with Fuller and Ossoli in the wreck of the *Elizabeth*.[50] Coverdale's immediate loathing for the ghost of Ossoli in Westervelt—the "spectral character" (3:95) of the man who appears to him in the forest with "almost the effect of an apparition" (3:91)—inscribes Hawthorne's own instinctive hatred of the man who both won and "ruined" Fuller, a passion that erupts again six years later in Rome when Mozier describes Ossoli to him. In Hawthorne's imagination, Ossoli becomes in Westervelt the very incarnation of decadence and duplicity, "a moral and physical humbug" whose handsome face "might be removeable like a mask," the mask of "perhaps but a wizened little elf, gray and decrepit, with nothing genuine about him, save the wicked expression of his grin" (3:95).

Westervelt's evil, it must be noted, is described in the distinctively European terms suggested by his very name and conforms in many respects to descriptions of Ossoli. In contrast to Coverdale's thoroughly American "rough hickory-stick" and plain "rustic garb" of a "linen blouse, with checked shirt and striped pantaloons," Westervelt is dressed like a European aristocratic fop. Carrying an elaborately carved serpent-headed stick, Westervelt wears "a summer-morning costume," with a "gold chain, exquisitely wrought, across his vest" and a "gem" that glimmers "like a living tip of fire" pinned to his extraordinarily white and well-pressed "shirt-bosom." Twenty-six years old when he met Fuller and twenty-nine when he died, Ossoli was tall, somewhat slight in build, and, by all accounts, extremely handsome. He had black eyes, black hair, and a black mustache. Employing what he had apparently heard about Ossoli, Hawthorne describes Westervelt as being "a little under thirty, of a tall and well-developed figure, and as handsome a man as ever I beheld" (3:91). Westervelt's "hair, as well as his beard and moustache, was coal-black" and "his eyes, too, were black and sparkling, and his teeth remarkably brilliant" (3:92), brilliant but, of course, false. Coverdale's repulsion originates not so much in his democratic disdain for Westervelt's decadent, vaguely Italian aristocratic "beauty" as it does in his recoil from his perception of Westervelt's aggressive sexuality, which is intimated by what Millington has termed Coverdale's "language of erection":[51]

> His countenance—I hardly know how to describe the peculiarity—had an indecorum in it, a kind of rudeness, a hard, coarse, forth-putting freedom of expression, which no degree of external polish could have abated, one single jot. Not that it was vulgar. But he had no fineness of nature; there was in his eyes (although they might have artifice enough of another sort) the naked exposure of something that ought not to be left prominent. With these vague allusions to what I have seen in other faces, as well as his, I leave the quality to be comprehended best—because with an intuitive repugnance—by those who possess least of it. . . .
>
> My dislike for this man was infinite. At that moment, it amounted to nothing less than a creeping of the flesh, as when, feeling about in a dark place, one touches something cold and slimy, and questions what the secret hatefulness may be. And, still, I could not but acknowledge, that, for personal beauty, for polish of manner, for all that externally befits a gentleman, there was hardly another like him. (3:91–92, 172)

Coverdale's association of Westervelt with the "naked exposure" of an aggressive sexuality is evident later at the Village Hall. Prefacing his description of the performance with a condemnation of the "mystic sensuality" of mesmerism that grants one "miraculous power . . . over the will and passions of another," Coverdale reports hearing an account of that power that suggests mesmerism's alliance with the force of a dark sexual attraction in its ability to lead a woman to betray those she once loved: "At the bidding of one of these wizards, the maiden, with her lover's kiss still burning on her lips, would turn from him with icy indifference; the newly made widow would dig up her buried heart out of her young husband's grave, before the sods had taken root upon it; a mother, with her babe's milk in her bosom, would thrust away her child" (3:198). Hawthorne's concern here and elsewhere with mesmerism arises from his identification with the male mesmerist's exploitation of his female subject. That concern, of course, is evident in the stranger's examples. Also evident perhaps is Hawthorne's concern for the power that he imagined Ossoli must have exercised over Fuller to make her betray the self that Hawthorne had known and, in a sense, to betray those friends who loved her.

Just as Fuller's friends then and scholars today have yet to determine whether Fuller and Ossoli were ever married, Coverdale never learns the exact nature of Zenobia's entanglement with Westervelt. In Coverdale's curiosity about her sexual past and his references to contemporary gossip, Hawthorne alludes to the gossip about Fuller and her Italian lover that reached America during the last four or five months of 1849 and continued long after her death. In an allusion that affirms the presence of those rumors by speculating on their very absence (true of Fuller in 1841 but not in 1849–52), Coverdale admits he "perplexed" himself "with a great many conjectures" about "whether Zenobia had ever been married" (46):

> If the great event of a woman's existence had been consummated, the world knew nothing of it, although the world seemed to know Zenobia well. It was a ridiculous piece of romance, undoubtedly, to imagine that this beautiful personage, wealthy as she was, and holding a position that might fairly be called distinguished, could have given herself away so privately, but that some whisper and suspicion, and, by degrees, a full understanding of the fact, would eventually be blown abroad. But, then, as I failed not to consider, her original home was at a distance of many hundred miles. Rumors might fill the social atmosphere, or might once have filled it, there, which would travel but slowly, against the wind, towards our north-eastern metropolis, and perhaps melt into thin air before reaching it. (3:46)

"Giving herself away privately" and "the world knew nothing of it" until the "whisper and suspicion" that "would eventually be blown abroad" from her distant home "against the wind" to "our north-eastern metropolis"—

Hawthorne's phrasing suggests the progress of the gossip through which Fuller's relationship with Ossoli came to be known first among the Anglo-American colony in Rome and then by her friends in America. Coverdale later confirms that rumors in fact did exist: "There were whispers of an attachment, and even a secret marriage, with a fascinating and accomplished, but unprincipled young man" (3:189). These rumors, however, did not destroy the high regard with which Zenobia's extraordinary character was held, just as they did not alienate any of Fuller's friends. Hawthorne explains why:

> Nor was her reputation seriously affected by the report. In fact, so great was her native power and influence, and such seemed the careless purity of her nature, that whatever Zenobia did was generally acknowledged as right for her to do. The world never criticised her so harshly as it does most women who transcend its rules. It almost yielded its assent, when it beheld her stepping out of the common path, and asserting the most extensive privileges of her sex, both theoretically and by her practice. The sphere of ordinary womanhood was felt to be narrower than her development required. (3:189–90)[52]

Fuller, in fact, made no apologies for her conduct, nor deemed any necessary. She presumed, in fact, that her friends, if not the public, would assent to her actions.[53]

Fuller has long been identified as informing Hawthorne's characterization of Zenobia as an outspoken feminist who was a powerful speaker but weaker writer, but because Zenobia is presented as being an Eve-like beauty who inspires Coverdale's sexual fantasies, even those most sympathetic to Fuller have qualified their assessment of Fuller's influence on Hawthorne and on his creation of Zenobia's character. Fuller was supposedly just too "plain" to inspire the erotic imagination of Hawthorne. On closer examination, Zenobia's beauty and her erotic attractiveness for Coverdale have little to do with her features, which are but vaguely described. Like Fuller, like Beatrice, Zenobia's purported beauty is primarily an impression created by the effect of the passionate intensity of her character—her look, gesture, and speech.[54] As a testimony to the power she exerted over Coverdale, Coverdale's descriptions of her have exerted a similar power over Hawthorne's readers, whose impressions of her physical beauty are in fact based on descriptions of her character and its physical, dynamic expression. Consider the focus of emphasis in the following descriptions:

> Assuredly, Zenobia could not have intended it—the fault must have been entirely in my imagination—but these last words, together with something in her manner, irresistibly brought up a picture of that fine, perfectly developed figure, in Eve's earliest garment. I almost fancied myself actually beholding it.

Her free, careless, generous modes of expression often had this effect of creating images which, though pure, are hardly felt to be quite decorous, when born of a thought that passes between man and woman. I imputed it, at that time, to Zenobia's noble courage, conscious of no harm, scorning the petty restraints which take the life and color out of other women's conversation. There was another peculiarity about her. We seldom meet with women, now-a-days, and in this country, who impress us as being women at all; their sex fades away and goes for nothing, in ordinary intercourse. Not so with Zenobia. One felt an influence breathing out of her, such as we might suppose to come from Eve, when she was just made, and her Creator brought her to Adam, saying "Behold, here is a woman!" Not that I would convey the idea of especial gentleness, grace, modesty, and shyness, but of a certain warm and rich characteristic, which seems, for the most part, to have been refined away out of the feminine system. . . .

Zenobia had a rich, though varying color. It was, most of the while, a flame, and anon a sudden paleness. Her eyes glowed, so that their light sometimes flashed upward to me, as when the sun throws a dazzle from some bright object on the ground. Her gestures were free, and strikingly impressive. The whole woman was alive with a passionate intensity, which I now perceived to be the phase in which her beauty culminated. Any passion would have become her well, and passionate love, perhaps, the best of all. (3:17, 102)

The latter passage names the "passionate intensity" that inspired the former passage, and the former passage locates that passionate intensity in the evocative power of Zenobia's look, gesture, and, particularly, speech.[55] Zenobia's speech alone inspires Coverdale's erotic images. That passage also provides a corrective gloss on what Hawthorne in 1858 would call the absence in Fuller of the "charm of womanhood" (14:155). Zenobia's attractiveness as a woman, Coverdale is careful to note, does not arise from those "charms" typically associated with contemporary constructions of femininity—"gentleness, grace, modesty, and shyness"—but "a certain warm and rich characteristic, which seems, for the most part, to have been refined away out of the feminine system" (3:17). He had made the same point earlier in describing her as "an admirable figure of a woman, just on the hither verge of her richest maturity, with a combination of features which it is safe to call remarkably beautiful, even if some fastidious persons might pronounce them a little deficient in softness and delicacy" (3:15). Zenobia has the "fulness and tenacity of life" in face and figure that Emerson described in Fuller, but both lacked the "softness" and "delicacy" of the conventionally beautiful woman, who is represented in *Blithedale* by Priscilla, that combination of "disease" and "beauty," whom Westervelt describes, in phrases that intertextually allude to Coverdale's earlier comment, as "one of those delicate, nervous young creatures, not uncommon in New England" who "have become what we find them by the gradual refining away of the physical system" (3:95).[56]

Zenobia's lack of conventional "delicacy" is, in fact, a sign both of her health and her sexuality. The "passionate intensity" of Zenobia's character is expressed in the dynamic of her body in motion. Note, for instance, Coverdale's contrast between the lifeless poses, the tableaux vivants, of conventional women with the natural vitality of Zenobia's movements:

> Not one woman in a thousand could move so admirably as Zenobia. Many women can sit gracefully; some can stand gracefully; and a few, perhaps, can assume a series of graceful positions. But natural movement is the result and expression of the whole being, and cannot be well and nobly performed, unless responsive to something in the character. I often used to think that music—light and airy, wild and passionate, or the full harmony of stately marches, in accordance with her varying mood—should have attended Zenobia's footsteps." (3:155–56)

Coverdale then links the natural beauty of her movement with the "large amount of physical exercise" that Zenobia, unlike "most of her sex," needed for "her moral well-being," and he specially illustrates his point by observing that "no inclemency of sky or muddiness of earth had ever impeded her daily walks" (3:156). That Fuller was noted for grace and vitality of movement and gesture or that she was an inveterate walker is not so much an indication that Hawthorne had Fuller in mind here as is that last detail, her willingness to walk during inclement weather or over wet, muddy ground. Hawthorne seems to be thinking here of his last walk through the wet woods of Sleepy Hollow with Fuller before she left Concord in the summer of 1844. In her journal, Fuller describes it: "Walk with H. in the woods long paths, dark and mystical. We went far & it was quite dark when we returned: we lost the path & I got wet in the long grass & had much scrambling. Yet this was pleasant too in its way."[57]

Westervelt may dismiss the conventional "charms of womanhood" in the "delicacy" of Priscilla's sexlessness, but for Coverdale, Westervelt is even more incapable of comprehending, much less being worthy of, the passionate intensity of Zenobia's rich and warm character. Coverdale's contempt for the "miserably incomplete" (3:103) Westervelt and his anger over Zenobia's having wasted herself on such a man anticipate Hawthorne's outburst in 1858 when he once again wonders of Fuller and the "half an idiot" Ossoli "what attraction she found in this boor, this hymen without the intellectual spark . . . except it were purely sensual," for Ossoli "could not possibly have had the least appreciation" of her (14:155). For Hawthorne, Fuller's connection with Ossoli led to "a total collapse in poor Margaret, morally and intellectually" (14:156). Similarly, Coverdale faults Westervelt's intellectual and spiritual inadequacy with "the moral deterioration" caused by the "false and shallow life" (3:103) Zenobia found with him:

> It was a crisis in which his intellectual perceptions could not altogether help him out. He failed to comprehend, and cared little for comprehending, why Zenobia should put herself into such a fume; but satisfied his mind that it was all folly, and only another shape of a woman's manifold absurdity, which men can never understand. How many a woman's evil fate has yoked her with a man like this! Nature thrusts some of us into the world miserably incomplete, on the emotional side, with hardly any sensibilities except what pertain to us as animals. No passion, save of the senses; no holy tenderness, nor the delicacy that results from this. Externally, they bear a close resemblance to other men, and have perhaps all save the finest grace; but when a woman wrecks herself on such a being, she ultimately finds that the real womanhood, within her, has no corresponding part in him. Her deepest voice lacks a response; the deeper her cry, the more dead his silence. The fault may be none of his; he cannot give her what never lived within his soul. But the wretchedness, on her side, and the moral deterioration attendant on a false and shallow life, without strength enough to keep itself sweet, are among the most pitiable wrongs that mortals suffer. (3:102–3)

Hawthorne's choice of the verb "wrecks" in "when a woman wrecks herself on such a being" is part of a pattern of imagery that foreshadows the tragic end of Zenobia's passions, and it is a pattern that suggests Fuller's death by drowning in the wreck of the *Elizabeth*. Westervelt's "cold scepticism smothers what it can of our spiritual aspirations" (3:101), and Zenobia "wrecks" herself on Westervelt (3:103) in a "miserable bond" that Zenobia fears "will strangle" her "at last!" (3:104). Taking leave of Coverdale and Blithedale for her "European" drawing room in the city, in despair over Hollingsworth's relationship with Priscilla and over Westervelt's reappearance to exert his mysterious claim over her, bitterly speaking of herself as "a tragedy-queen," Zenobia rejects Coverdale's offer to be her counselor with a foreboding metaphor of her determination to act upon her passions: "It needs a wild steersman when we voyage through Chaos! The anchor is up! Farewell!" (3:142).

Zenobia's final passionate act on her "voyage through Chaos" is to commit suicide. As many have suspected, Zenobia's "Chaos" is Fuller's "storm"; Zenobia's suicide, Fuller's refusal to attempt to save herself. Read outside its biographical context, *Blithedale* seems designed by Hawthorne to confirm Coverdale's early assessment that Zenobia's "quarrel of woman against man" arose from her own romantic disappointments (3:120–21). Read within its biographical context, however, *Blithedale* dramatizes Hawthorne's anger at himself and at Fuller for having betrayed herself and him by seeming to live up to Coverdale's masculine reduction of feminine desire to the single dimension of romantic fulfillment, an anger that Emerson shared with Hawthorne.[58] With Fuller's life, from Hawthorne's perspective, "hopelessly entangled with a villain's," facing the prospect of pining "among familiar scenes," of blushing "under the eyes that knew her secret," of her "heart" throbbing "uncomfortably," of being mortified for having "sacrificed the honor of her sex, at the foot of proud, contumacious man" (3:225), Hawthorne, as he states explicitly in 1858, envisioned the once dazzling and proud Fuller humbled, becoming, as Zenobia herself fears, the object of a ridicule whose "humor" would center on the comic collapse of her pretensions to a womanhood that transcended the narrow boundaries established for her sex. In the romantic theatricality that Coverdale imagines Zenobia acting out her suicide, Hawthorne seems to be saying that rather than see her life written for her as a bitter comedy, Fuller wrote it for herself as the tragedy she always feared it would be. By so interpreting Fuller's death, Hawthorne reclaims for Fuller not only the redemption of a tragic recognition of her failure to live up to her ideal of self but also the capacity, at the very end, to embrace once again that betrayed self, to reassert her power to define in death the part that she would live, if live only briefly. She will not end as a comic object lesson to prove the ridiculous pretensions of women who resist the narrow boundaries of their sex but as a tragic victim of those boundaries. That is why Zenobia seems to kneel in a prayer of submission yet makes her final gesture an immitigable defiance of that submission.

At her burial, Coverdale reenacts Zenobia's self-canceling gestures of submission to and defiance of the values of the "secret tribunal" that judges and condemns a woman who attempts to extend the boundaries of her sex. Challenging Westervelt's contention that Zenobia "was the last woman in the world to whom death could have been necessary," Coverdale finds himself first justifying Zenobia's suicide on the grounds that she faced both financial and emotional failure and poverty, that "she had tried life fully, had no more to hope, and something, perhaps, to fear" (3:239). In a rough draft of what Hawthorne would write in 1858 about the "kindness" of "Providence" saving Fuller from "ridicule" by putting her aboard that "fated ship," Coverdale then tells Westervelt pointedly, "Had Providence taken her away in its own holy hand, I should have thought it the kindest dispensation that could be awarded to one so wrecked" (3:239). Coverdale's sentiments here, it must be noted, were shared by many of Fuller's friends, who were as decid-

edly uncomfortable with them as is Coverdale, as is Hawthorne.[59] Assigning
to Westervelt the voice of his own self-doubt, Hawthorne has Westervelt
tell Coverdale that he "mistake[s] the matter completely," that with a mind
"various in its powers," a heart of "manifold adaptation," and a constitution
of "infinite buoyancy," Zenobia would have survived her disappointments
and been "borne . . . upward, triumphantly" in "a hundred varieties of brilliant success" (3:239–40). Still clinging to law of the world's "tribunals," for
Coverdale the "hundred varieties of brilliant success" would not compensate
for her having "nothing to satisfy her heart" (3:240).[60] He blames Westervelt
for being her "evil fate" and speculates that "the connection may have been
indissoluble, except by death," in which case he "cannot deem it a misfortune that she sleeps in yonder grave!" (3:240). Like Beatrice, Zenobia becomes in Coverdale's final judgment "a character of admirable qualities"
who "loses its better life, because the atmosphere, that should sustain it, is
rendered poisonous by such breath as this man mingled with Zenobia's"
(3:241). Despite his wish to have Heaven "annihilate" Westervelt, Coverdale,
in the end, and to himself only, admits that Westervelt "possessed" his "share
of truth" (3:241). In attempting to justify Zenobia's despair, Coverdale had
been complicitly enforcing the very values that had caused it:

> It was a wo[e]ful thought, that a woman of Zenobia's diversified capacity
> should have fancied herself irretrievably defeated on the broad battle-field of
> life, and with no refuge, save to fall on her own sword, merely because Love
> had gone against her. It is nonsense, and a miserable wrong—the result, like
> so many others, of masculine egotism—that the success or failure of woman's
> existence should be made to depend wholly on the affections, and on one
> species of affection; while man has such a multitude of other chances, that
> this seems but an incident. (3:241)

Fuller's death had to be a suicide. For Hawthorne to accept—as Sophia
had so readily—that Fuller had become so humbled in "bond-slavery" to an
unworthy love that she was willing to die rather than face life without Ossoli
would be an incomprehensible betrayal of the Fuller he had known. But
then to believe that Fuller had chosen death over humiliation was to see
Fuller's reassertion of pride as serving only to confirm the power of that
masculine egotism to destroy, if not subdue, those who defy it. To endorse
her death as a "kindness" of "Providence" is to become complicit in the
miserable wrong of a society that condemns her to the narrow sphere of
having but those two choices—humiliating submission or self-destructive
defiance. The former kills the spirit, the latter the body. Either way it is
murder, not suicide, and it is a murder that claims not one, but three victims,

one in the body, two in the spirit. One of them returns to the site of his regret and nostalgic longing to stand beside the body's grave and translate the words of the spirit who still speaks to him in the Cassandra's voice of an unquiet heart that refuses to be silenced. The other hears that voice but cannot acknowledge it, can only hope that by leaning away from its "vindictive shadow" and pressing "close, and closer still" to his Priscilla, he will be close enough to be absorbed by her, close enough then, finally, to have no spirit to haunt, no "side where Priscilla was not."

The Venus of the Tribune, the Pearl Diver, and THE MARBLE FAUN

> Nothing is more unaccountable than the spell that often lurks in a spoken word. A thought may be present to the mind, so distinctly that no utterance could make it so; and two minds may be conscious of the same thought, in which one or both take the profoundest interest; but as long as it remains unspoken, their familiar talk flows quietly over the hidden idea, as a rivulet may sparkle and dimple over something sunken in its bed. But, speak the word; and it is like bringing up a drowned body out of the deepest pool of the rivulet, which has been aware of the horrible secret, all along, in spite of its smiling surface.
>
> KENYON ON SPEAKING THE WORD "MIRIAM" TO DONATELLO IN
> *The Marble Faun*

When Kenyon finally says the word that lies "sunken in its bed" like a "horrible secret," the word that rises like a "drowned body out of the deepest pool," he confronts Donatello with the name of the woman that Donatello has fled but not forgotten (4:229). Donatello's reconciliation begins at that moment, but does not end until, in the marketplace of Perugia, in front of the Bronze Pontiff's statue, he too can speak her name. By calling her, he acknowledges that her crime is his as well and that they are forever bound in a communion of love and guilt, a "sad marriage-bond" (4:323), which Kenyon nevertheless blesses as "a true one" that should never "except by Heaven's own act . . . be rent asunder" (4:321). The very statue of Pope Julius seems to join Kenyon in extending a benediction on their reconciliation. In the marketplace, in front of the populace, under the eyes of the symbolic representative of the religious and political powers of the state, Donatello does what Dimmesdale could not do.

When Hawthorne left Coverdale at Zenobia's grave and Hollingsworth at Priscilla's side, he left behind him the most productive creative period in his life, the two-and-a-half-year period that began with *The Scarlet Letter* and ended with *Blithedale*. In his portrayal of Coverdale's middle-aged artistic incapacity, Hawthorne reexamines in *Blithedale* the sources in his own past that had led, he feared, to his own sense of literary sterility. The next few years would seem to prove that his fears had been well founded. Except for the campaign biography of Pierce and another collection of children's stories, *Tanglewood Tales,* Hawthorne would not write again for six years, and when he did, he could do so only after someone spoke the name of the "drowned body" whose "horrible secret" had lain "sunken in the bed" of his consciousness. The name was Margaret Fuller, and the person who would speak it was Joseph Mozier.

If Mozier's gossip on 2 April 1858 served to resurrect the body of Fuller in Hawthorne's consciousness, Hawthorne the next day tried with a fierce intensity to bury it again in what seems like his final "solution to the riddle"—his tragic narrative of a Fuller who spends a lifetime attempting to "re-create and refine" herself, to become "the greatest, wisest, best woman of the age," only to discover "in the twinkling of an eye" that "all her labor" could not prevent a rude old potency from erupting and shattering the dazzling surfaces of a brilliantly constructed life.[1] "There never was such a tragedy as her whole story," he wrote. "On the whole, I do not know but I like her the better for it," he concluded with some hesitation, "—the better, because she proved herself a very woman, after all, and fell as the weakest of her sisters might" (14:156–57). Instead of burying Fuller finally in this grave of the extraordinary but ultimately—tragically, maybe blessedly—ordinary woman, Hawthorne discovered that he was as dazzled as ever by the mystery of the Fuller who still eluded him despite his own latest re-creation of her, who would remain still "sunken in the bed" of consciousness, just below the surface. Employing one of the hieroglyphics that Kenyon claims is the only language capable of communicating the most intense experiences (4:258), Hawthorne has Miriam demonstrate the suggestiveness that Hilda claims for great art by reading Kenyon's interest in her mystery through the suggestiveness of the statue of the Pearl Diver. Her reading seems Hawthorne's reading of himself, imagined through Miriam as Fuller's likely response to his attempt to solve the riddle of her character, to possess the "pearl" that means "Margaret"—a hieroglyphic suggested perhaps by a poem Fuller wrote while staying with Hawthorne in July 1844, a poem that she suggested was inspired by her conversation with Hawthorne during a five-hour evening boat ride on the Concord. Punning on the meaning of "Margaret" as "pearl," Fuller states that "the ray of sufficient day" will one day

> break the spell
> of the slimy oyster shell
> Showing a pearl beyond all price so round and clear.
> For which must seek a Diver, too, without reproach or fear.[2]

In a statement that seems at first to refer to her "winning" of Donatello, Miriam tells Kenyon: "If we cannot all win pearls, it causes an empty shell to satisfy us just as well." Her next statement, however, not only suggests her understanding of the danger of Kenyon's interest in her but also revises the referent for the "empty shell" from, possibly, Donatello to Hilda: "My secret is not a pearl," she warns him. "Yet a man might drown himself in plunging after it." Following Fuller's footsteps in Rome, in Perugia, and in Florence, making her friends his friends, Hawthorne took the plunge one last time in *The Marble Faun.*

To a great extent *The Marble Faun* is a sympathetic revision of the tragic narrative Hawthorne constructed for Fuller's life that day in April 1858. The intensity of Hawthorne's reaction to Mozier's gossip seems to suggest that it was written spontaneously in the heat of shock and moral outrage, but a closer examination of that passage reveals that it was a narrative that Hawthorne had been a long time plotting and replotting. Mozier may have said the word that brought the "drowned body" of Fuller to the surface and onto Hawthorne's writing desk again, but for Hawthorne that body had never really been buried.

To understand why Hawthorne reacted so strongly that day in April 1858 and then why, as I argue, he retracted much of it in the writing of *The Marble Faun,* we may turn to Hawthorne himself for an explanation. In a critical passage in *Blithedale,* Hawthorne explains through Coverdale and Zenobia the powerful alternation of repulsion and attraction, condemnation and admiration, he felt for Fuller. Confronting Zenobia in the Europeanized luxury of her drawing room, Coverdale describes the "costly robes," the "flaming jewels around her neck," and the "exquisitely" jeweled flower in her hair, which adds "the last touch" that "transformed" Zenobia "into a work of art" (3:164). Powerfully attracted to her, Coverdale catches a glimpse of himself in the act of admiring Zenobia when he sees the "whole [room] repeated and doubled by the reflection of a great mirror, which showed me Zenobia's proud figure, likewise, and my own" (3:164). He sees himself in the act of seeing her and reflects on his reflection:

> It cost me, I acknowledge, a bitter sense of shame, to perceive in myself a positive effort to bear up against the effect which Zenobia sought to impose on me. I reasoned against her, in my secret mind, and strove so to keep my footing. In the gorgeousness with which she had surrounded herself—in the redundance of personal ornament, which the largeness of her physical nature and the rich type of her beauty caused to seem so suitable—I malevolently beheld the true character of the woman, passionate, luxurious, lacking simplicity, not deeply refined, incapable of pure and perfect taste. (3:164–65)

As Giovanni with Beatrice, Coverdale "malevolently" beholds the "art" of Zenobia's "true character" as passionate, unrefined, and impure because those are the very qualities within himself that so powerfully attract him to her. If his secret mind is successful in reasoning against her, he will be able to resist his powerful attraction to her by condemning in her, himself. His "bitter sense of shame," of course, results from this very recognition that his reading of the "art" of Zenobia is as much a revelation of his own character as it is of hers.

Hawthorne's description of Fuller's character in April 1858 also suggests more about his own character than it does of Fuller's, and what it suggests is precisely the passionate attraction and defensive reasoning against that attraction that Coverdale confesses to here. The terms of that reasoning are strikingly parallel. The passion of Zenobia is the sensuality of Fuller. The "largeness of . . . physical nature" in Zenobia is the "strong and coarse nature" in Fuller. A "not deeply refined" Zenobia is a Fuller "incapable of pure and perfect taste" who cannot "refine" but only "superficially change" her "strong and coarse nature." The brilliance of the "flaming jewels" and the jeweled flower, the very ornamentation that Zenobia gives her setting and person, transform her "into a work of art" just as Fuller ornaments her character with "a mosaic of admirable qualities . . . polishing each separate piece, and the whole together, till it seemed to shine afar and dazzle all who saw it," becoming "far more a work of art than any of Mr. Mozier's statues" (14:155–57). While this last parallel may seem to compare the brilliance of appearance with character, an earlier passage confirms that for Coverdale setting and ornamentation serve only to accent the already dazzling effect of Zenobia's nature: "Zenobia had a rich, though varying color. It was, most of the while, a flame, and anon a sudden paleness. Her eyes glowed, so that their light sometimes flashed upward to me as when the sun throws a dazzle from some bright object on the ground. . . . The whole woman was alive with a passionate intensity. . . . Any passion would have become her well, and passionate love, perhaps, the best of all" (3:102).

It is, of course, Coverdale's own desire that causes him to identify "passionate love" as the culmination of the "passionate intensity" of her character, and he makes this observation because he is both baffled and bitter about Zenobia's former relationship with Westervelt, a man who, much like Ossoli in the 1858 description, cannot "comprehend" Zenobia, who is so "miserably incomplete" that he has "hardly any sensibilities except what pertain to us as animals . . . no passion, save of the senses," who causes Zenobia, like Fuller with Ossoli, to "wreck herself" on him and suffer "the moral deterioration attendant on a false and shallow life" (3:102–3). Coverdale's immediate and obsessive loathing of Westervelt, very much like Hawthorne's of Ossoli, arises from his identification with Westervelt: "I detested this kind of man, and all the more," as Coverdale admits but Hawthorne will not, "because a part of my own nature showed itself responsive to him," responsive, that is, to a "cold scepticism" that "smothers what it can of our spiritual aspirations, and makes the rest ridiculous," as "ridiculous" as Hawthorne bitterly felt that Ossoli had made Fuller's high "aspirations" (3:101–2).

Denigrating what he desires, shamefully aware that his very disgust is but the symptom of that desire, Coverdale is able only for a moment to avoid succumbing to Zenobia's power to excite his self-confessed admiration: "But, the next instant, she was too powerful for all my opposing struggles. I saw how fit it was that she should make herself as gorgeous as she pleased, and should do a thousand things that would have been ridiculous in the poor, thin, weakly characters of other women" (3:165). Though Hawthorne ends his notebook passage on Fuller exploring the dubious comfort of the possibility that he might like her better for having proven herself "a very woman, after all," and capable of "falling" just "as the weakest of her sisters might," the grandeur with which he imagines Fuller's aspirations and tragic fall and the bitter perplexity with which he considers "the wonder" of her attraction to this "half-idiot . . . this boor, this hymen without the intellectual spark" (14:155) clearly suggests the extraordinary power that Fuller still possessed, eight years after her death, over Hawthorne's own "secret mind."

Finding in Hawthorne's praise and condemnation of women writers his conflicted identification with them, James D. Wallace has argued persuasively that Hawthorne's account of Fuller's "moral and intellectual collapse" links her surrender to the sexuality that she worked so hard to refine out of her nature with her failure as a writer and is Hawthorne's "confrontation" with "what . . . [he] feared as a particularly repellant form of his own failure."[3] By April 1858 Hawthorne had perhaps good reason to fear his own possibly imminent moral and intellectual collapse. Arriving in Rome free of the distractions that had occupied him over the last few years as a consul, not having published a new romance or tale in six years, Hawthorne was expected to write another "classic" in Rome, just as Fuller had claimed to have begun there and finished in Florence.[4] Ill and miserable throughout most of his first two months in Rome, Hawthorne had in fact finally begun writing on 1 April, two days before he penned the passage on Fuller. Besides the usual writing anxieties attendant on the commencement of a new project, Hawthorne perhaps already sensed the failure awaiting him; between 1 April and 19 May 1858 he would write eighty-eight pages of his new romance, *The Ancestral Footstep,* but he would give up on the project.[5]

The failure was permanent, despite efforts years later to complete the manuscript. To compound his fears of suffering, or having suffered, an "intellectual collapse" of his own literary powers, Hawthorne may have had good reason at the time to fear the power within himself of the "rude old potency" that he attributed to Fuller's "moral collapse." Between late January and the middle of April 1858, Hawthorne became intimate with the attractive thirty-three-year-old Salem sculptress Maria Louisa Lander, who had sought him out within days of his arrival and persuaded him to sit for a bust. Hawthorne visited her studio, usually alone, seventeen times for sittings. Herbert has speculated that though that relationship may have been "proper," it may not have been "innocent." He argues that Hawthorne's later ostracism of Lander in the fall of 1858 (caused apparently by rumors of her attachment to a man and of her posing as a nude model) "re-enacts" Hawthorne's "repudiation of Fuller" and arose from his resentment on discovering Lander's interest in other men and his "guilty alarm" over possible misrepresentations of the nature of his intimacy with her when he sat as her model.[6] For these reasons, Lander has often been proposed as the model for Miriam. Hawthorne's uneasy relationship with Lander was indeed likely on Hawthorne's mind as he created Miriam. She provided Hawthorne with an intimate view of the life of a woman artist living alone in Rome; she and Hawthorne seemed to share for a time a close relationship; and she committed some vaguely scandalous offense, which caused Hawthorne abruptly to break off all ties with her—all very much like Miriam, but also all very much like Fuller. For Hawthorne, Lander indeed seems to "reenact" Fuller's relationship with him and Fuller's "fall" in Rome. Lander may have contributed to Hawthorne's conception of Miriam, but Miriam, as I hope to show, is Hawthorne's re-creation of the role that Lander reenacted.

Whatever may have been Hawthorne's own concerns about the possibility that Rome would also be the site of his own collapse as a man and as an artist, the spark that ignited his attempt at "reasoning against" Fuller in his "secret mind" clearly began with Mozier's characterization of Ossoli and a baffled Hawthorne's sense of anger and betrayal over Fuller's choice: "He could not possibly have had the least appreciation of Margaret; and the wonder is, what attraction she found in this boor, this hymen without the intellectual spark—she that had always shown such a cruel and bitter scorn of intellectual deficiency" (14:155). The "cruel and bitter scorn" of Hawthorne's own disgust for the "intellectual deficiency" of Fuller's choice for a lover and "clownish husband" becomes his cruel and bitter scorn of Fuller for having made that choice (14:156). The "solution to the riddle" of her character becomes, thus, an attempt to solve the mystery of her attraction to a man that Hawthorne thinks totally unworthy of her. It is the mystery that will continue to plague Hawthorne. His final attempt at a solution will be the creative impetus that gives birth to *The Marble Faun,* the romance in which Kenyon asks again and again just what could possibly account for Miriam's relationship with such an "incomplete" man as the faunlike aristocrat, the Count of Monte Beni. The narrator, in fact, admits as much when, in a parallel to Hawthorne's curiosity about Mozier's crude characterization of the Marquis Ossoli, he locates the origins of his narrative in his curiosity over the still "unfinished" bust of Donatello: "It was the contemplation of this imperfect portrait of Donatello that originally interested us in his history, and impelled us to elicit from Kenyon what he knew of his friend's adventures" (4:381).

Hawthorne documented only Mozier's gossip about Fuller and Ossoli, but given his and Sophia's known friendship with Fuller, even if he had not attempted to elicit additional information about his friend's adventures in Italy, as he almost certainly would have, Hawthorne would still have been subjected to accounts from many others about Fuller's activities during the Roman revolution and her relationship with Ossoli, accounts that would have supplemented those he had already read in the 1852 *Memoirs.*[7] What he would have heard would have provided him with a significantly more sympathetic portrait of Fuller's life in Italy and her relationship with Ossoli. William Wetmore and Emelyn Story, for instance, were particularly close to both Fuller and the Hawthornes and were much more supportive of Fuller and Ossoli's relationship than Mozier was. Emelyn was the person Fuller turned to in Rome when she feared she might die in the final French siege of the city, temporarily entrusting to her a packet of documents that, among other matters, she assured Emelyn would verify her marriage to Ossoli—an incident Hawthorne converts into the packet of documents Miriam entrusts to Hilda.[8] When Hawthorne and family traveled to Florence to spend the summer months of 1858, they were following Fuller's path of exile from conquered Rome, and in Florence as in Rome, they moved in essentially the same circle of friends. Though the Brownings were to depart from Florence less than a month after the Hawthornes' arrival, they and others would have provided Hawthorne with firsthand accounts of Fuller's last days and of her relationship with Ossoli.

The Ossoli that emerges from the written accounts of those who knew him as Fuller's "husband" is that of a handsome but unworldly, reserved but affable, young man who seemed completely and affectionately devoted to Fuller and their child.[9] Though intelligent, and according to one observer, possessing "a quick and vivid fancy, even a share of humor," he had been poorly educated, and neither he nor Fuller ever pretended that he possessed intellectual powers that, if ever developed, would make him more nearly Fuller's intellectual equal.[10] That did not seem to bother him or Fuller, however, though Fuller was very much aware that her friends in America would have difficulty accepting him and understanding her need for him. According to Elizabeth Barrett Browning, Ossoli was "amiable & gentlemanly," was known for "having fought well . . . at the siege" and made "no pretension to cope with his wife on any ground appertaining to the intellect." Given Fuller's intellectual reputation, Browning, like most, at first wondered "at that species of marriage," but quickly accepted it, as did others who came to know them.[11]

Whatever complex of emotional and sexual needs may have brought and kept them together, Fuller and Ossoli were clearly bound by their commitment to the failed revolution and their present status as political and military exiles who had lost everything but themselves and now depended on each other. As potential threats to the conservative regime governing Florence, they were kept under surveillance, yet Ossoli's fidelity to the republican cause that had cost him his inheritance as well as the affections of his family (who had long served the papal government) was such that he defiantly wore indoors the Republican Guard uniform he could not risk wearing in public. Fuller, of course, became even more radical in her politics as she struggled to finish her history of the republican revolution. Bound by their losses and their love for their child, they faced the future with foreboding.

Fuller wrote of the "severe struggle" that she expected the rest of her life to be, if she was "able to live through it," and of Ossoli's suffering, which had "ploughed furrows in his life since first we met." "Our destiny is sad," she wrote. "We much brave it as we can." Reflecting on Fuller's death, Browning records retrospectively that no one "ever seemed to want peace more than she did" and that she left Italy in "such gloom," spending her last evening with Browning talking of the prophecy that Ossoli would die by drowning.[12]

Arriving in Florence having given up on *The Ancestral Footstep* as a failure, Hawthorne, by mid-July, would have to return again to the "riddle" that had inspired his greatest work before he could begin plotting the last romance he would be able to write.[13] This time the riddle Fuller presented to Hawthorne's imagination would be framed as the question Hawthorne had asked himself in April and attempted to answer in his notebook, the question he pondered as he sat in his study overlooking the garden of the Casa del Bello or later, like Donatello, as he walked the battlements of the tower of the Villa Montauto. While Hawthorne struggled to finish the first draft in Rome during the winter and spring, whatever his provisional answers to the "riddle" may have been, his final answer was shaped by a sympathy that grew out of his own intimate confrontation with death. While he looked into the chasm that had engulfed Fuller in Rome and attempted to re-create her in art, in another room in the house, Una, gripped intermittently for months by fever, seemed at times certain to step over into that abyss herself.

1

"In the study of my art, I have gained many a hint from the dead, which the living could never have given me."

"I can well imagine it," answered Miriam. "One clay image is readily copied from another."

KENYON AND MIRIAM IN *The Marble Faun*

In her works, Fuller wrote of her own life under the thin disguise of the names Miranda and Mariana. "Miriam" will be the name of the character she inspired, but like Fuller's "Miranda" and "Mariana" or like the woman at Blithedale whom Coverdale will denote by the name "Zenobia," "Miriam" will be only the character's "ghost-name," the name that she takes on to mask her identity, the name she is only "called" by her friends (4:7). Even the torturous Model "will forbear to speak another name" (4:94), and Hawthorne, of course, will refuse to the end to name the name of the woman that he believes his readers should be able to "surmise" unless, as he has

Kenyon explain to the tale's narrator, "your feelings have never been har-
rowed by one of the most dreadful and mysterious events that have occurred
within the present century" (4:467). "There never was such a tragedy" as
Fuller's, Hawthorne had earlier decided, and as he contemplates Fuller's
tragedy in his tale of Miriam's, the "drowned body" of Fuller rises frequently
to the figurative surface of his imagination. Miriam, as Margaret, is the
"pearl" that Kenyon could drown in "plunging" after. Miriam is a Corinne
whose desire to see a lover's reflection in the waters of the Fountain of Trevi
is granted, but only as a vision of the death that that love will bring. When
Hawthorne has Miriam reenact Corinne's recognition of her lover, Lord Nel-
vil, through his reflection in the placid pool, he seizes the opportunity to
have his character's imitation of art become his imitation of life. Miriam's
fountain evokes Fuller's tempestuous sea, and Miriam's premonition of disas-
ter parallels the premonitions of death that Fuller spoke of frequently in
Florence in the days preceding her fatal voyage:

> In Miriam's case, however, (owing to the agitation of the water, its transpar-
> ency, and the angle at which she was compelled to lean over,) no reflected
> image appeared; nor, from the same causes, would it have been possible for
> the recognition between Corinne and her lover to take place. The moon, in-
> deed, flung Miriam's shadow at the bottom of the basin, as well as two more
> shadows of persons who had followed her, on either side.
> "Three shadows!" exclaimed Miriam. "Three separate shadows, all so black
> and heavy that they sink in the water! There they lie on the bottom, as if all
> three were drowned together. This shadow on my right is Donatello; I know
> him by his curls, and the turn of his head. My left-hand companion puzzles
> me; a shapeless mass, as indistinct as the premonition of calamity! Which of
> you can it be? Ah!" (4:146–47)

For Hilda, who returned to the balcony over the precipice of Traitor's
Leap because she feared that Miriam might be tempted to commit suicide,
her promise to deliver Miriam's packet, now that they are forever separated,
has "the sacredness of an injunction from a dead friend" (4:387). In the Cata-
comb of Saint Calixtus, just after expressing her terror of "going astray" in
the endless "labyrinth of darkness, which broods around the little glimmer
of our tapers," Miriam suffers the fulfillment of her forebodings and is lost
in the darkness that the narrator, following Miriam's cue, identifies figuratively with death, significantly the death of friends: "While their collected
torches illuminated this one, small, consecrated spot, the great darkness
spread all around it, like that immenser mystery which envelopes our little
life, and into which friends vanish from us, one by one" (4:26–27). "'Why,
where is Miriam?' cried Hilda" in the very next sentence. And Miriam's is

the name, of course, that rises to consciousness "like a drowned body in the deepest pool of the rivulet" once Kenyon pronounces the unspoken name of the ghost haunting his conversation with Donatello.

Miriam is lost in the darkness of the grave of the catacombs in a chapter appropriately entitled "Subterranean Reminiscences." Indeed, most of the chapter is devoted to reminiscences of Kenyon and Hilda's now-lost friendship with Miriam, the chapter concluding with her disappearance into the darkness. The image of death that is associated with Miriam's vanishing within the catacombs is foreshadowed by the elusive, ghostly images with which she is described earlier in the chapter. In the first, the "riddle" of Miriam's ability to seem so "airy, free, and affable" in her intimacies with friends who are, nevertheless, kept unsuspectingly at a distance is compared to the specters conjured through occult rituals, a comparison that owes much to Hawthorne's recent participation with Sophia in seances in Florence: "She resembled one of those images of light, which conjurors evoke and cause to shine before us, in apparent tangibility, only an arm's length beyond our grasp; we make a step in advance, expecting to seize the illusion, but find it still precisely so far out of our reach" (4:21).[14] After relating the rumors surrounding Miriam, most of them concerning inappropriate marriages that she fled to Rome to avoid, the narrator associates her beauty not with her features but with her somewhat otherworldly "mystery": "Miriam, fair as she looked, was plucked up out of a mystery, and had its roots still clinging to her. She was a beautiful and attractive woman, but based, as it were, upon a cloud, and all surrounded with misty substance, so that the result was to render her sprite-like in her most ordinary manifestation" (4:23).

Such descriptions as these not only suggest the "ghostly" presence of Fuller inspiring Hawthorne's conception of Miriam but also serve, on closer inspection, to render Miriam's beauty—very much like Beatrice's or Zenobia's—as one of Hawthorne's own conjured illusions. Hawthorne subtly suggests his method and its effect in Miriam's self-portrait by painting his own portrait of the representational practices of memory. The image of Miriam in the portrait is "so beautiful, that she seemed to get into your consciousness and memory, and could never afterwards be shut out, but haunted your dreams, for pleasure or for pain; holding your inner realm as a conquered territory, though without deigning to make herself a home there" (4:47–48). The narrator suggests that the portrait rendered by Miriam is "a flattered likeness" by raising that possibility without resolving it. What is made explicit, however, is that much of the woman's beauty in the portrait and in memory's representation of it arises from "traits, expressions, loftinesses, and amenities, which would have been invisible, had they not been painted from within." Though not discernible to the eye, the narrator insists, "Yet their reality and truth is none the less." The truth of the portrait's beauty, however, lies far deeper than features, deeper even than the effects of personality: It lies in its representation "of the intimate results of . . . heart-knowledge" (4:49).

The "ghost" of Fuller inhabiting Miriam's characterization appears in both old and new guises. As Beatrice and Zenobia before her, Miriam was reared solely by a father. His attempt to impose his will on Miriam through a prearranged marriage leads to her rebellion and the mysterious "crime" and is something of a parallel to Dr. Rappaccini's experiment in selecting and preparing Giovanni as Beatrice's mate. Like Hester, Beatrice, and Zenobia, her beauty is exotically foreign ("a certain rich Oriental character in her face" [4:22]) and is largely the effect of a "nature" with "a great deal of color" (4:21), "warmth and passionateness" (4:20), and mystery. She is extraordinarily intelligent, independent, and artistic, and she speaks vehemently against the arbitrary barriers imposed on women. Like Zenobia, her works lack "technical merit" but appeal to "the patrons of modern art" because they reflect the passion of her character (4:20) and challenge the tradition of the Old Masters through their original and disturbing portrayals of passionate women. Though Hawthorne describes her as painting in oils, he refers to her as attempting in Rome "to support herself by the pencil" (4:23), a reference that is ambiguous enough to be consistent with her role as a painter yet also to serve as an allusion to Fuller's attempt, once she had left the Springs as a tutor and returned to Rome and Ossoli, to support herself exclusively through writing dispatches for the *Tribune*.

Despite these and other similarities between Miriam and her three predecessors, Miriam is unique in being primarily Hawthorne's imaginative re-creation of the Fuller he never knew—the Fuller who attracted the devoted love of a young, handsome, innocently simple, intelligent but undereducated aristocrat, the Marquis Giovanni Angelo Ossoli, and who eventually accepted his love—who shared his liberal principles and supported him in his turn against the papal government for whom his father and two brothers served, who joined him in his fight for the republicans and suffered with him in defeat, in the loss of his inheritance, and in exile at Rieti, at Perugia, and, finally, at Florence, where both were kept under police surveillance as political enemies—who herself wrote with reluctant approval in her *Tribune* dispatches of the political assassination of the Pope's minister, the Count Pellegrino Rossi, and of the necessity to shed blood to prevent the triumph of despotism—who spoke fatalistically of her life, particularly in the final few months, as a tragedy whose end she feared might be near. Hawthorne imagines Fuller alive in Rome in 1858 through her "ghostly" presence in Miriam's character—still friends with him, as Kenyon, and with Sophia, as Hilda. The Roman revolution has passed, but its presence lingers—militarily in the deployments of French troops, politically in the church- and police-backed despotic government, and personally in the embodiment of Miriam's guilt, the Model, whose mysterious "crime" as, possibly, a "political assassin" Miriam shares some complicity. If the Model in some ways may represent the Ossoli who, under Fuller's influence, became the republican revolutionary soldier who killed to prevent the reimposition by the French of the civil despotism of the church "Fathers," Donatello is his resurrected double not yet bound to Fuller, not yet fallen from innocence through passion and violence—still alive for Hawthorne's imagination to interrogate.

Hawthorne's attempt to find an answer to the source of Fuller's attraction to Ossoli and its role in the precipitation of her "tragedy" is focused at the intersection between the sexual and the political. The contemporary political context in which Hawthorne's description of Rome is framed has long been ignored, but as Robert S. Levine has recently demonstrated, the presence of French troops to maintain order, the despotic government's link to the politically reactionary church, the revolutionary symbolism of the repressed but heavily policed energies of the Roman people during the carnival, the characterization of Miriam and her Model as likely linked to a revolutionary political assassination—all are emphasized by Hawthorne as part of a "culturally specific representation of Rome's body politic during a time in which the Roman Catholic authorities had overcome one revolutionary challenge to their governing power and were attempting to contain future subversive threats."[15] Levine, for instance, argues persuasively that Hawthorne intended to suggest that Miriam's "crime," like Beatrice Cenci's, was political as well as sexual in nature. Beatrice Cenci's incestuous father, in Shelley's version, is so strongly linked to the Pope that Beatrice, with no other protector and no other form of justice available to her, turns to an assassin to rid her of her father's despotism. Though incest is not alluded to, Miriam's father, also well connected with the church fathers, attempts to enforce his will on Miriam through a prearranged marriage, a form of sexual oppression that Miriam also resists. Because "political assassin" is given the weight of the last item in a series of possible identities for both the Model and Memmius, the legendary executor of early members of the Church of Rome, because both are associated with the traditional hiding place for Roman political and religious rebels, the catacombs, and because Miriam's "stain" relates in some way to her resistance to her father's governance— the Model's crime and Miriam's complicity in that crime, the novel suggests subtly, was likely, according to Levine, "the assassination of a patriarch connected with the Roman Catholic political authority," a patriarch much like Minister Rossi.[16]

Such an interpretation is given even greater weight if we consider more closely Miriam's paintings of Jael, Judith, and Salome, as well as her responsiveness to Kenyon's Cleopatra and Hilda's copy of Guido's "Beatrice Cenci." Levine mentions the allusions to Jael, Judith, and Cleopatra as being linked to Beatrice Cenci by virtue of their similarity in being "strongly independent women," an unaccountable interpretive myopia, considering his argument, but one encouraged by the narrator himself, who finds in Miriam's passionate, violent renderings of Jael, Judith, and Salome only the reductive similarity of "the idea of woman . . . acting the part of a revengeful mischief towards man" (4:44).[17] The "revengeful mischief" of each, however, is more political than sexual. Each, in fact, participated in a political assassination. Jael drove the tent spike through Sisera's head as part of the revolt of the Israelites against their twenty-year political subjugation by Jabin, King of Canaan, a subjugation that Sisera, as Jabin's chief military officer, had enforced. For Jael's "revengeful mischief," an "angel of the Lord" pronounces her "blessed above women . . . blessed shall she be above women in the tent."[18] Like Jael, Judith saves her people from Nebuchadnezzar's attempt to subjugate them by slaying his military commander, Holofernes. Miriam's conceptions of both Jael and Judith, as the narrator does recognize, promote "the moral . . . that woman must strike through her own heart to reach a human life" (4:44), a moral that, within the context, would suggest that women must be prepared, like men, to sacrifice the private pleasures of the heart for a political commitment that may entail brutal violence. Miriam's alterations in Jael's expression to suggest "a vulgar murderess" and her depiction of the "diabolical grin of triumphant malice" on Holofernes's severed head, however, suggest Miriam's ambivalence toward her own "moral," suggest, that is, the guilt gnawing at her for having committed or condoned similar acts of violence, regardless of their justice (4:43–44).

The third painting in that group—Salome receiving the head of John the Baptist—follows the narrator's enunciation of Miriam's "moral," thus implying its exemption from the generalization, and reenforces the suggestions of the previous two paintings of Miriam's ambivalent guilt. Whereas both Jael and Judith, like Beatrice Cenci, are nobly "innocent" in that they chose to take violent action on behalf of justice, of freedom from intolerable despotism, Salome is ignobly "innocent" as a passive agent of her mother's desire to exact personal as well as political revenge on John the Baptist's public criticism of her marriage to her former brother-in-law, King Herod, who also desired his death as a political troublemaker but feared the political consequences and is horror stricken to find his secret desire fulfilled in his promise to Salome. Herod, of course, was also frequently represented as a would-be Cenci whose lust for his stepdaughter led to his rash promise to grant any favor she demanded. Miriam's portrayal of the saint's "look of gentle and heavenly reproach, with sad and blessed eyes," which awakens Salome's "whole womanhood . . . to love and endless remorse," foreshadows the sympathy and forgiveness that both Miriam and Donatello will seek and find in Perugia under "the Bronze Pontiff's Benediction" (4:44).

In an attempt to find yet another "solution to the riddle" of Fuller, Hawthorne conflates Fuller's sexual and political activities in Rome with Miriam's relationships with the Model and with Donatello. Though Hawthorne's characterization of the Model is so melodramatically gothic that, as in the Fountain of Trevi passage cited earlier, he could represent something so nebulous as Miriam's tragic fate (her "premonition of calamity"), his vaguely political and sexual link with Miriam's past suggests that he represents to some extent Hawthorne's own past conceptions of the man responsible for Fuller's "moral and intellectual collapse"—the "boor" and "hymen" Ossoli of April 1858, the Westervelt of 1852. That representation is replaced—literally killed—by the much more sympathetic representation of an Ossoli that Hawthorne had come to know, or to reconcile himself with, through the gossip of Rome and Florence—the innocent, simple, devoted admirer of Fuller whose participation in the violent revolution to overthrow the government of the church fathers binds him to Fuller as both lover and political criminal in exile. Ossoli's revolutionary activities seem to be imagined within the romance's time frame as being both in the past—in his guise as the Model-assassin—and in the present—in his guise as Donatello, the murderer. In the Model's final exposure as Brother Antonio and in Miriam's endorsement of the execution of political traitors only seconds before Donatello hurls the Model to his death over the precipice known as, in fact, "Traitor's Leap," Donatello's "murder" of the Model suggests subtly a repetition of the Model's crime, not an "assassination" of a tyrant but an "execution" of a traitor. Executions of such traitors are just, according to Miriam's values as a democrat-socialist, because these men "are the bane of their fellow-creatures" for having "poisoned the air, which is the common breath of all, for their own selfish purposes" (4:170). Miriam's moral, but not legal, complicity in the "execution" and her attempts to assuage the shock of Donatello's moral transformation are parallel to Fuller's peaceful participation in the revolution as a political sympathizer, a foreign propagandist, and a nurse to the wounded. Indeed, in a parallel to Fuller's efforts to articulate an ideological justification for the republican insurrection in Rome by linking it to democratic revolutions of the past, Miriam directs Donatello to Pompey's forum immediately after the murder and, "treading loftily past," proclaims: "For there was a great deed done here! . . . a deed of blood, like ours! Who knows, but we may meet the high and ever-sad fraternity of Caesar's murderers, and exchange a salutation?" (4:176).

While Hawthorne's portrayal of Donatello is sympathetic throughout, his resistance to accepting the "purely sensual" as the basis of Fuller's and Ossoli's relationship seems paralleled in *The Marble Faun* by his not allowing the "unfallen" Donatello—the innocent, unintelligent faun-satyr—the merely physical man—to be worthy of Miriam's love. Miriam may envy his "happy ignorance" (4:15)—his spontaneity, his unburthened enjoyment of simple pleasures—but she patronizes him as the pure male animal that he is. In his seemingly instinctive subordination of himself to a creature vastly more complex and intellectually superior, in his absolute worship of her, in his protective loyalty, he resembles nothing so much as Miriam's "pet." Thus, when Miriam is pleased with his kissing of her hand, Miriam bestows "on him a little, careless caress . . . like what one would give to a pet dog" (4:14). She admits to thinking of him as "a child . . . a simpleton," an "underwitted" man that she finds herself treating, unavoidably, "as if he were the merest unfledged chicken" (4:15). Though he is "a gentle creature" with her, Miriam recognizes that Donatello is capable of savagery; at times, Miriam says, he can be "an odd mixture of the bull-dog, or some other equally fierce brute" (4:18). As Hawthorne was puzzled by Ossoli's attraction to Fuller, so neither Miriam nor Kenyon can fathom Donatello's attraction to one so unlike him. At one point Miriam simply asks him, "Why should you love me, foolish boy? . . . We have no points of sympathy at all. There are not two creatures more unlike, in this wide world, than you and I!" Unfazed, Donatello explains the mystery by, basically, articulating it: "You are yourself, and I am Donatello. . . . Therefore I love you! There needs no other reason" (4:79). Flattered perhaps, Miriam can also be irritated: "I wish he would not haunt my footsteps so continually," Miriam complains to Kenyon (4:18). The only explanation that Kenyon can offer Miriam for Donatello's infatuation is that Miriam has dazzled him the way Hawthorne says that Fuller, as a self-created human work of art, dazzled "all who saw" her (14:157). "You have bewitched the poor lad," Kenyon tells her. "You have a faculty of bewitching people" (4:18). The narrator describes the very qualities that may have "bewitched" Donatello, but accepts Donatello's "reason" that there is basically no reason:

> It might have been imagined that Donatello's unsophisticated heart would be more readily attracted to a feminine nature of clear simplicity, like his own, than to one already turbid with grief or wrong, as Miriam's seemed to be. Perhaps, on the other hand, his character needed the dark element which it found in her. The force and energy of will, that sometimes flashed through her eyes, may have taken him captive; or, not improbably, the varying lights and shadows of her temper, now so mirthful, and anon so sad with mysterious gloom, had bewitched the youth. Analyze the matter as we may, the reason assigned by Donatello himself was as satisfactory as we are likely to attain.
>
> (4:79–80)

What is interesting about the narrator's reasoning in the passage above is that the "feminine nature of clear simplicity" that Donatello might reasonably "be more readily attracted to" describes, rather aptly, Hilda's character, just as Donatello's need of "the dark element" might just as well describe Kenyon's need to re-create a Cleopatra, or for that matter, Hawthorne's need to create a Zenobia, a Hester, a Beatrice, or a Miriam.

Though Hawthorne will not allow Miriam to respond yet to Donatello's open avowals of love with anything more than a bemused tolerance, he allows his narrator to speculate on the emotional ambiguity of her tolerance. Despite her "dark element," Miriam is not so "world-worn" that she would find "Donatello's heart . . . so fresh a fountain, that . . . she might have found it exquisite to slake her thirst with the feelings that welled up and brimmed over from it," a euphemistic denial that Miriam was capable of being drawn to the relationship for purely sensual pleasure. More innocently, Miriam merely finds "an inexpressible charm in the simplicity" of Donatello's "words and deeds," but "unless she caught them in precisely the true light, they seemed but folly, the offspring of a maimed or imperfectly developed intellect": "Alternately, she almost admired, or wholly scorned him, and knew not which estimate resulted from the deeper appreciation" (4:80).

The alternation within Miriam's heart is paralleled by the alternative views of Hilda and Kenyon about the possibility of Miriam ever loving Donatello. When Kenyon raises that very possibility, Hilda dismisses it out of hand: "Miriam! She, so accomplished and gifted! . . . And he, a rude, uncultivated boy! No, no no!" Kenyon too thinks that "it would seem impossible," but in an echo of Coverdale on Zenobia's attachment to Westervelt or of Hawthorne on Fuller's attachment to Ossoli, he observes that "a gifted woman flings away her affections so unaccountably, sometimes!" (4:105). Exploring the possibility that Miriam might do likewise, Kenyon describes a psychological need that he, and perhaps his author, knew only too well:

> Miriam, of late, has been very morbid and miserable, as we both know. Young as she is, the morning light seems already to have faded out of her life; and now comes Donatello, with natural sunshine enough for himself and her, and offers her the opportunity of making her heart and life all new and cheery again. People of high intellectual endowments do not require similar ones in those they love. They are just the persons to appreciate the wholesome gush of natural feeling, the honest affection, the simple joy, the fulness of contentment with what he loves, which Miriam sees in Donatello. True; she may call him a simpleton. It is a necessity of the case; for a man loses the capacity for this kind of affection, in proportion as he cultivates and refines himself. (4:105)

Only moments later during that same walk on the Pincian, Kenyon virtually confesses to being drawn to Hilda's uncomplicated innocence out of the same need: "Dear Hilda, this is a perplexed and troubled world! It soothes me inexpressibly to think of you in your tower, with white doves and white thoughts for your companions, so high above us all, and with the Virgin for your household friend. You know not how far it throws its light—that lamp which you keep burning at her shrine!" (4:112). It is this need to retreat to the comforts of a vicariously experienced innocence that causes Kenyon, at the novel's close, to retreat from his own deepest but most disturbing insights into this "perplexed and troubled world" and ask Hilda to "guide" him "home," where he can worship her "as a household Saint" (4:461).

As Kenyon thought possible, Miriam did indeed find herself capable of loving Donatello, but as Kenyon did not expect, her love will develop not from the need to retreat from the perplexities and passions of the world, as Kenyon's will, but from the recognition that she and Donatello are now bound together by their joint confrontation with those very perplexities and passions—in the world and in themselves. When Donatello strikes out to protect Miriam from her oppressor, hurling Brother Antonio over Traitor's Leap, he submits to a passion that will transform him into a man complete enough for Hawthorne to allow Miriam to love. In April 1858 Hawthorne could not understand Fuller's attraction to the handsome "half-idiot" Ossoli, but as he learned more of Ossoli's military service in the revolution and of the bond that political exile as well as parenthood had formed between him and Fuller, he imagined Ossoli has having experienced a transformation under Fuller's influence, a transformation suggested perhaps by Hawthorne's own need to redeem the nature of Fuller's liaison with Ossoli through a "transformed" perception of that relationship. It is no accident, then, that having submitted to Miriam's influence and knowing real passion for the first time, Donatello not only kills the Model that represents to some extent the Ossoli-figure who had inspired Hawthorne's loathing but also kills within himself the innocent but mindless masculine faun-satyr who is unworthy of Miriam's love.

The immediate effect of sin on Donatello becomes the central paradox of the romance—his redemption as a man. It also seems significant that, to redeem Donatello, Hawthorne employs a variation of the very metaphor he had used to condemn Ossoli. Miriam looks "wildly at the young man, whose form seemed to have dilated, and whose eyes blazed with the fierce energy that had suddenly inspired him. It had kindled him into a man; it had developed within him an intelligence which was no native characteristic of the Donatello whom we have heretofore known" (4:172). Donatello may now captivate a Miriam, for he now has the "intellectual spark" that he and Ossoli had lacked. "Kindled" by passion, his face takes on "a higher, almost an heroic aspect" (4:175)—"heroic" becoming a frequent adjective of Kenyon's for the fallen Donatello—and his eyes now "blaze" with a "fierce energy" and "intelligence" just as, earlier, Miriam's eyes were said to captivate by the "flash" of her own "force and energy of will" (4:79). Once Donatello implicates himself in her fate, she is now inextricably implicated in his. The effect on Miriam is instantaneous. She presses "him close, close to her bosom, with a clinging embrace that brought their two hearts together, till the horrour and agony of each was combined into one emotion, and that, a kind of rapture" (4:173–74). Bound by "their deed—the crime which Donatello wrought, and Miriam accepted on the instant," their union through shared guilt and mutual sympathy is "closer than a marriage-bond" (4:174).

With the ambivalence that lies at the very heart of Hawthorne's perception of Fuller's union with Ossoli, the narrator describes the bond between Donatello and Miriam as having "the ever-increasing loathsomeness of a union that consists in guilt," and yet in a virtual paraphrase of Milton's conception of the purpose of the "sacred consecration" of marriage, that union saves Miriam from "an icy solitude," and for her, "there can be no more loneliness" (4:175). Though Donatello will temporarily reject Miriam as responsible for his "crime," when he finally, unequivocally, accepts mutual responsibility, he develops the capacity to reciprocate Miriam's sympathy. Both repentant, the permanence of their bond is blessed as a form of "marriage" by both the "Bronze Pontiff" and Kenyon, but not, of course, Hilda, whose "merciless" (4:209) inability to give Miriam the sympathy that she needs wounds Miriam, in the imagery of the battlefield, "like a steel blade" (4:384). Significantly, that blessing occurs in the village of Perugia, the very spot where Fuller and Ossoli were detained for more than a month until, as she wrote Lewis Cass Jr., the "Police" recognized that "the Pontifical Authorities at Perugia" had "blessed" Ossoli's papers by allowing him to live "undisturbed." In a passage that Hawthorne would have read in the *Memoirs,* Fuller describes their rejuvenation in Perugia through the "perfect elixir" of "the pure mountain air." "Every morning," she also wrote, she and Ossoli went "to some church rich in pictures." [19]

Kenyon, of course, had condescendingly imagined Miriam capable of a love for Donatello that would be something of a refuge from passion, but he has difficulty accepting the passionate abandon that Miriam eventually develops for Donatello. When they meet in the Marble Saloon to discuss the possibility of her reconciliation with Donatello, Kenyon is shocked to see in Miriam the physical and emotional devastation of Donatello's rejection. Having determined to devote her "too much life and strength," her "too redundant energy," to Donatello, she has been left by his rejection with nothing to do but "brood, brood, brood, all day, all night, in unprofitable longings and repinings" (4:280). "Cherishing a love which insulated him from the wild experiences" of such passion, the Kenyon who seeks a refuge from passion in an "insulated" love cannot understand "how Miriam's rich, ill-regulated nature impelled her to fling herself, conscience and all, on one passion, the object of which, intellectually, seemed far beneath her" (4:280). Like Hawthorne of Fuller, Kenyon finds Miriam's passion for Donatello ultimately unfathomable, but as Coverdale had admitted of his own resistance and submission to Zenobia's character, so Kenyon had earlier acknowledged to Hilda of Miriam, "My heart trusts her, at least—whatever my head may do" (4:109). Finding nobility in Miriam's willingness to sacrifice herself for another, finding a redeeming purpose for their marriage of guilt if Miriam can, as she claims, serve "to instruct, to elevate, to enrich" Donatello's mind," Kenyon listens to his "heart" and, finally, deems Donatello worthy of Miriam:

> Kenyon could not but marvel at the subjection into which this proud and self-dependent woman had wilfully flung herself, hanging her life upon the chance of an angry or favourable regard from a person who, a little while before, had seemed the plaything of a moment. But, in Miriam's eyes, Do-

natello was always, thenceforth, invested with the tragic dignity of their hour of crime; and, furthermore, the keen and deep insight, with which her love endowed her, enabled her to know him far better than he could be known by ordinary observation. Beyond all question, since she loved him so, there was a force in Donatello worthy of her respect and love. (4:283–84)

If Hawthorne had earlier reasoned against Fuller's union with Ossoli, if his "head" still could not quite understand nor condone their relationship, here, through Kenyon, he seems to acknowledge, to himself at least, that his "heart" places its faith in Fuller's character. If Fuller deemed Ossoli worthy of her love, then despite what "ordinary observation" suggests, he will accept him as worthy. At Perugia, he will bless these tragedy-bound lovers as having a union as "true" as any marriage would have been.[20]

2

"It is Donatello's prize. . . . The eyes of us three are the only ones to which she has yet revealed herself. Does it not frighten you a little, like the apparition of a lovely woman that lived of old, and has long lain in the grave?"

"Ah, Miriam, I cannot respond to you. . . . Imagination and the love of art have both died out of me."

MIRIAM AND KENYON COMMENTING ON THE "VENUS OF THE TRIBUNE" IN
The Marble Faun

As the last complete romance that Hawthorne would write and the only one that features art as an explicit subject of interest to both the characters and the author, *The Marble Faun* has quite understandably been read for revelations it might yield for the creative failure that would torment Hawthorne for the final four years of his life.[21] The historical tidiness of such retrospective criticism just as understandably makes one a bit uneasy, a bit suspicious of the neatness of a critical narrative of a narrator's own beginnings and endings. It is an uneasiness that Hawthorne shared, for when Hawthorne wrote *The Marble Faun,* he did more than simply express his fears of his own impending "moral and intellectual collapse" as an artist. He announced its advent.

Sophia always maintained that Hawthorne never recovered from the trauma of Rome, from the excruciating anxiety of watching Una daily, for weeks, seem to die.[22] As Carton and Herbert have demonstrated, Hawthorne's relationship with Una was so close, so ambivalent, and in some ways, so intimately related to his role as an artist as well as a father, that the ordeal of watching her seem to die could not have but taken a severe toll on him. If it affected him in no other way, Una's illness forced the fifty-five-year-old Hawthorne to confront in the Eternal City his own eternal end. "The great darkness . . . into which friends vanish from us, one by one" seemed greater than ever for Hawthorne as "this one, small, consecrated spot" of light in which Una lived first flickered, then dimmed perilously close to extinction. "It is almost the worst trial in all this to see his face," wrote Ada Shepard, for "Mr. Hawthorne said that he had given up all hope . . . and wished no-one to try to inspire any in him."[23] Everywhere Hawthorne turned in Rome, he confronted the ruins of life left by death—the ghosts of civilizations, of artists, of a friend. Writing the first draft of *The Marble Faun* as Una battled with death, he began to see that the "rude old potency" that Fuller "could not possibly come at, to re-create and refine," that "bestirred itself" beneath the brilliant "mosaic of admirable qualities" and "undid all her labor in the twinkling of an eye," was not her sensuality so much as it was her mere mortality (14:156–57).

That "rude old potency" that shattered the dazzling surface of Fuller's life finds its parallel in the chasm of Curtius, "one of the orifices of that pit of blackness that lies beneath us, everywhere." Thinking perhaps of the tragedy of Fuller's death and its commencement with the republican revolution and the destruction of her personal and political hopes by the French, Hawthorne has Kenyon interpret the legend of the chasm as an "intimation" from the past of "all the future calamities of Rome—shades of Goths and Gauls, and even of the French soldiers of to-day" (4:161). Appropriately, Miriam serves for Kenyon and Hilda as the prophetic voice of that "intimation": "The firmest substance of human happiness," she warns them, "is but a thin crust spread over it, with just reality enough to bear up the illusive stage-scenery amid which we tread. It needs no earthquake to open the chasm. A footstep, a little heavier than ordinary, will serve; and we must step very daintily, not to break through the crust, at any moment. By-and-by, we inevitably sink!" (4:161–62). Talent, nobility, heroism, self-sacrifice—nothing can prevent the crust from breaking and shattering a life. For all of Curtius's nobility of purpose in attempting to prevent Rome's calamities by descending into the chasm himself, Miriam points out that "all the armies . . . all the heroes, the statesmen, and the poets," all of them have "piled upon poor Curtius" (4:162). Hilda, of course, refuses to accept Miriam's tragic fatalism. She imagines the chasm as very much like the "defective and evil nature" that Hawthorne in April 1858 had identified as Fuller's "rude old potency." For Hilda, the chasm is nothing more than man's "evil," a pit that can be bridged "with good thoughts and deeds" or, in a shift of metaphor, filled up by "heroic self-sacrifice and patriotism" and other virtuous acts. For Miriam, however, it all comes "to the same thing at last" (4:162). Confronted with the radically divergent visions of life offered by Miriam and Hilda, Kenyon responds sympathetically, even passionately, to Miriam's, not Hilda's. His "imagination," as the narrator tells us, "was greatly excited by the idea of this wondrous chasm," the chasm, that is, that could not be bridged or filled (4:163).

Until that moment when he confronts his inability to re-create the "Venus of the Tribune" from the broken fragments of that "apparition of a lovely woman who lived of old, and has long lain in the grave," Kenyon proves himself again and again to be more responsive to Miriam than to Hilda. For Hilda, Guido's representation of an unblemished, unruffled archangel Michael conquering with ease the demon dragon whose face he refuses to confront is "the most beautiful and the divinest figure that mortal painter ever drew" (4:139). For Kenyon, however, it is "the wild energy" of Miriam's conception of Michael that would be the masterpiece—a tattered and wounded Michael fiercely confronting in violent struggle an evil that inspires "unutterable horrour," that has the strength to defeat Michael if he does not battle it "as if his very soul depended upon it" (4:184). Despite Kenyon's repeatedly more sympathetic responses to Miriam and her passionate and tragic vision of life and art, early in the romance, the narrator attempts to thwart any inclination the reader might have to imagine a romantic attraction between Kenyon and Miriam. He feels for her only "a manly regard," the narrator tells us, but perhaps sensing the ambiguity of the phrase, he adds with a seemingly unambiguous certainty that his "regard" was "nothing akin to what is distinctively called Love" (4:36). The qualification, however, seems anything but unambiguous. The capitalization of "Love" and the phrase "what is . . . called" would alone suggest that the narrator is carefully excluding only a socially and literarily conventional "Love" expected of heroes and heroines of romances. The addition of the qualifier "distinctively," however, emphasizes the possibility that Kenyon's friendship with Miriam is complicated by an attraction not defined precisely by either "Love" or mere friendship. If "what is distinctively called Love" is the emotion arising from the need that draws Kenyon to Hilda, then indeed Kenyon's "manly regard" for Miriam is quite different from the passion-insulated "Love" he seeks in Hilda.

Whatever reasons we may give for the final years of Hawthorne's failure as an artist, *The Marble Faun* suggests that, for Hawthorne, his sense of present and impending failure, of the chasm opening beneath his very feet, is intimately related to his relationships with Sophia and with Fuller, with the

Strophe and Antistrophe of his life and of his art. More explicitly than either Phoebe or Priscilla, Hilda resembles the Sophia of the love letters that Hawthorne transformed into the Dove of his redemption. By 1858 the virginal Dove had seemed so thoroughly to inhabit that ideal that he now represents her as the sainted keeper of the Virgin's eternal flame, a light without heat shining down from a shrine towering above him, above all humanity, his object of worship now worshiped herself by a whole flock of Doves, an ideal idealized.

Like Hilda, Sophia as a young woman had shown great promise as an artist but had forsaken that promise by becoming instead a copyist of the Old Masters. Later, she gave up art entirely and, as Herbert has argued, subordinated her talent forever to her lifelong dedication to her husband's genius, to becoming the ideal that he had first imagined.[24] Hawthorne represents Sophia's "self-sacrifice" in Hilda's perfection as a copyist, worshiping so thoroughly the Old Masters and sympathizing so deeply with their work that she loses her self in their vision, becoming the living tool for the endless reproduction of their spirit in her work—like a mesmerized Priscilla with a brush in her hand. Hilda's loss of a creative self, as Sophia's was, is personal as well as artistic. Just as she dedicates her art to reproducing faithfully the works of the Old Masters, so she dedicates her life to the worship and reproduction of another masterwork of their patriarchal legacy, their vision of an ideal woman—the eternally white, spotless Virgin who lives "on the hither side of passion"—the Dove (4:374). To succeed as a copyist, she must subordinate herself with absolute fidelity to the aesthetic authority of the master to whom she pays homage. Aspiring to become the ideal of innocence and purity that she worships (and for which she is in turn worshiped), she must also serve that ideal with an equally rigid fidelity. As the ideal is absolute, so must the life be. Good cannot be stained by contact with evil, nor the purity of innocence by the shades of passion.

Like Priscilla of Hollingsworth or Hilda of her Old Masters, Sophia seemed to idealize blindly what she worshiped and to stake her entire faith on the purity of her idol. Sophia would insist, for example, that Hawthorne could not have known what he wrote: his genius as an artist resided exclusively, she believed, in his ability to copy, like Hilda, what he had only observed and sympathized with in others. She believed this because this is precisely what Hawthorne had told her to believe.[25] It seemed impossible for her to entertain the notion that Hawthorne's often disturbing work was in any way an imaginative representation of his own inner life. In a letter to her mother, for instance, she describes Hawthorne—eight years after their marriage, no less—as being "like a stray Seraph, who had experienced in his own life no evil," who "has literally been so pure from the smallest taint of earthiness" that "it can only be because he is a seer that he knows of crime," only be because he possessed "the intuition of a divine intellect" that did not experience but only "saw and sorrowed over all evil." In terms stronger even than Hilda's rejection of Kenyon's speculation that sin can have beneficial consequences, Sophia in the same letter then links her faith in Hawthorne's purity to her faith in the absolute separation of good and evil: "Not Julian's little (no, *great*) angel heart and life are freer from any intention or act of wrong than his [Hawthorne's]. And this is best proof to me of the absurdity of the prevalent idea that it is necessary to go through the fiery ordeal of sin to become wise and good. I think such an idea is blasphemy and the unpardonable sin."[26] Is it any wonder then that, after "blasphemously" writing 459 pages of narrative support for Kenyon's interpretation of the "fortunate" consequences of "evil," Hawthorne would feel some pressure to redeem himself—as a husband, if not as an author—by having Kenyon turn apostate to his most deeply felt insights and acquiesce to Hilda's cry: "Oh, hush!" (4:460).

Given the ideal of the Dove that Hawthorne had imposed on Sophia, it is perhaps only simple justice that he too should have to suffer the burden of having to live up to an equally impossible ideal. Justice or not, the strain was enormous—on both the husband and the artist. As he did in *Blithedale*, Hawthorne suggests the weight of that burden. In a passage that could well describe the devastation of Fuller's "fall" on Hawthorne as well as his anxiety lest a "fall" of his own have a similar effect upon Sophia, Hawthorne describes a Hilda crushed by disillusionment:

> The character of our individual beloved one having invested itself with all the attributes of right—that one friend being to us the symbol and representative of whatever is good and true—when he falls, the effect is almost as if the sky fell with him, bringing down in chaotic ruin the columns that upheld our faith. We struggle forth again, no doubt, bruised and bewildered. We stare wildly about us, and discover—or, it may be, we never make the discovery— that it was not actually the sky that has tumbled down, but merely a frail structure of our own rearing, which never rose higher than the house-tops, and has fallen because we founded it on nothing. But the crash, and the affright and trouble, are as overwhelming, for the time, as if the catastrophe involved the whole moral world. Remembering these things, let them suggest one generous motive for walking heedfully amid the defilement of earthly ways! Let us reflect that the highest path is pointed out by the pure Ideal of those who look up to us, and who, if we tread less loftily, may never look up so high again! (4:328–29)

As we can see in her letter to her mother, Sophia had staked her "whole moral world" on the proof of Hawthorne's spotless innocence, and she had protected her idolization of Hawthorne's purity as an artist and as a man by detaching the man entirely from his work. For Sophia, Hawthorne's dark tales of guilt and suffering had to originate exclusively from "the intuition of a divine intellect." To admit the possibility that Hawthorne knew the pain and guilt he described would cause the whole frail structure of Sophia's moral vision to collapse. Hawthorne seems to imagine the recognition that would destroy Sophia in his description of the shattering disillusionment Hilda experiences with the Old Masters once she finally realizes that the inspiration for great art arises not in the transcendent visions of an artist's pure imagination but in his imaginative representation of lived experience, in the artistic transformation that makes the face of his mistress the image of the Madonna. "Walking heedfully" in art required that Hawthorne live up to Sophia's pure ideal by concealing the autobiographical origins of much of his art. As Sophia over time proved herself amazingly firm in her commitment to her belief in "divine intuition" as the only origins of his art, Hawthorne seemed (as in his characterizations of Coverdale, Zenobia, and Hilda) to take increasingly less trouble at concealment. "Walking heedfully" also required that he represent his powerful attraction to an alternative vision of a passionate womanhood in a Hester, a Zenobia, or a Miriam only if that vision were finally repudiated and the Dove-like vision of an "angel and apostle" of "sacred love," a Priscilla, or a Hilda allowed to prevail. The last chapter, even the last page, would suffice.

Sophia's absolute faith in Hawthorne provided him with the freedom to explore the "blasphemous" with some measure of certainty that she would be incapable of assigning to experience what she had to believe was only his sacred genius for observation. But as Kenyon's representation of his love for Hilda suggests, the vision of womanhood that Sophia had come to represent, and then live, exerted an even more profoundly censorious, chilling influence on Hawthorne's imagination.[27] Kenyon represents that love as the love of an abstracted, idealized part of her nature—a womanhood rendered bodiless, reduced to the perfection of a delicate marble hand too pure to touch, too pure to kiss. It is an image of woman so small that it may be wrapped in "fleecy cotton" and kept secure in a jeweled ivory coffer where it may be displayed at the discretion of its possessor (4:120).[28] This idealized amputation of Hilda's femininity, however, is not the product of a purely idealizing "divine intuition," as Kenyon makes clear. The hand in which he represents his love for Hilda is so close a replica of Hilda's actual hand that

Miriam immediately recognizes the resemblance. Like Sophia, however, Hilda "never knew," admits Kenyon, that he "stole it from her" (4:121). Later, again when "Kenyon's genius, unconsciously wrought upon by Hilda's influence, took a more delicate character," he models in clay a figure described not as a girl or as a woman but as "maidenhood" itself "gathering a snowdrop" rather than such "passionate flowers" as the "crimson rose" that Kenyon had vainly sought in Hilda's "snowy breast." As delicate, cold, and impermanent as the snowdrop itself, Kenyon's figure is too evanescent, too "fragile" and "true only to the moment," for Kenyon to deem suitable for the permanent art of marble (4:374–75). Just as Hilda's original works of art showed a "delicate" talent that might develop if she ever gave them "a darker and more forcible touch," a "reality which comes only from a close acquaintance with life," so Hilda inspires in Kenyon the very passionless "delicacy" that reduces woman's nature to the lifelessness of an untouchable hand or to the coolness of an abstraction, maidenhood gathering flowers of ice.

Hilda lacks what Kenyon needs. Hawthorne makes that point in a dramatic way. He juxtaposes Hilda's "hand" with "Cleopatra." With snow rather than passionate flowers in her breast, Hilda is muse to Kenyon's very weakness as an artist—his passionless idealization of a conventionally partial vision of humanity. Before Kenyon undrapes his "veiled" statue of Cleopatra for Miriam, she frankly rebukes him for being like a "magician" who "turn[s] feverish men into cool, quiet marble" (4:119). It is not the first time Miriam has criticized the coldness of Kenyon's art, and of course, it is not the first time Hawthorne has seemed to reinscribe into his work Fuller's critique of the "frigidity and thinness" of his characters, characters who would be painted "with blood-warm colors" were Hawthorne's "genius fully roused to its work."[29]

In his chapter "Cleopatra," Hawthorne seems to provide something of a concise metafictional representation of his complex response to Fuller as a woman, as a critic, and as the muse who inspired his most successful art. Incapable of "stealing from a lady," Hawthorne claims in the preface that he would liked to have used Harriet Hosmer's statue of Zenobia, but he did not. He chose instead to appropriate for his purposes the Cleopatra of William Wetmore Story, his and Fuller's friend (4:4). Like Zenobia, Cleopatra, of course, challenged and was defeated by the Roman Empire, and more appropriately than Zenobia, Cleopatra's revolt against the Romans more clearly involved the intermixture of sex, politics, and violence that characterizes Miriam's Judith, Jael, and Salome—or, of course, Hawthorne's Fuller veiled in Miriam's characterization. Kenyon had first displayed Hilda's "hand" for Miriam, whose delicacy she was capable of appreciating in a limited way just as she was capable of painting the shadow of herself on the margins looking longingly upon young lovers or upon baby shoes in a domestic scene. But he had brought her to his studio for the expressed purpose of unveiling, for her alone, his newest work, the masterpiece that seems clearly inspired not only by Miriam's representation of her inner life in her paintings of passionate, troubled women but also by Miriam herself, or perhaps importantly, as Person has recognized, by the self-fashioned image of Miriam in her own portrait.[30]

Kenyon seems, then, to be responding to Miriam's criticism of his art by demonstrating what he is capable of creating when he is inspired by a passion that cannot be "distinctively called Love." For this demonstration, Hawthorne assigns to Kenyon the former studio of Canova, the studio that Maria Louisa Lander occupied in 1858 but also, significantly, the studio of the artist whose views on art and the creative process Fuller had described in a lengthy 1843 article for the *Dial*. Not only did Hawthorne read the article and praise it (8:374), but as Sarah I. Davis has persuasively argued, he also responded to it—occasionally even closely paraphrasing it—by writing "Drowne's Wooden Image," affirming through it, with Fuller, "the greater emotional intensity of romantic art and its genesis in romantic love." If "Drowne's Wooden Image" responds to Fuller, Kenyon's Cleopatra, as Person notes, is "Kenyon's effort to express his response to Miriam" and "recalls Drowne's carving of the Portuguese lady."[31]

Drawing away the veil to reveal the statue that will answer Miriam's criticism, Kenyon teases Miriam with his own little mystery, telling her that she "must make out" for herself "the special epoch" of Cleopatra's life that he intended to represent. Significantly, however, Miriam is not drawn to reading the statue for a representation of Cleopatra's history so much as she is intrigued by what it reveals about Kenyon's life before and during the act of creating it. It is the narrator who tells us of the statue that the "magnificence of her charms" was designed to "kindle a tropic fire in the cold eyes of Octavius" but that Kenyon had captured the "great, smouldering furnace deep down in the woman's heart" as she experienced that brief moment between "the fever and turmoil of her life," the moment just after Octavius "had seen her" and "remained insensible to her charms," the moment when she experienced the "repose of despair." Kenyon's Cleopatra, in other words, is very much like another Zenobia rejected by Hollingsworth for a Priscilla, another Hester spurned by the narrator for an "angel and apostle" of "sacred love." Like the author of Zenobia and Hester, the sculptor had not shrunk "timidly from the truth" and chosen "the tame Grecian type" as his model (4:126). By portraying her with "courage and integrity" and not idealizing her into a conventional image of womanhood, he had captured her "richer, warmer" nature. Unlike Hilda, whose ethereally innocent optimism would build a bridge over the Chasm of Curtius or fill it up with good thoughts and deeds, Kenyon's Cleopatra, like Miriam, confronts tragic despair with "profound, gloomy, heavily revolving thought" (4:126–27). As Miriam's contradictory art suggests of her, Cleopatra is "strong and passionate" but is also capable of "softness and tenderness." In a catalog of "seemingly discordant elements" that could sum up the "lurid intermixture" of characteristics ascribed to Beatrice, Hester, Zenobia, and Miriam, Cleopatra is imagined as "fierce, voluptuous, passionate, tender, wicked, terrible, and full of poisonous and rapturous enchantment" (4:127).

Miriam's immediate response to Kenyon's Cleopatra assumes precisely what Sophia refused to acknowledge about Hawthorne's work, namely, that Kenyon's imagination was fired by a passionate response to a woman in his life and, further, that in representing that passion he reexperienced it. "Did she never try—even while you were creating her—to overcome you with her fury, or her love," Miriam asks him: "Were you not afraid to touch her, as she grew more and more towards hot life, beneath your hand?" For Miriam, like Fuller, only a "genius fully roused" can "paint with blood-warm colors," and that arousal must come, as Fuller also said, by creating an art that responds dialogically with the voice of an Other, by hearing "a voice that truly calls upon his solitude to ope his study door."[32] The artist and his art cannot be detached. When Miriam asks Kenyon how he learned to create such a woman, Kenyon describes the creative process much like Coverdale did in his allusions to the "fires" of his memory or of Vulcan's workshop; he "kindled a great fire within my mind, and threw in the material." He does not identify the "material" that he transformed through the "fires" of passion, but Miriam assumes that a woman in Kenyon's life provided the inspiration for the "womanhood . . . so thoroughly mixed up with all those discordant elements": "Where did you get that secret? You never found it in your gentle Hilda. Yet I recognize its truth" (4:127).

Indeed, he did not find it in Hilda, as he admits, for she knows no "shadow of darkness or evil," but he did find it where Miriam recognizes it, as he will not admit. Implicitly acknowledging her recognition of herself in Kenyon's representation, Miriam immediately defends herself against the implication that her conscience is less "white" than Hilda's, but her defensiveness quickly fades as she recognizes, on the basis of his Cleopatra, that when moved by

passion Kenyon can "see far into womanhood," as Fuller had avowed of
Hawthorne. He was capable of being the intimate friend with whom she
has longed to share the secret that constitutes her mystery and her lonely
misery. "Perhaps—perhaps—but Heaven only knows—you might understand me!" she avows passionately: "Oh, let me speak!" Though Kenyon
encourages her to speak to him as Fuller claimed to speak to Hawthorne,
"as to a brother," Kenyon interprets her need to share her mystery with him
in a more intimate friendship as the need for a degree of "sympathy, and just
the kind of sympathy" that he feared he could not provide (4:128–29).
Though more euphemistically stated, Kenyon's fear is Giovanni's fear. Kenyon's failure of sympathy, like Giovanni's or like Theodore's in Zenobia's tale,
destroys the possibility of intimacy. Miriam will not reveal to him her "secret." He may search for it, as Zenobia allows Coverdale to search for it by
looking into her eyes, dropping "a plummet-line down into the depths of
her consciousness," but like Coverdale, he might be incapable of finding anything more than perhaps a ghost "laughing" at him "from the bottom of a
deep well" (3:48).

Fuller had written ambiguously in her review of *Mosses from an Old Manse*
that Hawthorne had still not uncovered "the mysteries of our being," and in
Miriam, who denies Kenyon the satisfaction of thinking he has or ever can
"petrify" her into a Cleopatra, Hawthorne seems to imagine the ghost of
Fuller still claiming her power to elude his understanding, warning him, as
though she had just read *The Scarlet Letter* rather than merely gazed upon
the statue of the Pearl Diver: "My secret is not a pearl. . . . Yet a man might
drown himself in plunging after it!" Indeed, it is not a "pearl." It is the gem
that Fuller identified as symbolizing her being. It is a "dark-red carbuncle—
red as blood" (4:129–30). In the *Memoirs,* Emerson wrote that Fuller "never
forgot that her name, Margarita, signified a pearl" but that "she chose carbuncle for her own stone," for "she valued what she had somewhere read,
that carbuncles are male and female" and that "the female casts out light"
while "the male has his within himself." "Mine," he quotes her as saying, "is
the male."[33] The "light" that Miriam could cast upon the mystery she had
come to represent for Kenyon would indeed remain within herself. However, in a later scene that is reminiscent of Coverdale's encounter with the
once rustically simple Zenobia in the jeweled luxuriance of her drawing
room, Kenyon confronts Miriam's secret, as it is read by him in the carbuncle.

After the "marriage" ceremony at Perugia, Miriam reappears in Rome
mysteriously as the passenger summoning Kenyon from the window of an

aristocratic coach. Kenyon is immediately "conscious of a change" in Miriam, which he at first assigns to her dress, being stunningly "richer than the simple garb that she had usually worn," but though he can never quite "satisfactorily define" the secret of her transformation, he locates its meaning as having something to do with the "clear, red lustre" of the gem glimmering on her breast: "Somehow or other, this coloured light seemed an emanation of herself, as if all that was passionate and glowing, in her native disposition, had crystallized upon her breast, and were just now scintillating more brilliantly than ever, in sympathy with some emotion of her breast" (4:396).

Miriam was perhaps wrong. Kenyon does not interpret her mystery in the virginally white symbolism of a pearl but in the blood-red passion that he attributes to the dazzling carbuncle. Though Miriam will never reveal her secret to Kenyon directly, she had earlier, in an internal monologue, referred to that secret in terms that would seem to confirm Kenyon's later interpretation of the meaning of the carbuncle. As Miriam leaves Kenyon's studio, Hawthorne imagines her identifying the conditions under which she could grant Kenyon access to her "secret," and those conditions seem to assign to Fuller, through Miriam, the recognition of what Hawthorne himself had seemed to have imagined, and feared, to be both the source of his attraction to Fuller's mystery and the only means of access to its solution: "I wonder how I ever came to dream of it," Miriam says of her desire for intimacy with Kenyon. "Unless I had his heart for my own, (and that is Hilda's, nor would I steal it from her,) it should never be the treasure-place of my secret" (4:130). The only secret she will give will be the bridal gift to Hilda of the bracelet of seven Etruscan gems, each symbolizing "in its entire circle . . . as sad a mystery as any that Miriam" (or Hawthorne) had ever represented the gems to signify, the secret that Hilda cannot read nor Miriam tell (4:462).[34]

How Kenyon ever came "to dream" of a Cleopatra may be suggested by Kenyon's indirect description of the creative process of the imaginations of lovers. Standing on the battlements of Donatello's tower, seemingly pained himself by an unnamed "anguish of remorse" that Donatello thinks was "just invented to plague him individually," Kenyon, as he does at similar moments of despair, longs for redemption in Hilda's ideal love and imagines her holding his "heart-strings" in her hand, pulling him toward her (4:262–63). And then, the narrator adds:

> But lovers (and Kenyon knew it well) project so lifelike a copy of their mistresses out of their own imaginations, that it can pull at the heart-strings al-

most as perceptibly as the genuine original. No airy intimations are to be trusted; no evidences of responsive affection less positive than whispered and broken words, or tender pressures of the hand, allowed and half-returned, or glances, that distil many passionate avowals into one gleam of richly coloured light. Even these should be weighed rigorously, at the instant; for, in another instant, the imagination seizes on them as its property, and stamps them with its own arbitrary value. But Hilda's maidenly reserve had given her lover no such tokens, to be interpreted either by his hopes or fears. (4:263–64)

Kenyon well knows this, as the narrator makes a point of telling us, but he does not know it from his experiences with Hilda. Giovanni, however, knows it from his experiences with Beatrice, her innocent touch of his hand seeming to turn it purple, the glances that become "appreciable signs" that they "looked love with eyes that conveyed the holy secret," despite "the physical barrier between them" (10:116). Coverdale knows it from "brooding over . . . incidents that seemed hardly to have left a trace in their passage" (3:194), incidents such as "the slightest touch" of his "fingers" to Zenobia's or her "full sisterly grasp of the hand" that conveyed "as much kindness in it as other women could have evinced by the pressure of both arms around . . . [his] neck" (3:163). Immediately after Kenyon's meditation on how the imagination can so convert a friend into a lover that the beloved is forever transformed into the lover's "property" and assigned "arbitrary value," Kenyon reassures Donatello that he "need not go to Rome to seek" the "friend" that, perhaps, Hawthorne had sought in Rome, Perugia, Florence: "If there were one of those friends, whose life-line was twisted with your own, I am enough of a fatalist to feel assured that you will meet that one again, wander whither you may. Neither can we escape the companions whom Providence assigns for us, by climbing an old tower like this" (4:264). Such friends, in other words, are like those friends transformed into lovers by the imagination. They become a "property" of the mind, ours, ourselves.

The creative process of lovers is the creative process by which Kenyon transforms friends into the "property" of his art. Passion provokes lovers to create of a friend a beloved. Passion sparks Donatello's intellectual growth, allowing him to transform himself into another man of his own making. And passion ignites in Kenyon's imagination the "great fire" and the "lambent flame" (4:127, 380) with which Kenyon both creates and invests his most powerful works of art, his statue of Cleopatra and his bust of Donatello. Both described as having at the moment "a fossil countenance" (a descriptive repetition we are made to notice), Hawthorne calls even further attention to what Kenyon had confessed was the inspiration he often gained from the dead, to what the narrator confessed was his inspiration for the tale he tells: "The reader is probably acquainted with Thorwaldsen's threefold analogy;—the Clay-model, the Life; the Plaister-cast, the Death; and the sculptured Marble, the Resurrection;—and it seemed to be made good by the spirit that was kindling up these imperfect features [of Donatello], like a lambent flame" (4:380).

The passion that redeems Kenyon, the artist, from the cold, delicate art that Hilda inspires arises from his imaginative response to his relationship with Miriam and hers with Donatello. Hawthorne's account of Kenyon's art is his account of the sources of his own art, his image in the mirror of Kenyon of the "resurrection" in art of Fuller and Ossoli through the passion that burned in his 1858 notebook description, that burns again in *The Marble Faun*. But, as also in the image of Kenyon and before him of Drowne, Hawthorne created passionate art from the fires of a passion experienced, not observed—a passion expressed, but never named, imagined, but never, except in the aesthetic intercourse between life and art, consummated. Like Drowne and Kenyon also, he seemed to know that once the passion had died, the art would die as well.

Hawthorne announces the death of both in the allegory of Kenyon and the Venus of the Tribune. In Kenyon's exhumation and attempt to piece together permanently the puzzle of the broken body of the Venus of the Tribune, Hawthorne seems to inscribe the failure of a diminished passion to resurrect and embody in art the spirit of the voice in Rome of the *Tribune*, the *New-York Daily Tribune*, the woman whose "rude old potency" shattered a lifelong labor to create and re-create herself just as it inevitably shatters Hawthorne's own capacity to re-create her in the image of his desire, in the monuments of art that cannot reanimate what time and decay eventually and forever bury. "How can you describe a Force? How can you write the life of Margaret?" Samuel G. Ward had asked in declining Emerson's invitation to participate in the writing of Fuller's *Memoirs*.[35] For a moment, however, it all seemed possible. Like the Fuller represented in Hawthorne's Beatrice, Hester, Zenobia, or Miriam, Kenyon's re-created Venus of the Tribune is either "the prototype or a better repetition" of the one the world knew, the one whose unconventional feminine beauty "dissatisfied" (4:424). Kenyon's Venus more accurately captures her "far nobler and sweeter countenance" (4:424) and the "Womanhood" that we recognize as being far more alive, more completely beautiful than "the poor little damsel" of the Venus de' Medici (4:427), for she is the woman of "personality, soul, and intelligence" who comes alive for Kenyon once he adds her "head" to her body (4:423).

As Hawthorne had discovered eventually from friends in Florence about Fuller's domestic intimacy with Ossoli, Kenyon also discovers of his Venus that this "poor, fragmentary" woman of personality and intelligence, once he had adjusted the broken parts to their "true positions," had "retained her modest instincts to the last" and had covered to the end what Hawthorne himself had concealed as the secret that constituted, in large part, the source of her mystery. "I seek for Hilda, and find a marble woman!" Kenyon exclaims, and indeed for a time he forgets his commitment to Hilda in his enchantment with the "forgotten beauty" that he had made "come back, as beautiful as ever" from "her long slumber" (4:423–24). Sophia's "Apollo," in the part of Kenyon who is also identified with Apollo (4:5), even imagines for a brief moment the Venus of the Tribune shining "lustrously as that of the Apollo Belvedere" in "another cabinet" beside him in the Vatican (4:424).

Kenyon's enchantment, however, is only temporary. In a passage that could just as well describe Hawthorne's own judgment of his efforts in *The Marble Faun* to revive a flagging passion for the woman now in her own "long slumber" and for the literary representations that she inspired, the narrator says: "Such were the thoughts, with which Kenyon exaggerated to himself the importance of the newly discovered statue, and strove to feel at least a portion of the interest which this event would have inspired in him, a little while before. But, in reality, he found it difficult to fix his mind upon the subject." The passion in his life is as dead as the woman, as dead as his art. He turns instead to "affection": "He could hardly, we fear, be reckoned a consummate artist, because there was something dearer to him than his art; and, by the greater strength of a human affection, the divine statue seemed to fall asunder again, and become only a heap of worthless fragments" (4:424).

Hawthorne will not leave it at that. The self-reflective allegory he writes of the failed art that he is writing is underscored when Donatello and Miriam enter the tomb in "disguise" and try to excite his passion over the Venus of the Tribune that is not his, as he had thought. As Miriam tells him pointedly, it is Donatello's "prize." Donatello had discovered her earlier, and they had wanted to share her secret with him. "The eyes of us three are the only ones to which she has yet revealed herself," she tells him (4:427).[36] The ghostly voice of the Fuller in Miriam appeals to his imagination one last time: "Does it not frighten you a little, like the apparition of a lovely woman that lived of old, and has long lain in the grave?" In a reply that likely haunted Hawthorne during the last four years of his life as he tried futilely without passion to force out one last romance, Kenyon admits wearily: "Ah, Miriam, I cannot respond to you. . . . Imagination and the love of art have both died out of me" (4:427).

He can no longer respond to her—or imagination and art—for he is indeed frightened. The body of the Venus of the Tribune is in fact "like the apparition of the lovely lady" that it attempted to revivify and make deathless through representation. Time has broken and buried both. Art cannot resurrect the dead nor rekindle for long a passion that flames only and now fitfully in memory.

Unable to respond to Miriam, Kenyon turns to Hilda and responds to her, as he must, with silence. "I shall tell Hilda nothing that will give her pain," Kenyon had vowed (4:287). To keep that vow, he must indeed say nothing. To have Hilda, he must renounce the search for some meaning to the riddle of Miriam's and Donatello's lives, to the Chasm of Curtius, to the "immortal agony" that he had found epitomized in the Laocoön by the human figures intertwined, like friends, by the twin snakes of "Errour and Evil." They were "sure to strangle him and his children, in the end," unless "Divine help intervene" (4:391). But to prevent driving Hilda away from him, he must recant the "Divine help" he had found in the belief that from evil and error, guilt and suffering, humans redeem themselves through the development of the moral and intellectual powers, the powers of deeper sympathy. He must turn to the closest approximation to "Divine help" he knows and worship her as his "household Saint" (4:461). He must turn to Hilda. She will "guide" him to that home far from the place where memories haunt the imagination, from the place where genius is "roused" by passion to a "blood-warm" art. She will do that if he will now respond to her voice alone, if he will now, finally, just "Hush!"[37]

The very moment that he does "hush," begs Hilda to forgive him, and cries to her, "Oh, Hilda, guide me home!" (4:460–61), he recognizes Miriam for the last time as the now-silent woman bidding him farewell. She is the figure kneeling in prayer beneath the open roof of the Pantheon, gazed upon by the Eye of Heaven. She extends her hands to them, not in the gesture of a Zenobia kneeling in prayer yet defying man and heaven, but in the gesture of the Bronze Pontiff blessing the union that he forgives. Miriam signals in silence her forgiveness, her benediction on their union, but she signals also a warning that qualifies that benediction. She is "on the other side of a fathomless abyss," and they must not approach her again. They must allow her to "glide out of the portal" and out of their lives in silence. She will not speak to them again, and they must not speak to her, must not draw too near the abyss and speak the word that lies like a "drowned body" in the "deepest pool" of consciousness. They do not.

Hawthorne does not.

$\mathcal{N}$ o t e s

CHAPTER ONE *The "Riddle" of Margaret Fuller*

1. Ralph Waldo Emerson, William Henry Channing, and James Freeman Clarke, *Memoirs of Margaret Fuller Ossoli,* 2 vols. (1852; rpt. 1884; rpt. New York: Burt Franklin, 1972), 1:98. Hereafter cited as *Memoirs;* the particular writer being cited will be identified within the text.

2. Margaret Fuller, "Margaret Fuller's 1842 Journal: At Concord with the Emersons," ed. Joel Myerson, *Harvard Library Bulletin* 21 (1973): 320–40; 329.

3. *Memoirs,* 1:232, 238. Of the reaction of his own "slow circulation" to Fuller's "torrent," Emerson cast himself in the seriocomic role of passive male victim of Fuller's "urgent assault" (*Memoirs,* 1:203): "When I found she lived at a rate so much faster than mine, and which was violent compared with mine, I foreboded rash and painful crises, and had a feeling as if a voice cried, *Stand from under!* . . . This feeling partly wore off, on better acquaintance, but remained latent; and I had always an impression that her energy was too much a force of blood" (*Memoirs,* 1:228). Much, of course, has been written of the extraordinarily intense intellectual and ambivalently romantic relationship between Emerson and Fuller. Most recently, Robert D. Richardson Jr., *Emerson: The Mind on Fire* (Berkeley: University of California Press, 1995) has asserted not only that Fuller "took less" from and "gave" more to Emerson intellectually than either Thoreau or Whitman but also that he "guarded his heart with her" because "he loved her, and he knew he loved her" (239–40). In addition to standard biographies of both figures, see particularly Christina Zwarg, *Feminist Conversations: Fuller, Emerson, and the Play of Reading* (Ithaca: Cornell University Press, 1995); Carl F. Strauch, "Hatred's Swift Repulsions: Emerson, Margaret Fuller, and Others," *Studies in Romanticism* 7 (1968): 65–103; and Marie Mitchell Olesen Urbanski, "The Ambivalence of Ralph Waldo Emerson towards Margaret Fuller," *Thoreau Journal Quarterly* 10, no. 3 (1978): 26–36.

4. For a current study of the linkage between the development in women of an independent sense of "self" and the not-so-metaphorical development of a "voice," see the important intellectual developmental study by Mary Field Belenky et al., *Women's Ways of Knowing: The Development of Self, Voice, Mind* (New York: Basic Books, 1987). Fuller's struggle to reconcile the masculine and the feminine within the self conforms at every

point to the developmental model proposed by this study of contemporary women. The difficulty that Fuller herself encountered in developing a "voice" of her own is suggested by Emerson's revision of the Fuller journal entry being quoted. To protect Fuller posthumously from herself, Emerson participates in the Clarke-Channing effort to convert Fuller through the redemption of editorial revision to conventional Christianity. For Fuller's statement, "We need great energy, and self-reliance to endure to day," Emerson rewrites it in the *Memoirs* to read, "We need great energy, faith, and self-reliance to endure to-day" (1:211). For an account of Emerson, Channing, and Clarke's attempt to memorialize an ideologically "acceptable" Fuller, see Bell Gale Chevigny, "The Long Arm of Censorship: Mythmaking in Margaret Fuller's Time and Our Own," *Signs* 2 (1976): 450–60; see also her "To the Edges of Ideology: Margaret Fuller's Centrifugal Evolution," *American Quarterly* 38 (1986): 173–201.

5. Fuller, "Margaret Fuller's 1842 Journal," 329. Three days earlier (25 August 1842), Fuller had written a letter to William Henry Channing describing her initial "excitement of intimacy" with Emerson, which was followed by the disappointments of "the questioning season." She has now, she claims, learned to accept and even appreciate the value of his "limitations," his "cool mind," which he described to her as "shut up in a crystal cell." She denies Channing's charge that she "had imbibed much of his [Emerson's] way of thought." She claims, in fact, that as she looks "forward to eternal growth" she is "always aware" that she is "far larger and deeper for him." Men, she asserts, have little to offer her: "When I am with God alone, I adore in silence. With nature I am filled and grow only. With most men I bring words of now past life, and do actions suggested by the wants of their natures rather than my own" (*The Letters of Margaret Fuller,* ed. Robert N. Hudspeth, 6 vols. [Ithaca, N.Y.: Cornell University Press, 1983–94], 3:90–92. Hereafter cited as *Letters*).

6. *Memoirs,* 1:346–47.

7. For Fuller's *Tribune* columns, see her *Papers on Literature and Art,* 2 vols. (New York: Wiley and Putnam, 1846) and her brother's posthumous editions, *At Home and Abroad* (Boston: Crosby, Nichols, 1856) and *Life Within and Life Without* (Boston: Brown, Taggard, and Chase, 1860). For a reliably edited selection of Fuller's *Tribune* columns written in New York, see Joel Myerson, ed., *Margaret Fuller: Essays on American Life and Letters* (New Haven: College and University Press, 1978); Bell Gale Chevigny, *The Woman and the Myth: Margaret Fuller's Life and Writings,* 2d rev. ed. (Boston: Northeastern University Press, 1992); and Catherine C. Mitchell, *Margaret Fuller's New York Journalism: A Biographical Essay and Key Writings* (Knoxville: University of Tennessee Press, 1995). For a complete and reliable edition of Fuller's European dispatches for the *Tribune,* see Larry J. Reynolds and Susan Belasco Smith, eds., *"These Sad but Glorious Days": Margaret Fuller's Dispatches from Europe, 1846–1850* (New Haven: Yale University Press, 1991). No similarly complete and scholarly edition currently exists of Fuller's New York columns.

8. Though Elizabeth Barrett Browning, who came to know Fuller during her postrevolutionary exile in Florence, claimed that Fuller had become "one of the out & out *Reds*" (*The Letters of Elizabeth Barrett Browning to Mary Russell Mitford, 1836–1854,* ed. Meredith B. Raymond and Mary Rose Sullivan, 3 vols. [Winfield, Kans.: Wedgestone Press, 1983], 3:285), Reynolds and Smith, introduction to *"These Sad but Glorious Days,"* argue that Fuller's final political position was more akin to Christian socialism than commu-

nism (35). See their edition of Fuller's final *Tribune* dispatch from Italy, 6 January 1850 (320–23) for Fuller's revolutionary prophecy.

9. *Memoirs*, 2:111, 2:58. Fuller continually sought to negotiate a reconciliation between the dual claims of intellect and instinct, thought and "life" (see, for instance, *Letters*, 3:143), which Fuller identified, respectively, as the masculine and feminine sides of her nature.

10. *Memoirs*, 1:61.

11. In his Bancroft Prize–winning *Margaret Fuller: An American Romantic Life, the Private Years* (New York: Oxford University Press, 1992), Charles Capper admits, for instance, that "Fuller has remained elusive and enigmatic," that his work is an attempt at "historical recovery," and that he makes no pretense of having encountered or presented the "real" Margaret Fuller, for she "is a phantom" (x). Recognizing as much, Joan von Mehren's precisely subtitled *Minerva and the Muse: A Life of Margaret Fuller* (Amherst: University of Massachusetts Press, 1994) makes no claim to having presented "the life"; her recreation is "strictly focused" on "the strategies . . . [Fuller] used to balance her private and her public life" (4). Later chapters explore critically the biographical history of Fuller representations and the permutations of the "Margaret myth"; the discussion that follows is meant merely to introduce the inception of the process.

12. "Death of Margaret Fuller" and "The Wreck of the Elizabeth," *New-York Daily Tribune*, 23 July 1850, 4. All quotations are from Greeley's tribute, "Death of Margaret Fuller."

13. *Memoirs*, 1:3, 1:132.

14. Review of *Memoirs of Margaret Fuller Ossoli*, *Prospective Review* 8 (1852): 199–218; 199, 200.

15. "Vanity *versus* Philosophy: Margaret Fuller Ossoli," *United States Magazine and Democratic Review* 30 (June 1852): 513–29; 513.

16. Clarke qtd. in Perry Miller, ed., *Margaret Fuller: American Romantic* (Gloucester, Mass.: Peter Smith, 1963), vii; O. W. Firkins, *Ralph Waldo Emerson* (Boston, 1915), 82, qtd. in rpt. of pp. 82–85 in Joel Myerson, ed., *Critical Essays on Margaret Fuller* (Boston: G. K. Hall, 1980), 141; David Watson, *Margaret Fuller: An American Romantic* (Oxford: Berg, 1988), xv.

17. James R. Mellow, *Nathaniel Hawthorne in His Times* (Boston: Houghton Mifflin, 1980), 494–95.

18. Nathaniel Hawthorne, *The Centenary Edition of the Works of Nathaniel Hawthorne*, ed. William Charvat et al., 23 vols. (Columbus: Ohio State University Press, 1963–97), 14:155. Unless otherwise noted, further quotations from the works of Hawthorne are taken from the Centenary edition and parenthetically cited within the text by volume and page number.

19. Hayden White, *The Content of the Form: Narrative Discourse and Historical Representation* (Baltimore: Johns Hopkins University Press, 1987), 45.

CHAPTER TWO *The "Scandal" of Margaret Fuller*

1. Ralph Waldo Emerson, *Emerson in His Journals*, ed. Joel Porte (Cambridge: Harvard University Press, 1982), 429.

2. Joel Myerson, *Margaret Fuller: A Descriptive Bibliography* (Pittsburgh: University of Pittsburgh Press, 1978), 39. Myerson's source for the first day's sale of the *Memoirs* is the *New York Home Journal,* 3 March 1852, 3. All bibliographic information regarding Fuller's works is derived from Myerson.

3. Ezra Greenspan, "Evert Duyckinck and the History of Wiley and Putnam's Library of American Books, 1845–1847," *American Literature* 64 (1992): 677–93; 685–86.

4. Duyckinck qtd. in Perry Miller, *The Raven and the Whale: The War of Words and Wits in the Era of Poe and Melville* (New York: Harcourt, Brace, 1956), 170. Horace Greeley, *Recollections of a Busy Life* (1868; rpt. New York: Arno and the New York Times Press, 1970), 171, 191, 175.

5. According to Ellen B. Ballou, *The Building of the House: Houghton Mifflin's Formative Years* (Boston: Houghton Mifflin, 1970), Horace Scudder sought through the three series of American biographies to advance his faith in "patriotism" as "a spiritual essence" that is "derived from . . . an 'identity with antecedent life,' from a knowledge of the country's history and the men who made it" (338–39).

6. Lowell gained the editorship of the series after the death of its first editor, James T. Fields, largely on his promise to write the Hawthorne volume for the series. The Hawthorne volume, however, did not appear until 1902 and was written by George E. Woodberry largely because Lowell first delayed the project and then asked for too much money, three thousand dollars (Ballou, *Building of the House,* 340–41).

Thomas Wentworth Higginson, *Margaret Fuller Ossoli* (1884; rpt. New York: Confucian Press, 1980), 2–5.

7. Henry James, *Hawthorne* (1879; rpt. London: Macmillan, 1967), 83.

8. Myerson's *Margaret Fuller: A Descriptive Bibliography* is once again the source of bibliographic information. The reprint house for the *Memoirs* is Burt Franklin, an imprint of Lennox Publishing, and the press run was limited to 350 copies.

9. Fuller's *Papers on Literature & Art* (1846) would be reissued only once after 1884 (in 1889 and not since then); *Summer on the Lakes, 1843* not until 1970; *At Home and Abroad* its twelfth and thirteenth printings in 1890 and 1895 but not again until 1971; and *Life Without and Life Within* its sixth and seventh printings in 1890 and 1895 but not again until 1970. Edited selections from Fuller's works did appear, however, in Mason Wade's 1941 *The Writings of Margaret Fuller* (New York: Viking) and Perry Miller's 1963 *Margaret Fuller: American Romantic* (Gloucester, Mass.: Peter Smith), but it was not until the late sixties and early seventies with the rise of the feminist movement that Fuller's works began to appear again in unabridged form.

10. My views on the formation and reformation of the American literary canon have been especially influenced by the following: Richard H. Brodhead, *The School of Hawthorne* (New York: Oxford University Press, 1986), 3–16, 48–66; Gerald Graff, "American Criticism Left and Right," in *Ideology and Classic American Literature,* ed. Sacvan Bercovitch and Myra Jehlen (Cambridge: Cambridge University Press, 1986), 91–121; Giles Gunn, *The Culture of Criticism and the Criticism of Culture* (New York: Oxford University Press, 1987); Russell Reising, *The Unusable Past: Theory and the Study of American Literature* (New York: Methuen, 1986); and Jane Tompkins, *Sensational Designs: The Cultural Work of American Fiction, 1790–1860* (New York: Oxford University Press, 1985).

11. Tompkins, *Sensational Designs,* 3–39; Brodhead, *The School of Hawthorne,* 48–66.

12. Brodhead, *The School of Hawthorne*, 51–52, 58–59.

13. Ballou, *Building of the House*, 313. The annuity contracts offered by Osgood in the mid-1870s to his stable of writers suggests clearly Hawthorne's commercial value. Whereas Oliver Wendell Holmes settled for less than $1,000 and Emerson and Lowell for $1,500, Hawthorne's children rejected an offer of $1,800. Bargaining hard and still immensely popular, Longfellow was to sign for $4,000, the only contract higher than that offered Hawthorne's heirs (242–43).

14. Tompkins, *Sensational Designs*, 37; C. E. Frazer Clark Jr., *Nathaniel Hawthorne: A Descriptive Bibliography* (Pittsburgh: University of Pittsburgh Press, 1978), 363, 365, 396.

15. Barbara Welter, *Dimity Convictions: The American Woman in the Nineteenth Century* (Athens: Ohio University Press, 1976). According to Margaret Gibbons Wilson, *The American Woman in Transition: The Urban Influence, 1870–1920* (Westport, Conn.: Greenwood Press, 1979), the phrase "New Woman" first appears in the mid-1890s (11 n. 2).

Kate Gannett Wells, "The Transitional American Woman," *Atlantic Monthly*, December 1880, 817–23; 818–20. Wells also states, "Formerly, to be a good housekeeper, an anxious mother, an obedient wife, was the *ne plus ultra* of female endeavor,—to be all this *for others' sakes*. Now, it is to be more than one is, for *one's own* sake" (821; her emphasis).

16. Beth Millstein and Jeanne Bodin, *We, the American Women: A Documentary History* (N.p.: Jerome S. Ozer, n.d.), 146.

17. Wilson, *American Woman in Transition*, 14 n. 27. The figures exclude enrollments in women's colleges and technical schools.

18. Millstein and Bodin, *We, the American Women*, 147.

19. Wilson, *American Woman in Transition*, 112. Wilson's statistics are a "percentage of aggregate population" of "native whites of native born parents" in "urban" areas.

20. Julian Hawthorne, *Nathaniel Hawthorne and His Wife*, 2 vols. (Boston: n.p., 1884), 1:v–vi. Hereafter cited as *NH and HW*.

21. Ibid., 1:v.

22. The exception is Thomas Wentworth Higginson, whose counterattack on Julian and the Hawthornes' marriage is discussed in detail later in this chapter.

23. "Hawthorne," review of *Nathaniel Hawthorne and His Wife*, *New York Times*, 23 November 1884, 6; [G. E. Woodberry], "Hawthorne in His Own Family," review of *Nathaniel Hawthorne and His Wife*, *Nation*, 18 December 1884, 525–26; 525; "The Real Hawthorne," *New-York Daily Tribune*, 16 November 1884, 4. The relief that such male reviewers expressed in the "manly" Hawthorne Julian made available to them suggests that the need for defensive assertions of masculinity among the classic writers of the American Renaissance was still felt among the inheritors and preservers of their canon (see David Leverenz, *Manhood and the American Renaissance* [Ithaca, N.Y.: Cornell University Press, 1989]). Hattie Tyng Griswold, "Genius at Home/Hawthorne's Secluded Life and His Enjoyment of Its Pleasures," *Chicago Tribune*, 19 July 1885, 18.

24. Griswold, "Genius at Home/The Reasons for Hawthorne's Dislike of Margaret Fuller," *Chicago Tribune*, 26 July 1885, 18.

25. Evidence was cited in the feud between Julian and Fuller's defenders by James Freeman Clarke and Frederick Fuller (discussed and cited later in this and other chapters).

26. NH and HW, 1:252, 256–257.

Julian also includes a letter written on the same day on the same subject by Sophia's mother, Mrs. Peabody, which he claims was written "from very much the same viewpoint" (1:257), a claim that is apparently meant to prefocus the reader's attention on his grandmother's critical remarks, for her philosophy is antithetical to her daughter's. Though Mrs. Peabody objects that Margaret could have used "language less offensive to delicacy" in her book, had the letters not been identified by name, Mrs. Peabody's position on women's rights would make a reader think that she, rather than Sophia, was the daughter of Fuller's generation. "Seems to me I could have written on the very same subjects," she proclaims. Though she assents to Margaret's portrayal of "what woman should be," she states that a "woman must wait till the lion shall lie down with the lamb, before she can hope to be the friend and companion of man" because "he has the physical power, as well as conventional, to treat her like a plaything or a slave, and will exercise that power till his own soul is elevated to the standard set up by Him who spoke as man never spoke" (1:258). Julian apparently reprints his grandmother's remarks because she later complains not only about Fuller's "offensive" language but also her "bad" style and the book's "look of absolute irreligion" (1:258). In any case, his preface to his mother's letter clearly identifies his sympathies, and he ignores his grandmother's essential agreement with Fuller's depiction of woman's state.

27. Ibid., 1:256.

28. John J. McDonald, "A Guide to Primary Source Materials for the Study of Hawthorne's Old Manse Period," Studies in the American Renaissance, 1977, 261–312, clearly suspects Julian of questionable editing. McDonald argues that he "can make no sense out of" Julian's assertion that Sophia's letter on Fuller was written on the same day as her mother's, which McDonald dates as "1845?" Because of the reference to Emerson's review of Past and Present in the July 1843 Dial and the appearance of Fuller's "Great Lawsuit" in the same issue and because the "tone of the reference is not retrospective," Sophia's letter, McDonald further argues "if it is one letter rather than a composite of several . . . seems most likely" to have been written "sometime in July, shortly after the articles appeared" (288–89). Sense could be made out of Julian's misdating of the letters if Julian did not want his grandmother's letter of 1845 to appear to be a response to— and gentle rebuke of—his mother's condemnation of Fuller's feminism (in the lost letter of 1843 cited by Julian or in the extant letter of 6 March 1845).

29. Sophia and Hawthorne wrote Fuller concerning the book sometime in the spring of 1845, and though the now-lost letter may have been critical of Woman in the Nineteenth Century, it apparently was friendly enough for Fuller to long to see them again and to make plans to visit them once more as a guest at the Manse. Here is her 22 May 1845 reply to the lost letter written that spring:

> I received your letter and read it with attention, then laid it aside and thought I would not reply, for so much had been said and written about my pamphlet, that I was weary of it and had turned to other things. When my interest revives, I shall, probably, make reply, but I hope viva voce.
>
> Yes! I hope to see you once more at the dear old house, with the green fields and lazy river and have, perhaps, sweet hours [ ] of last summer [ ] [i]f things work well, I hope to come. Una alone will be changed, yet still I think the same. Fare-

well, dear friends, now, for this is only meant as a hasty sign of affection from M. (*Letters*, 4:103)

30. Sophia to her mother, 6 March 1845 (Berg Collection of the New York Public Library; hereafter cited as Berg).

31. *NH and HW*, 1:257.

32. In a 22 August 1842 letter to her mother (Berg), Sophia does refer to Fuller as "Queen Margaret," but the reference is anything but sarcastic: "In the afternoon, as we were sitting in the parlor, a gentle step we heard in the hall. I sprang from my husband's embrace & found Queen Margaret! We were delighted. 'She came in so beautifully' as Mr. Hawthorne truly said, & he looked full of a gleaming welcome. We put her into the easiest chair, for she was pale & weary, & disrobed her of shawl & bonnet, & prevailed upon her to stay to tea. . . . [S]he returned the favor by distilling into our ears Sydnean showers of discourse—She was like the moon, radiant & gentle."

33. I should make it clear that I am not necessarily arguing that Sophia's views of marriage differ from those expressed in the letter cited by Julian, only that Julian may not be representing Sophia's reaction to Fuller's book accurately. In a 6 June 1843 letter to her mother (Berg), for instance, Sophia argued in response to her sister Elizabeth's contention that Sophia and Hawthorne had an Emersonian marriage of "self-sufficing worlds" that "no one who has ever become one with another being, as true husband & wife must become if really united, will ever, can ever, say that each is wholly independent of the other, except intellectually. Heart & spirit are forever indissolubly one."

34. Richard Henry Stoddard, "Hawthorne and His Wife," *Independent*, 1 January 1885, 11.

35. Julian Hawthorne, "Hawthorne and Margaret Fuller," *Boston Evening Transcript*, 2 January 1885, 4.

36. *NH and HW*, 1:259.

37. Hawthorne's assessment of Mozier was that he surprisingly lacked "the polish, the close grain, and white purity of marble . . . but, after all, he handles clay, and, judging from the specimens I have seen . . . is apt to be clay, not of the finest, himself." He is "sensible, shrewd, keen, clever," and on the night that he gossiped about Fuller's marriage, he "talked for about two hours in a very amusing and interesting style" on "topics . . . taken from his own personal experience, and shrewdly treated" (14:154–55). All references to Hawthorne's version of the Fuller notebook entry are taken from the Centenary edition; all references to Julian's version are from *NH and HW*, 1:259–62.

38. *NH and HW*, 1:259–60. Thomas Woodson suggests that the substitution of "man" for "hymen" was "probably a misreading" (14:766), but given the pattern of Julian's other editorial changes and the motives I have suggested, such a misreading would have been fortuitous indeed. Woodson's notes on the Fuller notebook passage (14:766–73) provide a concise history and summary of the furor created over Julian's publication of the Fuller passage.

39. Sarah F. Clarke, "Margaret Fuller Ossoli and Hawthorne," *Boston Evening Transcript*, 12 December 1884, 4; Julian Hawthorne, "Hawthorne and Margaret Fuller," 4.

40. C. A. Ralph, "With Regard to Margaret Fuller," *Boston Evening Transcript*, 15 January 1885, 6.

41. See Anna Mary Wells, *Dear Preceptor: The Life and Times of Thomas Wentworth Higginson* (Boston: Houghton Mifflin, 1963); and Tilden G. Edelstein, *Strange Enthusiasm: A Life of Thomas Wentworth Higginson* (New Haven: Yale University Press, 1968).

42. Higginson, *Margaret Fuller Ossoli*, 4.

43. Ibid., 314. By my count Higginson devotes 51 of the book's 314 pages to Fuller's married life: all of chapters 15 and 16 and most of 17. By contrast, he devotes only 17 pages to the chapter "Books Published," 14 pages to her life in New York, and 11 pages to her European travels. Ironically, Higginson himself had criticized the editors of the *Memoirs* for emphasizing Fuller's life over her work, noting the "curious fact" that "but two pages and a half" in the two-volume *Memoirs* were devoted to her work on the *Dial* (*Margaret Fuller Ossoli*, 130–31).

44. The discussion that follows of the split in the suffrage movement and the Beecher scandal was drawn chiefly from the following sources: Milton Rugoff, *America's Gilded Age: Intimate Portraits from an Era of Extravagance and Change, 1850–1890* (New York: Holt, 1989), 268–75; Wells, *Dear Preceptor,* 246–66; and James MacGregor Burns, *The Workshop of Democracy* (New York: Alfred A. Knopf, 1985), 122–27.

45. Qtd. in Wells, *Dear Preceptor,* 266. Higginson left after the election.

46. Clark, *Nathaniel Hawthorne,* 396. Clark also notes that customized editions were available in four and six volumes and supplemented with Hawthorne materials (signed Custom House document in one).

47. "The Real Hawthorne," 4; "Hawthorne," *New York Times*, 23 November 1884, 6; "Margaret Fuller in a New Light," *Boston Herald*, 23 November 1884, 12.

48. Review of *Nathaniel Hawthorne and His Wife, Boston Evening Transcript*, 15 November 1884, 6; "Nathaniel Hawthorne," *Boston Evening Transcript*, 28 November 1884, 6.

49. H[enry] B. B[lackwell], "Literary Notices," *Woman's Journal*, 6 December 1884, 394–95.

50. Sarah Clarke, "Margaret Fuller Ossoli and Hawthorne"; Caroline Healey Dall, "The Hawthorne Book Censured," *Springfield Republican*, 15 December 1884, 2.

51. Thomas Wentworth Higginson, "Wedded Isolation," *Woman's Journal*, 20 December 1884, 407. See T. Walter Herbert, *Dearest Beloved: The Hawthornes and the Making of the Middle-Class Family* (Berkeley: University of California Press, 1993).

52. Julian Hawthorne, "Hawthorne and Margaret Fuller."

53. [Thomas Wentworth Higginson], review of *Nathaniel Hawthorne and His Wife, Atlantic Monthly*, February 1885, 259–65. Rpt. in Kenneth Walter Cameron's *Hawthorne among His Contemporaries* (Hartford, Conn.: Transcendental Books, 1968), 266–69; 266–67.

54. Cameron, *Hawthorne among His Contemporaries*, 268. According to Maurice Bassan, *Hawthorne's Son: The Life and Literary Career of Julian Hawthorne* (Columbus: Ohio State University Press, 1970), Thomas Bailey Aldrich had asked Higginson "to give Julian a rap on the knuckles for his shabby treatment of Fields" and later congratulated Higginson for his "cruelly good" review (163).

55. Higginson, "Wedded Isolation," 407; Higginson, review of *Nathaniel Hawthorne and His Wife*, in Cameron, *Hawthorne among His Contemporaries*, 267–68.

56. James Freeman Clarke, "Hawthorne and Margaret Fuller," *Independent*, 1 January 1885, 1–2; 1.

57. Christopher Cranch, "Hawthorne and Margaret Fuller," *Boston Evening Transcript,* 9 January 1884, 6.

58. Julian Hawthorne, "Mr. Julian Hawthorne Rejoins," *Boston Evening Transcript,* 16 January 1885, 4.

59. James Freeman Clarke, "Hawthorne and Margaret Fuller," 2. Emerson's statement was taken from the *Memoirs,* 1:306. Hawthorne, "Mr. Julian Hawthorne Rejoins."

60. Hawthorne, "Mr. Julian Hawthorne Rejoins."

61. Frederick T. Fuller, "Hawthorne and Margaret Fuller," *Literary World,* 10 January 1885, 11–15. Rpt. in Joel Myerson, ed., *Critical Essays on Margaret Fuller,* 117–28; 126–27.

62. Qtd. in Myerson, *Critical Essays,* 125–26. Almost three years later, Elizabeth Peabody was to join the then finished, but not forgotten, feud by confirming Hawthorne's authorship of the Fuller description but stating that "he never meant" the passage to ever be printed ("Notes," *Critic,* 17 [September 1887], 146).

63. Qtd. in Myerson, *Critical Essays,* 125–26.

64. "Hawthorne and Margaret Fuller," *Springfield Republican,* 11 January 1885, 4. The *Springfield Republican's* review of Frederick Fuller's defense was itself excerpted two days later in the *Transcript* ("Hawthorne and Margaret Fuller," 13 January 1885, 6). The next day the *Transcript* ran its own editorial endorsement of Frederick Fuller's defense ("Literary Items," 14 January 1885, 6) and promoted Higginson's *Atlantic Monthly* review of the biography and attack on Julian as "spicy" ("The Atlantic," 27 January 1885, 6). Fuller's defense of his aunt was also excerpted in the *Critic* on 17 January ("Hawthorne as His Own Critic," 30) and Julian's 16 January rejoinder to Fuller and others on 24 January ("Notes," 47). *Woman's Journal,* as a final example, ran for comparison's sake both Sarah Clarke's defense of Fuller and Julian's "ill-natured" 2 January reply ("Margaret Fuller and Nathaniel Hawthorne," 10 January 1885, 10) and a week later on 17 January ran two additional articles defending Fuller ("A Reminiscence of W. H. Channing," 17, and Jennie Collins, "Nathaniel Hawthorne vs. Margaret Fuller," 17; two major articles in the feud had appeared earlier in *Woman's Journal,* Blackwell's on 6 December and Higginson's on 20 December).

65. Julian Hawthorne, "Mr. Hawthorne and His Critics," *Boston Evening Transcript,* 5 February 1884, 4.

66. Ibid.

67. Ibid; [George William Curtis], "Editor's Literary Record," review of *Nathaniel Hawthorne and His Wife, Harper's Monthly,* February 1885, 490.

68. Julian Hawthorne, "Mr. Julian Hawthorne and His Critics." For the full story of Julian's fraudulent scheme, see Bassan, *Hawthorne's Son,* 212–31.

69. Quotations from the following sources are identified within the text: Christopher Cranch, W. C. Burrage, and Unsigned Correspondent, "Hawthorne and Pharisaism," *Boston Evening Transcript,* 10 February 1885, 6. "Hawthorne and Pharisaism" is the *Transcript's* headline for its grouping of the three letters on the subject.

70. Oscar Cargill, "Nemesis and Nathaniel Hawthorne," *PMLA* 52 (1937): 848–62, briefly reignited the feud in 1937 when he suggested that Hawthorne's attack on Fuller was motivated by his lingering resentment of Fuller's brother-in-law Ellery Channing, an argument that was quickly and effectively challenged by Austin Warren, "Hawthorne,

Margaret Fuller, and 'Nemesis,'" *PMLA* 54 (1939): 615–18; and William Pierce Randel, "Hawthorne, Channing, and Margaret Fuller," *American Literature* 10 (1939): 472–76.

71. Nina Baym, "Thwarted Nature: Nathaniel Hawthorne as Feminist," in *American Novelists Revisited: Essays in Feminist Criticism,* ed. Fritz Fleischmann (Boston: G. K. Hall, 1982), 58–77; 58, 61–62. See Larry J. Reynolds, "Hawthorne and Emerson in 'The Old Manse,'" *Studies in the Novel* 23 (1991): 60–81; Joel Pfister, *The Production of Personal Life: Class, Gender, and the Psychological in Hawthorne's Fiction* (Stanford: Stanford University Press, 1991); and Herbert, *Dearest Beloved.* For excellent readings of gender issues in Hawthorne that do not challenge the conventional view of the Hawthornes' marriage, see Leland S. Person Jr., *Aesthetic Headaches: Women and a Masculine Poetics in Poe, Melville, and Hawthorne* (Athens: University of Georgia Press, 1988); and Leverenz, *Manhood and the American Renaissance.*

72. Margaret Fuller, "'The Impulses of Human Nature': Margaret Fuller's Journal from June through October 1844," ed. Martha L. Berg and Alice de V. Perry, *Massachusetts Historical Society Proceedings* 102 (1990): 38–126; 105–6.

73. Margaret Fuller, *Love-Letters of Margaret Fuller, 1845–1846* (New York: D. Appleton, 1903); Mason Wade, *Margaret Fuller: Whetstone of Genius* (New York: Viking, 1940), xi; Mason Wade, *The Writings of Margaret Fuller* (New York: Viking, 1941).

74. Chevigny, *The Woman and the Myth,* 1–12. See also Chevigny, "Growing Out of New England: The Emergence of Margaret Fuller's Radicalism," *Women's Studies* 5 (1977): 65–100; and Chevigny, "To the Edges of Ideology." Chevigny writes in the foreword to the second, expanded edition of *The Woman and the Myth* of the cultural and autobiographical contexts in which her interpretation of Fuller took shape. The foreword also provides an insightful historical review of the directions Fuller scholarship has taken since the late 1970s.

Paula Blanchard, *Margaret Fuller: From Transcendentalism to Revolution* (New York: Delacorte Press, 1979); Larry J. Reynolds, *European Revolutions and the American Literary Renaissance* (New Haven: Yale University Press, 1988), 54–78.

75. Reynolds, *European Revolutions,* 57. See also Reynolds and Smith, introduction to *"These Sad but Glorious Days,"* 1–35.

76. Zwarg, "Emerson as 'Mythologist,'" 214. Julie Ellison, *Delicate Subjects: Romanticism, Gender, and the Ethics of Understanding* (Ithaca, N.Y.: Cornell University Press, 1990), like Zwarg, repositions Fuller for poststructural American feminism by challenging Chevigny's "centrifugal" thesis and assessing Fuller's early "romantic" work as consistent with her revolutionary activism in Europe (xii, 225). Jeffrey Steele, *The Representation of the Self in the American Renaissance* (Chapel Hill: University of North Carolina Press, 1987), 105. See also Jeffrey Steele, introduction to *The Essential Margaret Fuller,* ed. Jeffrey Steele (New Brunswick, N.J.: Rutgers University Press, 1992), xi–xlvi.

CHAPTER THREE *"This Mutual Visionary Life"*

1. The 1879 statements were made in James, *Hawthorne,* 83; the 1903 statements were quoted in Chevigny, *The Woman and the Myth,* 420–21. For an assessment of how Fuller's sexuality and marriage have had an overwhelming influence on assessments of her life and work, see Chevigny, "To the Edges of Ideology," and "The Long Arm of Censorship"; and Marie Mitchell Olesen Urbanski, "Margaret Fuller: Feminist Writer and Revo-

lutionary," in *Feminist Theorists: Three Centuries of Key Women Thinkers,* ed. Dale Spender (New York: Pantheon Books, 1983), 73–89, especially 86–89.

Julia Ward Howe, introduction to *Love-Letters of Margaret Fuller, 1845–1846* (New York: D. Appleton, 1903), v–vi.

2. Katharine Anthony, *Margaret Fuller: A Psychological Biography* (New York: Harcourt, Brace and Howe, 1920), identifies the sources of Hawthorne's attitude toward Fuller as "only comprehensible as a symptom of his hidden misery, a cover for his fascinated interest in a Bacchante type. . . . No doubt he received the same sort of emotional satisfaction from vilifying her that his near ancestor had received from whipping a witch through the streets of Salem" (92–93). V. L. Parrington, *The Romantic Revolution in America,* vol. 2 of *Main Currents in American Thought* (New York: Harcourt, Brace and Company, 1927), 433, 448; 434; 428; 433, 428; 428, 426.

3. Parrington, *The Romantic Revolution in America,* 427, 448–49; Margaret Bell, *Margaret Fuller* (New York: Charles Boni, 1930), 120–21.

4. Wade, *Whetstone of Genius,* 113–14.

5. Randall Stewart, *Nathaniel Hawthorne: A Biography* (New Haven: Yale University Press, 1948), 66.

6. Baym, "Thwarted Nature," 58–60.

7. Arlin Turner, *Nathaniel Hawthorne: A Biography* (New York: Oxford University Press, 1980), 148, 324; Blanchard, *Margaret Fuller,* 194; Margaret Vanderhaar Allen, *The Achievement of Margaret Fuller* (University Park: Pennsylvania State University Press, 1979), 20.

8. Nina Baym, "Hawthorne's Women: The Tyranny of Social Myths," *Centennial Review* 15 (1971): 250–72; 250–51.

9. Baym, "Thwarted Nature," 60.

10. Nina Baym, *The Shape of Hawthorne's Career* (Ithaca, N.Y.: Cornell University Press, 1976), 199 n. 7.

11. Baym, "Thwarted Nature," 61.

12. Gloria C. Erlich, *Family Themes and Hawthorne's Fiction: The Tenacious Web* (New Brunswick, N.J.: Rutgers University Press, 1984), especially 61, 84–99; Persons, *Aesthetic Headaches,* 94–104; Evan Carton, "'A Daughter of the Puritans' and Her Old Master: Hawthorne, Una, and the Sexuality of Romance," in *Daughters and Fathers,* ed. Lynda E. Boose and Betty S. Flowers (Baltimore: Johns Hopkins University Press, 1989), 208–32; Robert K. Martin, "Hester Prynne, *C'est Moi*: Nathaniel Hawthorne and the Anxieties of Gender," in *Engendering Men: The Question of Male Feminist Criticism,* ed. Joseph A. Boone and Michael Cadden (New York: Routledge, 1990), 122–39; 138; Reynolds, *European Revolutions,* 79–80; Pfister, *The Production of Personal Life,* 67–68, 95–96, 131–34; and Herbert, *Dearest Beloved,* 12–14, 226, 228, 269. As an illustration of the need for greater attention to the Hawthorne-Fuller relationship, Pfister ruins several excellent points about Fuller's influence on Hawthorne by getting his facts dreadfully wrong. He has Hawthorne thinking of "his recently deceased friend, Margaret Fuller," when writing a descriptive statement about Hester (134), though Fuller was then very much alive and would be for more than five months after Hawthorne wrote the last sentence of the romance. He also mistakes Hawthorne's 1858 notebook entry for a letter and either states or allows ambiguous syntax to imply that Hawthorne condemned Fuller in 1850 rather than 1858:

"But her [Fuller's] independence gradually caught up to her 'brother,' who, after her death by drowning in 1850, two years before *Blithedale,* maligned her in a letter in terms that echo Weld's dressing down of Hutchinson: 'She set to work on her strange, heavy unpliable, and in many respects, defective and evil nature'" (96).

13. Hawthorne and Sophia first met Fuller on 28 October 1839 at a party hosted by Connie Park (15:383 n. 3). Leland S. Person Jr., "Hawthorne's Love Letters: Writing and Relationship," *American Literature* 59 (1987): 211–27; Marlon Ross, *The Contours of Masculine Desire: Romanticism and the Rise of Women's Poetry* (New York: Oxford University Press, 1989).

14. Person, for instance, states that "self-creative relationship requires Hawthorne's self-surrender; he becomes a form that Sophia will fill and then quicken into life—a male Galatea to her Pygmalion" ("Hawthorne's Love Letters," 213). I argue that Hawthorne is asking Sophia to surrender her substance to his form.

15. 30 August–9 September 1842 letter from Sophia to her mother (Berg); 1856–57 (?) letter from Sophia to her sister Elizabeth (qtd. in Edwin Haviland Miller, *Salem Is My Dwelling Place: A Life of Nathaniel Hawthorne* [Iowa City: University of Iowa Press, 1991], 416).

16. In addition to the Centenary edition of *The American Notebooks,* from which I quote here, I also cite from the valuable notes in Randall Stewart's edition of *The American Notebooks* (New Haven: Yale University Press, 1932).

17. Karen Lystra, *Searching the Heart: Women, Men, and Romantic Love in Nineteenth-Century America* (New York: Oxford University Press, 1989), 38.

18. This too is one of Person's major arguments throughout "Hawthorne's Love Letters."

19. In a complex but persuasive argument, Herbert, *Dearest Beloved,* argues that Hawthorne's success in inducing Sophia to inhabit his "ideal" was the happy (or unhappy) coincidence of both of them having "already imagined one another before they met" and finding that "on meeting . . . that their two narratives were already one" (34). The relationship that Hawthorne constructs in these letters, of course, is but an individual application of the broader cultural movement among the middle class in England and America during the early and middle nineteenth century to redefine male-female relations, specifically by defining the "true woman" as the spiritualized "angel" of the home providing refuge and redemption for her husband from the brutal materialism of the business and political world, the movement known as "the cult of domesticity" or the ideology of "true womanhood." My only reservation about such ideological analyses is that I feel the economic sources and consequences often overshadow the spiritual; the need to transform love into a religion and women into gods says as much about spiritual vacuity and despair as it does about man's needs to rationalize crass and patriarchal capitalism, the two actually being intimately interrelated. Nina Auerbach, *Woman and the Demon: The Life of a Victorian Myth* (Cambridge: Harvard University Press, 1982), though focusing primarily on British middle-class culture, makes much the same argument. That cavil aside, I focus on the particularity of Hawthorne's participation in the construction of that ideology rather than foreground that interpretative frame and supplement redundantly the many excellent studies already in existence—to name a few, Ann Douglas, *The Feminization of American Culture* (New York: Knopf, 1978); Gillian Brown, *Domestic Individualism: Imagining Self in Nineteenth-Century America* (Berkeley: University of Cali-

fornia Press, 1990); and, related to Hawthorne, Pfister, *The Production of Personal Life*, especially 1–11, and Herbert, *Dearest Beloved*.

20. Susan Gubar, "'The Blank Page' and the Issues of Female Creativity," in *The New Feminist Criticism: Essays on Women, Literature, and Theory*, ed. Elaine Showalter (New York: Pantheon, 1985), 292–313; 293. Hawthorne rewrites and explicitly refers to the Pygmalion myth in "Drowne's Wooden Image" and in "The Birth-mark." Immediately after the birth of Una, Hawthorne wrote to Horatio that he is happy to have had a daughter because "there is something so especially piquant in having helped to create a future woman" (16:25).

Person, *Aesthetic Headaches*, 114. Person's remarks are made specifically about Drowne, but Drowne is presented by Person as a model of Hawthorne's artistic project.

21. Herbert, *Dearest Beloved*, 117–18. Herbert's *Dearest Beloved* predicates its analysis of Hawthorne's marriage on the thesis that it "teemed with covert sexual politics . . . with inward debates about the axioms of its own constitution" (5), that, in other words, Sophia did, covertly, rebel against Hawthorne's assertion of power over her.

22. Hawthorne's attempt to find redemption in the idol of a woman of his own creating illustrates Nina Auerbach's thesis in *Woman and the Demon* that the "ethos of religious humanism" in Victorian life "exhorted man to stretch to godhead," which, in an age of religious crisis and disbelief, led man to imagine woman in "unorthodox" and "sometimes frightening" myths as "new vehicles for transfiguration" (7). Herbert, *Dearest Beloved*, contends that "Sophia's religious authority as the angel of Hawthorne's self-making" arose from Hawthorne's "own desperate need to reinforce the conviction that his selfhood as a man and artist had actually taken form during the years of solitary labor he had sustained before he met her" (77).

23. Herbert, *Dearest Beloved*, asserts that Hawthorne met Sophia's "dissociated fury [an "unvanquished will to power" concealed within her "groveling protestations of absolute devotion"] not only with acquiescent guilt but also with covert reciprocal rage" (28–29).

24. Qtd. in Ralph Waldo Emerson, *The Journals and Miscellaneous Notebooks of Ralph Waldo Emerson*, ed. William H. Gilman et al., 16 vols. (Cambridge: Harvard University Press, 1960–82), 7:48.

25. Blanchard, *From Transcendentalism to Revolution*, 102, 137. Hawthorne biographer Edwin Haviland Miller, *Salem is My Dwelling Place*, refers to Fuller's "erotic and intellectual aggressiveness" as the source of her power, and problems, in friendships (219).

26. For a discussion of Fuller's complex relationship with Ward and Barker, see Capper, *Margaret Fuller*, 276–87. In "Freeing the 'Prisoned Queen': The Development of Margaret Fuller's Poetry," *Studies in the American Renaissance, 1992*, 137–75, Jeffrey Steele argues that most of Fuller's poems between 1835 and 1838 were written to Barker and that many of her poems describing her spiritual crisis between 1839 and 1843 originate from the emotional turmoil inspired by the Ward-Barker engagement and marriage.

27. *Memoirs*, 1:213, 2:58.

28. Having examined these and other similar testaments from Fuller friends, Capper concludes that "whatever the cause" it is clear that Fuller possessed a "strong propensity at this time [1838–40] and for the next several years for throwing a brilliant glow of psychic, social, and moral excitement around her friendships" (*Margaret Fuller*, 268).

29. *Memoirs,* 1:64–66.

30. Qtd. in Higginson, *Margaret Fuller Ossoli,* 117–18.

31. *Memoirs,* 2:22–23.

32. Ibid., 1:202–3, 1:213, 1:205.

33. Emerson, *The Journals and Miscellaneous Notebooks,* 16:21–22.

34. Ibid., 11:495. Emerson proceeds to define that "total intimacy" as "an absolute all-confiding intimacy between her & another, which seemed to make both sharers of the whole horizon of each other's & of all truth" (11:495).

35. While I am more than a little hesitant to conclude, as Gloria Erlich has in *Family Themes* that Hawthorne harbored incestuous feelings toward Elizabeth, clearly Elizabeth was a seminal influence on Hawthorne's development as a man and as a writer. Her strength, her intelligence, her wit, her talent as a critic and a writer, her unswerving faith in Hawthorne's artistic potential, and her tough insistence that he fulfill her expectations all played an important lifelong role in Hawthorne's commitment to literature. Hawthorne, in fact, began writing in his boyhood as collaborator with Elizabeth and later turned to her when he needed help filling the pages of the *American Magazine of Useful and Entertaining Knowledge.* As a dramatically personal example of the debilitating effects of the cultural limitations imposed on women, Hawthorne would become the literary success Elizabeth insisted he be, while Elizabeth imprisoned herself in her room and devoted her talents for years to a translation of another man's writing, *Don Quixote.* As a tribute to her, poignant in the unspoken implication of the waste of what he so admired, Hawthorne would write late in his life that she was "the most sensible woman I ever knew in my life, much superior to me in general talent and of fine cultivation" (18:456). He would also say that Elizabeth "had more genius" than he had. His respect for her expressed itself as well in his need to earn her approval: "The only thing I fear," he said, "is the ridicule of Elizabeth" (*NH and HW,* 1:5).

36. Erlich, *Family Themes,* 61.

37. Margaret Fuller, review of *Grandfather's Chair, Dial* 1 (January 1841): 405. The essay "American Literature: Its Position in the Present Time, and Prospects for the Future" was first published in Fuller's 1846 *Papers on Literature and Art,* 2:122–43 and is reprinted in Joel Myerson, ed., *Essays on American Life and Literature* (Albany, N.Y.: College and University Press, 1978), 381–400; 399.

38. Turner, *Nathaniel Hawthorne,* 132–33; 55. Miller, *Salem is My Dwelling Place,* 190.

39. Sophia Peabody to Margaret Fuller, 11 May 1842 (fMS AM 1086, Houghton, by permission of the Houghton Library, Harvard University); Turner, *Nathaniel Hawthorne,* 147.

40. *Memoirs,* 1:280–81; Sophia to Fuller, 11 May 1842 (Houghton). Sophia's sonnet assigns to Fuller the role of the divinely inspired prophetess that Hawthorne will deny to Hester:

> GOD granteth not to man a richer boon
> Than low'rd Himself to draw the waiting soul,
> Making it swift to pray His high control
> Would with according grace its jars attune:
> So man on man the largest gift bestowd,
> When from the vision-mount he sings aloud,

> And pours around the unascended crowd
> Pure Order's heavenly stream that o'er him flows.
> My Priestess! Thou hast risen through thought supreme
> To central insight of eternal law;
> Thy golden-cadenced intuition seem
> From that new heaven which John of Patmos saw—
>   Behold! I reverent stand before thy shrine,
>   In recognition of thy words divine.

41. *Letters*, 3:66.

42. Ibid., 1:198.

43. Ibid., 3:66.

44. Ibid., 3:70.

45. Margaret Fuller, review of *Twice-Told Tales*, *Dial* 3 (July 1842): 130–31.

46. Fuller, "Margaret Fuller's 1842 Journal," 326, 330.

47. Ibid., 324.

48. Ibid., 324–25.

49. Miller, *Salem is My Dwelling Place*, asserts that Hawthorne's burning of Sophia's love letters to him "served as an epitaph of the Edenic relationship, which had in some ways proved but another bubble" (397). Herbert, *Dearest Beloved*, describes the act as an "assertion and effacement of his rage," arising from Hawthorne's "impulse to obliterate" Sophia's "worship" (29).

50. Sophia to her mother, 22 August 1842 (Berg).

51. Ibid.

52. Two years later, Hawthorne and Fuller did get lost during a walk in the woods (see Fuller, "'The Impulses of Human Nature,'" 108).

53. Reynolds, "Hawthorne and Emerson in 'The Old Manse,'" argues persuasively that in "The Old Manse" Hawthorne records his attempt during this period to reestablish an original, maternal, and pre-Oedipal relationship with nature that Emerson—as father figure, literary and personal rival, and author of *Nature*—obstructed (60–81). Fuller, I would argue, experiences to a great extent a similar conflict with Emerson, and in the summers of 1842 and 1844 begins to align herself with Hawthorne's sensuous earthiness against Emerson's brilliant but frigid abstractness.

54. Hawthorne apparently walked to Emerson's after lunch and returned by late afternoon. In her 22 August letter to her mother, Sophia says that because her Irish maid Sarah had gone to Waltham to attend a mass conducted by a visiting priest she had to cook for the first time since their marriage (cold meat, boiled corn and squash, rice in milk, and baked apples). Tired from standing over the stove, Sophia took a nap. After the nap, she made tea for Louisa, "(my husband & I do not drink it)," she adds, and then "we went up on the hilltop to see the sunset & the moon rise." She does not mention Hawthorne's walk to Emerson's.

55. Fuller, "Margaret Fuller's 1842 Journal," 325.

56. *NH and HW*, 1:252, 256. Stewart, ed., *American Notebooks*, for instance, calls this and the Charles Newcomb letter from Fuller "untactful suggestions" and "blunders" that "perhaps diminished" the "cordiality of relations" between Fuller and Hawthorne.

Stewart terms Hawthorne's replies "models of diplomatic correspondence" (315–16 n. 372). Following Julian's lead, Turner, *Nathaniel Hawthorne,* terms Hawthorne's reply to the first request "a *masterly* letter" (149; my emphasis). Even Fuller biographer Paula Blanchard, *From Transcendentalism to Revolution,* paraphrases Stewart in calling the Ellery letter a "tactless blunder" that Hawthorne "declined gracefully" but "privately doubtless resented even the suggestion of intruders" (193).

57. Fuller contrasted the letters from the two Hawthornes in her journal: "I enclose here a letter received from Hawthorne in answer to a question put at Ellery's earnest request, and with it one from Sophia received several days since. It is a striking contrast of tone between the man and woman so sincerely bound together by one sentiment" ("Margaret Fuller's 1842 Journal," 328). Unfortunately, the "striking contrast" remains a mystery since Sophia's letter has never been recovered.

58. As an example of Julian's influence on future Hawthorne biographers, Sophia's initial sentence expressing her regret that Hawthorne had been interrupted is the only sentence of Sophia's quoted by Turner, *Nathaniel Hawthorne,* in his account of the incident. Convinced that "Hawthorne recoiled from the excessive admiration of Margaret Fuller he found in Sophia and her associates" (147) and that Hawthorne and Sophia had for years carried on a debate about her (324), Turner, by omitting the remainder of the entry, obscures Fuller's friendly relations with both Hawthornes. Turner, however, apparently did not have access to the 1844 Fuller journals, as Hawthorne's most recent biographer, Edwin Haviland Miller, did. Though Miller, *Salem is My Dwelling Place,* devotes a full chapter to Fuller, his own animus toward Fuller is but thinly veiled. Of Fuller's relationships with Emerson, Channing, and Hawthorne, Miller, for instance, proclaims: "Her greed, as Carlyle noted, was insatiable, but she trifled with three married men" (234). And, remarkably for a biography that insightfully explores the psychological and sexual ambivalences haunting Hawthorne, he exceeds even Julian in editing the 1858 notebook passage to obscure Hawthorne's preoccupation with Fuller's sexuality, omitting the entire first sections of the passage in which Hawthorne's interest in Fuller's sexuality is evident (236).

59. Qtd. in Stewart, ed., *American Notebooks,* 317 n. 391.

60. Fuller, "Margaret Fuller's 1842 Journal," 334.

61. Qtd. in Stewart, ed., *American Notebooks,* 317 n. 391.

62. Fuller, "Margaret Fuller's 1842 Journal," 339.

63. *Letters,* 3:115–17.

64. Herbert's *Dearest Beloved* brilliantly explores the cultural and psychic origins and consequences of what Thomas Wentworth Higginson in 1885 called the Hawthornes' "wedded isolation" ("Wedded Isolation," 407; and review of *Nathaniel Hawthorne and His Wife,* 259–65). Herbert, for instance, contends that Hawthorne's "elaboration of the union of souls between himself and Sophia . . . arrives at a contradiction that points toward anxieties built into its structure" (120–21). Hawthorne "dreads disturbances of their sacred intimacy that threaten from multiplying sources" because he "can have communion with his 'Dove' only so long as that sweet bower is protected from connections to the life beyond it" (121). Within the broader range of a full-scale biography, Miller's *Salem is My Dwelling Place* explores some of the same territory, concluding for instance that Sophia's insistence on maintaining the facade of an "ecstatic Eden . . . exacted a toll [on her] physically as well as emotionally" (225).

65. Reynolds, "Hawthorne and Emerson in 'The Old Manse,'" 70.

66. On 22 February, Sophia fell while walking with Hawthorne over the frozen Concord and lost the baby a few days later. Mellow, *Nathaniel Hawthorne in His Times,* has concluded that based on Sophia's letters to her mother after her recovery the Hawthornes endured an "emotional disturbance" during this time (219). We can only imagine what Hawthorne must have felt when the dark drama of "The Birth-mark" played itself out on the Concord ice. See Pfister, *The Production of Personal Life,* for an intriguing historical reading of "The Birth-mark" as "complicit with and critical of a cultural process that discursively produces the female body as pathological" (38). Though Pfister alludes to the biographical contexts of the story, he does not pursue a full argument for a biographical influence.

67. Stewart, ed., *American Notebooks,* cites the proposals concerning boarders as possible causes of Hawthorne's change in attitude toward Fuller (315–16 n. 372), and Turner, *Nathaniel Hawthorne,* argues that both of the Hawthornes "grew impatient" with Fuller as she became "more dedicated to the cause of women's rights" (324). Julian, of course, is responsible for the latter theory, which, I think, suffers from the terminal weakness of ignoring the fact that Fuller had long been committed to women's rights and had first published on the subject in "The Great Lawsuit" in 1843. Stewart and Turner, however, did not have access to Fuller's 1844 journal.

68. The editors of the 1844 journal, Martha L. Berg and Alice De V. Perry, "'The Impulses of Human Nature,'" conclude that the "missing pages suggest that there was intention in or a design to their removal, perhaps because their content was too revealing or inappropriate to the image of Fuller that her editors wanted to communicate to the world" (54). They further conclude that the row of Xs that frequently appear at the bottom or top of pages were made by Fuller to denote "a break in the text, a thought interrupted, or some material omitted," leading them to conclude that the journal we have is a copy that Fuller made from the original journal, a copy that she intended to circulate "among her friends perhaps, as a 'letter-journal'" (54). Berg, however, has recently discovered a letter by William Clarke (see note 83 below) that suggests the journal we now have is his "tracing" of Fuller's original. Miller, *Salem is My Dwelling Place,* also suggests that "in recopying her journal at a later date she or someone else bowdlerized some of the accounts of her walks with Hawthorne" and denoted the omissions with the series of Xs (234). For a complete discussion of the state of the text, see Berg and De V. Perry ("'The Impulses of Human Nature,'" 51–55); for a general discussion of editorial changes made to Fuller's work, see Chevigny, "The Long Arm of Censorship" and "To the Edges of Ideology."

69. Fuller writes frequently of her love for Una in her journal, several times stating her preference for Una over her newly born niece Margaret Fuller "Greta" Channing and other babies, and Sophia verifies the mutual attraction between Fuller and Una in a notebook entry. Fuller's relationship with Una is discussed in chapter 5. Miller, *Salem is My Dwelling Place,* 234.

70. Among the adjustments, of course, was an increase in the already great financial pressures; Hawthorne at one point envisions his baby daughter in the almshouse (16:23).

71. Miller, *Salem is My Dwelling Place,* 230–31.

72. Fuller, "'The Impulses of Human Nature,'" 66.

73. Steele, "Freeing the 'Prisoned Queen,'" 156, 155; Fuller, "'The Impulses of Human Nature,'" 38–51.

74. Fuller, "'The Impulses of Human Nature,'" 66, 71.

75. Ibid., 83.

76. Blanchard, *From Transcendentalism to Revolution,* states that "no more telling evidence exists of the Hawthornes' friendship to the Fullers as a family" than Sophia's willingness to nurse daily Margaret Fuller Channing as well as Una (192).

77. Fuller, "'The Impulses of Human Nature,'" 84. This is pure speculation, of course, but the context of the entry, the location of the conversation, the fact that Emerson seems rarely to have visited the Hawthornes at night, and the mysteries surrounding the editing of the original manuscript suggest the possibility that Hawthorne, rather than Emerson, may have been the speaker.

78. Ibid., 54. For William Clarke's role as a possible "editor" of the journal, see note 68 above and 83 below.

79. Ibid., 92–93.

80. Ibid., 89.

81. Ibid., 85.

82. Ibid., 90.

83. Ibid., 105–6. Editors Berg and De V. Perry identify "William" as William Hull Clarke rather than, as has often been the case, William Henry Channing (105 n. 142).

84. Ibid., 105–6. The poems are not copied under the entry. Two poems, however, are copied later in the journal. In the first, Fuller puns on the meaning of "Margaret" as "pearl" to suggest that "the ray of sufficient day" will one day

> break the spell
> of the slimy oyster shell
> Showing a pearl beyond all price so round and clear.
> For which must seek a Diver, too, without reproach or fear. (112)

In the other poem (or fragment), Fuller writes a farewell to Emerson on 23 September and follows it with the two couplets:

> Winding hence afar.
> O mild and steady star
> The oft deserted stream
> Will ne'er forget thy silver beam! (118)

Both poems suggest Fuller's romantic longings at the time and employ sexually suggestive metaphors—the feminine associated with water and unopened shells and the masculine with the phallic penetration of beams and divers. If Fuller read the Margaret-pearl-diver poem to Hawthorne, it suggests much about Miriam's warning to Kenyon that a "diver" might drown in seeking to find her "pearl" (4:258). For an analysis of Fuller's poetry, see Steele, "Freeing the 'Prisoned Queen.'"

85. Fuller, "'The Impulses of Human Nature,'" 105, 93.

86. Ibid., 106, 92, 93.

87. Ibid., 108.

88. Ibid., 122, 107.

89. Ibid., 118.

90. *Letters,* 4:103.

CHAPTER FOUR *"Rappaccini's Daughter" and the Voice of Beatrice*

1. Reviewing the criticism of the tale, Lois A. Cuddy, "The Purgatorial Gardens of Hawthorne and Dante: Irony and Redefinition in 'Rappaccini's Daughter,'" *Modern Language Studies* 17 (1987): 39–53, concludes that "ambiguity, obscurity, and inexplicable complexity" have become critical "assumptions" (53 n. 9). Indeed, Roy R. Male, *Hawthorne's Tragic Vision* (Austin: University of Texas Press, 1957), complains that the tale is "almost too complex, too rich in meaning for a completely satisfactory analysis" (55). His complaint is common. Richard H. Fogle, *Hawthorne's Fiction: The Light and the Dark,* rev. ed. (Norman: University of Oklahoma Press, 1964), confesses that for him the tale is "the most difficult of Hawthorne's stories" (91), and Nina Baym, *The Shape of Hawthorne's Career,* praises the tale's richness but laments that it is perhaps "too rich" for "any wholly satisfactory reading" (107). Like Baym, Lea Newman, *A Reader's Guide to the Short Stories of Nathaniel Hawthorne* (Boston: G. K. Hall, 1979), praises the tale's "complexities" as "part of the story's virtues" but condemns "an excess of [these] virtues" as being "an integral fault" of the tale (269).

2. *NH and HW,* 1:360.

3. During the heyday of deconstruction, Deborah L. Jones, "Hawthorne's Post-Platonic Paradise: The Inversion of Allegory in 'Rappaccini's Daughter,'" *Journal of Narrative Technique* 18 (1988): 153–69, observed that the tale is an "autodeconstructive" text that is itself "premised upon an inability to reveal a final, totalizing reading except by recourse to misguided hermeneutic allegiances" (168). John Downton Hazlett, "Rereading 'Rappaccini's Daughter': Giovanni and the Seduction of the Transcendentalist Reader," *Emerson Society Quarterly* 35 (1989): 43–68, similarly reads the tale as a critique of an allegorical and transcendental symbolization of experience; Hawthorne, claims Hazlett, seeks to "seduce his readers into making the very kind of symbolizing errors he wanted to criticize" (43). In a similar vein, see also Beverly Haviland's "The Sin of Synecdoche: Hawthorne's Allegory against Symbolism in 'Rappaccini's Daughter,'" *Texas Studies in Language and Literature* 29 (1987): 278–301.

4. For an opposing view, see Julie E. Hall, "'Tracing the Original Design': The Hawthornes in Rappaccini's Garden," *Nathaniel Hawthorne Review* 21 (spring 1995): 26–35. Hall argues for Sophia as the inspiration of Beatrice.

5. Richardson, *Emerson: The Mind on Fire,* 388–89.

6. Emerson, *The Journals and Miscellaneous Notebooks,* 8:368–69.

7. Fuller, review of *Twice-Told Tales,* 130–31.

8. Ibid. Hawthorne's praise of Aubépine seems also to be influenced somewhat by the organic metaphors Fuller employed to praise Hawthorne's work. Fuller commended Hawthorne's work in general for "the soft grace, the playfulness, and genial human sense" and compared the limited revelation of his life in his art to "gleams of light on a noble tree which stands untouched and self-sufficing in its fulness of foliage on a distant hill-slope" or to "slight ripples wrinkling the smooth surface, but never stirring the quiet depths of a wood-embosomed lake" (review of *Twice-Told Tales,* 130). Hawthorne, in turn, used wind, water, and light to praise Aubépine's own "human sense": "Occasion-

ally a breath of Nature, a raindrop of pathos and tenderness, or a gleam of humor will find its way into the midst of his fantastic imagery, and make us feel as if, after all, we were yet within the limits of our native earth" (10:92).

9. Reflecting on the varied interests and personalities of those identified as "Transcendentalists," Emerson identified Fuller as the single force that drew them together: "Margaret with her radiant genius & fiery heart was perhaps the real centre that drew so many & so various individuals to a seeming union" (*The Journals and Miscellaneous Notebooks*, 16:21–22).

10. Fuller, "'The Impulses of Human Nature,'" particularly 83, 93, 105–6. For earlier but more vivid expressions of her discontent with Emerson's passionless commitment to ideas, see Fuller, "Margaret Fuller's 1842 Journal," particularly 323–24, 326, 330, 340.

11. Margaret Fuller, review of Emerson's *Essays: Second Series, New-York Daily Tribune*, 7 December 1844, 1. Rpt. as "Emerson's Essays" in Myerson, *Essays on American Life and Letters*, 240–47; 245–46. Fuller had first read the essays in Concord while staying with the Hawthornes, and while we do not know for certain, it is likely that Fuller discussed them with Hawthorne. In a 13 July 1844 letter to Emerson (*Letters*, 3:209–10), she expresses privately the concerns that will inform her public criticism. "You are intellect, I am life," she writes. "Were I a Greek and an artist I would polish my marbles as you do, as it is, I shall be content whenever I am in a state of unimpeded energy and can sing at the top of my voice, I dont care what," she adds, for "whatever is truly felt has some precious meaning." Quoting this passage, David Robinson has recently contended that this letter expresses Fuller's "intellectual declaration of independence" from Emerson, her recharting of the path she must take to find "fulfillment as a writer and thinker"—moving away from Emerson's too exclusive "concern with intellect and form" and toward a recognition of "the importance of a kind of Dionysian energy" ("Margaret Fuller's Letters as Transcendentalist Texts," paper delivered on 28 December 1994, MLA Convention, San Diego).

12. *Letters*, 3:143.

13. Reynolds, "Hawthorne and Emerson in 'The Old Manse.'" As much of this chapter amply demonstrates, I am deeply indebted to Reynolds's insights into the Hawthorne-Emerson relationship and, more generally, the autobiographical origins of Hawthorne's work.

14. *Letters*, 3:66.

15. Ibid., 3:70; Fuller, "Margaret Fuller's 1842 Journal," 340.

16. *Letters*, 1:175.

17. Fuller, "'The Impulses of Human Nature,'" 108.

18. Miller, *Salem is My Dwelling Place*, in a single sentence concluding a note, suggests that "perhaps the portrait of Beatrice . . . was influenced by Fuller's involvement with flowers" (548 n. 21).

19. Margaret Fuller, "Autobiographical Romance," in *The Essential Margaret Fuller*, 24–43. The work was first published in 1852 in the *Memoirs* (1:11–42).

20. Pfister, *The Production of Personal Life*, 67–70. Pfister notes that "flower imagery sprouted everywhere in the well-ordered feminine culture industry" (65–66). His brief discussion of the importance of flower imagery in the pseudonyms and titles adopted by women authors during this period is valuable (65–67). Pfister's interpretation of Haw-

thorne's deployment of "flowers" to symbolize female sexuality and "blooming flowers" to suggest menstruating women is part of his general argument that Hawthorne was participating in a "cultural tendency to *biologize* masculine social or literary anxieties about women" (70). Pfister assumes, as tradition would have it, that Hawthorne was repelled by what Pfister terms throughout his study the "monstrosity" of Fuller, her "commixture" of masculine and feminine traits. His study is provocative throughout, and his association of Fuller with Beatrice is insightful but limited by his assumptions about their relationship.

21. Fuller, "Autobiographical Romance," 32, 37, 32.

22. Margaret Fuller, "The Great Lawsuit: Man *versus* Men. Woman *versus* Women," *Dial* 4 (July 1843): 1–47; 15–16.

23. Steele, *Representations of the Self*, 100–133; 105, 109. See also Steele's, "Freeing the 'Prisoned Queen,'" particularly 145–47.

24. Margaret Fuller, "The Magnolia of Lake Pontchartrain," *Dial* 1 (January 1841): 299–305. Rpt. in *The Essential Margaret Fuller*, 44–49; 47–49; Steele, *Representations of the Self*, 111.

25. Margaret Fuller, "Yuca Filamentosa," *Dial* 2 (January 1842): 286–88. Rpt. in *The Essential Margaret Fuller*, 50–52; 51–52. Hawthorne first mentions the name of "Margaret" as meaning "pearl" and notes its potential as a character name during Fuller's extended visit with the Hawthornes in July 1844 (8:242). Emerson writes: "She never forgot that her name, Margarita, signified a pearl" (*Memoirs*, 1:219).

26. Fuller, "The Magnolia of Lake Pontchartrain," 48. In her "Autobiographical Romance," Fuller claims that she "had no natural childhood" (27), that "much" of her "life was devoured in the bud" (37), and clearly lays responsibility for her overwhelming sense of isolation from others on her father's intellectual influence, on her mother's absence ("My mother was in delicate health, and much absorbed in the care of her younger children" [27]), and on her first sister's death in infancy: "She who would have been the companion of my life was severed from me, and I was left alone. This has made a vast difference in my lot. Her character . . . would have been soft, graceful and lively; it would have tempered mine to a gentler and more gradual course" (25–26). Fuller describes "embracing" her mother's flowers with "passionate emotions" she "has never dared express to any human being" (32). For Fuller, as for Beatrice, flowers substitute for the absent mother and sister.

27. Auerbach, *Woman and the Demon*, 9, 8.

28. *Memoirs*, 1:219; Margaret Fuller, "Leila," *Dial* 1 (April 1841): 462–67. Rpt. in *The Essential Margaret Fuller*: 53–58; 53–57.

29. Pfister, *The Production of Personal Life*, makes a similar point about "The Birth-mark" and "The Writings of Aubépine," namely, that both suggest "that Hawthorne sees himself penned up in an allegorizing mode that *produces* the masculine obsession to stereotype how women read themselves. He sees his allegorical form producing his content" (45; his emphasis).

30. Reynolds, "Hawthorne and Emerson in 'The Old Manse.'" Reynolds argues that Hawthorne's difficulty in completing "The Old Manse" arose from his inability to "place his life within a moral framework without indulging in public confession" but that in the fictional narratives of "The Birth-mark" and "Rappaccini's Daughter" "whatever au-

tobiographical elements they contain pose[d] no threat of exposure" (76). Reynolds argues that Hawthorne's rivalry with Emerson "forms a subtext for not only 'The Old Manse,' but also later works," *The Scarlet Letter* being the most notable (76).

31. Fuller, "'The Impulses of Human Nature,'" 83.

32. Hawthorne's use of "Oriental" to describe Beatrice's beauty will appear again in his description of Zenobia's type of beauty. "Oriental" during this period, indeed through the early and late romantic period, was synonymous with "exotic" and "sensual." As Emerson's account and others suggest, Fuller's passionate nature, use of flowers and gems, and other very "un-New Englandish" qualities made her seem, in Emerson's words, "a little pagan," like "a foreigner" (*Memoirs*, 1:219–27).

33. Fuller, review of *Twice-Told Tales*, 130–31. At the Fuller session of the 1994 MLA Convention, David Robinson argued: "Needing not only the confirmation, but more crucially, the sense of purpose, that dialogue with another could provide, Fuller approached all her literary work as a sort of highly charged personal conversation" ("Margaret Fuller's Letters as Transcendentalist Texts"). At that same session, Larry J. Reynolds provided a striking illustration of Robinson's point, arguing that under Fuller's editorship but not Emerson's (who had a different vision of the periodical's design as well as purpose), the *Dial* was an extension of the conversations previously published through packets of letters, journals, poems, and essays exchanged between members of Fuller's "coterie" of friends ("Margaret Fuller and the Face of the *Dial*," paper presented 28 December 1994, MLA Convention, San Diego; revised as "From *Dial* Essay to New York Book: The Making of *Woman in the Nineteenth Century*, in *Periodical Literature in Nineteenth-Century America*, ed. Kenneth M. Price and Susan Belasco [Charlottesville: University Press of Virginia, 1995], 17–34).

34. Fuller, review of Emerson's *Essays*, 245.

35. Fuller, "Margaret Fuller's 1842 Journal," 324. In terms parallel to those at issue in "Rappaccini's Daughter," Fuller reinstates this contrast in "The Great Lawsuit" as one between those, like Emerson, who seek through "intellect" to "gather from every growth of life its seed of thought" and "look behind every symbol for its law," believing that if they can *"see* clearly, the rest will follow" and those who seek perfection through the imperfections of "life," never shrinking "from incessant error," trusting their "faith" in themselves and others as the way to truth, and living by the following credo: "Help others, without blame that they need thy help. Love much, and be forgiven" (4–5; her emphasis).

36. Fuller, "Margaret Fuller's 1842 Journal," 324–25.

37. Reynolds, "Hawthorne and Emerson in 'The Old Manse,'" 70.

38. Reynolds, "Hawthorne and Emerson in 'The Old Manse,'" explains much of Hawthorne's sense of rivalry with Emerson as arising from his resentment over Sophia's worshipful admiration of Emerson, an admiration that Hawthorne subtly worked to undercut (73).

Hawthorne completes the passage (after supper, apparently) by summarizing Emerson's assessment of the intellectual development of his other friends—Ellery Channing, Henry David Thoreau, and Charles Newcomb (8:371–72). In each case, Hawthorne presents Emerson ever so slightly as playing the role of "mentor-schoolmaster" patronizing in his presumption of evaluating his friends' intellectual developments. Despite the "spin" that Hawthorne places on his depiction of Emerson, Hawthorne seemed to have enjoyed the conversation. Taken out of context (as I have admittedly done), the Fuller passage has been used by those who cannot conceive of Hawthorne's admiring Fuller more than Emerson as an example of Hawthorne's contempt for Fuller, not Emerson (see, for example, Turner, *Nathaniel Hawthorne,* 148).

39. Fuller, "The Magnolia of Lake Pontchartrain," 47–48.

40. Curiously, Fuller's 1840 "Autobiographical Romance" describes her mother's garden as having a back gate opening "into the fields" that was "embowered in the clematis creeper." Fuller describes her childhood joy at watching sunsets from the open gate, but she notes that she never allowed herself to step through the gate, for she "loved the silvery wreaths of my protecting vine" (31–32). Later in the same passage she describes passionately embracing her mother's flowers, vowing to be "as perfect as they," and expresses her regret that with "the blights, the distortions, which beset the human being" she could never be as perfect as "ye golden autumn flowers, which so strive to reflect the glories of the departing distant sun and ye silvery flowers, whose moonlight eyes I knew so well" (32). For a discussion of Fuller's association of her mother with her garden, see Annette Kolodny, *The Land before Her: Fantasy and Experience of the American Frontiers, 1630–1860* (Chapel Hill: University of North Carolina Press, 1984), 112–30.

41. Fuller, "Margaret Fuller's 1842 Journal," 325; Fuller, "'The Impulses of Human Nature,'" 108.

42. Baym, "Thwarted Nature," 65–66. Of Giovanni, Baym writes that "it is the entire physical presence of Beatrice, her very body itself especially as concentrated in her fragrance, her physical perfume, that revolts him" (65).

43. Richard Brenzo, "Beatrice Rappaccini: A Victim of Male Love and Horror," *American Literature* 48 (1976): 152–64; 158. Brenzo states outright that "it is hard to believe" Beatrice's statement describing her love for Giovanni as being only temporary, that she is simply "ignorant of the power of her sexuality" and the sexual nature of their relationship, and that thus Giovanni's "insight seems deeper than hers" (158).

44. *Letters,* 3:66.

45. Brenzo, "Beatrice Rappacchini," makes this point also: "For Giovanni, sexual commitment to Beatrice means 'death' in the sense of being dominated by a woman, being robbed of his independence, and having his personality swallowed up." Brenzo also argues, as I do, that "Giovanni has a real compulsion to possess Beatrice, to change and control her, a compulsion revealed by his attempts to know her sexually, and by his persistent desire to shape her into his personal image of the divine woman" (157–58). I would stress, however, as Baym does, that much of Giovanni's response is motivated by displaced self-revulsion, by his inability to meet the challenge of an "intellectual friendship."

46. Fuller, "The Magnolia of Lake Pontchartrain," 48.

47. See Person, "Hawthorne's Love Letters," particularly 212–14.

48. Herbert, *Dearest Beloved,* has demonstrated that Hawthorne had good reason to be worried, for, in his reading of Hawthorne family life, Una's early manifestations as a Pearl-like child of the emotional problems that would plague her beginning in adolescence were signs of the strain of her having to live up to the impossible ideals imposed on her by Sophia and Hawthorne (see especially 177–83).

49. Baym, "Thwarted Nature," 65.

50. Ibid., 58–60; Raymond Williams, *Marxism in Literature* (New York: Oxford University Press, 1977), 121–27.

51. "The Legal Wrongs of Women," *United States Magazine and Democratic Review* 14 (May 1844): 477–82; 478–79, 477; W. A. Jones, "Female Novelists," *United States Magazine and Democratic Review* 14 (May 1844): 484–89; 488–89.

Elizabeth Barrett was a frequent contributor in 1844, having pieces in the July through October issues. Of interest also is the publication in two parts in the August and September issues of an unsigned story entitled "The Draper's Daughter." Besides the suggestive parallel of the title (appearing as it does in the two issues preceding Hawthorne's writing of "Rappaccini's Daughter"), the tale seems to have few parallels with Hawthorne's tale, though a more thorough examination than mine might uncover some.

52. Fuller, review of *Twice-Told Tales*, 61.

53. Fuller, *Papers on Literature and Art*, 2:122–43. Rpt. in *Essays on American Life and Letters*, 381–400; 399.

54. Margaret Fuller, review of Hawthorne's *Mosses from an Old Manse*, *New-York Daily Tribune*, 22 June 1846, 1. Rpt. in *Essays on American Life and Letters*, 371–74.

55. Ibid.

CHAPTER FIVE *"Speak Thou for Me!"*

1. Stephen Nissenbaum, introduction to Nathaniel Hawthorne, *The Scarlet Letter and Selected Writings*, Modern Library Edition (New York: Random House, 1984), vii–xlii, has made the strongest argument for the influence of Hawthorne's "firing" on the "fiction" of "The Custom-House" and on the "*real* autobiography" of *The Scarlet Letter* (xix); see also his "Firing of Nathaniel Hawthorne," *Essex Institute Historical Collections* 114 (1978): 57–86. Nina Baym, "Nathaniel Hawthorne and His Mother: A Biographical Speculation," *American Literature* 54 (1982): 1–27, has made the best case for the influence of Hawthorne's mother and her death on the writing of *The Scarlet Letter*; along similar lines, see also, more recently, Miller, *Salem is My Dwelling Place*, 278–98. Erlich, *Family Themes*, on the other hand, argues that Louisa and Elizabeth, along with the mother, inform Hawthorne's conception of Hester (99). See also, James M. Cox, "*The Scarlet Letter*: Through the Old Manse and the Custom House," *Virginia Quarterly Review* 51 (1975): 432–47.

2. Sophia was perhaps more resentful than worried. The only passages from Sophia's 27 September 1849 letter to her mother (Berg) that are frequently quoted are her statements that Hawthorne "is writing morning & afternoon" and that he "writes immensely—I am almost frightened about it." Sophia makes these statements, however, to explain why *she* has had no time of her own to devote to her drawing and why she needs her parents to send writing paper and ink. Having asked her mother to send two more yards of material, she writes:

> I have been wholly absorbed by making this dressing-gown myself—cutting it out and all—Tell Livy that I have to get ready for winter before I can draw. Also tell her that if I did *not* have to sew now, I still could not do anything yet—because Mr. Hawthorne is writing morning & afternoon, & I have no time yet. I must take care of the children now all day long—& sew at the same time. . . . Will you

ask father to buy half a ream of good letter paper for as cheap as possible. I have no paper. And I want some yellow envelopes. I have no ink down stairs & cannot disturb Mr. Hawthorne. He writes immensely—I am almost frightened about it. But he is well now & looks very shining.

Herbert, *Dearest Beloved,* does not quote this letter, but he might well have, for it seems to support much of what he says about the tensions within the Hawthorne marriage.

3. The most noted of these studies are Charles Ryskamp, "The New England Sources of *The Scarlet Letter,*" *American Literature* 31 (1959): 257–72; and Michael J. Colacurcio, "Footsteps of Anne Hutchinson: The Context of *The Scarlet Letter,*" *ELH* 39 (1972): 459–94. See also Colacurcio's more recent essay "'The Woman's Own Choice': Sex, Metaphor, and the Puritan 'Sources' of *The Scarlet Letter,*" in Michael J. Colacurcio, ed., *New Essays on "The Scarlet Letter"* (Cambridge: Cambridge University Press, 1985), 101–35; and Frederick Newberry, "A Red-Hot *A* and a Lusting Divine: Sources for *The Scarlet Letter,*" *New England Quarterly* 60 (1987): 256–64.

4. Nathaniel Hawthorne, *The English Notebooks,* ed. Randall Stewart (New York: Russell and Russell, 1941), 225. Hawthorne recalled this moment on 14 September 1855.

5. Person, *Aesthetic Headaches,* finds in this episode a metaphor for the creative origins and purposes of Hawthorne's, Poe's, and Melville's art.

6. Herbert, *Dearest Beloved,* 151–52. Herbert attributes Sophia's headache to the "thunderbolt" of Hawthorne's "depiction of the burdens" imposed on women by the domestic ideal praised in the final sentence of the penultimate paragraph (209).

7. Sophia Hawthorne to Elizabeth Peabody in a 21 June 1850 letter (Berg). Elizabeth had apparently written to Sophia the comments of a Mr. Bellows and endorsed them. Sophia's letter responds not only to that comment but to another similar one by Ellery Channing that Elizabeth reported to her. Sophia's explanation is that Hawthorne "sees men & he sees passions & crimes & sorrows by the intuition of genius, & all the better for the calm, cool, serene height from which he looks." In the next sentence, however, she states: "Doubtless all the tendencies of powerful, great natures lie deep in his soul; but they have not been waked, & sleep fixedly, because the noblest only have been called into action." I contend, of course, that these "tendencies" were awakened more than she was willing to admit and took "action" in art. Sophia's other sister, Mary Peabody Mann, agreed with Elizabeth, writing her son Horace that incidents in Hawthorne's life inevitably found themselves "bye and bye in books, for he always put himself into his books; he cannot help it" (Antioch College Library; qtd. in Miller, *Salem is My Dwelling Place,* 9). Elizabeth's approval of the assessment of Hawthorne's art as an exorcism of private demons accords with Hawthorne's own frequent "complaint" that the demonic seemed to overtake him in the act of writing, a fear first expressed jokingly to his mother in the 13 March 1821 letter in which he announced that he would become a writer (15:139).

8. In his rhetorical, not biographical, study, Gordon Hutner, *Secrets and Sympathy: Forms of Disclosure in Hawthorne's Novels* (Athens: University of Georgia Press, 1988) identifies Dimmesdale's Election Day sermon as a paradigm for the purposes and methods of *The Scarlet Letter* and, indeed, of art in general (25–26). Hawthorne's identification with Arthur, of course, has often been made by critics who read the romance as veiled autobiography. Nissenbaum, introduction to *The Scarlet Letter and Other Writings,* for instance, argues that Arthur Dimmesdale, as "priest-artist" (Arthur/author and *Arthur*) embodies Hawthorne's guilt for having compromised through ambition his artistic in-

tegrity ("celibacy") in the politics of the Custom House (xxviii–xxxvi). Evan Carton, "'A Daughter of the Puritans,'" reads Dimmesdale as epitomizing the "contradictions" in the novel between the "diverse sexual and familial roles" plaguing Hawthorne and informing his characterizations not only of Dimmesdale but also of Chillingworth, Hester, and Pearl (222). Miller, *Salem is My Dwelling Place*, argues for Hawthorne's "being the sum total" of all four of his characters (296–97). See also William C. Spengemann, *The Forms of Autobiography: Episodes in the History of a Literary Genre* (New Haven: Yale University Press, 1980), who discusses the work within the generic context of American autobiography (132–65).

9. Nissenbaum, introduction to *The Scarlet Letter*, explores in some depth Hawthorne's identification of himself with Dimmesdale as both artist and "priest." As more of a "priest" than a "minister," Dimmesdale in committing "adultery" violates his vows of "chastity," and his subsequent hypocrisy is rooted in his professional ambition. Nissenbaum argues that in Dimmesdale, Hawthorne expresses his own guilt over violating his professional integrity as an artist by soiling himself politically and then hypocritically proclaiming his innocence (xxix–xxxvi). I argue that Hawthorne's identification of Dimmesdale as a "priest" arises more from personal rather than professional guilt and is also associated with an "adultery" in Rome, not New England, by a Catholic, not a Protestant.

10. Fuller's praise for George Sand was truly bold, but as Chevigny, *Woman and the Myth*, points out it was always hedged by qualifiers while Fuller remained in America and remained a virgin and praised chastity. In Europe her attitudes changed toward both Sand and virginity, and she praised Sand, in fact, for having "bravely acted out her nature" (300–301).

11. Fuller, "The Great Lawsuit," 29–30. Fuller revised and expanded "The Great Lawsuit" during the fall and winter of 1844 into *Woman in the Nineteenth Century* (1845). Except where noted, all the citations from "The Great Lawsuit" may be found extant in *Woman in the Nineteenth Century*, the most recent and accessible edition being Steele's in *The Essential Margaret Fuller*, 243–378.

12. Fuller, "The Great Lawsuit," 30. In *Woman in the Nineteenth Century*, Fuller attempts to explain what she had meant by "severe lawgivers to themselves" by revising the paragraph following that sentence to read:

> They must be religious students of the divine purpose with regard to man, if they would not confound the fancies of a day with the requisitions of eternal good. Their liberty must be the liberty of law and knowledge. But, as to the transgressions against custom which have caused such outcry against those of noble intention, it may be observed, that the resolve of Eloisa to be only the mistress of Abelard, was that of one who saw in practice around her, the contract of marriage made the seal of degradation. Shelley feared not to be fettered, unless so to be was to be false. Wherever abuses are seen. . . . (286)

13. Fuller, Ossoli, and their son, Angelo, were not to set sail for America, however, until 17 May 1850. At the time Hawthorne completed *The Scarlet Letter*, Fuller and Ossoli were living in Florence after having fled Rome in July and Rieti in September. With Ossoli cut off from his inheritance and with Fuller struggling to complete her manuscript on the recent revolutions, they were entirely dependent on loans and gifts from family and friends. Their politics also kept them at some risk, for they were kept under surveillance during their stay in Florence (see Joseph Jay Deiss, *The Roman Years of Marga-*

ret *Fuller* [New York: Thomas Y. Crowell, 1969], 278–307; and Blanchard, *From Transcendentalism to Revolution*, 314–30). Though Fuller did not begin making actual arrangements for a return to America until the spring of 1850, she wrote of her general plans to return during the fall of 1849 (see, for example, *Letters*, 5:300–301). Her increasingly precarious financial and political situation in Italy since midsummer made a return not only likely but virtually inevitable. Her friends—among them Emelyn Story, William Channing, and Caroline Sturgis Tappan—had anticipated as much and, as Blanchard says, had "all discreetly warned her of what she might have to face at home" (318). Her friends in New England had long been confronting the gossip on her behalf. As a Swedish visitor to New England in early 1850, Frederika Bremer wrote of the attacks against Fuller's character and the vehement defenses by her friends caused by the gossip of "a Fourierest or Socialist marriage, without the external ceremony" (qtd. in Chevigny, *The Woman and the Myth*, 393). Her friends were hard-pressed in their defense, however, for as Sarah Clarke noted in a blunt letter to Fuller, without any evidence of a marriage, they found themselves "in a most unpleasant position" in responding to "the world," which "said such injurious things of you which we were not authorized to deny." Clarke herself had decided that "it seemed that you were more afraid of being thought to have submitted to the ceremony of marriage than to have omitted it" (qtd. in Chevigny, *The Woman and the Myth*, 393–94). "What you say of the meddling curiosity of people repels me," Fuller wrote to Caroline Sturgis in December 1849 (*Letters*, 5:303).

14. While Fuller's dispatches from Europe eloquently condemn broader economic, social, and political injustices, clearly her passion for rectifying the wrongs committed against women had also intensified. Though the following passage from a *Tribune* dispatch written on 2 December 1848 reflects Fuller's exhaustion and despondency over having to leave her three-month-old baby in Rieti in order to return to Ossoli and Rome, it clearly reveals that Fuller planned to keep working to transform "the whole relation between men and women." It may also suggest in her references to the need for a woman "younger and stronger" and "more worthy" to take up the "battle" on behalf of women that she anticipated that the scandal of her new status as an unwed mother would compromise her effectiveness as an advocate for women:

> Another century, and I might ask to be made Ambassador myself . . . , but woman's day has not come yet. They hold their clubs in Paris, but even George Sand will not act with women as they are. They say she pleads they are too mean, too treacherous. She should not abandon them for that, which is not nature but misfortune. How much I shall have to say on that subject if I live, which I hope I shall not, for I am very tired of the battle with giant wrongs, and would like to have some one younger and stronger arise to say what ought to be said, still more to do what ought to be done. Enough! if I felt these things in privileged America, the cries of mothers and wives beaten at night by sons and husbands for their diversion after drinking, as I have repeatedly heard them these past months, the excuse for falsehood, "I *dare not* tell my husband, he would be ready to kill me," have sharpened my perception as to the ills of Women's condition and remedies that must be applied. Had I but genius, had I but energy, to tell what I know as it ought to be told! God grant them me, or some other more worthy woman, I pray.
> (*"These Sad but Glorious Days,"* 245–46)

15. Richard Millington, *Practicing Romance: Narrative Form and Cultural Engagement in Hawthorne's Fiction* (Princeton: Princeton University Press, 1992), 100–103. Millington's

argument is that for Hawthorne "freedom of mind" required both understanding "the sense in which the meaning of one's own life—even to oneself—belongs to the community" but refusing "nevertheless to accede to the coercive patterns of mind that the community attempts to enforce." Thus Hester "remains faithful to her acts of rebellion by choosing again the context that gave those acts their meaning" (100).

16. Sacvan Bercovitch, *The Office of "The Scarlet Letter"* (Baltimore: Johns Hopkins University Press, 1991). Bercovitch's argument for a chastened Hester finally integrated into the community and liberal ideology is weakened by his general failure to acknowledge that in practicing the Christian ethic that Dimmesdale only professed she became more a living part of the community than Dimmesdale, its hermetic ideological hero. A more common interpretation of the ending is that Hawthorne attempts to constrain Hester and the sympathies that he has unleashed on her behalf by inserting her squarely within the ideology of domesticity and condemning her, by contrast, with her foil, the "domestic angel." Reynolds, *European Revolutions,* terms it "a veiled compliment to Hawthorne's little Dove, Sophia" (79). For Milton R. Stern, *Contexts for Hawthorne: "The Marble Faun" and the Politics of Openness and Closure in American Literature* (Urbana: University of Illinois Press, 1991), Hawthorne's sudden evocation of "the unfallen spotless heroine of the marketplace ideologies" is a "failure of nerve," the "voice of the one who would belong, unmaking in political rhetoric what he has painstakingly created in image, characterization, and event" (157–58). Millington's specific argument against the view that Hawthorne turns on Hester and his novel or that he engages Hester and the reader in the compromises of patience counseled by liberal consensus is that such views ignore Dimmesdale's torture at the hands of his "unexamined conformity to a dominant ideology," assume that Hester's advice to wronged women is "palliative" when in fact Hester herself has never repented of her own sin with Dimmesdale, and disregard the fact that even talking about the need for a "social transformation" would have been extraordinarily unwelcome to the patriarchy of seventeenth-century Puritan New England (*Practicing Romance,* 101–3). Millington's argument follows essentially Nina Baym's earlier contention, in *The Shape of Hawthorne's Career,* that in returning, Hester "does not acknowledge her guilt" but "admits that the shape of her life has been determined by the interaction between that letter, the social definition of her identity, and her private attempt to withstand that definition," an attempt that is successful in that she eventually brings "the community to accept that letter on her terms rather than its own" and thus brings "about a modest social change" (129–30).

17. Reynolds does claim that the closing reference to the feminist prophetess and "angel" of "sacred love" is both a "veiled compliment" to his "little Dove, Sophia" and "a veiled criticism of Margaret Fuller" (79), but he does not note Hawthorne's editing of Fuller's text. Charles Swann, "Hester and the Second Coming: A Note on the Conclusion to *The Scarlet Letter,*" *Journal of American Studies* 21 (1987): 264–68, comes closer to this recognition. In countering Colacurcio's seventeenth-century contextual reading of the ending, Swann mentions that Fuller's "Great Lawsuit" "equally clearly bears on Hester's case" and quotes one sentence ("Those who would reform the world. . . ."), but he immediately moves on to consider Mother Ann's relevance without making any further claims for Fuller's personal or authorial influence on Hawthorne (265). His interpretation of the ending as Hester's vision of a literal Second Coming of Christ as a woman is clearly far removed from what Fuller or Hawthorne had in mind. Donna Dickenson,

introduction to Margaret Fuller, *Woman in the Nineteenth Century and Other Writings,* World's Classics (New York: Oxford University Press, 1994), cites the penultimate paragraph of *The Scarlet Letter* and Fuller's comments on George Sand to assert that "Fuller anticipates Hawthorne's belief that the female Messiah must herself be pure" (vii–xxix; xiii). More recently, Robert Milder, *"The Scarlet Letter* and Its Discontents," *Nathaniel Hawthorne Review* 22 (spring 1996): 9–25, cites the passage as evidence that Fuller had prophesied her own (and Hester's) fate as a feminist who commits a sexual transgression (12). When I first made the observation in a 1989 seminar paper for Professor Larry J. Reynolds that Hawthorne's penultimate paragraph paraphrased Fuller, it was original. As Fuller's work becomes better known, however, that is no longer quite the case.

18. Fuller, "The Great Lawsuit," 7–8, and *Woman in the Nineteenth Century, 253.*

19. Fuller, "The Great Lawsuit," 8, and *Woman in the Nineteenth Century, 253–55.*

20. Francis E. Kearns, "Margaret Fuller as a Model for Hester Prynne," *Jahrbuch für Amerikastudien* 10 (1965): 191–97; Reynolds, *European Revolutions,* 79–80. Reynolds's explanation for the underlying causes of Hawthorne's sudden denunciation of Fuller in the 1858 notebook passage was made earlier, but less explicitly, by Blanchard, *From Transcendentalism to Revolution* (195), whom Reynolds acknowledges. Bercovitch, *The Office of "The Scarlet Letter,"* 85.

21. Fuller, "These Sad but Glorious Days," 238–47. Dates of publication in the *New-York Daily Tribune* are given parenthetically in the notes occasionally when the appearance of those columns seems to me important in terms of Hawthorne's writing of *The Scarlet Letter.*

22. Ibid., 285 (24 July 1849), 278 (23 June 1849), 154 (25 December 1847). For an account of the great excitement with which Americans read Fuller's dispatches for news of the revolution, see Reynolds's *European Revolutions,* 1–24, 54–78, 137–39, and his and Smith's introduction to "These Sad but Glorious Days," 1–2.

23. Ibid., Fuller, "These Sad but Glorious Days," 303 (11 August 1849).

24. Ibid., 310 (11 August 1849).

25. Sophia referred to Hawthorne's "brain fever" in a 1 August 1849 letter to her mother (Berg; qtd. in Miller, *Salem is My Dwelling Place,* 273).

26. Fuller, "These Sad but Glorious Days," 237 (19 January 1849).

27. Hawthorne may have heard gossip about Fuller's baby before early September, but as Reynolds points out, Caroline Sturgis Tappan would almost certainly have informed Sophia during Sophia's visit with her in the Berkshires during 3–8 September 1849, if not earlier in their exchange of letters during the summer of 1849. Fuller had informed Caroline of her baby and of his father, Giovanni Angelo Ossoli, an Italian marquis, in the early spring of 1849, months before informing anyone else in America (*European Revolutions,* 187, n. 2). The original letter in which Fuller informed Caroline of her baby was lost or destroyed. The earliest extant letter describing the baby (not announcing his existence) is Fuller's letter to Caroline on 16 March 1849 (*Letters,* 5:207–11). As a revelation of the "gossip circuit" between New England and Rome, Fuller acknowledges in the same letter to Caroline that she had heard of Caroline's recent marriage in December long before Caroline announced it to her in her last letter. Reynolds argues persuasively that Hawthorne began writing *The Scarlet Letter* between 21 and 25 September (*European Revolutions,* 189, n. 30).

28. Fuller, review of *Grandfather's Chair*, 58.

29. Hawthorne admired Byron enough to have his portrait look down upon him from the walls of the Manse. In a 30 August–4 September 1842 letter to her mother (Berg), Sophia describes her progress in decorating the Manse, mentioning a portrait of Byron, a statue of Napoleon, and a statue of Apollo (this given as a wedding gift by Carolina Sturgis).

30. Nathaniel Hawthorne, "Main-street," in *Aesthetic Papers*, ed. Elizabeth P. Peabody (1849; rpt. New York: AMS Press, 1967), 145–74; 163. Peabody's positioning of "Main-street" establishes an ideological foundation within a historical context for the arguments of the two essays that immediately follow it—S. H. Perkins's "Abuse of Representative Government" and Thoreau's "Resistance to Civil Government [Civil Disobedience]." Read as a unit, Hawthorne's historical indictment of Puritan New England's "hard, cold, and confined . . . system," the "iron cage" of "that which they called Liberty" (153), leads into Perkins's condemnation of the intolerances and brutalities of contemporary partisan politics, where individuals and minorities, where principle itself, are sacrificed for power, and Perkins's indictment, of course, provides a powerful introduction for Thoreau's radical solution to the problem. Thoreau's essay influenced Hawthorne to some extent in his portrayal of Hester's "silence" on the scaffold and of her silence (for a time, at least) about her increasingly radical intellectual resistance to the "untrue" ground on which the relations between men and women have been established and institutionalized. Her resistance is more, not less, active in the closing view of her counseling other women.

31. Hawthorne, "Main-street," 163. Baym, *The Shape of Hawthorne's Career*, argues that in "Main-street," Hawthorne envisions the golden ages of New England history in the pre-European matriarchy of an Indian culture in harmony with nature and in the first phase of independent Puritan families, in which "personal freedom and human relation combine in a natural world free from social institution" (120–21). In subsequent generations, as the Puritans establish communities and oppressive institutions, "the matriarchy and the life of the yeoman family" are destroyed as, in Hawthorne's words, "the pavements of Main-street" are "laid over the red man's grave" (*The Shape of Hawthorne's Career*, 120; "Main-street," 150). It is "to the influence of these children and grandchildren" of the original Puritans, claims Baym, that "Hawthorne attributes much of the worst in American life and character even in the nineteenth century" (121). "Let us thank God," the narrator of "Main-street" urges, "for having given us such ancestors; and let each successive generation thank him, not less fervently, for being one step further from them in the march of ages" (162).

32. For excellent discussions of the implications of Hawthorne's decision of modeling "Pearl" on Una, see Carton, "'A Daughter of the Puritans,'" and Herbert, *Dearest Beloved*, 202–8.

33. In a passage that Hawthorne might well have recalled in his writing of *The Scarlet Letter*, Fuller praised William Godwin for writing "like a brother" in defense of his wife, Mary Wollstonecraft, one of those, like Sand, whom Fuller had described, in the present state of society, as becoming the world's "outlaws" for "breaking bonds." Of Sand, Wollstonecraft, and Godwin, Fuller wrote in *Woman in the Nineteenth Century*: "They find their way, at last, to light and air, but the world will not take off the brand it has set upon them. The champion of the Rights of Woman found, in Godwin, one who would plead

that cause like a brother. He who delineated with such purity of traits the form of woman in the Marguerite, . . . a pearl indeed . . . was not false in life to the faith by which he had hallowed his romance. He acted as he wrote, like a brother" (284). In a poem in her 1844 journal, for instance, Fuller defines the meaning of "Marguerite" as the fusion of "love, grief, hope and fear / In that one century-hallowed tear," which she then identifies as "a pearl beyond all price so round and clear / For which must seek a Diver, too, without reproach or fear" ("'The Impulses of Human Nature,'" 112).

34. I take this up in chapter 8.

35. Manuscript joint notebook, 1843–44, 8 (qtd. in Turner, *Nathaniel Hawthorne,* 148); Turner, *Nathaniel Hawthorne,* 148.

36. On 13 July, for instance, Fuller records "playing with the beautiful Una, reading." The next day she "staid with Una while H. & Sophia took a walk & then S. went to Ellen." In the following day's entry, she refers again to baby-sitting Una with Hawthorne after Sophia had left and records: "We had most pleasant communion. He is mild, deep and large" ("'The Impulses of Human Nature,'" 84–85; see also, 93).

37. Ibid., 81–82.

38. Ibid., 89.

39. Ibid. The "Waldo" to whom Fuller referred was Emerson's first child, whom she had adored.

40. Ibid., 90, 82.

41. Ibid., 108.

42. Ibid., 89.

43. *Woman in the Nineteenth Century,* 282. Compare to "The Great Lawsuit," 28.

44. See Alfred S. Reid, *The Yellow Ruff and "The Scarlet Letter"* (Gainesville: University of Florida Press, 1955), 96–97, and especially Mukhtar Ali Isani's "Hawthorne and the Branding of William Prynne," *New England Quarterly* 45 (1972): 182–95. Isani explores some parallels between Hester and Prynne and Roger and Prynne but generally confines himself to the implications of Prynne's conflict with Laud and does not explore Prynne's opposition to Milton's views of marriage and divorce.

45. My account of Prynne's life is based on Sir Leslie Stephen and Sir Sidney Lee, eds., *Dictionary of National Biography,* 22 vols. (London: Oxford University Press, 1922), 16:432–37; *Encyclopaedia Britannica,* 15th ed., s. v. "Prynne, William" and "History of England and Great Britain: Charles I"; and Clarence L. Barnhart, *The New Century Cyclopedia of Names* (New York: Appleton-Century-Crofts, 1954), 3264–65.

John Milton, *Means to Remove Hirelings,* in Frank Allen Patterson, ed., *The Student's Milton,* rev. ed. (New York: Appleton-Century-Crofts, 1933), 878–98; 886. Patterson notes of this allusion that Milton "never condescends to call him by name" ("Glossary," 38). James Holly Hanford and James G. Taaffe, *A Milton Handbook,* 5th ed. (New York: Appleton-Century-Crofts, 1970), identify Prynne as Milton's most explicitly identified target in *Colasterion.* Prynne "had stigmatized" Milton's argument for divorce as a "monstrous heresy of 'divorce at pleasure'" (75–76).

46. The phrase "arts of deception" is Michael Davitt Bell's. His essay "Arts of Deception: Hawthorne, 'Romance,' and *The Scarlet Letter*," in *New Essays on "The Scarlet Letter,"* 29–56, is a fine analysis of Hawthorne's duplicitous strategies for making acceptable his engagement with the imaginative fictions of "romance," whose "delusions" were

"clearly dangerous" to a culture that valued "reason or judgment," for it served "to undermine the basis of psychological and social order, to alienate oneself from 'the real businesses of life'" (37).

47. Reynolds, "*The Scarlet Letter* and Revolutions Abroad," *American Literature* 57 (1985): 44–67 (also, *European Revolutions*, 79–96), is the first to demonstrate the importance of "revolutionary" imagery and themes to Hawthorne's imagination as he wrote "The Custom-House" and *The Scarlet Letter*. Of particular importance are Hawthorne's references to the guillotine in "The Custom-House" and his association of it with the scaffold in *The Scarlet Letter*. For Hawthorne, according to Reynolds, the Jacobin mobs of the original French Revolution came to be associated with the revolutionary mobs of Paris during the "Bloody June Days" of 1848 and, in turn, with the Whig "mobs" out for his own head. As a representative of the spirit of Liberty as well as Eve, Hester's influence on Arthur is "revolutionary" and, as Reynolds argues (based on Arthur's unleashed passions after their meeting in the forest), destructive. While I agree that Hawthorne feared the anarchy of mobs, I contend that though Hawthorne indeed associated the guillotine with French revolutionaries, he would have specifically associated it in the fall of 1849 with those revolutionaries, the Jacobins, who on obtaining civil authority used that authority to betray their principles and their fellow republicans, destroying one tyranny in order to establish an even greater one. When the French, after their revolutions of 1848, marched on the fledgling Republic of Rome to reestablish a reactionary Papal government and foreign hegemony in Italy, they betrayed their republican principles and fellow revolutionaries, as Fuller so vehemently condemned them. As Hawthorne wrote that fall, French armies occupied Rome under martial law. While the Whigs were anything but revolutionaries, the "mob" of Whigs after Hawthorne's head, from his point of view, at least, had betrayed their promises to reform in the name of justice and tolerance what they had defined as the Democrats' practice of automatically replacing political appointees, promising instead to replace only those who had been maleficent in office (see Nissenbaum, "The Firing of Nathaniel Hawthorne," 65). As Hawthorne would portray them, once the Whigs gained authority, they too abandoned principle for the privileges of power, as he makes clear: "There are few uglier traits of human nature than this tendency—which I now witnessed in mean no worse than their neighbors—to grow cruel, merely because they possessed the power of inflicting harm" (1:40–41). Similarly, the Puritans, fleeing oppression in England, had established a government every bit as oppressive and intolerant as the one they had fled, establishing as one of their first institutions the "black rose" of the prison and the scaffold to extirpate the "red rose" of America. As Hawthorne was with the Whigs and Fuller with the apostate republicans of the French army, so Hester is with the Puritan authorities. She is a victim not of the anarchy of revolution but of the oppressive power of institutionalized authority. That such authority wields that power hypocritically is reenforced not only by Arthur's public role in her persecution and humiliation but also by Hawthorne's deliberate historical anachronism in making Bellingham the chief civil authority as governor presiding over her punishment.

48. See Nissenbaum, introduction to *The Scarlet Letter*, for the relationship between Arthur's guilt, hypocrisy, and need for confession and Hawthorne's political and artistic guilt (xxviii–xxxvi).

49. Henry David Thoreau, "Resistance to Civil Government [Civil Disobedience]," in Carl Bode, ed., *The Portable Thoreau*, rev. ed. (New York: Penguin, 1964), 109–37; 112–13.

50. Herbert, *Dearest Beloved,* 184–211. Though Herbert does not establish a connection between Milton, Fuller, and Hawthorne, he identifies the essential conflict between the civil and sacred conceptions of marriage at work in middle-class nineteenth-century culture and at issue in *The Scarlet Letter.* I find his cultural and biographical analysis persuasive, as my own views will amply demonstrate in their debt to his, but I find the biographical and literary context to be broader than Herbert presents.

51. John Milton, *Doctrine and Discipline of Divorce,* in *The Student's Milton,* 573–626, especially 582; quotations on 591, 594.

52. From Milton's point of view, "Chillingworth's" desire to assuage the pangs of loneliness and solitude through marriage would be appropriate but impossible since there was no "real" union between himself and Hester, and only an authentic union can vanquish solitude. Hester's physical "adultery" was thus inevitable, in fact, was faithful in its way to the absence of union that was the nature of that "marriage."

53. Fuller, "The Great Lawsuit," 30, and *Woman in the Nineteenth Century,* 286.

54. Reynolds, "From *Dial* Essay to New York Book," demonstrates the importance of Fuller's dialogue with her friends in 1842 and again in 1844 in Concord (including Hawthorne but especially Emerson) as the impetus for her articulation of her views of marriage and male-female friendships. Milton's vision of the Garden of Eden and the marriage of Adam and Eve, of course, was very much on Hawthorne's mind during his Old Manse days, as was Fuller's conception of his and Sophia's marriage, specifically her prediction in her letter of July 1842 that he and Sophia would develop the highest form of marriage. In Hawthorne's 1 February 1843 letter to Fuller, he mentions that he and Sophia had been reading "through Milton's Paradise Lost, and other famous books." He then states, significantly, that "it sometimes startles me to think how we, in some cases, annul the verdict of applauding centuries, and compel poets and prosers to stand another trial, and receive condemnatory sentence at our bar" (15:671). Though Hawthorne may have been thinking of Milton's literary reputation, I contend that, within the context of his lengthy description of his own marriage, he was thinking of Milton's conception of marriage and divorce and the "condemnatory sentence" he would have received at the "bar" of Hawthorne's own age.

55. *Letters,* 3:66.

56. For an analysis of Hawthorne's response to the personal, marital, and creative conflicts that followed upon his entry into "Emerson's" Concord, see Reynolds, "Hawthorne and Emerson in 'The Old Manse.'" See also Herbert, *Dearest Beloved,* 109–60.

57. Fuller, "Margaret Fuller's 1842 Journal," 330.

58. Ibid., 335. See Emerson, *The Journals and Miscellaneous Notebooks of Ralph Waldo Emerson,* 7:336, 8:144, 7:532–33.

59. Fuller, "Margaret Fuller's 1842 Journal," 331–32, 326.

60. Ibid., 325.

61. *Letters,* 3:96. See Reynolds, "From *Dial* Essay to New York Book," for an account of the influence of the 1842 and 1844 conversations between Fuller and Emerson on Fuller's views of marriage in "The Great Lawsuit" and her revisions in *Woman in the Nineteenth Century.*

62. Fuller, "The Great Lawsuit," 27. In *Woman in the Nineteenth Century,* Fuller revises the passage to make her position clearer that a "union of one with one is believed to be the only pure form of marriage" (281).

63. Fuller, "The Great Lawsuit," 28, and *Woman in the Nineteenth Century,* 282. Reynolds makes this same observation in "From *Dial* Essay to New York Book."

64. *Letters,* 3:66; "The Great Lawsuit," 28–32, and *Woman in the Nineteenth Century,* 282–87, 289. The debate between Fuller and Emerson continued, in a sense, after her death. To her good friend William Henry Channing's belief that Fuller's "view of a noble life" would have prevented her from compromising and submitting to "a legal tie" with Ossoli, Emerson responded in his journal that he believed Fuller would have sacrificed her principles once faced with the "practical question" and "a vast public opinion, too vast to brave" (*The Journals and Miscellaneous Notebooks,* 11:463). Without evidence, Emerson, of course, presented her in the *Memoirs* as "married."

65. Fuller, "'The Impulses of Human Nature,'" 92. Sophia also criticized Emerson's marriage in much the same terms as Hawthorne did to Fuller. As Reynolds has demonstrated ("Hawthorne and Emerson in 'The Old Manse,'" 73–77), Hawthorne had managed to convert Sophia, who had once idolized Emerson, to his and Fuller's opinion of Emerson's emotional deficiencies. Writing to her mother (6 June 1843 [Berg]) about a letter in which her sister Elizabeth had employed Emerson's conception of the "self-sufficiency" of the individual in marriage to praise the marriage of Sam and Ana Barker Ward, Sophia defends her own marriage and challenges her sister's praise of the Wards' marriage. In a true marriage, she insists, neither partner "is wholly independent of the other, except intellectually" because "heart & spirit are forever, undissolubly one." Emerson cannot understand this, she asserts, because he "knows not much of love" and "has never yet said any thing to show that he does." "He is an isolation," Sophia concludes. "He has never yet known what union meant with any soul." Citing this letter, Herbert, *Dearest Beloved,* concludes, rightly, I think, that Sophia's definition of the "oneness" of the "true husband and wife" and her critique of Emerson is, in effect, Sophia's condemnation of the Emersons' marriage as "an adulterous legal marriage," parallel to the marriage of Roger and Hester (188–89).

66. In his journal, Emerson obscured the target of Fuller's and Hawthorne's criticism by attributing Hawthorne's remark to himself. He changed the "H." in Fuller's journal to a "W." in his. In the *Memoirs* he continued the deception, but more "honestly," by simply leaving out the entire last sentence of the passage so it appears that Fuller is writing generally about friendship and marriage rather than paraphrasing a conversation about a specific person. See Emerson, *The Journals and Miscellaneous Notebooks,* 11:463; and *Memoirs,* 2:292.

67. Fuller, "'The Impulses of Human Nature,'" 83.

68. Despite Fuller's virulent anti-Catholic attacks on papal politics and particularly against Jesuits, Hawthorne was almost certain to have associated Fuller's Italian "husband" with Catholicism regardless of how little he had heard about him. He may well have heard that the family of the Marquis Ossoli was directly associated with the Pope and the Papal Guard, though Ossoli went against his own family in opposing the Pope during the revolution. Hawthorne was more likely to have heard that Fuller had named her son Angelo, which suggests that Hawthorne's choice of "Angel" as the people's epithet for the charitable Hester was inspired at least in part for its value as a covert allusion. Though Nissenbaum, introduction to *The Scarlet Letter,* pursues an entirely different interpretation, he does identify many of the key images of Catholicism associated with Dimmesdale (xxix–xxx). It should be noted, as well, that James Lowell reported in a 12

June 1860 letter to Jane Norton that Hawthorne had considered having Dimmesdale confess to a priest: "I have seen Hawthorne twice. . . . He is writing another story. He said that it had been part of his plan in 'The Scarlet Letter' to make Dimmesdale confess himself to a Catholic priest. I, for one, am sorry he didn't. It would have [been] psychologically admirable" (qtd. in Henry G. Fairbanks, "Hawthorne and Confession," *Catholic Historical Review* 43 (1957): 38–45; 40).

69. A few of the physical details of the setting in which Arthur encounters Hester in the forest even parallel the setting in which Hawthorne encountered Fuller in Sleepy Hollow on that Sunday afternoon in August 1842. Hawthorne came upon Fuller unexpectedly in a small clearing just off the pathway. Hawthorne emphasizes the fact that the clearing was obscured from the path by a surrounding ridge and the forest and that she reclined in the grass while he sat beside her (8:342–43). As Arthur walks along the forest path, of course, he encounters a waiting Hester, and they retire to a "little dell" that is obscured from the pathway by "a leaf-strewn bank rising gently on either side" and by the forest. They sit on the ground as they talk (1:186, 190).

70. Milton, *Doctrine and Discipline of Divorce*, 582, 591.

71. Fuller, "The Great Lawsuit," 43, and *Woman in the Nineteenth Century*, 343.

72. Fuller, *Woman in the Nineteenth Century*, 343.

73. For a general analysis of the importance of masculine obsession and terror to Hawthorne's work, see Nina Baym's important revisionist essay "Thwarted Nature."

74. Leverenz, *Manhood and the American Renaissance*, makes the point that both Chillingworth and Dimmesdale maintain "their intellectual or spiritual self-control by rejecting intimacy" (269). Leverenz sees the narrator as obsessed by a fear that both "Hester's passionate loving, like Chillingworth's passionate hating, leaves the self wide open to demonic possession" (264).

75. Colacurcio, "'The Woman's Own Choice,'" 101–35, especially 109–11.

76. Nathaniel Hawthorne, "Mrs. Hutchinson," *Tales, Sketches, and Other Papers*, vol. 12 of *The Works of Nathaniel Hawthorne* (Boston: Osgood, 1883), 218. Hawthorne's sketch of Anne Hutchinson originally appeared in the *Salem Gazette*, 7 December 1830, 4.

77. Yes, you might say, but what about those letters to his publishers in the mid- and late 1850s denigrating that "d——d mob of scribbling women" (17:304)? Those letters, of course, cannot be ignored, but they cannot be assumed to present a clear notion of Hawthorne's attitudes toward women or women writers. As James D. Wallace, "Hawthorne and the Scribbling Women Reconsidered," *American Literature* 62 (1990): 201–22, has demonstrated so persuasively Hawthorne praised women writers as profusely as he sometimes condemned them. Both the praise and the condemnation centered on just those qualities in their writings that characterized Hawthorne's own works and that caused him profound ambivalence. I would also add to Wallace's argument that any reading of those letters to his publishers in the 1850s should be placed within the context of Hawthorne's long period of creative inactivity (perhaps, creative sterility) and of their audience, written as they were to publishers whose list was made up overwhelmingly of male writers.

78. Fuller, "The Great Lawsuit," 29–30, and *Woman in the Nineteenth Century*, 284.

79. Fuller, "The Great Lawsuit," 30, and *Woman in the Nineteenth Century*, 286.

80. Fuller, "The Great Lawsuit," 30, 44, 47, and *Woman in the Nineteenth Century*, 286,

312, 347. Steele, *Representations of the Self,* demonstrates thoroughly how Fuller's concept of the power of virginity, symbolized by the goddess Minerva, is an attempt to relocate "the idea of woman" and her "independent spiritual authority" within "women's souls" by "advocating female self-reliance outside of male-female relations," a frontal assault "at nineteenth-century faith in motherhood as the ideal of female being" (127).

81. Fuller, "The Great Lawsuit," 47, and *Woman in the Nineteenth Century,* 347.

CHAPTER SIX   *"Silken Bands" and "Iron Fetters"*

1. To secure British copyrights, Fields had *The Blithedale Romance* released in England "shortly before 7 July 1852" and in the United States on 14 July (Clark, *A Descriptive Bibliography,* 210, 213). Four days before 7 July, an unsigned review in the English *Spectator* (25 [3 July 1852]: 637–38]; rpt. in J. Donald Crowley, ed., *Hawthorne: The Critical Heritage* [New York: Barnes and Noble, 1970], 243–44) asserted that notwithstanding Hawthorne's disclaimers "Margaret Fuller seems to have suggested the idea of Zenobia" (244). By October the *Westminster Review* (58 [October 1852]: 592–98; rpt. in *Hawthorne: The Critical Heritage,* 259–64) could allude to "the supposition that Zenobia is an apograph of Margaret Fuller," endorse it, and then proceed to speculate that Hawthorne may be giving his readers "a missing chapter in Margaret Fuller's life—unwritten hitherto, because never sufficiently palpable to come under the cognizance of the biographer, and only capable of being unveiled by the novelist." The reviewer even recommends the novel as "an excellent introduction to the study of her supposed prototype" (262–63). Contemporary reviewers were reluctant to comment much on Coverdale as a character, much less on Hawthorne's autobiographical purposes, but an unsigned review in the *Christian Examiner* (55 [September 1852]: 292–94; rpt. in *Hawthorne: The Critical Heritage,* 250–52) alluded to the critics' dilemma and resolved it by making it Sophia's: "We leave to the help-meet of the author to settle with him the issue that may arise from his description of himself as a bachelor" (252).

2. Miller, *Salem is My Dwelling Place,* 275.

3. Hawthorne justified his decision to rent a room rather than join Sophia and the children in the Peabody home in a letter in which he claims that "it would be a sin to add another human being to the multitudinous chaos of that house" (16:334). Miller, *Salem is My Dwelling Place,* argues that he likely just wanted to "escape from the two Elizabeths . . . as well as from his own family responsibilities and restrictions" (303). While Miller may be right about Hawthorne's reluctance under even ordinary circumstances to confront daily and in close quarters his sister-in-law and mother-in-law, much of that reluctance, especially under the circumstances in April 1850, originated not so much in temperamental differences as in his long-standing, but now aggravated, chagrin, if not shame, at having failed Sophia as a husband.

4. Miller, *Salem is My Dwelling Place,* 303.

5. Hawthorne and Sophia had variously inquired about houses at Portsmouth (near Bridge), Essex Falls, Hamilton, and West Cambridge (near Longfellow) (16:313 nn. 4, 6).

6. Mellow, *Nathaniel Hawthorne in His Times,* 320.

7. The original letter in which Fuller first informed Caroline of her baby is lost. Fuller's 16 March 1849 letter (*Letters,* 5:207–11) to Caroline describes in detail the child whose birth had been announced in the earlier letter. Soon after reaching Florence, Ful-

ler began writing to friends of her plans to return home. To William Henry Channing, for instance, she wrote that she had no intention of returning without Ossoli but that she had no illusions about the difficulties facing them in America. While Ossoli learned English, she would "be engaged in the old unhealthy way" and that their life would "probably be a severe struggle" (5:301). In a 17 December 1849 letter to Caroline, Fuller discussed her plans to return and indicated that she hoped to see her in her "Lenox home" within the year (5:303). In that same letter, she responded to Caroline's earlier letters describing the scandalous gossip about her: "What you say of the meddling curiosity of people repels me. It is so different here" (5:303).

8. Sophia to her mother, 9–16 June, 1 August 1850 (Berg).

9. Miller, *Salem is My Dwelling Place,* 305.

10. Sophia to her mother, 1 August 1850 (Berg). Sophia's consolation, however, only served to deepen her grief. "But Margaret is such a loss," she continued, "with her new & deeper experience of life in all its relations—her rich harvest of observation." Caroline knew the impact Fuller's death would have on the Hawthornes, for she apparently kept the news from them for a few days and, as Sophia, describes the dramatic moment, "when she did tell me—she gave me the papers & instead of overwhelming me with a shock—tried to break a way by a look of great sorrow & foreboding."

11. Greeley, "Death of Margaret Fuller"; "The Wreck of the *Elizabeth*" and "The Wreck on Fire Island," *New-York Daily Tribune,* 24 July 1850, 4; Higginson, *Margaret Fuller Ossoli,* 276. Though sources are not clearly identified, at least one of the *New-York Daily Tribune* accounts, "The Wreck of the *Elizabeth*," quotes directly from Mrs. Hasty, the widow of the *Elizabeth*'s original captain who died at sea with the smallpox that almost took Angelino's life. A Mr. Bangs commanded the ship for the remainder of the voyage. For a convenient summary of the incident, see Blanchard, *From Transcendentalism to Revolution,* 331–37. Chevigny notes in *The Woman and the Myth* that "so many at the time had the impression that Fuller wished to die that when Higginson was writing his biography of Fuller a number of friends pressed him to eradicate it" (401 n. 46). Chevigny herself attempts to counter Margaret Allen's argument in "The Political and Social Criticism of Margaret Fuller," *South Atlantic Quarterly* 72 (1973): 560–73, that Fuller's will to live was weakened by her despair over the triumph of reactionaries in Italy (401 n. 46).

12. Joel Myerson, *Margaret Fuller: An Annotated Secondary Bibliography* (New York: Burt Franklin, 1977), 24–31. As if Fuller's loss in such a dramatic and seemingly unnecessary way was not sensational enough, the *New-York Daily Tribune* reported between 23 and 31 July on the incompetence of the local life-saving crews and on massive plundering of flotsam from the wreckage and valuables stripped from bodies washed ashore—plundering that began even as Fuller and others waited helplessly on deck for rescue. As many as forty people were implicated, and rumors circulated that bodies were buried in the sand to conceal the crime. Thoreau, later joined by Ellery Channing, helped search for Fuller's body and manuscripts, and posted rewards, all of which received *Tribune* coverage. Fuller's desk with only a few of her papers was recovered. Plundered clothing belonging to Fuller was also later discovered in a home.

13. Sophia to her mother, 1 August 1850 (Berg).

14. Ibid.; Mellow, *Nathaniel Hawthorne in His Times,* 322.

15. Herbert, *Dearest Beloved,* does not quote this passage to illustrate his thesis, but

he might well have. See especially pp. 3–5 and 24–28 for persuasive readings of other notebook passages that illustrate Herbert's thesis.

16. George Hillard to Hawthorne, 28 March 1850 (qtd. in Rose Hawthorne Lathrop, "The Hawthornes in Lenox: Told in Letters by Nathaniel and Mrs. Hawthorne," *Century* 27 (November 1894): 86–98; 88).

17. Sophia to her mother 4 September 1850 (Berg).

18. It is, of course, Herbert's project in *Dearest Beloved* to approximate such a calculation. Herbert reads in Sophia's "groveling protestations of absolute devotion" to Hawthorne a concealed but "unvanquished will to power." Behind Hawthorne's apparent willingness to meet "Sophia's expectations," Herbert finds evidence in Hawthorne's fiction that "he met her disassociated fury not only with acquiescent guilt but also with covert reciprocal rage" (28–29).

19. See Emerson, *The Journals and Miscellaneous Notebooks*, 11:258.

20. Turner, *Nathaniel Hawthorne*, 225.

21. Sophia to her mother, 27 January 1851 (Berg).

22. *True Stories from History and Biography* was a collection of *Grandfather's Chair, Famous Old People, Liberty Tree*, and *Biographical Stories*.

23. Clark, *A Descriptive Bibliography*, is the source of all bibliographic information.

24. Herbert, *Dearest Beloved*, 5.

25. Miller, *Salem is My Dwelling Place*, 341.

26. Herbert, *Dearest Beloved*, 28, 18; Sophia qtd. in Miller, *Salem is My Dwelling Place*, 341.

27. Hawthorne also mentions several visits by Caroline Sturgis Tappan and several visits he made to her home to borrow books and magazines.

28. Sophia to Mary Peabody Mann, 22 June 1851 (Berg). Sophia praised her father's help during the delivery but is conspicuously silent about Hawthorne's: "He [her father] was invaluable to me at the momentous hour—so self-possessed, gentle, firm & patient—& he was actually alone when the baby came! He called bravely for Mr. Hawthorne, who had gone down to receive the nurse & I was sorry enough she had not arrived, for I meant my husband should never be present at such a time."

29. For Elizabeth Peabody's recollection of Sophia's statement, see Norman Holmes Pearson, "Elizabeth Peabody on Hawthorne," *Essex Institute Historical Collections* 94 (1958): 256–76; 276; Miller, *Salem is My Dwelling Place*, 344.

30. Herbert, *Dearest Beloved*, 27. See also page 291 n. 2.

31. Sophia to James T. Fields, 1 January 1862 (Boston Public Library; qtd. in Miller, *Salem is My Dwelling Place*, 43); Miller, *Salem is My Dwelling Place*, 231, 260.

32. Sophia to her sister Elizabeth Peabody, 10 July 1851 (Berg). Sophia also reports in the letter that Hawthorne had characterized her confinement for three months as "months of utter misery to him," yet when her confinement ended, "still he was separated." As Sophia acknowledged to her sister Mary (4 July 1851 [Berg]), it was Hawthorne who suggested that she needed to get away for a while. Hawthorne was not the only one miserable during this time. In her letters of June and July to her family, Sophia had complained of lack of energy, sleeplessness, headache, and toothaches. She had also complained bitterly of Rose's first nurse, of her father's extended visit having destroyed

Hawthorne's "activities" and "domestic life," and even, uncharacteristically, of Una's misbehavior over the last few months, which Sophia hoped the trip would cure. Of Una, Sophia wrote: "Una's naughtiness consists principally in her *impatience*—It is the root of the trouble. She has no grave faults—no disingenuousness—no falsehood—All is fair & open & conspicuously disagreeable—the pout, the frown, the angry tone—very apparent—seething [illegible] irritation & greater impatience. I cannot hope that any body will much like her just now except her mother" (4 July 1851 letter to Mary [Berg]).

33. Mellow, *Nathaniel Hawthorne in His Times*, 377.

34. William Ellery Channing to Ellen Fuller Channing, 30 October 1851 (Massachusetts Historical Society; qtd. in Miller, *Salem is My Dwelling Place*, 364). Caroline claimed the right to the apples growing on the property rented to the Hawthornes. The dispute seemed focused between Caroline and Sophia, but Hawthorne intervened in defense of Sophia and their tenant privileges. The incident compounded Hawthorne's discontent with Lenox and provided him with an excuse for accelerating his search for another home. See Miller, *Salem is My Dwelling Place*, 348–52; Mellow, *Nathaniel Hawthorne in His Times*, 379–81; and Turner, *Nathaniel Hawthorne*, 233–34.

35. Qtd. in Mellow, *Nathaniel Hawthorne in His Times*, 381–82. Hawthorne's "lack of society" outside the home was matched at this time apparently by his discomfort with society within the home. In her 10 July 1851 letter to her sister Elizabeth (Berg), Sophia explained her vow "never . . . to have guest for so long again" after her father completed his extended visit because "it fairly destroys both his [Hawthorne's] activities & his domestic life—He has no other life—never visiting & having nothing to do with the public—I do not know as any one but myself can estimate the cost to him of having a stranger in our courts—especially in these narrow ones." She then describes their "separation" during and after her recent three-month confinement and her sense of his being still, to her, like a "hermit."

After the birth of Rose, Una had been a troubled and troubling child, according to Sophia (see n. 32 above). An additional indication of Hawthorne's "misery" during this period and perhaps of his withdrawal or "separation" from his family during this stressful period may be gathered from Sophia's explanation for Una's bad behavior: "She has been as naughty as possible lately; all her sweet bells jangled—because she has been so long without a centre & hampered with by my abominable nurse who regularly taught her to flout Grandpapa . . . & 'do as she pleased' & Mama was not to be met with any where about" (Sophia to her sister Mary, 4 July 1851 [Berg]). Hawthorne's absence from Sophia's explanation suggests his absence as a "centre" for Una.

36. Ellery Channing invited him in December to inspect the Alcott house, which was for sale. Thinking perhaps of what he had seen in October of Hawthorne's family life, Ellery tried to encourage him to make the trip by letting him know that they could lead a bachelor's life during his stay, for his wife and children were gone and he was stocked with liquor. Besides, he wrote, "Emerson is gone, and nobody here to bore you. The skating is damned good" (qtd. in Julian Hawthorne, *NH and HW*, 1:432–33). Hawthorne, however, could not make the trip until February.

37. Greeley, "Death of Margaret Fuller," 4; review of *Memoirs of Margaret Fuller Ossoli*, 199.

38. Chevigny, "To the Edges of Ideology," argues that both the *Memoirs* and *Blithedale* were postmortems on Fuller's life that attempted to reinsert her into an ideological con-

struct of womanhood that Fuller had deconstructed. More recently, Louise D. Cary, "Margaret Fuller as Hawthorne's Zenobia," *American Transcendental Quarterly* 4 (March 1990): 31–48, expands on Chevigny's argument to analyze Hawthorne's romance as an "insidious treatment" of Fuller's life in a transparently "fictionalized biography" (32). While I find most of Cary's parallels between Fuller's life and Zenobia's character accurate, I think her account of Hawthorne's malicious purposes is far too simplistic, a perfect illustration, in fact, of the critical legacy that Julian Hawthorne made almost inevitable.

39. See Albert J. von Frank, "Life as Art in America: The Case of Margaret Fuller," *Studies in the American Renaissance, 1981*: 1–26.

40. Crowley, *The Critical Heritage*, 263.

41. Coverdale's description of the narrative flow of his book parallels Hawthorne's descriptions of the Concord in his notebooks and in "The Old Manse," a marked contrast of course to Melville's tempestuous ocean. Interesting possibilities present themselves if the passage is read with Fuller's descriptions of boat rides with Hawthorne on the Concord in mind ("'The Impulses of Human Nature'").

CHAPTER SEVEN *Dreaming the "Same Dream Twice"*

1. Qtd. in *NH and HW*, 1:444–45.

2. Lauren Berlant, "Fantasies of Utopia in *The Blithedale Romance*," *American Literary History* 1 (1989): 30–62, analyzes the tensions between "fantasies of communion" in subjective (tragic) and in collective (utopian) life and asserts that Coverdale's narrative is "an endless well-ordered love plot about his eternal lovelessness" (52).

3. The pervasive atmosphere of mystery in *Blithedale* has been much commented upon. C. J. Wershoven, "Doubles and Devils at Blithedale," *American Transcendental Quarterly* 58 (1985): 43–54, expresses the frustration of many a reader of the romance in calling *Blithedale* "a novel full of tricks": "Everywhere we are confronted by puzzles, riddles, disguises, amateur theatrics, and dreams. We must struggle through the mist of illusion to ask, what is real?" (43). Frederick Crews, *The Sins of the Fathers: Hawthorne's Psychological Themes* (New York: Oxford University Press, 1966), contends that Hawthorne could not have answered Wershoven's question: "If Hawthorne has blurred all his portraits except Coverdale's, backed away from the simplest explanations of fact, exploited literal scenes for a cabalistic meaning that is lost upon the reader, and included episodes that make virtually no sense apart from such meaning, then we must infer that Hawthorne as well as Coverdale is at the mercy of unconscious logic" (205).

4. Surprisingly little attention is paid to Hawthorne's use of "Coverdale" as a name for his narrator. One exception is Joan Magretta, "The Coverdale Translation: *Blithedale* and the Bible," *Nathaniel Hawthorne Journal* (1974): 250–56. Magretta argues that Coverdale "translates" his experiences at Blithedale into biblical-like parables; she does not, however, explore the autobiographical implications of Hawthorne's selection of the name "Coverdale."

5. Virtually everyone who knew Fuller testified to her power as a conversationalist, a power that few, including Fuller, believed was equalled by her writing. In 1840 Fuller wrote in her journal: "I will write well yet; but never, I think so well as I talk; for then I feel inspired, and the means are pleasant; my voice excites me; my pen never" (qtd. in

Emerson, *The Journals and Miscellaneous Notebooks,* 11:471). Fuller's reputation as a writer, I believe, has suffered because her power as a speaker and conversationalist was so remarkable that it made her writing seem "tame" to those who knew her. Unfortunately, this litany of negative contrasts does an injustice to her writing and creates a predisposition among readers to find the faults that were evident during her own day primarily to those who heard her words before reading them.

6. Fuller, "Leila," 53–54; Fuller, "The Magnolia of Lake Pontchartrain," 48.

7. Fuller, "The Magnolia of Lake Pontchartrain," 49.

8. Ibid., 48.

9. In one of the best essays on *Blithedale* in recent years, Richard Brodhead, "Veiled Ladies: Toward a History of Antebellum Entertainment," *American Literary History* 1 (1989): 273–94, demonstrates how *Blithedale* responds to the increasingly "public" creation of woman into "a creature of private space" (274) through the increasing presence of women in the literary marketplace, a presence granted, ironically, only if their works endorse the "private space" from which they, as authors, have escaped, and in the public theater, Jenny Lind's wildly popular and highly publicized performances of scenes from Shakespeare being the most notable example.

10. Hawthorne, for instance, signed a 21 October 1841 letter to Sophia from Brook Farm as "Thine Ownest, Theodore de l'Aubépine" (15:592). Sophia initially considered naming Julian "Theodore," but Hawthorne objected (16:201–2).

11. That truth, according to Person, *Aesthetic Headaches,* is "to encounter a woman in her fully human nature," Zenobia's purpose in telling the tale being to "subvert" Coverdale's "inclination to idealize" women (152).

12. Pfister, *The Production of Personal Life,* 70. See especially Pfister's chapter "Monsters in the Hothouse," 59–79.

Fuller, *Woman in the Nineteenth Century,* 310. In the very next sentence, Fuller attacks those who would "biologize" cultural constructions of gender by claiming that "Nature" itself exposes the folly of such efforts: "History jeers at the attempts of physiologists to bind great original laws by the forms which flow from them. They make a rule; they say from observation, what can and cannot be. In vain! Nature provides exceptions to every rule" (310).

13. Fuller, *Woman in the Nineteenth Century,* 343.

14. Hawthorne frequently conceived of himself as a worker in fire. *The Scarlet Letter,* of course was a "h-ll-fired story," and in *Blithedale,* as he neared the end, he wrote Grace Greenwood that he had "been brooding over a book" and had "latterly got under a high pressure of steam" (16:533). He could not "promise to amend" *Blithedale,* he wrote E. P. Whipple in the letter in which he asked Whipple for his advice on the finished draft, because, he asserted, "the metal hardens very soon after I pour it out of my melting pot into the mould" (16:536). Hawthorne, as blacksmith molding from his past the characters of *Blithedale* in his creative fire, has his narrator employ "fire" as a metaphor for his own creations. Coverdale re-creates the "fireside" at Blithedale on that arctic April day by raking "away the ashes from the embers in my memory" (3:9). In re-creating the "fires" of memory, Coverdale animates the self-created "monsters" of his mind while kindling the "fires" of "youth, warm blood, . . . hope," and the "so very beautiful"

women, the "fires" for which he would now spend his "last dollar" if he could "prolong" their "blaze" (3:24).

15. Person, *Aesthetic Headaches,* makes the similar point that "Zenobia's presence always implies more than Coverdale or Hawthorne can denote," that Coverdale's allusions to Eve and Pandora are failed attempts to conform her "to type" in order "to contain her frightening power," and that even the figures that he selects, Pandora being the exemplar, symbolize "resistance to containment and the power to break out of 'moulds'" (149). As with most of his insights into the importance in Hawthorne of the feminine to the creative, Person is certainly right in this, but I would give both Coverdale and Hawthorne more credit for being self-consciously critical of this masculine desire.

16. Pfister, *The Production of Personal Life,* says of this statement that it "is surely the most provocative statement in Hawthorne's novel" because an "awareness" of the cultural constructedness of gender "appears to have been rare in the mid-nineteenth century, although it can be found in the writings of Sarah Grimké and Margaret Fuller and in the works of female authors who wrote later in the century" (85).

17. For Person, *Blithedale* is the "best example" in Hawthorne "of the way a woman's presence and voice challenge masculine literary forms and disrupt or dazzle male discourse" (*Aesthetic Headaches,* 146).

18. For a reading of *Blithedale* as a "parody" of contemporary sentimental literature, see Ken Egan Jr., "Hawthorne's Anti-Romance: *Blithedale* and Sentimental Culture," *Journal of American Culture* 11 (1988): 45–52. Egan asserts that "the critical side of Hawthorne's imagination rejects the comforting conclusion of *House*" and that *Blithedale* "reads like a pastiche of parodized sentimental conventions," but he does not explore the biographical origins of Hawthorne's change of heart, only noting that Hawthorne "felt divided toward popular culture in general" (45).

19. Fuller, *Woman in the Nineteenth Century,* 283.

20. Emerson, *Emerson in His Journals,* 414.

21. Herbert, *Dearest Beloved,* 23–24. Herbert, I think, is certainly correct in his argument that Hawthorne attempts to do what Hollingsworth does not—to free himself from Zenobia's ghost by attempting to expose "the subversive tensions" that were inherent in the "romantic ontology of domestic relations" on which Hollingsworth and Priscilla's and his own marriage to Sophia were based (17).

22. Emerson's position is well known; Fuller's, less so. Fuller, like Zenobia, frequently stayed at Brook Farm for short visits and sympathized with its ideals but had little faith that its utopian goals could be accomplished. In an 1840 letter to, apparently, William H. Channing, Fuller explains: "Utopia it is impossible to build up. At least, my hopes for our race on this one planet are more limited than those of most of my friends. I accept the limitations of human nature, and believe a wise acknowledgment of them one of the best conditions of progress. Yet every noble scheme, every poetic manifestation, prophesies to man his eventual destiny" (*Letters,* 2:109). Coverdale's skeptical commitment to the "experiment" of *Blithedale* (3:10–11) is similar in many points to Fuller's, as the following passage from the same letter attests: "It was not meant that the soul should cultivate the earth, but that the earth should educate and maintain the soul. Man is not made for society, but society is made for man. No institution can be good which does not tend to improve the individual. In these principles I have confidence so profound,

that I am not afraid to trust those who hold them, despite their partial views, imperfectly developed characters, and frequent want of practical sagacity" (*Letters,* 2:109).

23. Miller, *Salem is My Dwelling Place,* 189. Miller speculates that Hawthorne's commitment to Brook Farm was "but another tactic to postpone marriage" (189).

24. Reynolds, "Hawthorne and Emerson in 'The Old Manse,'" 65, 73–77.

25. Ibid., 76. Leverenz, *Manhood and the American Renaissance,* makes the similar point that Hawthorne's major romances feature "two contradictory stories: a woman's struggle for strength and autonomy within patriarchy, and the rivalry of several men for dominance" (246).

26. Hawthorne may have had Zenobia command Coverdale to write a ballad rather than another genre because he may have associated Brook Farm, Fuller, Emerson, and himself with a conversation held there by the three on 27 September 1841, the day of the masquerade for Frank Dana's birthday. In a Coverdale-like self-portrait, Hawthorne describes in his notebook the scene while he, "whose nature it is to be a mere spectator both of sport and serious business, lay under the trees and looked on." He then adds: "Meanwhile, Mr. Emerson and Miss Fuller, who had arrived an hour or two before, came forth into the little glade where we were assembled. Here followed much talk" (8:202). In a note to that entry, Claude Simpson states that while no one left a clearly identified record of that conversation he believes (and I am convinced that the context within *Blithedale* supports that belief) that the following journal entry by Emerson (between 28 September and 8 October 1841) may be a summary of the trio's talk: "Margaret Fuller talked of ballads, and our love for them: strange that we should so value the wild man, the Ishmaelite, and his slogan, claymore, and tomahawk rhymes, and yet every step we take, everything we do, is to tame him. . . . Margaret does not think, she says, in the woods, only 'finds herself expressed'" (8:605–6).

27. Indeed, Emerson invited the comparison by making it himself. In an 11–12 April 1839 journal entry, for instance, he wrote: "I told S[arah] M[argaret] F[uller] that I was a cross of Plato & Aristotle" (*The Journals and Miscellaneous Notebooks,* 7:186). I thank Larry J. Reynolds for pointing out the Hollingsworth-Plato-Emerson associations to me.

28. Lauren Berlant, "Fantasies of Utopia," 43. In her notes, Berlant points out that Eliot began his ministry at Roxbury but did not begin his missionary work with the Indians nor preach to them until he went to Concord. She also notes that Hawthorne's association of Eliot with a "rock" pulpit is an emphasis not shared by historians (58 n. 15). "Eliot's Pulpit" by allusion thus melds Brook Farm with Concord, one the site of the romance, the other the site of the memory.

29. Hollingsworth's power as a speaker affects Coverdale in much the same way that Emerson's did for the "multitudes" who came to hear him. Hawthorne, in effect, describes Hollingsworth as something of an undiscovered Emerson: "He talked to us, his few disciples, in a strain that rose and fell as naturally as the wind's breath among the leaves of the birch-tree. No other speech of man has ever moved me like some of those discourses. It seemed most pitiful—a positive calamity to the world—that a treasury of golden thoughts should thus be scattered, by the liberal handful, down among us three, when a thousand hearers might have been the richer for them; and Hollingsworth the richer, likewise, by the sympathy of the multitudes" (3:119).

30. Hawthorne had first paired the "seamstress" and the "feminist," a woman with too much to do and a woman with too little, in "The Christmas Banquet" (10:303).

31. To Whipple's suggestion to Hawthorne that Hollingsworth had not been "sufficiently punished for his cruelty to Zenobia," Hawthorne replied, "I hate the man ten times worse than you do, . . . but I don't now see how such a nature can feel the remorse he ought to feel." When Whipple reports Hawthorne's joy in having discovered a way to "punish" Hollingsworth, he cites only the material related to Coverdale's visit with Hollingsworth and Priscilla. He does not cite "Coverdale's Confession," which I contend was then added as his "punishment" of Coverdale (16:537 n. 2).

32. Richard H. Millington, "American Anxiousness: Selfhood and Culture in Hawthorne's *The Blithedale Romance*," *New England Quarterly* 63 (1990): 558–83; 580. Millington reads the "inauthenticity" of Coverdale's confession as largely unconscious, representing his "last, best hope for selfhood" but, in failing, revealing "the depth of his anxiousness and guilt about having nothing to confess, nothing to say, because he has succeeded in being nothing" (580). I argue that given his depiction of the consequences of Hollingsworth's choice of Priscilla, Coverdale self-consciously and self-contemptuously betrays Zenobia once again.

33. For Sophia's comments, see her letter to her mother on Fuller's *Woman in the Nineteenth Century* (*NH and HW,* 1:257). Emerson records hearing that from childhood onward she "idealized herself as a sovereign" and "believed that she was not her parents' child but a European princess confided to their care"; he then quotes her as having written that "I take my natural position always: and the more I see, the more I feel that it is regal. Without throne, sceptre, or guards, still a queen" (*Memoirs,* 1:235). See also Emerson's depiction of her as "like a queen of some parliament of love" (*Memoirs,* 1:214).

34. See Pfister, *The Production of Personal Life,* 96–99, and John C. Hirsh, "Zenobia as Queen: The Background Sources to Hawthorne's *The Blithedale Romance*," *Nathaniel Hawthorne Journal* (1971): 182–91. Hirsh surveys the "literary tradition" that had developed around the historical Zenobia and makes his case for the "literary origins" of Zenobia against "the preoccupation with Margaret Fuller as source" (182). Pfister's examination, however, is a much more insightful examination of the uses to which the historical Zenobia served as a contemporary literary figure. Pfister stresses the "conquered" rather than "defiant" Zenobia, claiming that she had become "the stereotype of a proud and able woman feminized and privatized into silence" (99). Unlike Hirsh, Pfister links Fuller to Zenobia, but unaccountably does not make the connection between Fuller's militancy in Rome and her liaison with Ossoli. Fuller, by the way, had chosen William Ware's *Letters from Palmyra* (later entitled *Zenobia*) for one of her first literary reviews (*Western Messenger* 5 [April 1838]: 24–29).

35. Louise D. Cary, "Margaret Fuller as Hawthorne's Zenobia," as mentioned in the previous chapter, examines *Blithedale* as a "fictionalized biography" that presents an "insidious treatment" of Fuller's life (32).

36. Chevigny, *Woman and the Myth,* xxxii–xxxiii; Millington, "American Anxiousness," 570.

37. Person, *Aesthetic Headaches,* points out that not only does Zenobia resist all efforts to "contain" her in a "mold," she in fact succeeds, like "a sculptress within the narrative," to shape "other characters to her own designs" (151).

38. Christina Zwarg, "Womanizing Margaret Fuller: Theorizing a Lover's Discourse," *Cultural Critique* 16 (1990): 161–91; 162–65.

39. Fuller, for instance, is quoted in her *Memoirs* as writing the following about a

transcendent moment in her life: "Since that, I have never more been completely engaged in self; but the statue has been emerging, though slowly, from the block. Others may not see the promise even of its pure symmetry, but I do, and am learning to be patient. I shall be all human yet" (1:142). See also *Memoirs*, 1:238, for an unnamed contemporary on Fuller's perception of herself as both artist and art object, and, recently, Frank, "Life as Art in America."

40. Reynolds and Smith, introduction to *"These Sad but Glorious Days,"* 28, 32, 26.

41. Fuller, *"These Sad but Glorious Days,"* 321–22 (13 February 1850).

42. Fuller's final three dispatches from Europe are, in Reynolds and Smith's words, "melancholy reflections on the state of the world as well as fierce, apocalyptic jeremiads directed at the unjust who have triumphed." While they seem to denote a turn toward "a revolutionary socialism," Reynolds and Smith find them more indicative of Fuller's "Christian socialism" (introduction to *"These Sad but Glorious Days,"* 35). They were, nevertheless, too radical for the tamer image being created for her by her friends and relatives after her death. Fuller's brother Arthur left them out of his collection *Home and Abroad,* and they were not reprinted in full until Reynolds and Smith's edition in 1991.

43. As Gay Wilson Allen, *Waldo Emerson* (New York: Viking, 1981) concluded from his subject's return again and again in his journals to meditate on the meaning of Fuller's life and death, Emerson just "could not get Margaret out of his mind" (336).

44. *Memoirs*, 1:205.

45. Fuller wrote, for instance, "I must follow my own law, and bide my time, even if, like Oedipus, I should return a criminal, blind and outcast, to ask aid from the gods. Such possibilities, I confess, give me great awe; for I have more sense than most, of the tragic depths that may open suddenly in the life" (*Memoirs*, 2:111). Or consider:

> Though no one loves me as I would be loved, I yet love many well enough to see into their eventual beauty. Meanwhile, I have no fetters, and when one perceives how others are bound in false relations, this surely should be regarded as a privilege. And so varied have been my sympathies, that this isolation will not, I trust, make me cold, ignorant, nor partial. My history presents much superficial, temporary tragedy. The Woman in me kneels and weeps in tender rapture; the Man in me rushes forth, but only to be baffled. Yet the time will come, when, from the union of this tragic king and queen, shall be born a radiant sovereign self. (*Memoirs*, 2:136)

46. Emerson, for instance, describes his, and others', initial reluctance to become Fuller's friend by noting that she then had a "dangerous reputation for satire" and "great scholarship": "The men thought she carried too many guns, and the women did not like one who despised them" (*Memoirs*, 1:202). He then narrates the development of their friendship as a tale of the "hunter" and the "hunted," with Fuller practicing every "art of winning," having "studied" his "tastes" and "challenged" his "frankness by frankness," concluding, "[o]f course, it was impossible long to hold out against such urgent assault" (*Memoirs*, 1:202–3). As their friendship developed, Fuller's passionate nature and her demands on his friendship led Emerson, in his words, to forebode "rash and painful crises" and he "had a feeling as if a voice cried, *Stand from under!*" (*Memoirs*, 1:223).

Sarah Freeman Clarke employs military metaphors even more explicitly to describe Fuller's initial effect: "She broke her lance upon your shield. . . . Your outworks fell before her first assault, and you were at her mercy. . . . [T]hough she broke down your little shams and defenses, you felt exhilarated by the compliment of being found out, and even that she had cared to find you out" (qtd. in Higginson, *Margaret Fuller Ossoli,* 117–18).

47. Fuller's dispatches from Rome may also have inspired Hawthorne's description of the look in Zenobia's eyes when she is gripped by the "wild passion" of her jealousy of Priscilla. He has Coverdale imagine her as having the look of a woman about to plunge a dagger into her rival, an act of passion, he says, more appropriate to Italy than New England (3:78). On 2 December 1848 Fuller described in detail the assassination by dagger of the Pope's agent, Minister Rossi, an act she terms "an act of summary justice on an offender whom the laws could not reach" (Fuller, *"These Sad but Glorious Days,"* 240).

48. Hawthorne, of course, bases his literal description of Zenobia's suicide and her recovery on his July 1845 notebook account of Martha Hunt's suicide and his own participation in the recovery of her body (8:261–67). The pole damaged Hunt's eye, not her heart.

49. Chevigny, "To the Edges of Ideology," 196. Chevigny argues that "Zenobia is best understood as reflecting Hawthorne's interest in the sexual rebel in Rome as well as in the Brook Farm feminist. Narrator Coverdale's prurient anxiety about Zenobia's sexual secrets mimics Hawthorne's preoccupation. . . . Zenobia's bitter fall before Hollingsworth simply allegorizes Fuller's 'fall' in her liaison with Ossoli" (196). While Chevigny's assertions are on target, she does not develop them or support them, the purposes of her essay being much broader in scope.

50. Cargill, "Nemesis and Nathaniel Hawthorne," 860. Cargill discovered the connection in the article "From the Wreck on Fire Island," *New-York Daily Tribune,* 24 July 1850, 4. The *Tribune* reported that the body of Henry Westervelt, a seaman on the *Elizabeth,* washed up on shore three days after the wreck. The article listed the names of the eight who drowned and the fourteen who survived.

51. Millington, "American Anxiousness," 564.

52. Compare Coverdale's description of Zenobia's "stepping out of the common path" because it was "felt to be narrower than her development required" to Fuller's explanation to her sister Ellen Fuller Channing in an 11 December 1849 letter of why she "did not hesitate a moment" to form a relationship with Ossoli though "the connexion seemed so every way unfit": "I acted upon a strong impulse. I could not analyze at all what passed in my mind. I neither rejoice nor grieve, for bad or for good I acted out my character. Had I never connected myself with any one my path was clear, now it is all hid, but in that case my development must have been partial" (*Letters,* 5:292).

53. In response to reports of gossip about the legitimacy of her relationship with Ossoli, Fuller, for instance, wrote on 30 November 1849 to Emelyn Story:

> I am sure your affection for me will prompt you to add, that you feel confident whatever I have done has been in a good spirit and not contrary to *my* ideas of right; for the rest, you will not admit for me, as I do not for myself, the rights of the social inquisition of the U.S. to know all the details of my affairs. If my mother is content, if Ossoli and I are content, if our child when grown up is content, that is enough. You and I know enough of the U.S. to be sure that many persons there will blame whatever is peculiar, the lower persons everywhere, are sure to think that whatever is mysterious must be bad, but I think there will remain for me a

sufficient number of friends to keep my heart warm and help me to earn my bread; that is all that is of any consequence. (*Letters,* 5:285)

Emerson attests to the accuracy of Hawthorne's description, through Zenobia, of Fuller's immunity from the moral condemnation accorded most women who stepped "out of the common path" because it was "narrower than her development required," and he proves Fuller's assumptions of her friends' loyalty to be well founded. Just after her death, Emerson recorded in his notebooks contemptuously that "the timorous said, What shall we do? how shall she be received, now that she brings a husband & child home?" But he was confident that Fuller would have quickly silenced them: "She had only to open her mouth, & a triumphant success awaited her. She would fast enough have disposed of the circumstances & the bystanders. For she had the impulse, & they wanted it. Here were already mothers waiting tediously for her coming, for the education of their daughters" (*Emerson in His Journals,* 414). Note the parallel between Emerson's anticipation of Fuller's continued involvement in the education of women on her return to America and Hawthorne's deployment of Hester as a "counselor" to women on *her* return from Europe.

54. Besides Cary's recent study of the similarities, and more importantly the differences, between Fuller and Zenobia ("Margaret Fuller as Hawthorne's Zenobia"), four other studies, three of them master's theses, have been devoted to parallels between Fuller and Zenobia. Kelley Thurman, "Margaret Fuller in Two American Novels: *The Blithedale Romance* and *Elsie Venner,*" master's thesis, University of Kentucky, 1945, locates nineteen separate parallels between the two. Useful for its thorough enumeration of the superficial similarities, the study makes no attempt to explore why Hawthorne would be so interested in Fuller. Anne Elizabeth Gushee, "Nathaniel Hawthorne and Margaret Fuller," master's thesis, Columbia University, 1955, examines the parallels between Zenobia and Fuller but concludes that Zenobia was solely a product of Hawthorne's imagination (39–49). Working under Arlin Turner at Duke, Veda Bagwell Sprouse, "The Relationship between Margaret Fuller and Nathaniel Hawthorne," master's thesis, Duke University, 1965, finds, like Turner (see his introduction to the Norton Library edition of *The Blithedale Romance* [New York: Norton, 1958], 13), that Mrs. Almira Barlow served as a model for Zenobia's beauty, Fanny Kemble for her theatricality, and Fuller for her feminism ("to counter-balance the contemporary praise" of Fuller [54]). The least useful study of the group, Jessie A. Coffee's "Margaret Fuller as Zenobia in *The Blithedale Romance,*" *Proceedings of the Conference of College Teachers of English* 48 (1973): 23–27, concludes that Fuller was only vaguely on Hawthorne's mind, Fuller not having the sexual allure of a Zenobia.

Edward Wagenknecht, *Nathaniel Hawthorne: The Man, His Tales and Romances* (New York: Continuum, 1989), for instance, dismisses Fuller's influence on Zenobia's characterization by asserting that Fuller, unlike Zenobia, "was decidedly plain," and besides, Hawthorne "decidedly disliked her" (114). Even Blanchard, *From Transcendentalism to Romance,* asserts that though there are numerous parallels between Fuller and Zenobia there is one major difference: Zenobia "is dark and beautiful, as Margaret certainly was not" (193). Following Chevigny's earlier argument that Hawthorne modeled Zenobia after Fuller but encoded Fuller's "unmentionable sexuality" in Zenobia's beauty ("To the Edges of Ideology," 196), Cary adds that to do so was "a truly terrible condescension to Fuller" in that it betrays Hawthorne's concern that "his audience would simply fail to credit the sexual allure of any homely woman" ("Margaret Fuller as Hawthorne's Zenobia," 36–37).

Interestingly, no one seems to employ the same standards to question the credibility of Hawthorne's sexual attraction to Sophia, and Sophia was never characterized, by anyone, as being anything more than attractive, never certainly a beauty. One contemporary, in fact, thought that Sophia looked like Fuller. Evert Duyckinck in an August 1850 letter to his wife from the Berkshires wrote that Sophia "resembles Margaret Fuller in appearance" but that Sophia was "more robust than she was" (qtd. in Mellow, *Nathaniel Hawthorne in His Times,* 333).

What emerges from the *Memoirs* and indeed from all other contemporary accounts of Fuller is that, whatever she may have looked like, her friends testify again and again to her passionate intensity and the powerful attraction she exerted on them and on others, an attraction that left them often testifying to Fuller's "beauty." Emerson tries to explain this in a passage in which he contrasts the greater power of her speech to her prose:

> But in discourse, she was quick, conscious of power, in perfect tune with her company, and would pause and turn the stream with grace and adroitness and with so much spirit, that her face beamed, and the young people came away delighted, among other things, with "her beautiful looks." When she was intellectually excited, or in high animal spirits, as often happened, all deformity of features was dissolved in the power of the expression. So I interpret this repeated story of her sumptuousness of dress, that this appearance, like her reported beauty, was simply an effect of a general impression of magnificence made by her genius, and mistakenly attributed to some external elegance. (*Memoirs,* 1:337)

55. Compare Coverdale's descriptions of Zenobia's effect on him with the following from a March–April 1843 Emerson notebook description, only a small part of which I give here:

> Unable to find any companion great enough to receive the rich effusions of her thought, so that her riches are still unknown & seem unknowable. . . . All natures seem poor beside one so rich, which pours a stream of amber over all objects clean & unclean that lie in its path, and makes that comely & presentable which was mean in itself. We are taught by her plenty how lifeless & outward we were, what poor Laplanders burrowing under the snows of prudence & pedantry. Beside her friendship, other friendships seem trade. . . . She excels other intellectual persons in this, that her sentiments are more blended with her life; so the expression of them has greater steadiness & greater clearness. . . . An inspirer of courage, the secret friend of all nobleness . . . in her presence all were apprised of their fettered estate & longed for liberation; of ugliness & longed for their beauty; of meanness, & panted for grandeur.
>
> Her growth is visible. . . . She rose before me at times into heroical & godlike regions, and I could remember no superior women, but thought of Ceres, Minerva, Proserpine, and the august ideal forms of the Foreworld. She said that no man give such invitation to her mind as to tempt her to a full expression; that she felt a power to enrich her thought with such wealth & variety of embellishment as would no doubt be tedious to such as she conversed with. And there is no form that does seem to wait her beck—dramatic, lyric, epic, passionate, pictorial, humourous.

She has great sincerity, force, & fluency as a writer, yet her powers of speech throw her writing into the shade. What method, what exquisite judgment, as well as energy, in the selection of her words, what character and wisdom they convey! . . . a silver eloquence. . . . You cannot predict her opinion. . . . Meanwhile, all the pathos of sentiment and riches of literature & of invention and this march of character threatening to arrive presently at the shores & plunge into the sea of Buddhism & mystic trances, consists with a boundless fun & drollery, with light satire, & the most entertaining conversation in America. (*Emerson in His Journals,* 302–3)

56. See Emerson's description of Fuller in *Memoirs,* 1:202. See also *Memoirs,* 1:91 and 2:35, for Clarke's and Channing's descriptions.

57. Fuller, "'The Impulses of Human Nature,'" 108.

58. While reading Fuller's private papers in preparation for writing the *Memoirs,* Emerson made the following entry into his journal: "The unlooked for trait in all these journals to me is the Woman; poor woman: they are all hysterical. 'I need help. No, I need a full, a godlike embrace from some sufficient love.' &c. &c. . . . This I doubt not was all the more violent recoil from the exclusively literary & 'educational' connections in which she had lived. Mrs. Spring told me that Margaret said to her, 'I am tired of these literary friendships, I long to be wife & mother'" (*The Journals and Miscellaneous Notebooks,* 11:500).

59. Fuller's friend in Florence during the last months of her life, Elizabeth Barrett Browning, in a 24 September 1850 letter to Mary Russell Mitford, wrote that "it was better for her [Fuller] to go," for had she lived and published her book on the Italian revolutions, she "would have drawn the wolves on her with a still more howling enmity both in England & America" because of what Browning suspected would be "those blood-colours of socialistic views" that Fuller's book would have promoted. Fuller's unhappiness, according to Browning, further endorses "Providence": "Was she happy in anything, I wonder? She told me that she never was. May God have made her happy in her death!" (*Letters . . . to Mary Russell Mitford* 3:463).

Emerson's views on her death, I believe, best appropriate the contradictoriness of Hawthorne's. Immediately after her death, he wrote in his notebooks that "to the last her country proves inhospitable to her; brave, eloquent, subtle, accomplished, devoted, constant soul!" He then states his contempt for those "timorous" souls who anticipated her return to America with anxiety, who said, "What shall we do? How shall she be received now that she brings a husband & child home?" He was confident that "she had only to open her mouth, & triumphant success awaited her" (*Emerson in His Journals,* 413–14). However, on 5 August 1850, he wrote to Carlyle that her death was perhaps appropriately well-timed: "She died in happy hour for herself. Her health was much exhausted. Her marriage would have taken her away from us all, & there was a subsistence yet to be secured, & diminished powers, & old age" (*The Letters of Ralph Waldo Emerson,* ed. Ralph L. Rusk, 6 vols. [New York: Columbia University Press, 1939], 4:224). Three years later, in his journal, Emerson seems to have forgotten that he once expressed what he now so angrily denounces:

It is a bitter satire on our social order, just at present, the number of bad cases. Margaret Fuller having attained the highest & broadest culture that any American woman has possessed, came home with an Italian gentleman whom she had married, & their infant son, & perished by shipwreck on the rocks of Fire Island, off New York; and her friends said, "Well, on the whole, it was not so lamentable, & perhaps it was the best thing that could happen to her. For, had she lived, what could she have done? How could she have supported herself, her husband, & child?" And, most persons, hearing this, acquiesced in this view that, after the education has gone far, such is the expensiveness of America, that the best use to put a fine woman to, is to drown her to save her board. (*Emerson in His Journals,* 444)

60. Hutner, *Secrets and Sympathy,* makes the excellent point that both Coverdale and Hollingsworth "drown themselves in their own self-reflective pools," their lives "deadened" for the same reason as Zenobia's supposedly was—because their existences proved dependent on the affections (136).

CHAPTER EIGHT *The Venus of the Tribune, the Pearl Diver, and* The Marble Faun

1. Hawthorne's representation of Fuller's "rude old potency" may have been inspired by the following passage in the *Memoirs.* Having quoted Fuller as writing, "I have no belief in beautiful lives; we are born to be mutilated," Channing writes: "In a word, to her own conscience and to intimate friends she avowed, without reserve, that there was in her much rude matter that needed to be spiritualized" (*Memoirs,* 2:101). Fuller's conception of her life as a work of art, specifically as a "statue" in the making (see *Memoirs,* 1:238), also influenced Hawthorne's choice of metaphorical representation in the 1858 notebook entry.

2. Fuller, "'The Impulses of Human Nature,'" 105–6.

3. Wallace, "Hawthorne and the Scribbling Women Reconsidered," 215.

4. Brodhead, *The School of Hawthorne,* presents the persuasive argument that Hawthorne's very status as a living "classic" disabled him from producing future "classics," which is both demonstrated by and is the very implied subject of *The Marble Faun* (67–80). My reading of the romance owes much to Brodhead's.

5. Mellow, *Nathaniel Hawthorne in His Times,* 498.

6. Herbert, *Dearest Beloved,* 228, 230–32. Herbert finds it "plausible" that Hawthorne saw in Lander the "'delightful freedom' that he himself yearned to regain, the innocent compulsiveness he had cherished with Sophia in their paradise at the Old Manse," a "renewed contact with his own 'feminine' creativeness" (230). I would modify this line of speculation by identifying Fuller as the woman Hawthorne had come to associate with his "'feminine' creativeness." Alone in Rome practicing her art in the former studio of Canova, the artist on whom Fuller had written a lengthy *Dial* article that had influenced Hawthorne's "Drowne's Wooden Image" (a matter I will take up later), Lander could well have reminded Hawthorne of Fuller's situation in Rome. At thirty-three, Fuller's age in 1843, Lander could also have reminded Hawthorne of the woman Fuller had been during the most intense years of their friendship.

7. See *Memoirs,* 2:281–329.

8. Emelyn Story's account was published, in part, in the *Memoirs,* 2:281–93. For the full, unedited version, see Chevigny, *The Woman and the Myth,* 403–10. For some indica-

tion of the intimacy of Fuller's friendship with the Storys, see Fuller's letters to them from Florence, *Letters*, 5:284–88.

9. For accounts of Fuller and Ossoli after the defeat of the Roman republicans, see *Memoirs*, 2:269–330; Chevigny, *The Woman and the Myth*, 365–401 and 410–13; Deiss, *The Roman Years of Margaret Fuller*, 274–313; and volume 5 of Fuller's *Letters*.

10. Chevigny, *The Woman and the Myth*, 412. Informing her mother for the first time in a 31 August 1849 letter of her relationship with Ossoli and her baby, Fuller describes Ossoli thus:

> He is not in any respect such a person as people in general would expect to find with me. He had no instructor except an old priest, who entirely neglected his education; and of all that is contained in books he is absolutely ignorant, and he has no enthusiasm of character. On the other hand, he has excellent practical sense; has been a judicious observer . . . ; has a nice sense of duty, which . . . may put most enthusiasts to shame; a very sweet temper, and great native refinement. His love for me has been unswerving and most tender. I have never suffered a pain that he could [not?] relieve. His delicacy in trifles, his sweet domestic graces, remind me of E——. In him I have found a home, and one that interferes with no tie. (*Letters*, 5:261)

11. For Fuller's awareness of how Ossoli would likely be received in America, see her *Letters*, 5:261, 283–85, 291, 300–303. Browning, *Letters . . . to Mary Russell Mitford*, 3:285.

12. *Letters*, 5:301; Browning, *Letters . . . to Mary Russell Mitford*, 3:309.

13. At this point it is only proper to recognize the earlier work of Harry De Puy, "The Marble Faun: Another Portrait of Margaret Fuller?" *Arizona Quarterly* 40 (1984): 163–78. Despite De Puy's superficial knowledge of Fuller's life, he does point out some of the basic parallels between Fuller and Miriam and Ossoli and Donatello that I also find evident, as well as some that I do not find convincing. His reading of her presence in the novel, however, is superficial and condescending. In fact, more than any other that I have encountered, his essay could serve as an extreme example of the type of misogynist readings Julian made inevitable and that Baym deplored. Expanding upon Cargill's discredited thesis that *Blithedale* was written by Hawthorne as revenge on Fuller for a supposed affront by Ellery, De Puy reads *The Marble Faun* as Hawthorne's effort to "fix Margaret's wagon good" (178). Here's a sample of De Puy at work: "If the title is only an *apparent* misnomer, as any sensible scholar would believe, then Miriam—rather, Margaret, that wild, ill-bred, unattractive, cold, unapproachable, 'immoral,' hulking, masculine, 'soft marble' offspring of Nature—*is* the Marble Faun!" (177).

14. See Hawthorne's notebook and pocket diary for the frequent discussions in Florence regarding spiritualism, for his participation and opinions, and for Sophia's experiences, through Ada Shepard, of communicating with the dead (14:302–3, 397–401, 415–19, 523, 608).

15. Robert S. Levine, "'Antebellum Rome' in *The Marble Faun*," *American Literary History* 2 (1990): 19–38; 20. Levine argues that Hawthorne uses the Roman political situation to explore "more generalized cultural tensions" relevant and recognizable to antebellum America (20). Stern, *Contexts for Hawthorne*, should also be consulted, for though he does not explore the specific politics of Hawthorne's Rome, he reads the novel as Hawthorne's final ambivalent and contradictory depiction of the more general politics of perceiving

history as "romance" (allied with liberal-progressive politics) or as "tragedy" (allied with conservative-traditional politics).

16. Levine, "'Antebellum Rome,'" 26.

17. Ibid., 25.

18. Judges 5:24. See Judges 4:17–24 for Jael's role in Sisera's death and in liberating the Israelites.

19. *Letters,* 5:267; *Memoirs,* 2:303.

20. In having Kenyon "bless" Miriam's union with Donatello yet having Hilda continue to condemn Miriam for her "crime," Hawthorne may perhaps be suggesting the divergent attitudes toward Fuller in his own household as well as within himself.

It is worth noting that such a good friend as William Henry Channing believed Fuller would not have marred the quality of her relationship with Ossoli by forming "a legal tie [that] was contrary to her view of a noble life," a view Emerson records but does not accept (*The Journals and Miscellaneous Notebooks,* 11:463).

21. See especially, Brodhead, *The School of Hawthorne,* 67–80, and Herbert, *Dearest Beloved,* 256–72.

22. Miller, *Salem is My Dwelling Place,* 441.

23. Carton, "'A Daughter of the Puritans'"; Herbert, *Dearest Beloved,* 248–83. Shepard qtd. in Herbert, *Dearest Beloved,* 256.

24. Herbert, *Dearest Beloved,* 37–58.

25. In the 27 February 1842 letter to Sophia in which Hawthorne explains his inability to inform his mother and sisters of his plans to marry, Hawthorne, after describing the "cloudy veil . . . over the abyss of . . . [his] nature" that he has no intention of unveiling for anyone, including Sophia, he asserts that "it is this involuntary reserve, I suppose, that has given the objectivity to my writings. And when people think that I am pouring myself out in a tale or essay, I am merely telling what is common to human nature, not what is peculiar to myself. I sympathize with them—not they with me" (15:612–13).

26. Sophia to her mother, 4 September 1850 (Berg; qtd. in Lathrop, "The Hawthornes in Lenox," 91).

27. Gloria Erlich, "Deadly Innocence: Hawthorne's Dark Women," *New England Quarterly* 41 (1968): 163–79, observes that all Hawthorne's "virgins"—Phoebe, Priscilla, Hilda—"seem to affect the creativity of their men" but that whether this effect is positive or negative depends upon one's perception of the value of the men's creativity. Hawthorne, she reminds us, was considerably more ambivalent about the nobility of the artist than we are (175).

28. Person, *Aesthetic Headaches,* remarks similarly that Hilda inspires "the full dehumanizing power of his medium" as illustrated by his objectification of "the smallest and most 'delicate' part of her to stand for the whole," the part that instead of "encouraging a deeply passionate response" from him "keeps him at a distance" (165). My reading of Hilda's and Miriam's influence on Kenyon's art is parallel at numerous points to Person's fine discussion (160–72).

29. Fuller, review of *Twice-Told Tales,* 131.

30. Person, *Aesthetic Headaches,* 164.

31. Sarah I. Davis, "Margaret Fuller's 'Canova' and Hawthorne's 'Drowne's Wooden

Image,'" *American Transcendentalist Quarterly* 49 (1981): 73–78; 76; Person, *Aesthetic Head-aches*, 164.

32. Fuller, review of *Twice-Told Tales*, 130–31.

33. *Memoirs*, 1:219.

34. Emerson notes that Fuller often identified friends with certain gems that she would put on when she wrote to them (*Memoirs*, 1:219). In his notebook, Emerson wrote that Fuller "put on the carbuncle and the bracelet to write to her friend" (*The Journals and Miscellaneous Notebooks*, 11:472). He does not indicate which friend he was referring to. The "carbuncle" and the "bracelet" of the seven Etruscan gems given to Hilda are thus linked as symbolizing Miriam's and Fuller's "mystery."

35. Qtd. in Emerson, *The Journals and Miscellaneous Notebooks*, 11:488.

36. Early excavators had been so clumsy that they had only buried the Venus of the Tribune deeper. Hawthorne is perhaps making a wry comment on the efforts of Emerson, Channing, and Clarke in the *Memoirs*.

37. Brodhead, *The School of Hawthorne*, asserts that Hilda "wants to silence . . . expression itself," for "her version of the world sustains itself by suppressing art in one of its forms, as a meaning-constructing action" (79).

Index

Aldrich, Thomas Bailey, 264n. 54
Allen, Gay Wilson, 301n. 43
Allen, Margaret, 293n. 11
American Men of Letters Series, 14
American Suffrage Association, 25, 29
Anthony, Katherine, 42
Apollo and Nathaniel Hawthorne, 126, 253, 286n. 29
Aristotle, and Ralph Waldo Emerson, 299n. 26
Auerbach, Nina, 105–6, 268n. 19, 269n. 22

Ballou, Ellen B., 16, 260nn. 5, 6, 261n. 13
Bancroft, George, 60–61
Barker, Anna, 56, 80, 269n. 26, 290n. 65
Barlow, Almira, 303n. 54
Bassan, Maurice, 264n. 54, 265n. 68
Baym, Nina, 38, 44–46, 120, 275n. 1, 279n. 42, 280n. 1, 284n. 16, 286n. 31, 291n. 73, 307n. 13
Beecher, Rev. Henry Ward, 26–27, 264n. 44
Belenky, Mary Field, 257n. 4
Bell, Margaret, 43
Bell, Michael Davitt, 287–88n. 46
Bellingham, Governor Richard, 154, 288n. 47
Bercovitch, Sacvan, 130–32, 284n. 16
Berg, Martha L., 85, 87, 273n. 68, 274n. 83
Berlant, Lauren, 197, 296n. 2, 299n. 28
Blackwell, Henry, 26, 29
Blanchard, Paula, 39, 45, 56, 272n. 56,
274n. 76, 283n. 13, 285n. 20, 293n. 11, 303n. 54
Bremer, Frederika, 283n. 13
Brenzo, Richard, 117, 279nn. 43, 45
Bridge, Horatio, 58, 100, 161–63
Brodhead, Richard, 15–16, 260n. 10, 297n. 9, 306n. 4
Brown, Gillian, 268n. 19
Browning, Elizabeth Barrett, 227–28, 280n. 51, 305n. 59
Burns, James MacGregor, 264n. 44
Burrage, W. C., 38
Byron, Lord, and Nathaniel Hawthorne, 136, 286n. 29

Canova, 247
Capper, Charles, 259n. 11, 269n. 28
Cargill, Oscar, 210, 265n. 70, 302n. 50
Carton, Evan, 46, 240, 267n. 12, 282n. 8, 286n. 32
Cary, Louisa D., 296n. 38, 300n. 35, 303–4n. 54
Cenci, Beatrice, 232–33
Channing, Ellen Fuller, 25, 77, 138
Channing, Ellery, 25; and Margaret Fuller, 1, 70, 138, 293n. 12; and Nathaniel Hawthorne, 77, 176–77, 265n. 70, 295n. 36
Channing, Margaret Fuller ("Greta"), 25, 86, 138–39, 273n. 69
Channing, William Ellery ("Dr. Channing"), 61
Channing, William Henry: characterization of Margaret Fuller, 57–58, 258n. 5;

Channing, William Henry (continued)
friendship with Margaret Fuller, 1–2,
274n. 83, 293n. 7; on Margaret Fuller's
"marriage," 283n. 13, 290n. 64, 306n.
1, 308n. 20
Chevigny, Bell Gale, 4, 39, 205, 210,
258nn. 4, 7, 266nn. 74, 1, 273n. 68,
282n. 10, 293n. 11, 295–96n. 38, 302n.
49, 303n. 54, 306n. 8
Clark, E. E. Frazer, Jr., 264n. 46
Clarke, James Freeman, 4–5, 32, 57
Clarke, Sarah Freeman, 23, 29–30, 57,
283n. 13, 301–2n. 45
Clarke, William Hull, 84–85, 87, 89, 273n.
68, 274n. 83
Cleopatra, 246–48
Cleveland, Grover, 27
Coffee, Jessie A., 303n. 54
Colacurcio, Michael J., 154, 281n. 3
Coleman, Ann, 136–37
Comstock, Anthony, 26
Coverdale, Miles, 161, 182, 296n. 4
Cox, James M., 280n. 1
Cranch, Christopher P., 33, 37
Crews, Frederick, 296n. 3
Croly, Jan ("Jennie June"), 17
Cuddy, Lois A., 274n. 1
Curtis, George William, 36–37

Dall, Caroline Healey, 29–30
Dana, Frank, 299n. 26
Dante Alighieri, and "Rappaccini's Daugh-
ter," 94–95
Davis, Sarah I., 247
Deiss, Joseph J., 282–83n. 13
Democratic Review. See United States Maga-
zine and Democratic Review
De Puy, Harry, 307n. 13
de Staël, Madame, 97
Dial, 3, 55, 278n. 33
Dickens, Charles, 17, 178
Dickenson, Donna, 284–85n. 17
Douglas, Ann, 268n. 19
"The Draper's Daughter," 280n. 51
Duyckinck, Evert, 5, 13–14, 121–22, 304n.
54

Egan, Ken, Jr., 298n. 18
Eliot, Samuel ("Apostle Eliot"), 196–97,
299n. 28
Emerson, Edward Waldo, 138
Emerson, Ellen, 139

Emerson, Lidian, 80, 138
Emerson, Ralph Waldo: and Roger Chillingworth, 146–50, 195; and Dante
Alighieri, 94–95; and Samuel Eliot
("Apostle Eliot"), 196–97; and Margaret Fuller, editing of her works, 149,
258n. 4, 290n. 66; and Margaret Fuller,
relationship with, 2, 5, 12, 70, 85–87,
89, 91, 97–98, 113, 207, 257n. 3, 301nn.
42, 46; and Margaret Fuller, statements about, 1, 12, 58, 94–95, 105,
207, 249, 257n. 3, 270n. 34, 276n. 9,
278n. 32, 290n. 64, 299n. 26, 300n. 33,
301n. 46, 303–4n. 53, 304–5n. 55, 305n.
58, 305–6n. 59, 308n. 20, 309n. 34; and
Nathaniel Hawthorne, 66–67, 72–73,
98–101; and Hollingsworth, 193, 195–
98, 299n. 29; identification with Aristotle, 299n. 26; identification with
Plato, 196–97, 299n. 27; literary market value of, 261n. 13; and marriage,
147, 290n. 65; and the masculine and
the feminine, 152; in "The Old
Manse," 99–100; and Rappaccini,
106–9, 115, 195
Emerson, Waldo, 80, 139, 287n. 39
Eminent Women Series, 14
English Men of Letters Series, 14
Erlich, Gloria, 46, 59–60, 267n. 12, 280n.
1, 308n. 27

Fields, James T., 161–62, 167, 169–70, 175,
260n. 6, 264n. 54, 292n. 1
Firkins, O. W., 6
Fogle, Richard H., 275n. 1
Fuller, Arthur B., 5, 13, 301n. 42
Fuller, Frederick T., 34–36
Fuller, Margaret: and Anna Barker, 56, 80,
269n. 26; and Beatrice, 94–95, 106,
109–20, 276n. 18; and Brook Farm,
298–99n. 22; and the carbuncle as a
symbol, 249–50, 309n. 34; and celibacy, 156–57, 292n. 80; and Ellery
Channing, 1, 7, 70; character of, 3–4,
28, 32–35, 41, 56–60, 94–95, 205–6,
227–28, 269nn. 25, 28, 274n. 54, 278n.
32, 283n. 13, 290n. 64, 300n. 39, 301–
6nn. 45, 46, 52, 53, 54, 55, 58, 59, 306n.
1, 307n. 13; on character of Giovanni
Ossoli, 302n. 52, 307n. 10; and James
Freeman Clarke, 4; and Ann Coleman,
136–37; contested biographical repre-

sentations of, 4–11, 22–46, 259n. 11; and "Conversations," 2, 55, 62, 110; and Coverdale, 298n. 22; as cultural icon, 14, 24–25, 29–30, 35–43; death of, 3, 160, 164–66, 210, 216–19, 293nn. 10, 11, 12, 303n. 53, 305–6n. 59; and the *Dial*, 55–56, 278n. 33; edited/censored journals of, 84, 87, 273n. 68; and Lidian Emerson, 80; and Ralph Waldo Emerson, correspondence with, 100; —, relationship with, 2, 55–56, 58, 70, 85–86, 111–12, 258n. 5, 274nn. 77, 276n. 11, 278n. 35, 289n. 61; —, statements about, 86–87, 89, 91, 97–98, 108, 111, 147–48, 150, 258n. 5, 274n. 84, 276n. 11; and Waldo Emerson, 72; and feminism, 38–41, 129–30, 155–57, 191, 205, 208–9, 262n. 26, 266n. 76, 282nn. 10, 12, 283n. 14, 286–87n. 33; and flowers, 101–4, 185–86, 276n. 18, 277n. 26, 279n. 40; and friendship, 1–2, 56–60, 70–71, 269n. 28, 270n. 34, 278n. 32, 301–2n. 46; and Horace Greeley, 4–5, 91; and Sophia Hawthorne, 32, 66–69, 99 (*see also* Hawthorne, Sophia: and Margaret Fuller, relationship with); and Una Hawthorne, 84–88, 92, 137–40, 273n. 69, 287n. 36; and Hester, 129–33, 135, 137, 140–41, 145–46, 150–58, 160–61, 284–85n. 17, 303n. 53; as a journalist, 3, 97–98, 133–34, 206–9, 258n. 7, 285n. 22, 301n. 42, 302n. 47; literary reputation of, 12–15, 24, 29–31, 39–42, 260n. 9, 264n. 43, 266nn. 74, 1; as Mariana, 228; and marriage, ideas about, 82, 99, 139–40, 147–50, 192, 208, 289nn. 54, 61, 62; and "marriage" of, 6–10, 25, 29, 133–35, 150–51, 163–66, 190, 212, 226–28, 237–39, 266n. 1, 282n. 13, 285n. 27, 290nn. 64, 68, 292–93n. 7, 302n. 52, 302–3n. 53, 305–6n. 59, 307n. 10, 308n. 20; and the masculine and the feminine, 101–5, 112–14, 118–19, 152–57, 184–86, 189, 208, 257–58n. 4, 262n. 26, 274n. 84, 297n. 12, 298n. 16, 301n. 45; as Miranda, 102, 228; and Miriam, 137, 221–22, 225–32, 234–35, 237–42, 244, 246–56, 307n. 13; in "The Old Manse," 85–86; parents and childhood of, 75, 101–2, 112–13, 277n. 26, 279n. 40; and Elizabeth Peabody, 62–63; and Pearl, 137; and the

pearl as a symbol, 221–22, 249, 274n. 84, 277n. 25, 288–87n. 33; physical appearance of, 213, 215, 303–4n. 54; as a political radical, 132–34, 206–9, 258–59n. 8, 266n. 76, 301n. 42, 302n. 47, 305n. 59; and Priscilla, 160; and the Revolution in Rome, 39, 133–34, 209, 205–7, 227–28, 231–32, 237–39, 246, 283n. 14, 302n. 47; and George Sand, 97, 129, 155–56, 282n. 10, 283n. 14; on self-reliance, 1–3; as a sexual rebel against Puritanism, 41–43; as a social critic, 3, 98, 131–32, 206–7, 298–99n. 22; and Caroline Sturgis Tappan, 163; and Transcendentalism, 39–40, 55, 276n. 9; and the "Venus of the Tribune," 252; visits the Old Manse, 71–72, 84–92; and Samuel Ward, 56, 79–80; and Zenobia (from *The Blithedale Romance*), 160–61, 177–78, 184–87, 191–92, 203–19, 222–24, 292n. 1, 296n. 38, 300n. 34, 302nn. 47, 49, 303–4n. 54; and Zenobia (Queen of Palmyra), 204–5. Works: *At Home and Abroad*, 13, 260n. 9; "Autobiographical Romance," 101–2, 277n. 26; "Canova," 247; *Eckermann's Conversations with Goethe*, 55; "The Great Lawsuit: Man versus Men; Woman versus Women," 56, 84, 91, 102, 129–31, 139–40, 148–49, 155–57; "Leila," 105, 184–85; *Life Without and Life Within*, 13, 260n. 9; *Love-Letters of Margaret Fuller, 1845–46*, 39, 41–42; "The Magnolia of Lake Pontchartrain," 101–3, 118–19, 184–86; *Memoirs of Margaret Fuller Ossoli*, 4–5, 14–15, 25, 165, 177, 227, 260nn. 2, 8, 304n. 54; *Papers on Literature and Art*, 13, 122, 260n. 9; *Poems*, 222, 269n. 26, 274n. 84; *Summer on the Lakes, 1843*, 13–14, 56, 260n. 9; "Yuca Filamentosa," 101–4, 184; *Woman in the Nineteenth Century*, 13–14, 56, 84, 91, 140, 153, 155–56, 192, 262n. 26, 282n. 12

Fuller, Margaret, and Nathaniel Hawthorne: correspondence with, 81, 91–92, 262–63n. 29; literary criticism of, 60, 63, 66–69, 92, 96–97, 122–24, 135, 246, 248–49, 275n. 8; literary influence on, 98–106, 129–33, 184–87, 189, 192, 247, 275n. 8, 284–85n. 17; as literary inspiration for, 10–11, 45–47, 132–33,

Fuller, Margaret, and Nathaniel Hawthorne (*continued*)
135–37, 160, 186–87, 208–19, 246–48, 252–55; relationship with, 20, 28, 34–35, 137–41, 287n. 36 (*see also* Hawthorne, Nathaniel: and Margaret Fuller, relationship with); statements about, 38, 66–69, 71, 80, 86–92, 99–100, 138–40, 272n. 57, 274n. 77

Gender. *See* "the masculine and the feminine" under Emerson, Ralph Waldo; Fuller, Margaret; Hawthorne, Nathaniel
Graff, Gerald, 260n. 10
Greeley, Horace, 14, 91, 165–66
Greenwood, Grace, 297n. 14
Grimké, Sarah, 298n. 16
Griswold, Hattie Tyng, 19
Godwin, William, 286–87n. 33
Goethe, Johann Wolfgang von, 2, 55
Gubar, Susan, 48
Gunn, Giles, 260n. 10
Gushee, Anne Elizabeth, 303n. 54

Hall, Julie E., 275n. 4
Hanford, James Holly, 287n. 45
Hathorne, Elizabeth ("Ebe"), 59–60, 65–66, 69, 75–76, 172, 270n. 35, 280n. 1
Hathorne, Elizabeth (mother), 65–66, 69, 75–76, 280n. 1
Hathorne, Louisa, 65–66, 69, 72, 75–76, 172, 271n. 54, 280n. 1
Haviland, Beverly, 275n. 3
Hawthorne, Julian: as child, 173–74, 176; condemnation of, 24, 29–35, 37–38, 264n. 54, 265n. 64; as editor (unscrupulous), 21–23, 262n. 28; and Margaret Fuller, 11, 13, 20–22, 30, 34–37, 78, 84, 262n. 26; and Nathaniel Hawthorne, 13, 18, 22–24, 31–36, 173–74, 176; on Sophia Hawthorne, 18, 20; imprisonment of, 37, 265n. 68; influence of, on literary history, 11, 13, 15, 18, 20, 28, 37–46, 262n. 28, 265n. 64, 260n. 9, 273n. 67, 296n. 38, 307n. 13; on the marriage of his parents, 18–20; and *Nathaniel Hawthorne and His Wife*, 13; —, defense of, 30–37; —, reviews of, 18, 27–29, 31, 33–38; —, sales of, 27; on role of women in society, 16, 19–21, 173
Hawthorne, Nathaniel: and *American Magazine of Useful and Entertaining Knowledge*, 270n. 35; and Aubépine, 95–98, 275n. 8; and Brook Farm, 63–65, 181, 193–94, 299nn. 23, 26; and Byron, 136, 286n. 29; and Catholicism, 150–51, 290–91n. 68; and celibacy, 157; character of, 9, 10, 18, 22, 28–32, 34–38, 42–47, 65–70, 82–83, 161–64, 167–69, 171–79, 240–41, 243–45, 272n. 58, 273n. 66, 281n. 7; childhood of, 75–76, 83; and Roger Chillingworth, 141–44; and Coverdale, 160–61, 172, 175, 178–79, 181–83, 186–88, 194–98, 222–23, 292n. 1, 296n. 4; creative processes of, 93–100, 125–37, 140–46, 150–51, 154, 158, 160–61, 166–72, 174–79, 181–84, 186–88, 190–98, 202, 207–19, 221–26, 228–32, 234–35, 237–56, 277–78n. 30, 280n. 1, 280–81n. 2, 281nn. 3, 7, 281–82n. 8, 284nn. 16, 17, 287–88n. 46, 296n. 3, 297–98n. 14, 298n. 15, 306n. 4, 308nn. 25, 27, 28, 309n. 37; and Arthur Dimmesdale, 127–28, 141, 143, 151, 182, 195, 281–82n. 8, 282n. 9, 291n. 69; on Ralph Waldo Emerson, 72–73, 99, 101; and Ralph Waldo Emerson, relationship with, 61, 94–95, 98–101, 106–9, 114, 146–50, 193–98, 271n. 53, 276n. 13, 277–78n. 30, 278–79n. 38, 289n. 56, 299n. 26; and fatherhood, 46, 83, 85, 120, 240–41, 269n. 20, 273n. 70, 279n. 48, 294n. 28; and feminism, 38, 43–47, 84, 91, 136–37, 173–74, 273n. 67, 284n. 16, 291n. 77; and Giovanni, 95–96, 98–101, 104–20, 151, 195; and Elizabeth ("Ebe") Hathorne, 59–60, 270n. 35; and Louisa Hathorne, 59–60; and Sophia Peabody Hawthorne, correspondence with, 47–54, 162, 199–200; —, courtship of, 46–54, 146, 199–200, 268nn. 13, 14, 18, 19; and Holgrave, 192; and Hollingsworth, 188, 190–93, 298n. 21, 300n. 31; identification with Apollo, 126, 253, 286n. 29; and intimacy, 65, 68–70, 98, 99, 118–20, 291n. 74, 308n. 25; and Kenyon, 221–22, 226, 229, 235–56; literary reputation of, 13, 15–16, 18, 38, 121–23; as male mesmerist, 47–55, 199–200; and Robert Manning, 83; marketing and sales of, 15–16, 170, 261n. 13; and marriage, ideas about,

144–49, 157–58, 289nn. 50, 54; marriage of, 30–32, 38, 44–48, 65–67, 71, 78–80, 82–84, 118–19, 162, 166, 172–77, 192–95, 198–201, 243–46, 263nn. 32, 33, 266n. 71, 268n. 19, 269nn. 21, 22, 23, 271n. 49, 272n. 64, 273n. 66, 280n. 2, 292n. 3, 294n. 18, 294–95n. 32, 295nn. 35, 36, 298n. 21, 299n. 23; and the masculine and the feminine, 18–19, 45–47, 59, 66–69, 98–100, 104–5, 116–21, 151–58, 245–46, 184–93, 199–202, 213–19, 266n. 71, 268nn. 14, 19, 269n. 23, 273n. 66, 276–77n. 20, 277n. 29, 279nn. 43, 45, 281–82n. 8, 284n. 16, 286n. 31, 298nn. 15, 16, 17, 299n. 25, 306n. 6, 308nn. 27, 28; and Herman Melville, 166, 169, 172, 178–79; and mesmerism, 53–54, 211–12; and Milton, 289n. 54; and *Moby-Dick,* 178–79; and mother and sisters, relationship with, 65–66, 69, 75–76, 280n. 1; and Joseph Mozier, 6, 263n. 37; and Napoleon, 286n. 29; and Nature, 72–73, 76–77; and Giovanni Angelino Ossoli, 7–9, 209–12, 215, 226–28, 237; and Elizabeth Peabody, 62–63; and Pearl, 137; politics of, 288n. 47; and the Salem Custom House, 133, 280n. 1, 282n. 9, 288n. 47; and spiritualism, 307n. 14; and Caroline Sturgis Tappan, 163–64, 176, 285n. 27, 294n. 27, 295n. 34; and Theodore (de l'Aubépine), 186, 297n. 10; and Transcendentalism, 106–11; and women, 42–43, 59–60, 173–74, 225–26. Works: *The Ancestral Footstep,* 225, 228; "The Birth-mark," 83, 263n. 20, 273n. 66, 277nn. 29, 30; *The Blithedale Romance,* 51, 75, 159–61, 167, 175, 177–79, 180–219; "The Christmas Banquet," 155, 299n. 30; "The Custom-House," 126, 143–44, 183, 280n. 1; "Drowne's Wooden Image," 247, 269n. 20; "Endicott and the Red Cross," 133, 135; "Ethan Brand," 50; *Famous Old People,* 63; "The Gentle Boy," 62, 66; *Grandfather's Chair,* 63; *The House of the Seven Gables,* 167, 169–72; "Mrs. Hutchinson," 155; "Main-Street," 136, 143, 286nn. 30, 31; *The Marble Faun,* 51, 220–56; "Monsieur du Miroir," 93; *Mosses from an Old Manse,* 121–24;

"The Old Manse," 99–101, 105, 194–95, 197, 277n. 30; *Passages from the American Notebooks,* 60; "Rappaccini's Daughter," 92–124, 128, 135–36, 150–51, 182, 184–87, 275nn. 2, 3; *The Scarlet Letter,* 125–58, 160–61, 167, 169, 171, 179, 181, 278n. 30; *The Snow-Image,* 170, 172, 175, 188; *True Stories from History and Biography,* 170; *Twice-Told Tales,* 170–71; "The Writings of Aubépine," 95–98, 182, 277n. 29; *A Wonder-Book for Girls and Boys,* 167, 170; "Young Goodman Brown," 72
Hawthorne, Nathaniel, and Margaret Fuller: character of, 7–10; correspondence with, 78–79, 81–84, 91; death of, 8–9, 164, 175, 216–19, 241, 229; "marriage" of, 6–10; relationship with, 21, 27–28, 30, 38, 43–47, 54–92, 111–16, 118–24, 137–41, 150–51, 195–98, 207, 216–19, 221–22, 224–28, 240, 247, 250–53, 262n. 29, 267nn. 2, 12, 271n. 56, 272n. 58, 273n. 67, 276–77n. 20, 285n. 27, 291n. 69, 299n. 26, 308n. 20. *See also* Fuller, Margaret, and Nathaniel Hawthorne
Hawthorne, Rose, 173–74, 295n. 35
Hawthorne, Sophia Peabody: as an artist, 243; and Beatrice, 275n. 4; character of, 30–32; and editing of Hawthorne's notebooks, 71; on Ralph Waldo Emerson, 290n. 65; on Margaret Fuller, 20–22, 71–72, 79–80, 137–38, 164–65, 262nn. 26, 29, 263n. 32, 270–71n. 40; and Margaret Fuller, relationship with, 32, 44–45, 61–62, 77–78, 84, 112; on Nathaniel Hawthorne, 47–48, 79–80, 163–64, 172, 174–75, 243–44, 271n. 54, 280–81n. 2, 281n. 7, 295n. 35; and Nathaniel Hawthorne, love-letters to, 48; on Nathaniel Hawthorne's work, 126, 170, 201, 243–45, 248, 281nn. 6, 7; and Hilda, 232, 242–43, 245–46; and marriage, 18–19, 263n. 33, 290n. 65 (*see also* Hawthorne, Nathaniel: marriage of); and mesmerism, 53–54; miscarriage of first child, 273n. 66; and Phoebe, 170, 192, 198; physical appearance of, 176, 304n. 54; and Priscilla, 192–93, 198;
Hawthorne, Una, 172–74, 176, 295n. 35; and Margaret Fuller, 84–88, 92, 137–

Hawthorne, Una (*continued*)
40, 273n. 69; illness in Rome, 228,
240–41; and Pearl, 137, 279n. 48, 286n.
32
Hazlett, John Downton, 275n. 3
Herbert, T. Walter, 30, 38, 46, 50, 71, 144,
166, 172, 174, 193, 225, 240, 243, 266n.
71, 268n. 19, 269nn. 21, 22, 23, 271n.
49, 272n. 64, 279n. 48, 281nn. 2, 6,
286n. 32, 289n. 50, 290n. 65, 293–94n.
15, 294n. 18, 298n. 21, 306n. 6
Higginson, Thomas Wentworth: on Margaret Fuller, 14, 25, 165, 264n. 43; on
Julian Hawthorne, 31, 261n. 22, 264n.
54; on Nathaniel Hawthorne, 30–32;
and *Margaret Fuller Ossoli*, 14, 24; and
women's suffrage movement, 25–27,
264n. 45
Hillard, George, 161, 167–68
Hirsh, John C., 300n. 34
Hoar, Elizabeth, 55, 166
Holmes, Oliver Wendell, 261n. 13
Hosmer, Harriet, 246
Howe, Julia Ward, 14, 24, 41
Hudspeth, Robert N., 258n. 5
Hunt, Martha, 302n. 48
Hutchinson, Anne, 125, 155
Hutner, Gordon, 281n. 8, 306n. 60

Isani, Mukhtar Ali, 287n. 44

Jael, Sisera, and Jabin, 233, 308n. 18
James, Henry, 14, 41, 205
Jones, Deborah L., 275n. 3
Jones, W. A., 121
Judith, Holofernes, and Nebuchadnezzar,
233

Kearns, Francis E., 132
Kemble, Fanny, 303n. 54
Kolodny, Annette, 279n. 40

Lander, Maria Louisa, 225–26, 247, 306n.
6
Laocoön, 254
Laud, Archbishop, 141–42
Leverenz, David, 261n. 23, 266n. 71,
291n. 74, 299n. 25
Levine, Robert S., 232–33, 307n. 15
Library of American Books, 13, 122
Lind, Jenny, 297n. 9
Literary history: canonization in, 24, 33,

35, 38–40, 260n. 10; and gender, 13,
16, 18–22, 24, 27, 39–47, 121; marketing of, 15–16; politics of, 13–16, 38–40,
260n. 5
Literary propriety, 28–29, 33, 35–38
Longfellow, Henry Wadsworth, 127, 163,
261n. 13
Lowell, James Russell, 260n. 6, 261n. 13,
290–91n. 68
Lystra, Karen, 48

Magretta, Joan, 296n. 4
Male, Roy R., 275n. 1
Mann, Horace, 177
Mann, Mary Peabody, 65, 177, 281n. 7
Martin, Robert K., 46, 267n. 12
Mathews, Cornelius, 168
Marriage, 16–22, 25, 27, 144–49, 157,
261n. 15, 262n. 26, 263n. 33, 267n. 19,
289nn. 50, 52, 54, 61, 62, 290nn. 64,
65, 298n. 21, 302n. 52. *See also* "marriage" under Emerson, Ralph Waldo;
Fuller, Margaret; Hawthorne, Nathaniel; and Hawthorne, Sophia
McDonald, John J., 262n. 28
Mellow, James R., 6, 166, 273n. 66, 295n.
34
Melville, Herman, 166, 169, 172, 178–79
Milder, Robert, 285n. 17
Miller, Edwin Haviland, 64, 71, 84, 161–
62, 174, 193, 269n. 25, 271n. 49, 272n.
58, 273n. 68, 276n. 18, 280n. 1, 282n.
8, 292n. 3, 295n. 34, 299n. 23
Miller, Perry, 260n. 9
Millington, Richard, 130, 202, 205, 211,
283–84n. 15, 284n. 16, 300n. 32
Milton, John, 94, 142–45, 287n. 45
Mitchell, Catherine C., 258n. 7
Mother Ann, 284n. 17
Mozier, Joseph, 6–8, 221, 263n. 37
Myerson, Joel, 258n. 7, 260n. 2

Napoleon, and Nathaniel Hawthorne,
286n. 29
Nathan, George, 39
National Woman Suffrage Movement, 26
Newcomb, Charles, 81, 271n. 56, 278n. 38
Newberry, Frederick, 281n. 3
Newman, Lea, 275n. 1
New-York Daily Tribune, 3–4, 97, 133, 166,
206. *See also* Fuller, Margaret: as a
journalist

Nissenbaum, Stephen, 280n. 1, 281–82n. 8, 282n. 9, 288nn. 47, 48
Norton, Andrews, 108

Ossoli, Angelo Eugenio Filippo (Fuller's son), 130, 135, 163–65, 282n. 13, 285n. 27, 290n. 68
Ossoli, Marquis Giovanni Angelo: and Brother Antonio (the Model), 234; character of, 227–28, 231–32, 282n. 13, 302–3n. 53, 307n. 10; and Donatello, 231, 234–35, 237–40; and Margaret Fuller, relationship with, 163–64, 282n. 13, 293n. 71, 302n. 52, 302–3n. 53, 307n. 10; and revolution in Rome, 231–32; and Westervelt, 209–13, 224

Parrington, V. L., 42–43
Patterson, Frank Allen, 287n. 45
Peabody, Elizabeth Palmer (mother), 21, 262n. 26
Peabody, Elizabeth Palmer (daughter): and *Aesthetic Papers*, 136, 286n. 30; on Nathaniel Hawthorne, 126, 265n. 62, 281n. 7; on marriage, 263n. 33, 290n. 65; as patron and publisher of Margaret Fuller, 62–63; as patron and publisher of Nathaniel Hawthorne 55, 60, 62–63
Peabody, Mary. *See* Mann, Mary Peabody
Pearson, Norman Holmes, 294n. 29
Perkins, S. H., 136, 286n. 30
Perry, Alice de V., 85, 87, 273n. 68, 274n. 83
Person, Leland S., Jr., 46–47, 49, 247, 266n. 71, 267n. 12, 268n. 14, 18, 281n. 5, 297nn. 15, 17, 300n. 37, 308n. 28
Pfister, Joel, 38, 46, 101, 189, 266n. 71, 267–68n. 12, 273n. 66, 276–77n. 20, 277n. 29, 297n. 12, 298n. 16, 300n. 34
Pierce, Franklin, 100
Pike, William, 181
Plato, and Ralph Waldo Emerson, 196–97, 299n. 27
Prynne, William, 141–46, 287n. 45

Ralph, C. A., 12, 24
Randel, William Pierce, 266n. 70
Reid, Alfred S., 287n. 44
Reising, Russell, 260n. 10
Reynolds, Larry J., 39–40, 46, 83, 98, 113, 132, 135, 148, 194, 206, 258nn. 7, 8,
261nn. 71, 75, 271n. 53, 276n. 13, 277–78n. 30, 278nn. 33, 38, 284nn. 16, 17, 285nn. 17, 20, 22, 27, 288n. 47, 289nn. 54, 61, 290n. 63, 299n. 27, 301n. 42
Richardson, Robert D., Jr., 94, 257n. 3
Ripley, George, 55
Ripley, Sophia, 65
Robinson, David, 276n. 11, 278n. 33
Ross, Marlon, 47
Rossi, Count Pellegrino ("Minister Rossi"), 231, 233, 302n. 47
Rugoff, Milton, 264n. 44
Ryskamp, Charles, 281n. 3

Salome, John the Baptist, and King Herod, 233–34
Sand, George, 97, 129, 155–56, 282n. 10
Scudder, Horace, 14, 250n. 5
Shelley, Percy Bysshe, 232
Shepard, Ada, 241, 307n. 14
Simpson, Claude, 299n. 26
Smith, Susan Belasco, 206, 258nn. 7, 8, 301n. 42
Spengemann, William C., 282n. 8
Spouse, Veda Bagwell, 303n. 54
Stanton, Elizabeth Cady, 26
Steele, Jeffrey, 40, 85, 103, 266n. 76, 269n. 26, 274n. 84, 292n. 80
Stern, Milton R., 284n. 16, 307–8n. 15
Stewart, Randall, 44, 268n. 16, 271n. 56, 273n. 67
Stone, Lucy, 26–27
Story, Emelyn, 226–27, 283n. 13, 306–7n. 8
Story, William Wetmore, 226
Strauch, Carl F., 257n. 3
Swann, Charles, 284n. 17

Taaffe, James G., 287n. 45
Tappan, Caroline Sturgis: and Margaret Fuller's death, 164, 293n. 10; and Margaret Fuller's "marriage" and motherhood, 176, 210, 283n. 13, 285n. 27, 292–93n. 7; and Hawthorne's identification with Apollo, 286n. 29; influence on the inception of *The Scarlet Letter* 135, 285n. 27; as landlord to the Hawthornes at Lenox, 163–64, 294n. 27, 295n. 34
Thoreau, Henry David: and Emerson, 278n. 38; and Margaret Fuller's death, 12, 293n. 14; influence of "Resistance

Thoreau, Henry David (*continued*)
  to Civil Government" on "The
  Custom-House" and *The Scarlet Letter,*
  136–37, 143–44, 286n. 30
Thurman, Kelley, 303n. 54
Tilton, Theodore, 26
Tompkins, Jane, 75–76, 260n. 10
Transcendentalism, 18, 39–40, 55, 106–11
Turner, Arlin, 44–45, 64, 137–38, 272nn.
  56, 58, 273n. 67, 279n. 38, 295n. 34,
  303n. 54

Union Association, 26
*The United States Magazine and Democratic
  Review,* 5, 121
Urbanski, Marie Mitchell Olesen, 257n. 3,
  266n. 1

Von Frank, Albert, 206, 296n. 39
Von Mehren, Joan, 259n. 11

Wade, Mason, 39, 43–44, 260n. 9
Wagenknecht, Edward, 303n. 54
Wallace, James D., 224–25, 291n. 77
Ward, Samuel, 56, 79–80, 252, 269n. 26,
  290n. 65
Ware, William, 300n. 34
Warren, Austin, 265n. 70

Wells, Anna Mary, 264nn. 41, 44
Wells, Kate Gannett, 16, 261n. 15
Wershoven, C. J., 296n. 3
Westervelt, Henry, 302n. 50
Whipple, E. P., 297n. 14, 300n. 31
White, Hayden, 8
Wilson, Margaret Gibbons, 261nn. 15, 17,
  19
Williams, Raymond, 121
Wollstonecraft, Mary, 155–56, 286–87n.
  33
Woman's Journal, 25–26, 29
Women: club/organization movement in
  the late nineteenth century, 17; "cult
  of domesticity" ("true womanhood"),
  18, 20–21, 29, 38, 268n. 19; education
  of, 17; role in society and feminism,
  16, 18–21, 24, 29, 39–40, 121, 279n. 9;
  suffrage movement, 17, 25–27; in the
  work place, 17, 261nn. 15, 19, 297n. 9
Woodberry, George E., 17, 260n. 6
Woodhull, Victoria Claflin, 26–27
Woodson, Thomas, 263n. 38

Zenobia (Queen of Palmyra), 204–5,
  300n. 34
Zwarg, Christina, 40, 206, 257n. 3, 266n.
  76

Thomas R. Mitchell was born and raised in Louisiana and received his Ph.D. in English from Texas A&M University in 1994. He is an associate professor of English at Texas A&M International University and a contributor to *Hawthorne and Women: Engendering and Expanding the Hawthorne Tradition* (University of Massachusetts Press, 1999). He lives in Laredo, Texas, with his wife, Linda Marie, and their three children, Lesley, Ashley, and Jackson.